Eng^d by A.H. Ritchie.

U. S. Grant
Lt. Gen.

THE CAMPAIGN LIVES OF ULYSSES S. GRANT, AND SCHUYLER COLFAX.

BY GEN. JAMES S. BRISBIN.

CINCINNATI:
C. F. VENT & CO., PUBLISHERS.
CHICAGO: J. S. GOODMAN & CO.
1868.

STEREOTYPED AT THE FRANKLIN TYPE FOUNDRY, CINCINNATI.

PREFACE.

An author's first book must necessarily be defective, especially if that book be written about events in which hundreds of thousands of persons were actors. In this volume I have aimed to do justice only to two characters. If, therefore, soldiers and statesmen, who may chance to read it, do not find their own names recorded, or a full account of the events with which they were connected given, let them remember I am not writing of them and of the events, only so far as they relate to Grant and Colfax.

It is always difficult to write of a man who is still living, for, whether it be to censure or praise him, the writer must feel more or less embarrassed. Remembering Lossing's motto, that "he who writes the truth should write all of it," I have endeavored to gather, from every possible source, such information concerning the illustrious General Grant as would be of interest to the reader; and I desire, in advance, to give credit to Mr. Larke, Abbott, Badeau, Reid, General Rawlins, and others, for such matter as I have used from their books, letters, and papers. A number of officers, who served with General Grant in Mexico and Oregon, and several of his personal friends, have been good enough to write me much that is interesting; and to them, one and all, I beg leave, in this public manner, to return my sincere thanks.

A careful investigation of all the facts connected with the life of General Grant will convince any impartial person that he is really a *great man*. Reason as we may on his career, prove that at but few times he has shown any marked evidence of genius, praise his subordinates as we will, still he stands the first soldier of his country, unique, remarkable, peculiar, the study of a nation. Here we behold a man silent, modest, unambitious, by his great talents in times of public danger, heaping benefactions on his country, until the nation, proud, grateful, unanimous, showers upon him all its honors, and raises him to an office which it has to create in order that the office may be worthy of the man. He, the poor son of a tanner, unpretending, without friends or influence, until his deeds had won both, unused to the world, rises, not suddenly, but step by step, in spite of the machinations of enemies and jealousies of men of lesser talents, to the head of our armies, and there, undazzled by his eminence, unspoiled by his honors, strong and self-poised, exhibits new talents, and maintains himself with so great credit that his fellow-citizens lay at his feet the crown of the republic and beg him to wear it, not to honor him, but to honor them.

Before he was forty-three years of age he had participated in two great wars, captured five hundred guns, more than one hundred thousand prisoners, a quarter of a million of small arms, redeemed from rebel rule over fifty thousand square miles of territory, re-opened to the commerce of the world the mightiest river on the globe, and stubbornly pursued his path to victory, despite of all obstacles. Since then, he has crushed out the rebellion in the East, reëstablished the authority of the Union over a territory larger than France, taken two hundred battle-flags, scores of canon, thousands upon thousands of prisoners, and hundreds of thousands of small arms, and then modestly returned to the capital of the nation, to disband his army of a million of men, lay his sword at the feet of the Congress of the people, and wait their pleasure whether he should fill a high station or become an humble private citizen. The world furnishes few such examples of greatness and humility, and our country only one other—that of George Washington.

Will any reasonable man say all these events in the life of Grant are the result of accident or mere good luck? Surely to assert that would be as foolish as unjust, and subject the person to the jeers and contempt of the world. His acts are the result of great wisdom and talents, and not the caprice of fortune. Consider his tribulations at Shiloh, his toils at Vicksburg, his battles of the Wilderness, his siege of Petersburg and capture of Lee, his conduct in the difficult Cabinet position forced upon him by the President, and, lastly, his measures during the impeachment excitement. When our President was bursting with rage; when the War Minister was hedged about with bayonets; when the country was trembling from center to circumference with excitement; when the Executive and the Congress seemed about to call out under arms their respective partisans and inaugurate another civil war, to whom did the people look with confidence and hope? Ulysses Grant, and none other. Unmoved by the tempest of passion raging over the land, conscious of his own strength and ability to control the storm, he sat calmly and serenely in his head-quarters, now receiving anxious inquiries from the President's friends, and anon receiving a delegation of grave but excited Senators, assuring all, nay, convincing all that the republic was safe. Was this accident, or greatness? If not greatness, why did not some other man of the hundred great men in the capital calm the elements and give confidence to the country? If an accident, it was such a one as retrieved the misfortunes of Shiloh, stormed the fortresses of Vicksburg, pushed Lee from the Wilderness, and finally broke his sword at Five Forks.

Some men are born great, others have greatness thrust upon them, while others again wring greatness from the world. To the latter class emphatically belongs Ulysses Grant; and yet it may with truth be said that he belongs to the second class, for, being as modest as he was great, he claimed nothing for his services, and honors and greatness had to be thrust upon him. I am nobody's puffer. I do not say these things of Grant to bring him out for the Presidency, for to commend *him* to the American people would be like recommending Alexander, or Cæsar, or Napoleon, to historians as subjects worthy of their consideration. I do not say them for the purpose of currying favor with Grant, or for any selfish or improper reason, but I utter them because I believe them to be true, because I think Grant a great and good man, because I admire him as a soldier and statesman, and feel grateful to him for reëstablishing the Union of these States, and thus preserving for me and my children the Government which the fathers founded. What Washington established, he, with his mighty sword, has preserved; and hereafter the names of Washington and Grant will stand side by side, and, in marble and brass, fill every niche of our country's fame to the latest posterity.

Of the other person named in this volume, I need only say that he has been in the civil department of the Government what General Grant has been in the military—as eminent in legislation as he in war. A young man of brilliant talents, an eminent statesman, the purity of whose public and private character has made his name a word of honor throughout the land, he of all men is fittest to be associated in high honor and power with the illustrious hero of the age. Bespeaking for my work the liberal treatment of critics, with serious misgivings I launch it upon the public, conscious that it is not without defects.

THE AUTHOR.

LEXINGTON, KY., July 1st, 1868.

CONTENTS.

INTRODUCTION.

(Page 17—23).

CHAPTER I.

(Page 24—28).

GRANT'S ANCESTORS—HIS PARENTS—WHERE AND WHEN HE WAS BORN—ANECDOTES OF GRANT—HIS FIRST PISTOL-SHOT—HE GOES TO SCHOOL AT GEORGETOWN—WHAT HE SAID TO HIS TEACHER—THE BUMBLE-BEE FIGHTER—GRANT BUYS A HORSE OF FARMER RALSTON—HE THRASHES HIS COUSIN JOHN FOR CALLING WASHINGTON A REBEL—MORE ANECDOTES ABOUT GRANT—HE SWIMS WHITE OAK CREEK IN A WAGON—HOW HE FLANKED THE LOGS—MR. HAMER GETS HIM AN APPOINTMENT TO WEST POINT—HIS ENTREE INTO THAT INSTITUTION.

CHAPTER II.

(Page 29—47).

GRANT AS A CADET AT WEST POINT—HIS PROGRESS IN THE CLASSES—HE GRADUATES NO. 21 IN A CLASS OF THIRTY-NINE—WHO GRADUATED IN GRANT'S CLASS, AND WHAT BECAME OF THEM—WHAT GRANT LOOKED LIKE WHEN HE LEFT WEST POINT—ANECDOTE OF THE HERO—HE FALLS IN LOVE WITH MISS JULIA DENT—IS ORDERED OFF TO MEXICO—PARTICIPATES IN THE BATTLES OF PALO ALTO AND RESACA DE LA PALMA—IS APPOINTED QUARTERMASTER—DISTINGUISHES HIMSELF AT CHEPULTEPEC—WHAT THE OFFICIAL REPORTS SAY OF HIM—HIS OLD COMRADES IN MEXICO, AND WHAT BECAME OF THEM—RETURNS FROM THE MEXICAN WAR AND MARRIES.

CHAPTER III.

(Page 48—63.)

GRANT AND CHANDLER—GRANT IS STATIONED AT DETROIT AND SACKETT'S HARBOR—GOES TO CALIFORNIA AND THENCE TO OREGON—GARRISON LIFE ON THE FRONTIER—HE IS APPOINTED A FULL CAPTAIN—RESIGNS FROM THE ARMY AND RETURNS TO ST. LOUIS—BECOMES A FARMER—SKETCHES OF GRANT IN CIVIL LIFE—GOES INTO THE REAL ESTATE AND AUCTIONEERING BUSINESS—MOVES TO GALENA, ILLINOIS—RAISES A COMPANY FOR THE WAR—IS APPOINTED COLONEL OF THE TWENTY-FIRST ILLINOIS INFANTRY.

CHAPTER IV.

(Page 64—83.)

GRANT AS A COLONEL—IS ASSIGNED TO COMMAND OF A BRIGADE—IS APPOINTED BRIGADIER-GENERAL, AND ASSIGNED TO COMMAND AT CAIRO—GRANT'S ENEMIES—HE CUTS THE NEUTRALITY KNOT IN KENTUCKY—CAPTURE OF PADUCAH—THE BATTLE OF BELMONT—WHY THAT BATTLE WAS FOUGHT—THE EXPEDITION INTO KENTUCKY—PREPARATIONS TO ATTACK FORT HENRY—FALL OF FORT HENRY—PREPARATIONS TO ATTACK FORT DONELSON—CAPTURE OF FORT DONELSON—REJOICING OF THE PEOPLE—GRANT PROMOTED BY THE PRESIDENT TO MAJOR-GENERAL—NEW DISTRICT CREATED FOR HIM—HE GETS UNDER A CLOUD—IS RELIEVED FROM HIS DISGRACE—PREPARATIONS FOR THE BATTE OF SHILOH.

CHAPTER V.

(Page 84—99.)

GRANT RECEIVES A HANDSOME PRESENT—GRANT AT SAVANNAH—GENERAL C. F. SMITH AND GRANT—COMPOSITION OF THE TWO ARMIES—THE BATTLE-FIELD OF SHILOH—POSITION OF THE TROOPS—A. S. JOHNSTON'S ADDRESS TO HIS SOLDIERS—SKIRMISHING BEFORE THE BATTLE—THE BATTLE—CONDUCT OF LEWIS WALLACE AND NELSON—BUELL ARRIVES ON THE FIELD—WHAT HE SAID TO GRANT—THE SECOND DAY'S BATTLE—GRANT AND THE FIRST OHIO REGIMENT—THE NEW YORK HERALD'S ACCOUNT OF THE BATTLE—REJOICING OVER THE NEWS—COMPLIMENTARY ORDER TO GRANT AND BUELL—GRANT'S CONDUCT IN THE BATTLE.

CHAPTER VI.

(Page 100–117.)

HALLECK ASSUMES COMMAND OF THE ARMY—GRANT'S ENEMIES AGAIN BUSY—WASHBURN'S DEFENSE OF HIM—ADVANCE ON CORINTH—DIGGING AND DITCHING—LETTERS FROM A UNION SOLDIER—ELLIOT'S RAID—PURSUIT OF THE ENEMY FROM CORINTH—GRANT'S POSITION—HE IS PLACED IN COMMAND OF THE DISTRICT OF TENNESSEE—HALLECK SUCCEEDS M'CLELLAN—GRANT AND THE REBELS—GRANT AND THE NEWSPAPERS—HOW HE TREATED GUERRILLAS—PRICE'S RAID—ADVANCE ON IUKA—THE BATTLE—DEFEAT AND ESCAPE OF THE REBELS—BATTLE OF CORINTH—DEFEAT AND RETREAT OF THE REBELS—GRANT'S CONGRATULATORY ORDER TO HIS ARMY—MR. LINCOLN'S DISPATCH.

CHAPTER VII.

(Page 118–134.)

CHARACTER OF GRANT—HALLECK AND GRANT COMPARED—OPENING OF THE MISSISSIPPI—ADVANCE TO GRAND JUNCTION—COLONEL LEE'S RAID—GRANT'S ADMINISTRATIVE ABILITY—HE ESTABLISHES CONTRABAND CAMPS—SEVERITY OF HIS DISCIPLINE—THE COTTON TRADE—ANECDOTE OF GRANT—GRANT AND THE JEWS—HE REDUCES THE BAGGAGE OF HIS ARMY—ADVANCE ON VICKSBURG—SURRENDER OF HOLLY SPRINGS—GRANT FALLS BACK—ORGANIZATION OF HIS ARMY—SHERMAN'S EXPEDITION AGAINST VICKSBURG—REPULSE OF SHERMAN—FULL ACCOUNT OF THE FIRST ATTACK ON VICKSBURG—CAPTURE OF ARKANSAS POST—GRANT DETERMINED TO CAPTURE VICKSBURG—HIS TELEGRAM TO HALLECK.

CHAPTER VIII.

(Page 135–149.)

THE PRESIDENT'S EMANCIPATION PROCLAMATION—GRANT ENFORCES THE POLICY OF THE GOVERNMENT—YOUNG'S POINT—THE WILLIAMS CANAL—ROUNDABOUT BAYOU EXPEDITION—MOON LAKE—YAZOO PASS EXPEDITION—ADMIRAL FARRAGUT—ADMIRAL PORTER—M'CLERNAND'S MARCH—RUNNING THE BATTERIES—GRIERSON AND HATCH'S RAID—BATTLE OF PORT GIBSON—GRANT'S FIGHTING APPEARANCE—EVACUATION OF GRAND GULF—PERPLEXING SITUATION OF GRANT—HIS PLANS DISAPPROVED BY THE PRESIDENT AND HALLECK—PEMBERTON AND JOHNSTON MARCH AGAINST HIM—BATTLE OF RAYMOND—ADVANCE ON JACKSON—PRELIMINARY MOVEMENTS—GRANT LEADS THE ADVANCE IN PERSON AND ON FOOT.

CHAPTER IX.

(Page 150—162.)

PEMBERTON DECEIVED BY GRANT—DEFEAT OF JOHNSTON—CAPTURE OF JACKSON—DESTRUCTION OF REBEL PROPERTY—JOHNSTON DECEIVED BY GRANT—MEETING OF SHERMAN, GRANT AND M'PHERSON AT THE STATE CAPITAL—ADVANCE ON PEMBERTON—BATTLE OF CHAMPION HILLS—DETAILS OF THE BATTLE—RETREAT OF PEMBERTON—SHERMAN'S OPINION OF THE CAMPAIGN—GRANT'S REPLY—FIRST ASSAULT ON VICKSBURG—DETAILS OF THE ACTION—THE NAVAL OPERATIONS ON THE RIVER—COMMUNICATION WITH GRANT ESTABLISHED—HAINES' BLUFF SEIZED FOR A NEW BASE—PREPARATIONS FOR THE SIEGE.

CHAPTER X.

(Page 163—190.)

SECOND ATTACK ON VICKSBURG—FULL ACCOUNT OF THE BATTLE—MISUNDERSTANDING BETWEEN GRANT AND M'CLERNAND—POSITION OF THE ARMY—PEMBERTON'S ADDRESS—SHERMAN'S EXPEDITION—THE MINES AT VICKSBURG—TERRIFIC EXPLOSION OF A MINE—FIGHT IN THE CRATER—PEMBERTON GIVES UP THE GHOST—HIS LETTERS TO GRANT—THEIR INTERVIEW—GRANT'S LETTERS TO PEMBERTON—SURRENDER OF THE REBEL GARRISON—ADVANCE OF THE UNION TROOPS INTO VICKSBURG—GRANT AT PEMBERTON'S HEAD-QUARTERS—IMPORTANCE OF THE SURRENDER OF VICKSBURG—LINCOLN'S LETTER TO GRANT.

CHAPTER XI

(Page 191—212.)

PREPARATIONS TO ATTACK JOHNSTON—SURRENDER OF PORT HUDSON—INVESTMENT OF JACKSON—JEFF. DAVIS' LIBRARY—JOHNSTON'S ADDRESS TO HIS ARMY—RETREAT OF THE REBELS—GRANT AND THE REBEL MAJOR—HIS TREATMENT OF SUBORDINATE OFFICERS—FRIENDSHIP BETWEEN GRANT AND SHERMAN—MRS. GRANT VISITS HER HUSBAND—ANECDOTE OF MRS. GRANT—GRANT AND HIS SOLDIERS—ADMINISTRATIVE ABILITY OF GRANT—HONORS TO GRANT AT MEMPHIS—REVIEW AT NEW ORLEANS—TERRIBLE ACCIDENT TO GRANT—HE IS APPOINTED TO A NEW COMMAND—VISITS LOUISVILLE—HIS NEW ARMY AND GENERALS—BRAGG'S FORCES—THE CHATTANOOGA CAMPAIGN.

CHAPTER XII.

(Page 213–238.)

CHATTANOOGA—THE UNION ARMY—THE REBEL ARMY—BRAGG'S BLUNDER—WHAT JEFF DAVIS SAID—HOOKER'S BATTLE ON THE 28TH OF OCTOBER—BURNSIDE SHUT UP IN KNOXVILLE—HOOKER'S BATTLE ABOVE THE CLOUDS—FULL ACCOUNT OF SHERMAN'S ADVANCE—THRILLING BATTLE SCENES—GENERAL GRANT IN BATTLE—DEFEAT OF BRAGG—GRANT'S PURSUIT—FIGHT AT RINGGOLD—HEROIC CONDUCT OF GRANT—WHAT HIS STAFF OFFICERS SAY OF HIM—SHERMAN REACHES KNOXVILLE—DEFEAT AND RETREAT OF LONGSTREET—END OF THE CHATTANOOGA CAMPAIGN—CONGRATULATIONS AND REJOICING.

CHAPTER XIII.

(Page 239–252.)

GRANT'S VICTORIES—VOTE OF THANKS BY CONGRESS—BILL TO REVIVE THE GRADE OF LIEUTENANT-GENERAL—A MEDAL GIVEN HIM—APPOINTED LIEUTENANT-GENERAL AND ASSUMES COMMAND OF THE ARMY—HONORS TO GENERAL GRANT—HE RECEIVES VALUABLE PRESENTS—THE OLD SOLDIER'S GIFT—GRANT VISITS NASHVILLE AND KNOXVILLE—CROSSES THE CUMBERLAND MOUNTAINS ON HORSEBACK—HIS RECEPTION AT LEXINGTON, KENTUCKY—VISIT TO LOUISVILLE—HONORS AT MEMPHIS—A GRAND DINNER—SERENADE TO GRANT, AND HIS SPEECHES—GRANT LEAVES THE WEST—HIS LETTER TO SHERMAN, AND SHERMAN'S REPLY—HIS VISIT TO WASHINGTON—THE PRESIDENT PRESENTS HIM HIS COMMISSION AS LIEUTENANT-GENERAL.

CHAPTER XIV.

(Page 253–269.)

GRANT IN HIS NEW COMMAND—THE REBEL CHIEFTAIN LEE—GRANT'S COMBINATIONS—ALL READY TO ADVANCE—BATTLES OF THE WILDERNESS—GALLANTRY OF CRAWFORD—DEATH OF WADSWORTH—HANCOCK'S FIGHTING—DEATH OF SEDGWICK—BATTLE OF SPOTTSYLVANIA COURT-HOUSE—CAPTURE OF A REBEL DIVISION AND TWO REBEL GENERALS—BURNSIDE'S BATTLES—FORWARD ALONG THE WHOLE LINE—ANECDOTES OF GRANT—BATTLE OF COLD HARBOR—ORDER OF BATTLE—TERRIBLE FIGHTING—CROSSING THE JAMES—ASSAULTS ON PETERSBURG—INVESTMENT OF THE CITY—THE SIEGE BEGUN—PRESIDENT LINCOLN'S LETTER TO GRANT—GRANT'S REPLY.

CHAPTER XV.

(Page 270—280.)

SIGEL RELIEVED—HUNTER IN THE VALLEY—BATTLE ON NORTH RIVER—BRILLIANT SUCCESS OF HUNTER—HIS DEFEAT NEAR LYNCHBURG—SHERIDAN AT DEEP BOTTOM—HE MARCHES TO WITHIN TWELVE MILES OF RICHMOND—COLONEL PLEASANTS' MINE—THE EXPLOSION—SUCCESS OF THE MINE—FAILURE OF THE TROOPS—FIGHTING IN THE CRATER—EARLY'S ADVANCE ON WASHINGTON—GREGG'S ATTACK ON THE WELDON RAILROAD—HEAVY FIGHTING—SHERIDAN IN THE VALLEY—BATTLE OF OPEQUAN—DEFEAT OF SHERIDAN'S FORCES BY EARLY—SHERIDAN'S RIDE—HE REGAINS THE BATTLE—GRANT'S PRAISE OF SHERIDAN—THE PRESIDENT'S LETTER TO HIM—HE IS MADE A MAJOR-GENERAL IN THE REGULAR ARMY—SHERMAN'S MARCH TO THE SEA.

CHAPTER XVI.

(Page 281—305.)

THE SITUATION—BEGINNING OF THE END—ANECDOTES OF GRANT—SHERIDAN LOOSE AGAIN—INTERVIEW BETWEEN LINCOLN, GRANT, MEADE, SHERIDAN, AND SHERMAN—ADVANCE OF THE FIFTH CORPS—SHERIDAN AT FIVE FORKS—CAPTURE OF PETERSBURG—ADVANCE OF THE ARMY—THE FIGHTING—FALL OF RICHMOND—THE REBEL RAMS BLOWN UP—CORRESPONDENCE BETWEEN GRANT AND LEE—SHERIDAN AT THE APPOMATTOX—INTERVIEW BETWEEN GRANT AND LEE—TERMS OF SURRENDER PROPOSED—LEE SURRENDERS HIS ARMY—SCENES OF THE SURRENDER—FORM OF PAROLE—NUMBER OF PRISONERS TAKEN BY GRANT—SHERMAN'S MOVEMENTS—THE END—THE MARCH HOMEWARD—REVIEW AT WASHINGTON—GRANT TAKES LEAVE OF HIS ARMY—GRANT AT HOME.

CHAPTER XVII.

(Page 306—316.)

THE GRADE OF GENERAL—GRANT COMMISSIONED A GENERAL—HIS PERSONAL APPEARANCE, HABITS, MANNERS, CONDUCT, AND DRESS—GRANT IN BATTLE—HIS MILITARY FAME—HIS KINDNESS OF HEART—DEATH OF COLONEL O'MEARA—A PLEASANT LETTER—THE OLD SOLDIER AND GRANT—ANECDOTE OF STANTON AND LINCOLN—GRANT'S RELIANCE UPON DIVINE PROVIDENCE—HIS TREATMENT OF SUBORDINATE OFFICERS—WHAT HE SAID OF SHERMAN, THOMAS, SHERIDAN, AND OTHERS—ANECDOTE OF GRANT—HIS JUSTICE—A CANDIDATE FOR THE PRESIDENCY.

CHAPTER XVIII.

(Page 317–325.)

SOLDIERS AND SAILORS' NATIONAL CONVENTION AT CHICAGO—THE PROCESSION—THE EAGLE "OLD ABE"—THE HALL—THE SCENES—CONVENTION CALLED TO ORDER—GOVERNOR FAIRCHILD TEMPORARY CHAIRMAN—HIS SPEECH—THE COMMITTEES—GOVERNOR HAWLEY'S SPEECH—REMARKS OF GENERALS SICKLES, HALSTEAD, AND OTHERS—PERMANENT ORGANIZATION—GENERAL LOGAN'S REMARKS—GRANT'S FATHER—HIS SPEECH—ADDRESSES BY GENERAL COCHRANE, MAJOR HAGGERTY, AND O'CONNER—COLONEL STOKES, OF TENNESSEE—THE RESOLUTIONS—GRANT UNANIMOUSLY NOMINATED BY HIS COMRADES FOR PRESIDENT—GREAT ENTHUSIASM—THE LARGEST DELEGATED CONVENTION EVER ASSEMBLED—ADJOURNMENT OF THE CONVENTION.

CHAPTER XIX.

(Page 326–344.)

NATIONAL REPUBLICAN CONVENTION AT CHICAGO—GENERAL SCHURTZ MADE TEMPORARY CHAIRMAN—HIS SPEECH—PROCEEDINGS OF THE CONVENTION—THE COMMITTEES—PERMANENT ORGANIZATION—SPEECH OF GOVERNOR HAWLEY—SOLDIERS RECEIVED—ELOQUENT SPEECH BY GOVERNOR FAIRCHILD—SECOND DAY'S PROCEEDINGS—THE PLATFORM—ADDITIONAL RESOLUTIONS—LOGAN'S SPEECH—GENERAL GRANT UNANIMOUSLY NOMINATED—THE VOTE BY STATES—THE ANNOUNCEMENT—WILD SCENES IN THE CONVENTION—THE EFFECT OF THE NOMINATION UPON THE PEOPLE—NOMINATION OF A VICE-PRESIDENT.

CHAPTER XX.

(Page 345–352.)

HOW GENERAL GRANT RECEIVED THE NEWS OF HIS NOMINATION—THE ENTHUSIASM IN WASHINGTON—PROCESSIONS—ADDRESS TO GENERAL GRANT BY GOVERNOR BOUTWELL—GRANT'S REPLY—RECEPTION OF THE SOLDIERS' AND SAILORS' COMMITTEE—PRESENTATION BY COLONEL ALLEMAN—GRANT'S REPLY—RECEPTION AT GRANT'S RESIDENCE IN THE EVENING—PRESENTATION OF THE REPUBLICAN NATIONAL CONVENTION'S RESOLUTIONS BY GOVERNOR HAWLEY—ABLE SPEECH BY HAWLEY—GENERAL GRANT'S REPLY—GRANT FORMALLY ACCEPTS THE REPUBLICAN NOMINATION—CONCLUSION.

SCHUYLER COLFAX.

CHAPTER I.

(Page 355—356.)

BIRTH AND PARENTAGE OF COLFAX—DEATH OF HIS FATHER—POVERTY AND EARLY STRUGGLES OF THE FAMILY—HIS EDUCATION AND HABITS—HIS MOTHER MARRIES MR. MATTHEWS—SCHUYLER A CLERK—THEY REMOVE TO INDIANA—COLFAX DRIVES A WAGON ACROSS MICHIGAN—HIS STEP-FATHER SETTLES AT NEW CARLISLE—COLFAX A CLERK AGAIN—THE "STORE AND POST-OFFICE"—YOUNG COLFAX AS AN ORACLE—HIS FIRST ACQUAINTANCE WITH HON. JOHN D. DEFREES—A FRIEND IN NEED—GOES TO SOUTH BEND—READS LAW—IS DEPUTY COUNTY AUDITOR—THE MOOT LEGISLATURE—WRITES FOR THE NEWSPAPERS—IS APPOINTED SENATE REPORTER—ESTABLISHES THE VALLEY REGISTER, AND BECOMES AN EDITOR—HIS POVERTY AND STRUGGLES SUCCEEDS AT LAST—HIS POPULARITY WITH THE PEOPLE—HELPS TO FRAME THE CONSTITUTION OF INDIANA—OPPOSITION TO THE BLACK LAWS—IS NOMINATED FOR CONGRESS—HIS DEFEAT—IS A DELEGATE TO THE NATIONAL CONVENTIONS OF 1848 AND 1852, AND VOTES FOR TAYLOR AND SCOTT—HIS POLITICS—PURITY OF HIS CHARACTER—IS RENOMINATED AND TRIUMPHANTLY ELECTED TO CONGRESS—BEGINS HIS LEGISLATIVE CAREER.

CHAPTER II.

(Page 366—372.)

COLFAX AS AN ODD-FELLOW—HIS ENTRANCE INTO CONGRESS—SUPPORTS BANKS FOR THE SPEAKERSHIP—HIS FIRST SPEECH IN CONGRESS—IS A MEMBER OF IMPORTANT COMMITTEES—ENTERS THE PRESIDENTIAL CAMPAIGN OF 1856—IS RE-ELECTED TO CONGRESS—HIS IMMENSE POPULARITY—IS ELECTED SPEAKER OF THE XXXVIII CONGRESS—SUPPORTS THE WAR—MR. COLFAX'S VIEWS ON THE NATIONAL ENTERPRISES—HE SUPPORTS

LINCOLN—MR. LINCOLN'S FRIENDSHIP FOR HIM—COLFAX ON THE STUMP —IS AGAIN RE-ELECTED TO CONGRESS—RE-ELECTED SPEAKER OF THE XXXIX CONGRESS—HIS POPULARITY IN THE HOUSE—THE BEST SPEAKER SINCE CLAY—REMARKABLE ABILITY OF MR. COLFAX AS A PRESIDING OFFICER.

CHAPTER III.

(Page 373—388.)

PERSONAL MANNERS OF MR. COLFAX—WHY THE WOMEN LIKE HIM—HIS WIFE—MR. COLFAX AT HOME—HIS RECEPTIONS—WHY THEY ARE POPULAR—COLFAX AND HIS MOTHER—A GOOD SON—GRANT AND COLFAX—EARLY STRUGGLES AND POVERTY OF COLFAX—SUPPER TO HIM BY THE PRESS OF WASHINGTON—HIS REMARKS—COLFAX AS A POLITICIAN—HIS TALENTS—GRANT SAFE FROM ASSASSINATION IF COLFAX IS VICE-PRESIDENT—COLFAX'S SPEECHES—HIS PIETY—COLFAX AT SOUTH BEND—WHAT HIS NEIGHBORS THINK OF HIM—A TEMPERANCE MAN—HIS LIBERALITY AND SUPPORT OF GOOD CAUSES—PERSONAL APPEARANCE—ANECDOTE—COLFAX IN HIS OFFICE—HIS RECORD.

CHAPTER IV.

(Page 389—402.)

THE CHICAGO CONVENTION — NOMINATIONS FOR VICE-PRESIDENT — MR. PIERCE'S SPEECH—MR. CLAFLIN'S SPEECH—HON. HENRY LANE'S SPEECH —SPEECH OF MR. CUTCHESON—REMARKS OF FRED. HASSAUREK, CARL SCHURTZ, JUDGE JONES, ALEXANDER M'CLURE, AND OTHERS—HONS. BEN. WADE, COLFAX, WILSON, FENTON, HAMLIN, HARLIN, CURTIN, POMEROY SPEED, CRESWELL, AND KELLEY NOMINATED FOR VICE-PRESIDENT—FIRST BALLOT—SECOND BALLOT — THIRD BALLOT — FOURTH BALLOT — FIFTH BALLOT—COLFAX DECLARED THE UNANIMOUS NOMINEE OF THE CONVENTION—THE ENTHUSIASM—ADJOURNMENT.

CHAPTER V.

(Page 403—411.)

HOW MR. COLFAX RECEIVED HIS NOMINATION—GREETINGS FROM HIS BROTHER MEMBERS—THE CROWD AT THE CAPITOL—SERENADE TO MR. COLFAX—REPRESENTATIVE PIKE'S REMARKS—MR. COLFAX'S SPEECH—RECEPTION OF THE SOLDIER'S COMMITTEE—THE SPEECHES—RECEPTION OF THE REPUBLICAN COMMITTEE—SPEECH OF GOVERNOR HAWLEY—REPLY OF SPEAKER COLFAX—HIS FORMAL LETTER OF ACCEPTANCE—GENERAL REMARKS—THE END.

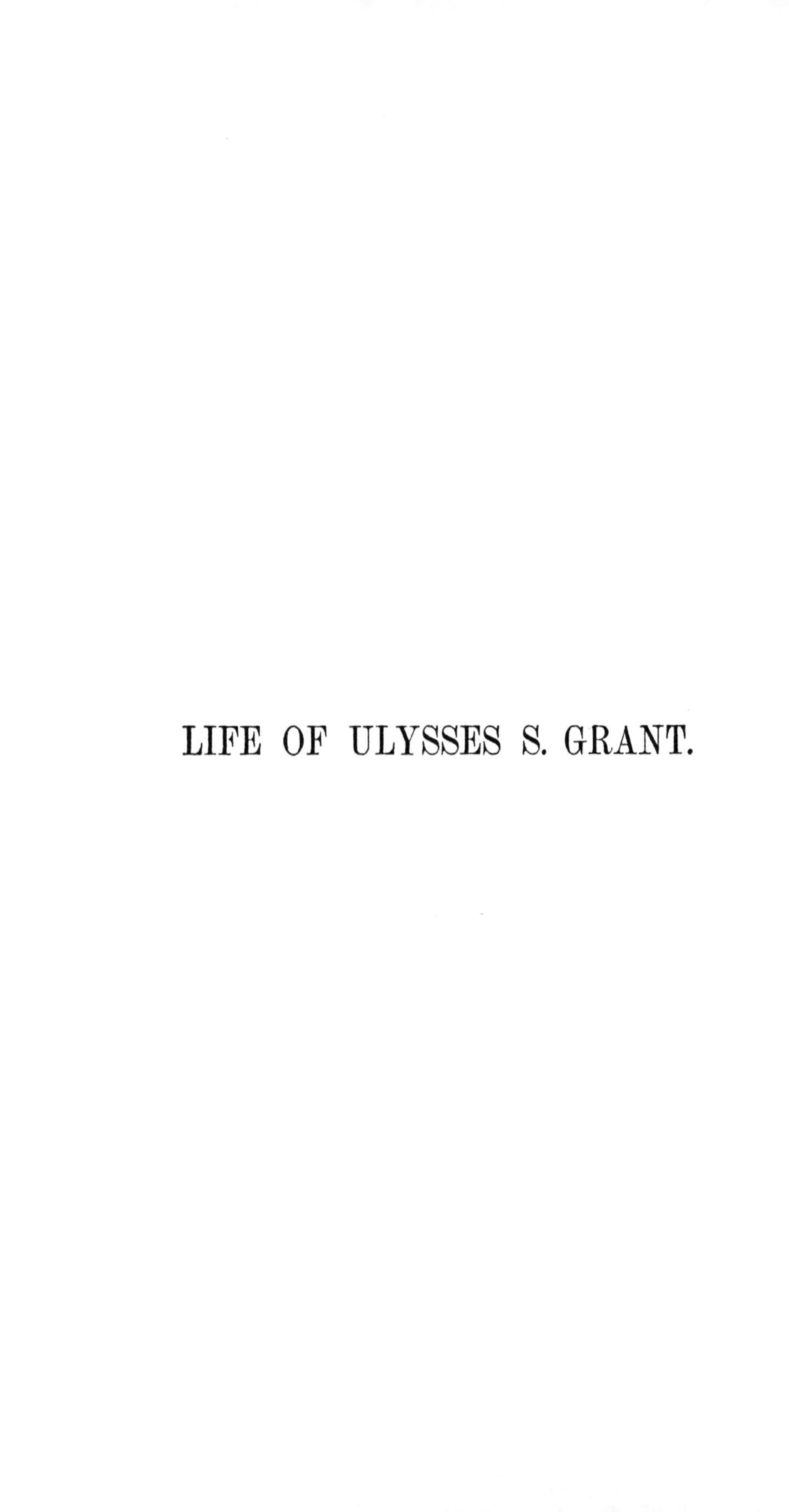

LIFE OF ULYSSES S. GRANT.

CHAPTER I.

GRANT'S ANCESTORS—HIS PARENTS—WHERE AND WHEN HE WAS BORN—ANECDOTES OF GRANT—HIS FIRST PISTOL-SHOT—HE GOES TO SCHOOL AT GEORGETOWN—WHAT HE SAID TO HIS TEACHER—THE BUMBLE-BEE FIGHTER—GRANT BUYS A HORSE OF FARMER RALSTON—HE THRASHES HIS COUSIN JOHN FOR CALLING WASHINGTON A REBEL—MORE ANECDOTES ABOUT GRANT—HE SWIMS WHITE OAK CREEK IN A WAGON—HOW HE FLANKED THE LOGS—MR. HAMER GETS HIM AN APPOINTMENT TO WEST POINT—HIS ENTREE INTO THAT INSTITUTION.

ULYSSES S. GRANT was born on the banks of the Ohio, about twenty-five miles above Cincinnati, at the village of Point Pleasant, in the county of Clermont, on the 27th day of April, 1822. In this country it is of little consequence who a man's ancestors were, or whether, in fact, he had any at all; but as a matter of gratification to the curious, it may be recorded that Grant's great grandfather, Noah Grant, commanded a company of *white and black men*, in 1756, and fell at the battle of White Plains, as also did his brother, Solomon Grant. The General's grandfather was a lieutenant under Washington, and fought from the beginning to the close of the Revolutionary War. The father of General Grant was born in Westmoreland County, Pennsylvania, January 23, 1794, and is still living at Covington, Kentucky. He learned the tanning business with his half-brother, at Maysville, Kentucky, and in 1820 settled at Point Pleasant, Ohio, where he set up his trade, and soon afterward married Miss Hannah Simpson, the mother of General Grant, who is still living.

Grant had five brothers and sisters. One brother and one

sister, both single, died of consumption during the late war; of the others, a brother lives in Chicago, another in Galena, and the younger sister at Covington, with her father. Many stories are told of the precociousness of Ulysses, and his father thinks Grant was a great little boy; indeed, he would be a poor father if he did not, but remembering the fate of our bee-fighter, we hesitate about relating these anecdotes. Reid is responsible for the following:

"The absence of fear was always a characteristic of Ulysses. When two years of age, while Mr. Grant was carrying Ulysses in his arms through the village on a public occasion, a young man wished to try the effect of a pistol report on the child; Mr. Grant consented, saying, 'The boy never saw a pistol or gun before in his life.'

"The baby hand was put on the lock, and the tiny finger curled around the trigger and pressed upon it until the hammer fell, and the charge exploded with a loud report. Ulysses hardly stirred, but delighted with the loud noise the powder had made, pushed the pistol away, and, clapping his hands, cried, 'fick again; fick again.' A bystander said, 'That boy will make a general some day, he neither winked nor dodged.' None will question but that the prediction has been verified; and this man, if living, can safely claim precedence over Mr. Washburne in having discovered the military talents of General Grant."

While Grant was still a lad, his parents, who were then living at Georgetown, in Brown County, Ohio, sent him to the village school, and from all we can learn, the future conqueror was considered a dull boy; but Larke tells the following anecdote of him during this period:

"One day Grant was puzzling his brains over a sum in arithmetic, when the teacher came along, and seeing his perplexed look, said to him, kindly:

"'Well, Ulysses, can't you master it?'

"'Can't!' returned Grant, 'what does that mean?'

"'Why, why, when we can't do a thing, we say we can't,' replied the teacher. The class had been studying definitions, and Grant took up his dictionary, and after looking through it for some time, said, 'I can't find it; there is no such word in my book.' The teacher was so struck with the boy's reply, that he commended him for it, and wound up by saying, 'You are quite right, Ulysses, and if, in the future struggles of your life, any one asserts that you can't do a thing that you have set your mind to do, and which is lawful and right, tell them, as you have me to-day, that there is no such word in your dictionary.' It is said, that Grant never forgot the lesson of his instructor, and that his reply to Pemberton and Lee, was only his old answer to his teacher, in another form."

Abbott tells the following story about Grant: "When Ulysses was twelve years old his father sent him to a neighboring farmer to buy a horse which he had been bargaining for. Before Ulysses started, his father said to him:

"'You can tell Mr. Ralston that I have sent you to buy the horse, and that I will give him $50 for it. If he will not take that, you may offer him $55, and rather than come away without him, give Mr. Ralston $60 for the horse.'

"Ulysses, getting the matter right in his mind, set out, but on arriving at Mr. Ralston's, his plans for bartering were knocked out of balance by Mr. Ralston asking him directly, 'How much did your father say you might give for the horse?'

"Grant's mother had told him he must never tell a lie, and believing it would be wrong to prevaricate in this case, he replied:

"'Father told me to offer you $50; if that would not do, to give you $55, and that he would be willing to give $60 rather than not get the horse.' 'Well,' replied farmer

Ralston, 'I can not sell the horse for less than sixty dollars.' 'I am sorry for that,' was the rejoinder of young Grant, 'for since I have seen the horse, although father said I might, I have determined not to give more than $50 for him.'

"Mr. Ralston took the fifty dollars and Grant rode the horse home."

Mr. Grant had a brother who had settled in Canada, and as there was no school in the neighborhood, he sent his son John over to Georgetown to board with his uncle and go to school with Ulysses. The Canadian youth was strongly tinctured with British prejudices, and one day the conversation turned upon Washington, when John denounced the father of his country as "a rebel who had fought against his king."

Ulysses had been taught by his mother to revere the character of Washington, and was indignant at the irreverent language of his cousin. The boys soon came to blows, and after pulling hair and pummeling each other for some time, Jack came off with a bloody nose and Ulysses with a black eye. On reaching home, Mrs. Grant desired to have her boy punished for fighting, and called in his father, but after hearing the case, the old gentleman said, "Wife, I tell thee the boy must not be whipped, he has done nothing but stand up for his country, and no boy should be punished for fighting in defense of his native land, and Washington."

Years after this, when the boys had grown to be men, they met in Canada, and John said to Ulysses, "Do you remember the thrashing you gave me for calling Washington a rebel?"

"Yes," replied Ulysses, "and you can get a fight out of me again, John, on that question."

Grant's father tells us, that in his early boyhood, Ulysses manifested the same fondness for horses that is still characteristic of him. He was always sure to go to the circuses that came around, and invariably volunteered to ride the vicious mule—sometime succeeding, despite the animal's tricks, to the no small amusement of the spectators and annoyance of the showman. He imitated the circus men, riding the horses to water, standing on their backs, and thus became a proficient horseman long before he entered West Point.

Young Grant was fond of driving horses, and frequently hauled loads of passengers from Georgetown to the neighboring villages and back. He would always rather drive team than work in the tannery of his father, and from the first seemed determined never to be a tanner.

Grant was a brave lad, and early manifested an indomitable will. His father relates the following anecdote of him:

"One day Ulysses was coming from Augusta, Ky., to Georgetown, with some young ladies in his wagon. It had been raining, and the water in the Ohio had backed into the tributary streams. Grant's route lay across White Oak Creek, and; not knowing the depth of the water, he drove in, when the wagon went down and the horses commenced swimming. The young ladies were terribly frightened, and commenced screaming, thinking they would surely all be drowned; but Grant, with great presence of mind, steered his horses toward the opposite bank, saying, coolly, 'Keep still, girls; I will take you through safe.' Ulysses was only about thirteen years old when this happened."

One day Ulysses was sent to the woods to haul some logs, when, finding the choppers gone, he hitched a horse to the logs, and dragging them to a tree that had fallen partly down, drew them up the slanting tree, and then backing the wagon under, pulled them over into the bed. This was considerable of a flank movement for a lad of fourteen.

Ulysses one day said to his father, when they were working together in the tannery: "Father, this tannery business is not the kind of work I like. I will work at it, to please you, until I am twenty-one, but I will never follow it another day after that."

Mr. Grant, with great good sense, said: "No, my son; I do not wish you to work at any thing that is distasteful to you. I want you to work at what you like, and stick to it. Now, what do you think you would like to do?"

"I would like to be a farmer, a down the river trader, or get an education," replied Ulysses.

"How would you like to go to West Point and learn to be a soldier?" said his father.

"First rate," answered Ulysses, "that would suit me exactly."

Mr. Grant immediately wrote to Mr. Morris, then a Senator in Congress from Ohio, asking him if there was any vacancy at West Point which he could control. Senator Morris replied at once that there was a vacancy from the congressional district in which Mr. Grant lived—the young man who had been appointed having failed to pass his examination. Mr. Grant wrote to Hon. Thomas L. Hamer, the Representative then in Congress from the district, asking him to appoint his son Ulysses. Mr. Hamer received the letter *the night before his term expired*, and at once appointed young Grant.

Grant's right name was Hiram Ulysses, but as his father, in his letter, only called him Ulysses, and Mr. Hamer knowing his mother's name was Simpson, wrote it Ulysses Simpson Grant, and as such the letter of appointment was issued to him from the War Department, and the authorities would never afterward change it.

Grant entered West Point in the spring of 1839, at the age of seventeen.

CHAPTER II.

GRANT AS A CADET AT WEST POINT—HIS PROGRESS IN THE CLASSES—HE GRADUATES NO. 21 IN A CLASS OF THIRTY-NINE—WHO GRADUATED IN GRANT'S CLASS, AND WHAT BECAME OF THEM—WHAT GRANT LOOKED LIKE WHEN HE LEFT WEST POINT—ANECDOTE OF THE HERO—HE FALLS IN LOVE WITH MISS JULIA DENT—IS ORDERED OFF TO MEXICO—PARTICIPATES IN THE BATTLES OF PALO ALTO AND RESACA DE LA PALMA—IS APPOINTED QUARTERMASTER—DISTINGUISHES HIMSELF AT CHEPULTEPEC—WHAT THE OFFICIAL REPORTS SAY OF HIM—HIS OLD COMRADES IN MEXICO, AND WHAT BECAME OF THEM—RETURNS FROM THE MEXICAN WAR AND MARRIES.

THE life of a "plebe" at West Point is, to say the least of it, not pleasant. The brutal practices indulged in by the older students have long been a matter of terror to young men joining the academy, and he who expects to avoid the mischievous jokes of the seniors reckons without his host. The predecessor of Grant having failed to pass the requisite examination, our young hero reached the Point full of fears and misgivings as to his ability to go through the ordeal of the board. He knew his opportunities had been poor, that he possessed little knowledge, and, the more he thought over it, the more probable seemed his rejection.

While he was racked with the horrible feelings of suspense his tormentors began. The first night Grant was at the Point a cadet, dressed as an officer, entered his room, and, after some conversation, gave him a lesson of twenty pages of printed matter to commit to memory by morning. Ulysses dove into it, but soon gave up in despair, and retired to bed, while other boys sat up all night endeavoring to master their hard tasks. After a sleepless night the boys were surprised, the next morning, to find that the lesson was not called for, and, as the day wore on, they began to suspect they had been made the victims of a joke. The sight of these youths, book in hand, waiting nervously for hours until the professors should summon them to recitation, must, indeed, have been amusing to the older students.

Grant passed a fair examination, but not so good as the boys from the large towns and cities, who had enjoyed better school advantages. The General is now the head of the army, and, as such, the "Father of the Point;" and let us here ask him to remember, sometimes, the days when he was young Ulysses, and, when a poor country youth fails to pass his first examination, give him another chance, just for the sake of the days of "auld lang syne."

Grant entered the fourth class of 1839, and, during the year, studied English grammar, rhetoric, mathematics, geography, composition, declamation, French, and tactics. He made good progress, but was not brilliant.

As is well known, the cadets have to camp out during part of the year, and go through all the mock usages of camp life in time of war. Ulysses seems to have liked this as the best part of his cadet experience, and it is said he always preferred the tents on the field to quarters in the barracks.

During 1840, our young soldier entered the third class, where he studied cavalry tactics, and continued the other studies of the fourth class. The only thing that can be said of him during this year is that he showed considerable pluck and pertinacity of purpose. He had entered the class low down, and, after holding on steadily for awhile, advanced a file, and soon another, always holding on to what he got. There were several young men in the class who were more brilliant than Grant, but hardly one except him who did not fluctuate, sometimes advancing, and then falling back again. At the close of this year he was commissioned a corporal.

In 1841, he entered the second class, and studied experimental philosophy, chemistry, drawing, horsemanship, infantry and artillery tactics, and rose to the high dignity of a sergeant of cadets.

An officer, who was at that time a member of the Military Academy, thus describes Grant:

"I remember him well. He was a small, tiny-looking little fellow, with an independent air about him, and a good deal of determination. It is a long time ago, but when I recall old scenes I can still see Grant, with his overalls strapped down on his boots, standing in front of the quarters. It seems as though it were but yesterday that I saw him going to the riding hall, with his spurs clanging on the ground, and his great cavalry sword dangling by his side. It is twenty-seven years since, and I am growing old now, but it is wonderful what a short time it seems since I was a young man, and saw the famous soldier, then a mere stripling lad, at the Point."

During 1842, Grant entered the first class of the Military Academy, and took rank as a commissioned officer of cadets. He commanded sometimes a section of a battery, sometimes a troop, and then, again, a company of foot, and seems to have been well liked and respected by those who served under him. All the cadets still living of Grant's company agree that he was a fair, upright, and kind-hearted young man, never playing the petty tyrant or acting the spy on his subordinates, as young cadets who find themselves for the first time dressed in a little brief authority too often do. His studies, during this year, were laborious and difficult, including ethics, constitutional law, international law, military law, and practical, civil, and military engineering. In the fall he camped out again with his company, and, although a pretty strict officer while on duty, he seems to have been a jolly fellow round the camp-fire, and much liked by his comrades. During his last year, Grant made an effort to obtain some knowledge of the science of mineralogy and geology, and the Spanish language, but he made only tolerable progress.

On the 30th day of June, 1843, Grant passed his final examination, and graduated from the Military Academy in a class of thirty-nine, standing No. 21, or about the middle of the class.

It is said that the companions of a man's youth nearly always exercise a controlling influence over his after life, and, if his fortunes be great, are sure to share with him his honors and authority. In this view of the case we ought, perhaps, to state who Grant's comrades were, where they are, and, if still living, what they are now doing.

The names of the young men who graduated at the Military Academy, in 1843, in the class with Grant, were:

1. William B. Franklin; 2. George Deshon; 3. Thomas Brereton; 4. John H. Grelaud; 5. W. P. Raynolds (not Reynolds); 6. Isaac F. Quimby; 7. Roswell S. Ripley; 8. John J. Peck; 9. John P. Johnstone; 10. Joseph J. Reynolds. The name of the next graduate does not appear. 11. James A. Hardie; 12. Henry F. Clarke; 13. —— Booker; 14. Samuel G. French; 15. Theodore L. Chadbourne; 16. Christopher C. Auger; 17. Franklin Gardner; 18. George Stevens; 19. Edward B. Holloway; 20. Louis Neill; 21. Ulysses S. Grant; 22. Joseph H. Potter; 23. Robert Hazlitt; 24. Boyer Wood; 25. William K. Van Bokelen. The next four graduates do not appear. 30. Frederick Steele; 31. Henry R. Selden; 32. Rufus Ingalls; 33. Frederick T. Dent; 34. J. C. McFerran; 35. Henry M. Judah; 36. Norman Elting; 37. Cave J. Couts; 38. Charles G. Merchant; 39. George C. McClelland.

Of these men, Deshon was assistant professor in the Military Academy for two years, and when he resigned, in

1851, was ordnance officer at Alleghany Arsenal, Pennsylvania. He was somewhat noted for having resigned his commission in the army to become a Roman Catholic priest. Brereton was brevetted for gallant conduct in the Mexican War, and resigned after a continuous and highly honorable service of over fifteen years. Grelaud died a captain in the Fourth Artillery, at Fort Meyers, Florida, in 1857.

Franklin entered the Topographical Engineers, fought through the Mexican War, became a major-general under Grant, and is now living in civil life. Raynolds entered the infantry, was a colonel on the staff of Fremont during the war, and, we believe, is now dead. Quimby entered the artillery, was a professor at West Point, resigned, and retired to civil life, but, at the beginning of the war, reëntered the army, was a brigadier-general in the Army of the Potomac, and is now in civil life. Ripley entered the artillery, fought in the Mexican war, wrote a book to injure General Scott, resigned before the late war, and, at the opening of hostilities, joined the rebel army. Peck entered the artillery, resigned, reëntered the army in 1861, was a major-general in the Army of the James, and is now in civil life. J. J. Reynolds was a professor at the Point, became noted for his knowledge of the sciences, resigned before the war, reëntered the service in 1861, became a major-general, and is now colonel of the Twenty-sixth Infantry, and is commanding in Texas. He is an able man, and fit for any position in the Government. Johnstone entered the artillery, was a gallant officer in Mexico, and fell at Contreras. Hardie entered the artillery, became an assistant adjutant-general in the War Department, and is now a colonel in the inspector-general's department, and lives in Washington. Clarke entered the artillery, served with distinction in Mexico, served through the war in the Army of the Potomac as a commissary, and is now a lieutenant-colonel in the subsistence department, and lives in Washington. Booker, who stood thirteenth on the list of graduates, in 1843, died, while a lieutenant, at San Antonio, Texas, June 26, 1849. French, though a native of New Jersey, deserted the United States Army, in 1861, entered the rebellion, and became a major-general. He was an able man, and we think is now dead. Chadbourne was killed in the battle of Resaca de la Palma, May 9, 1846, and was distinguished for his bravery and coolness. Gardner, a native of New York, deserted the United States Army in 1861, and joined the rebellion. He became a Confederate major-general, and surrendered at Port Hudson, July 9, 1863. The last time we saw Franklin, he was standing in the St. Charles Hotel, at New Orleans, looking bloated and very seedy, and we presume, if Louisiana rum has n't killed him, he is still living. Auger entered the Second Infantry, became a major-general, commanded the Department of Washington for a long time, is colonel of the Twelfth Infantry, and serving with his regiment in the West. Stevens was drowned, in the passage of the Rio Grande, May, 1846. Holloway, of Kentucky, fought through the Mexican War, and distinguished himself at Contreras; he was captain of infantry at the beginning of the war, threw up his commission and joined the rebellion. Neill, who stood just above Grant on the list of graduates, died, January 13, 1850, while in service at Fort Crogham, Texas. Potter, who stood next after Grant, entered the Second Infantry, was a brigadier-general during the war, is now a lieutenant-colonel of the Thirteenth Infantry, and serving with his regiment. Hazlitt was killed at the storming of Monterey, September 21, 1846. Lieutenant Edwin Howe, of whom we find some account as graduating in 1843, in the class with Grant, and who died at Fort Leavenworth, March 31, 1850, was probably one of the officers whose names we have failed to find on the rolls, and stood twenty-six or twenty-seven. Wood left the army several years before the rebellion, but is, we believe, still living. He was from Virginia. The name of Charles S. Hamilton also appears on the list of graduates in 1843, after Woods; he is probably one of the officers whose names are missing on the rolls of the army, and, it is likely, never entered the service; he stood twenty-eight or twenty-nine on the list, was a major-general of volunteers, under Grant, commanded for a time a district in Tennessee, resigned, and is in civil life. Bokelen was a native of New York, but was cashiered for embezzling two hundred and twenty-five dollars public funds, and for rebel proclivities. The name of Alfred St. Amand de Crozet, of New York, appears as a graduate in the class of 1843; he died at the Spencer House, in Cincinnati, April 23, 1855, a first lieutenant in the Eighth United States Infantry. Charles E. James also appears among the graduates of 1843; he died at Sonora, California, June 8, 1849. Steele, the thirtieth graduate with Grant, entered the Second Infantry, was a major at the beginning of the war, became a major-general under Grant, was with him at Vicksburg, and in the Mississippi campaigns, as a division commander; afterward commanded in Arkansas, was appointed colonel of the Twentieth Infantry when the army was reorganized, and died a month or two since in California. He was an able and gallant officer, and much beloved and trusted by the General of the army. Selden entered the infantry, and was afterward a captain in the Fifth Regiment, but is not now in the service, nor is it known what became of him. Ingalls entered the rifles, was a major-general during the war, and quartermaster-general of the Army of the Potomac; he is now a colonel in the Quartermaster's Department, and lives in Washington. Dent entered the Fourth Infantry, served in Mexico, was a brigadier-general during the war, is now major of the Fourteenth Infantry, and on the staff of General Grant, who married his sister. McFerran entered the Third Infantry, was a quartermaster during the war, is now a lieutenant-colonel in the Quartermaster's Department, and lives at Washington. Judah entered the infantry, was a brigadier-general during the war, and commanded a division of the Twenty-third Army Corps, in Kentucky, for some time; he is now dead. Elting resigned the service October 29, 1846; it is not known whether he is living or dead. Couts resigned soon after graduating, and, in the year 1849, was a member of the California State Constitutional Convention; it is not known whether he is living or dead. Merchant resigned soon after graduating, and, we believe, is still living in New York city. George C. McClelland, of Pennsylvania, was the last graduate, and is not now in service.

It is interesting to look over the list and see how the twenty-first graduate has outstripped all the rest; and when we remember that their chances in the race of life were equal, if not better than his, we can not but believe that it was true talent, and not accident, which brought Grant to the front, and gave him command over his thirty-eight associates.

Professor Coppee, in his history of the rebellion, thus describes Grant at the time he left the Military Academy, in 1843. He says:

"I had the honor of being Grant's comrade at West Point for two years. I remember him as a plain, straightforward, common-sense youth; quiet, rather of the old-head-on-young-shoulders order; shunning notoriety; quite contented while others were grumbling; taking to his military duties in a very business-like manner; not a prominent man in the corps, but respected by all, and very popular with his friends. His sobriquet of 'Uncle Sam,' where every good fellow has a nickname, came from these very qualities; indeed, he was a very Uncle Sam-like sort of a youth. He was then, and always, an excellent horseman, and his picture rises before me as I write, in an old torn coat, obsolescent, leather, gig-top, loose riding pantaloons. He exhibited little enthusiasm in any thing. His best standing was in the mathematical branches and their applications to tactics and military engineering."

A story is told of Grant during his cadet life which is worth repeating here, as it is characteristic of the man. The persecutions of his seniors were very annoying to him, and Grant believing them no longer tolerable, had made up his mind to fight. One day when the company was on mock-parade, the captain put some insult upon him, when Grant stepped suddenly out of the ranks, pulled off his jacket, and said:

"Now, captain, if you think you are as good a man as I am, pull off your coat and fight me."

The captain doffed his jacket, and at it they went. Grant was the smaller of the two, but he got the captain down and pummeled him until he cried enough.

"Now," said Grant, going up to the lieutenant, "you have been imposing on me, too, and I want a settlement with you."

Such a challenge was not to be declined, and the lieutenant pitched into him, but Grant knocked him down and thrashed him soundly, and then turning to the company, said:

"Who comes next? I want peace, and I am going to have it, if I have to lick the whole company."

At this his comrades set up a shout, and the captain coming up to him, said: "You'll do; I guess they won't bother you any more, Grant."

For a long time after this occurrence, Grant was known

at the Point as "Company Grant." The plucky little fellow had rid himself of his tormentors, the boys never afterward attempting to run any of their jokes on him.

When Grant left the Military Academy, he took the accustomed three months' leave of absence granted to graduates, and on the 1st day of July, 1843, was gazetted for the Fourth Infantry, and attached to that regiment by brevet. In the fall of the year, he joined his regiment, then stationed at Jefferson Barracks, Missouri. Among the young officers who graduated with Grant, and who were assigned to the Fourth Infantry, was his class-mate, Frederick Dent. Dent's parents lived about four miles from the barracks, and as he and Grant had been quite intimate at the Point, it was but natural that he should invite his young friend to visit his home. Here it was Grant saw, for the first time, the good woman who is now his wife; he soon won the girlish heart of Julia Dent, and they became engaged, but the rising troubles in Mexico caused them to postpone their marriage, and Grant was soon afterward ordered off with his regiment. The leaving of a sweetheart behind is a thing that often happens to officers in the army, and is about the hardest thing in all nature. Often have we seen a pale Hamlet stalking through our camp, with an order for the frontier in his pocket, and we have never failed, if it were possible, to give the poor fellow a short respite from his torments. Talk of sickness in the family, the death of a father; these things are as nothing when compared with the great grief that tears a fond fellow from a pair of loving arms. Having had some experience in such matters, we presume that Grant's feelings were any thing but comfortable when leaving his Julia, to take the chances of getting his head knocked off in Mexico.

The Mexicans and Americans had for some time held imaginary boundary lines in Texas, and the disputes daily arising between the settlers had at last broken out into open war. Corpus Christi had been seized by General Taylor, as a base of operations, and thither the Fourth Infantry was hurried. While stationed at this place, Grant received his full commission as second lieutenant in the Seventh Infantry, which bears date of September 30th, 1845, but having become attached to the officers of the Fourth, he determined to wait for a vacancy in his own regiment, and declined to accept the position tendered him in the Seventh Regiment. He had not long, however, to wait, for, on the 19th of November, 1845, his commission reached him as full second lieutenant in the Fourth Infantry.

War had not yet been formally declared by Congress against Mexico, but the matter was considered settled; and General Taylor, hearing that a large force of Mexicans was marching toward the Rio Grande, with the avowed intention of crossing over, and driving the American settlers out of Texas, he hastened to meet them, but learning that Fort Brown had been besieged, he changed his route, and marched to the relief of the garrison. In Taylor's command was the Fourth Infantry, and, among others toiling along on foot through the dreary sand, and thinking day and night of his sweetheart in the far-off States, was a love-sick lieutenant, named Ulysses Grant.

On the 8th day of May, 1846, the Mexican and American forces met in battle at Palo Alto, and here, for the first time, Grant smelt powder and saw war. No mention is made of him in any of the official reports; but his companions say he did well, and won the good opinion of his superiors. Next day Taylor followed up the Mexicans to Resaca de la Palma, and fought a battle, completely routing the enemy. Here again we find no official mention made of Grant; but his comrades say he behaved with great gallantry.

The Mexicans, in full retreat, rushed pell-mell over the Rio Grande, while General Taylor marched up the river, crossed over into the republic of New Leon, and moved against Monterey. Meanwhile, General Scott had arrived at Vera Cruz, and ordered a portion of the forces on the Rio Grande to coöperate with him. Among the regiments sent down was the Fourth Infantry, and Grant with it participated in the siege of Vera Cruz, which surrendered to the American forces on the 29th day of March, 1847.

The quartermaster, commissary and adjutant of a regiment are always selected by the commanding officer from the most intelligent, energetic, trusty, and best young officers in the regiment; and Grant must already have obtained considerable standing, and attracted the notice of his superiors, for in April, 1847, he was appointed quartermaster of the Fourth Infantry.

As a usual thing, quartermasters do not fight much, but Grant seems to have been an exception to the general rule; for he participated in all the battles in which his regiment was engaged. At the battle of Chepultepec, on the 13th of September, 1847, he behaved with distinguished gallantry, being appointed a first lieutenant and a brevet captain, to date from the day of the battle. In his report, Captain Horace Brooks, who commanded a battery of the Second Artillery in the battle, says:

"I succeeded in reaching the fort with a few men. Here Lieutenant U. S. Grant with a few more men of the Fourth Infantry, found me, and by a joint movement, after an obstinate resistance, a strong field work was carried, and the enemy's right completely turned."

The official report of Major Francis Lee, commanding the Fourth Infantry in the battle of Chepultepec, contains this paragraph:

"At the first barrier the enemy was in strong force, which

rendered it necessary to advance with caution. This was done; and when the head of the battalion was within short musket range of the barrier, Lieutenant Grant, Fourth Infantry, and Captain Brooks, Second Artillery, with a few men of their respective regiments, by a handsome movement to the left, turned the right flank of the enemy, and the barrier was carried." And he mentions Lieutenant Grant as "among the most distinguished for his zeal and activity," and as "behaving with great gallantry on both the 13th and the 14th." Brevet Colonel John Garland, Grant's brigade commander, in his report of the battle of Chepultepec, says:

"The rear of the enemy had made a stand behind a breastwork from which they were driven by detachments of the Second Artillery, under Captain Brooks, and the Fourth Infantry, under Lieutenant Ulysses Grant, supported by other regiments of the division. The conflict was sharp but decisive. . . . . . . I recognized the command as it came up, mounted a howitzer on the top of a convent, which, under the direction of Lieutenant Grant, quartermaster of the Fourth Infantry, and Lieutenant Lendrum, of the Third Artillery, annoyed the enemy considerably." . . . In closing his report, Colonel Garland says: "I must not omit to call attention to Lieutenant Grant, Fourth Infantry, who acquitted himself most nobly upon several occasions under my own observation."

In this report General Garland makes particular mention of only two officers besides his own staff, and these are Lieutenant Grant and Captain Brooks. General Worth, in his report of the operations of the army on the 16th of September, speaks highly of Lieutenant Grant, but the extract is too long to insert here.

Grant participated in sixteen battles in Mexico, and at the close of the war returned to St. Louis with his regiment, and in 1848 was married to Miss Julia S. Dent.

We must now turn aside again from the straight path of our narrative to make some mention of the men who were General Grant's comrades in Mexico. The roster of his regiment, the Fourth Infantry, stood at that time as follows:

Lieutenant-Colonel John Garland, commanding the regiment and brigade; brevetted colonel for Resaca de la Palma; brevetted brigadier for Cherubusco; severely wounded in the capture of Mexico City; made colonel of the Eighth Regular Infantry, May, 1848, and died in the city of New York, June 5, 1861.

Major Francis Lee, brevetted lieutenant-colonel for Cherubusco; brevetted colonel for Molino del Rey; appointed colonel of Second Regiment Infantry, October 18, 1855, and died at St. Louis, Missouri, January 19, 1859.

Captain George W. Allen, brevetted major for Florida war; brevetted lieutenant-colonel for Resaca de la Palma; appointed major Second United States Infantry, and died at Vera Cruz, March 15, 1848.

John Page, mortally wounded in first battle of Palo Alto, and died July 12, 1846.

William M. Graham, brevetted major for Florida war; promoted major Second United States Infantry, February 16, 1847; appointed lieutenant-colonel Eleventh Infantry; wounded three times in Mexico; killed at Molino del Rey, September 8, 1847.

Pitcairn Morrison, brevetted major for Resaca de la Palma; promoted major Eighth United States Infantry, September 26, 1847; promoted lieutenant-colonel Seventh Infantry, June 9, 1853; promoted colonel Eighth Infantry, June 6, 1861; retired from active service, October 20, 1863; still living, but over seventy years old.

George A. McCall, brevetted major and lieutenant-colonel for Resaca de la Palma; appointed in the Inspector-General's

Department, with the rank of major; resigned April 29, 1853; reëntered service April, 1861; appointed brigadier-general, May 17, 1861; appointed major-general, and assigned to command of Pennsylvania Reserve Regiments; resigned March 31, 1863; died about two months ago in Pennsylvania.

Gouverneur Morris, brevetted major for Resaca de la Palma; promoted major Third Infantry, January 31, 1850; promoted lieutenant-colonel First Infantry, 1857; retired from active service, September 9, 1861; still living, but very old and feeble.

R. C. Buchanan, brevetted major for Resaca de la Palma; brevetted lieutenant-colonel for Molino del Rey; appointed acting inspector-general, 1848; promoted major Fourth Infantry, September 9, 1851; appointed lieutenant-colonel Fourth Infantry, September 9, 1851; appointed brigadier, May, 1861, but was too old to take the field; promoted colonel First Regular Infantry, February 8, 1864; is still living, and at present in command of the Fifth District, in place of General Hancock, relieved.

Charles H. Larned, brevetted major for Resaca de la Palma; drowned in Puget's Sound, near Fort Madison, Washington Territory, March 27, 1854.

Benjamin Alvord, brevetted captain for Resaca de la Palma; brevetted major for National Bridge; appointed paymaster, with rank of major, June 22, 1854; appointed brigadier-general volunteers, 1863; appointed brevet major-general in the regular army, April 9, 1865; at present a major in the Paymaster's Department, and lives in Washington.

Henry L. Scott, appointed aid-de-camp and assistant adjutant-general on General Scott's staff, 1847; brevetted major for Cherubusco; brevetted lieutenant-colonel for Chepultepec; appointed special aid to General Scott, March 7,

1855; retired from service, October 30, 1861, and died about two years ago in New York City.

First Lieutenant Henry Prince, adjutant of the Fourth Infantry, 1846; brevetted captain for Cherubusco; severely wounded, and brevetted major for Molino del Rey; appointed paymaster, May 23, 1855; appointed brigadier-general volunteers, April 28, 1862; commanded a division Twenty-third Army Corps, during the rebellion; brevetted a brigadier in the regular army, March 13, 1865; is at present a major in the Pay Department, and lives in Washington.

Charles Haskins, at one time adjutant Fourth Infantry; killed at Monterey, September 21, 1846.

Richard Graham, mortally wounded at the battle of Monterey, September 21, 1846, and died October 12, 1846.

John H. Gore, brevetted captain for Cherubusco; brevetted major for Molino del Rey; died August 1, 1852, in Bay of Panama, New Grenada.

Richard E. Cochran, killed in the battle of Resaca de la Palma, May 9, 1846.

Theodore H. Porter, killed in a skirmish, near the Rio Grande, April 19, 1846.

Sidney Smith, wounded at Molino del Rey; mortally wounded in the attack upon Mexico City, September 14, 1847; died September 16, 1847.

Granville O. Haller, brevetted captain for Molino del Rey; brevetted major for Chepultepec; appointed full captain, January, 1848; appointed major Seventh Infantry, September 25, 1861; summarily dismissed from service, August, 1863.

Henry D. Wallen, wounded at Palo Alto, May 8, 1846; appointed adjutant, February, 1849; promoted captain, January 31, 1850; promoted major Seventh Infantry, November 25, 1861; promoted lieutenant-colonel, July 30, 1865; is at present commanding Fort Columbus, New York.

Henderson Ridgely, appointed assistant adjutant-general to General Lane, 1846; killed at Pass Gaudalaxara, November 24, 1847.

Jenks Beaman, participated in the battles of Palo Alto and Resaca de la Palma; commanded his company in the battle of Molino del Rey; died at Tampico, May 6, 1848.

SECOND LIEUTENANTS.

Christopher R. Perry, fought through the war; died October 8, 1848, on his road home.

C. C. Auger, of whom some account is given elsewhere in these papers.

Ulysses S. Grant, the subject of these narratives.

Henry M. Judah, of whom mention is made elsewhere.

James S. Woods, brevetted first lieutenant for Resaca de la Palma; killed at Monterey, September 21, 1846.

Alexander Hayes, brevetted first lieutenant for Resaca de la Palma; appointed assistant adjutant-general to General Lane, 1847; resigned April 12, 1848; entered the volunteer service, 1861; was a brigadier-general in the Army of the Potomac, and fell, we think, at Gettysburg.

Abraham Lincoln, wounded at Molino del Rey, and brevetted a first lieutenant; died at Pilatka, Florida, April 15, 1852.

Thomas J. Montgomery, commanded his company at Cherubusco and Molino del Rey; appointed first lieutenant, December, 1847; appointed captain, March, 1854; died at Fort Steilacoom, Washington Territory, November 22, 1854.

David A. Russell, brevetted first lieutenant for the National Bridge; remained in the regular army until the beginning of the late war; appointed a brigadier-general of volunteers; served in the Army of the Potomac as a division commander, and fell, we think, at Chancellorsville.

Delancy Floyd James, brevetted first lieutenant for Molino del Rey; was lieutenant-colonel (during the war) of the Nineteenth United States Infantry; is at present colonel of the Sixth United States Infantry, and serving with his regiment.

Alexander P. Rodgers, wounded and afterward killed at Chepultepec, September 13, 1847.

Maurice Maloney, brevetted first lieutenant for Molino del Rey; brevetted captain for Chepultepec; wounded at San Cosme Gate, September 13, 1847; promoted to full first lieutenant, May, 1848; promoted captain, November, 1854; promoted major First United States Infantry, September 16, 1862; promoted lieutenant-colonel, June 21, 1867, and, we believe, is at present serving in New Orleans.

Archibald B. Botts, died, January, 1847, at Camargo, Mexico.

Thomas R. McConnell, brevetted first lieutenant for Molino del Rey; brevetted captain for Chepultepec; promoted to full captain, February, 1855; resigned, March 11, 1856, and, if not dead, is in civil life.

Edmund Russell, wounded at Cherubusco; brevetted first lieutenant for Molino del Rey; killed by the Indians, near Red Bluff, California, March 24, 1853.

Abbott, in his "Life of Grant," tells the following story, which seems to be well authenticated:

"At Monterey, the brigade with which Lieutenant Grant served had pushed its way into the heart of the city. The firing was heavy. Suddenly it was discovered the ammunition was running out. There was no egress from the perilous position except through the narrow street, the houses on one side of which were held by the Mexicans, who fired from every door and window. General Gardner hesitated about ordering any one to make the perilous attempt to get out for ammunition. Grant, who was an accomplished horseman, volunteered, and, throwing himself on one of the officer's horses, he put the animal to the top of its speed, and on approaching the Mexican barricades caught his foot in the crupper of the saddle, and, grasping the mane with his hands, hung on the side of the horse, so as to shield his body, passed through the gauntlet in safety, and in an hour returned with a wagon loaded with ammunition."

As before stated, Grant, after the Mexican War, returned to St. Louis and married Miss Dent. Having obtained a short leave of absence, he set off to spend his honey-moon, and here we leave him for the present.

CHAPTER III.

GRANT AND CHANDLER—GRANT IS STATIONED AT DETROIT AND SACKETT'S HARBOR—GOES TO CALIFORNIA AND THENCE TO OREGON—GARRISON LIFE ON THE FRONTIER—HE IS APPOINTED A FULL CAPTAIN—RESIGNS FROM THE ARMY AND RETURNS TO ST. LOUIS—BECOMES A FARMER—SKETCHES OF GRANT IN CIVIL LIFE—GOES INTO THE REAL ESTATE AND AUCTIONEERING BUSINESS—MOVES TO GALENA, ILLINOIS—RAISES A COMPANY FOR THE WAR—IS APPOINTED COLONEL OF THE TWENTY-FIRST ILLINOIS INFANTRY.

At the expiration of his honey-moon leave of absence, Grant joined his regiment, and soon afterward went with it to Detroit. It was while stationed here that a little incident happened, out of which Grant's Democratic enemies have manufactured a very large story. In the Northern cities, where snow and ice lie on the ground for many months in the year, as every one knows, the corporation laws require the owners of property to keep clear their pavements. Senator Zechariah Chandler, then a merchant in Detroit, neglected to clear the ice away in front of his house, and one morning, as Grant was coming into town from the fort, he slipped and fell on Mr. Chandler's pavement, and hurt his leg severely. Knowing that the ice should have been cleared away, and enraged by his hurt, Grant entered a complaint before the town authorities against Chandler. The case came up, and Grant appeared against Chandler, and testified to the ice being on the pavement in violation of the city laws. Chandler, in person, defended his case, and, among other things, asked Grant how he knew there was ice on his pavement. "Why, I fell on it and hurt myself; besides, I saw it as I drove by in my cutter," replied Grant. "Oh, you saw it as you fell in the gutter, did you," said Chandler; and then, to mortify Grant, and pay him for the trouble he had given, Chandler continued: "If you soldiers would keep sober, perhaps you would not fall on people's pavements and hurt your legs."

This made Grant very wroth, and he talked about whipping Chandler, who was about twice his size, but no fight occurred, and, except some sharp words, there was no quarrel. The Democratic papers have it that Grant cowhided Chandler, but there is not one word of truth in that, and the above is the whole of the story as related to us by an officer who was serving in Grant's regiment at the time of the occurrence.

Chandler was fined, and made to clear the ice off his pavement, but he has, no doubt, long ago forgiven Ulysses for the trouble he gave him.

Grant's regiment went from Detroit to Sackett's Harbor, and from thence to Governor's Island, where it remained a short time.

The annexation of California, and the discovery of gold, drew thither a vast emigration from the States, and to protect our citizens, and keep peace and order among the thousands of desperate men who were pouring from all quarters in search of the glittering dust, it became necessary to send out troops; and the Fourth Infantry was one of the first regiments ordered off. Grant was obliged to leave his wife and child behind, and Mrs. Grant went to his father's, where their second child was soon afterward born. An officer, who was with Grant at the time, says he complained of the harsh orders of the Government compelling him to separate from his little family, and for several days meditated resigning. We doubt not that Grant fully resolved, if ever he became the head of the army, he would adopt a system of orders that would not necessitate the separation of officers from their families, but he seems to have forgotten it, for it is not long since the writer, "by order of General Grant," sent a young officer into the wilds of Texas, while his stricken, and well-nigh heart-broken wife, with her little one, was obliged to return North to his father's, just as Grant's wife did a quarter of a century ago. We hope the General will not forget his old resolve, but remedy the present unchristian system of orders used in the army. Whom God hath joined together, let no man put asunder, by orders or otherwise.

Grant saw but little of the scenes of violence and lawlessness enacted in California, in 1852 and 1853, by the reckless white men, treacherous Mexicans, and more bloodthirsty Indians that thronged thither; for the company to which he was attached, after making a brief stop at San Francisco, was hurried on to Fort Dallas, in the wilds of Oregon.

Life in garrison there must have been almost insupportably wearisome. The days came and went in the same solitary monotony; now and then an Indian hunt, a game of billiards for the beer, a mail from the States, or a scrub horse race, was all that broke the dreariness of life in that distant territory. It is charged that Grant drank a good deal at this time, and it is well known that officers, when stationed in such solitary garrisons, far away from their families, often drink more than they should; but we can find no officer, who was in garrison at that time with Grant, who will say that he ever saw him drunk, or under the influence of liquor. It is not to be denied that he sometimes took a glass, but we never knew an officer in a frontier garrison who did not occasionally drink. In large towns and cities, where we constantly breathe the air that has passed through the lungs of two or three Democratic topers, we get enough whisky in the atmosphere to do us: but out on the great plains of the West, where one gets air that was never breathed by mortal man, two or three nights' camping out, and long journeys by day, makes one feel wonderfully like taking something. If you do n't believe it, try it, and see if you do n't surprise yourself by taking a horn at the very first fort you come to. Not only do the officers, as a general thing, take their grog when on frontier duty, but we have yet to find the first minister who would refuse, when pressed, after he got as far out as Santa Fe, to "take a glass of something real good, just from the States." The mere mention of the States, in the far, far off regions, is enough to remove a man's objections, if he had any.

The Democrats have repeatedly charged General Grant with being a drunkard; and yet, perhaps, as a body, the Democrats drink more whisky than any people in the United States. Rum and Democracy seem to be one and inseparable, and, if Grant ever drank much liquor, it was while he lived at St. Louis, and was a member of the Democratic party. *We have made careful and honest inquiry, and say, most emphatically, that Grant, from the time he entered West Point, in* 1839, *until he resigned from the army, in* 1854, *and from the time he rejoined the army, in* 1861, *up to the present date, has always been a sober man.*

We well remember how the papers said that General McDowell lost the first battle of Bull Run because he was drunk, and we doubt not that thousands of good people, to this day, think McDowell is a drunkard, when, as scores of officers in the army can testify, he is a perfect old maid about whisky, never drinks a drop, and is constantly lecturing officers who do take a glass. John B. Gough is not a better temperance man than Irvin McDowell. It was a mighty hard cut on him, after being a temperance man all his life, and devoting his spare time to lecturing the young officers on the beauty of total abstinence, to give the old soldier a national reputation as a drunkard. As Charlie Norris, of the dragoons, used to say, "If Mac had n't talked temperance so much, and had taken his glass regularly, along with the rest of us, them newspaper chaps would never have cracked that joke about his getting drunk at Bull Run."

John Pope says, "If you want to injure a man, and can't think of any thing else to charge against him, just say he gets drunk, and, as half the people take their grog, they will be sure to believe it." There is a good deal of truth in that, and Pope might have added, "If you want to discredit a man, just say he is a liar;" and, although we can't say whether for the same reason that he advances in the case of whisky, yet certain it is that at one time the American people believed Pope the greatest liar living, when the facts of history go to show that he is really one of the most truthful men in the country.

At Shiloh, while riding fast, Grant's horse fell, and gave him a severe contusion; thereupon some newspaper writers gave out he was drunk, and fell off his horse, when the truth was Grant was just as sober at the battle of Shiloh as the ministers will be who will go into their pulpits to preach to the people next Sabbath day. These examples will serve to show how easy it is for the people to be mistaken in a man's character when they get their information from the teachings of a venal, unscrupulous, and partisan press.

While stationed at Fort Dallas, in August, 1853, Grant received his commission as full captain in the Fourth United States Infantry. While Grant was a first lieutenant he was quartermaster of his regiment, and bore the reputation of being a careless, good-natured fellow, and, withal, a very good officer. One day, either because he had no trunk of his own, or because he had more confidence in the care of his comrade, Grant gave Lieutenant Gore his quartermaster's funds to keep. Gore locked the money up (amounting, in all, to about six hundred dollars) in his trunk, and one day while all the officers were out of the quarters, a soldier who was a member of the Fourth Infantry band, stole the money from the trunk and deserted with it. As is often the case, Grant was obliged to carry this money on his returns up to the time when he quit the army, and it remained charged against him in the Treasury until after the capture of Vicksburg, when Mr. Arnold, of Illinois, introduced a bill in the House of Representatives, and had him relieved from all responsibility in the matter. This is the same money that the Democrats now charge Grant with being a defaulter for, only, under Democratic manipulation, it has grown from six hundred to seventeen thousand dollars—a slight increase, but not much when calculated by Copperhead arithmetic. Those Democrats who charge Grant with being a defaulter should turn over the files of the Globe, and they will find that every Democratic member then in Congress voted for the bill relieving Grant from all responsibility in the loss of the money, they believing that it was no fault of his whatever.

In 1854, Grant having become thoroughly home-sick, and seeing no chance of having his family with him for years to come, determined to resign. He wished to become a farmer, and wrote to his father-in-law, who owned some land near St. Louis. Mr. Dent offered to give Mrs. Grant a farm, and the General's father said he would stock it; so, on the 31st day of July, 1854, Grant tendered his resignation, which was accepted, and he returned to St. Louis, and soon afterward moved on to his wife's farm, near that city.

Although Grant worked hard, he got poorer every day, and finally gave up farming. True, he had made some improvements on his farm, having built fences, and a house, which is still standing, the logs of which he hewed with his own hands, but at the end of four years he found himself, pecuniarily, considerably worse off than when he began. During the last years of his farm life he hauled a great deal of wood to St. Louis, the Hon. Mr. Blow frequently buying from him.

A gentleman, who is now a citizen of St. Louis, thus speaks of Grant:

"I knew him well when he was a farmer. Often have I seen him driving home his wood-wagon, in his old felt hat and farmer coat. He was a sensible, plain, matter-of-fact man, and very industrious. I heard he sometimes drank, but I never saw him under the influence of liquor, nor did I ever hear any of his neighbors say they saw Grant tight. He was a hard-working, clever man, and we all liked him, but never thought he would be great some day."

The following anecdote is told of Grant, referring to his former life:

"Last winter the General gave a party in his fine house at Washington, and among the hundreds who came was Mrs. Blow, whom Grant had not seen since he lived at St. Louis. After shaking the lady warmly by the hand, and expressing his delight at seeing her under his roof, the General said:

"'Well, Mrs. Blow, times have changed a good deal with me of late.'

"'Yes,' replied Mrs. B., not wishing to refer to his days of poverty, and thinking the General spoke of the war, 'we have peace at last, and I suppose you are glad of it, as you can rest now.'

"'I am, indeed, happy to think the country is once more united, but I did not refer to the war when I spoke of the times having changed with me. I was thinking of when I used to haul wood to your house in St. Louis, and you used to give me orders on Mr. Blow at the office. Don't you remember it?'"

Mrs. B. replied she did, and the General then went on and spoke with simplicity and feeling of the times when he was a farmer and wood dealer.

In 1858, Grant gave up farming, rented out his land, and moved into St. Louis, where he and a Mr. Boggs opened a real estate office. They were not successful, and Grant, who soon saw there was not enough profit in the business to support two families, told his partner to take all of it, and he would look up something else to do. He next got a situation in the custom-house, but the collector dying soon afterward, he was either discharged or left of his own accord.* He now tried his hand at collecting debts, but for this business he was not at all qualified. It is said Grant always apologized for dunning a debtor, and when he was told by a fellow he had no money he believed him and went off, nor could he be induced to go back and trouble him again. Grant next became an auctioneer; it is amusing now to think of the silent General as an auctioneer, praising the quality of wares. Imagine Grant mounted behind the counter singing out to the crowd: "Here is an article, gentlemen, of use to every family, and such a one as can not be had anywhere else in the city for the money. Look at it; sound as a dollar, and I will sell it cheap. How much do I hear for this fine butter bowl? Say two fifty; one dollar. Start it at seventy-five cents, somebody. Seventy-five; I hear seventy-five? seventy-five, seventy-five, seventy-five; say one dollar; one dollar it is; one dollar, one dollar, one dollar, one dollar; are you all off at one dollar? It is a shame to let so fine a butter bowl go at that price. One dollar, once—one dollar, twice; and three—do I hear no

* An officer, who was stationed at Jefferson Barracks at this time, informs us that Grant applied to the Quartermaster's Department in St. Louis for a clerkship, and was refused.

more? t-h-r-e-e times. Gone at one dollar, and you have a real bargain in it, sir."

Grant found auctioneering a dull business; indeed, if he did not make longer speeches than he does now, it is a wonder he ever sold a single article at cost. In 1859, Grant's father, a thrifty, sharp old gentleman, came to look after his son's prospects, and seeing he was not prospering, offered him an interest in the successful leather house of Grant & Son, at Galena, Illinois. Grant gladly accepted his father's proposal to go into the leather trade, and began preparations for moving at once with his family to Galena.

Speaking of his residence at St. Louis, a leading merchant writes of Grant:

"I remember the General well when he occupied a little farm to the south-west of the city. He cut the wood off his place, and was in the habit of drawing it to Carondelet market, and there selling it. There are many of our citizens who bought wood by the cord from him, and can still call to mind the time when they made purchases of the great General. When he came into market he was usually dressed in an old felt hat, with a blouse coat, and his pants tucked in the top of his boots. He appeared, as he was, like a sturdy, honest woodman. From all I can learn, he was a hard-working, reliable, and truthful man. He was always at work at something, but although he farmed all summer and hauled wood all winter, he did not possess the knack of making money, and got poorer every year. He borrowed money sometimes, but, always strictly honorable, he promptly repaid it. His habits of life were hardy, inexpensive and simple, but he was one of those men of whom we often say, 'He has no luck in any thing he does, the fates are against him;' indeed, we guess poor Grant often thought so himself, as he struggled along with the world, but his time hadn't come yet, as we have all seen since, and there is not one of us but would gladly have endured all his hardships for such a glorious future. As to the inquiry about his being an inebriate, I can find nothing to confirm it. On a cold day, when he had brought a load of wood to Carondelet market, he would take something to keep himself warm, but would not drink too much. This, so far as I can trace, is the only foundation for the many reports about his inebriety at this time."

Professor Coppee, who was a cadet at West Point with Grant, thus speaks of him:

"I visited St. Louis at this time (1857), and remember, with pleasure, that Grant, in his farmer rig, whip in hand, came to see me at the hotel, where were Joseph J. Reynolds, then professor, now major-general, General (then major) D. C. Buell and Major Chapman, of the cavalry. Grant may have used spirits then, but I distinctly remember that upon the proposal being made to take a drink, Grant said, 'I will go in and look at you, but I never drink any thing;' and other officers, who saw him frequently afterward, told me that Grant drank nothing but water."

Grant and his two brothers succeeded well with their store at Galena. Grant was a good salesman and attended closely to business. His share of the profits soon enabled him to build a comfortable house, and about the beginning of the war the greatest concern of Grant was to get a good board-walk laid from his house to the store. He has often said that the only office he ever desired to hold, was mayor of Galena, so he could get that walk put down. It is related, that after one of his great victories, some gentlemen of Galena had the walk laid, and telegraphed the General: "Rest easy, the walk is down." Grant seems to have been little known to his fellow-citizens, for after he had become famous, his father tells us that the citizens would stop in the store to see which of the Grant boys it was that had gone to the war.

In 1861, when the news of the firing on Fort Sumter reached Galena, Grant was in his store; and after reading the account, he laid down the paper, and said to a friend who was standing by: "I shall go to the war. You know Uncle Sam educated me for the army, and though I have served him through one war, I feel I have not yet canceled the debt I owe the Government." Grant pulled on his coat, and going into the streets of Galena, commenced raising a company of volunteers. Sumter fell on the 13th of April, 1861. President Lincoln called for seventy-five thousand troops on the 15th, and on the 19th Grant was drilling his company at Galena. The men expected to elect Grant their captain; but a citizen confessing to Grant that he was anxious to go into the war, and thinking the captaincy would serve as a stepping-stone to something higher, Grant at once gave way, and he took the company to the State Capital. Grant at once wrote to the Adjutant-General of the army, at Washington—Lorenzo Thomas—stating he had been educated at West Point, and tendering his services in any capacity he could be useful; but the Government thought so little of the matter that they did not even reply to his letter.*

Hon. E. B. Washburn, who was then the Representative in Congress from the Galena District, had noticed the patriotic exertions of Grant, and one day sent for him, and learning his story, offered at once to go with him to Springfield, and urge Richard Yates, the Governor of the State, to give him something to do in the war. They set out together, and on reaching the Capital, Governor Yates, on the recommendation of Mr. Washburn, appointed Grant an aid-de-camp on his staff as commander-in-chief of the Illinois forces, and

*So little was thought of this letter that it was not even preserved, but torn up and thrown into the waste basket.

assigned him to the duty of mustering in the troops. Governor Yates soon perceived that Grant's practical knowledge of military matters would make him a valuable man to have about his person, and he appointed him Adjutant-General of the State. Grant worked with a will at the difficult task of mustering in the three-months' men, which, amid much confusion, he accomplished by the most indefatigable energy, but seeing Yates was disposed to keep him at the Capital, when he wanted to be in the field, and learning that an old West Pointer, McClellan, had been appointed to command at the West, and was then at Cincinnati, he determined to visit his father at Covington, and see if McClellan would not give him duty in the field. Grant secretly hoped that when General McClellan saw him, he would offer him a position on his staff, but, although he went twice to Cincinnati to see the young Napoleon, no offer of a place was made him, and Grant was about to return to Illinois without mentioning his aspirations to any one, when his father received a dispatch from Governor Yates, stating that "Ulysses Grant had been appointed colonel of the Twenty-first Illinois Infantry." Grant at once resigned his appointment as mustering officer, accepted the colonelcy of the Twenty-first, and joined his regiment, which was then organizing at Mattoon, Illinois.

After removing his men to Caseyville, and drilling them for a short time, Grant, on the 31st day of July, 1861, reported with his regiment to General John Pope, then commanding the District of Missouri, was assigned by that General to the command of the troops at Mexico, on the North Missouri Railroad, and here Grant began his first military operations in the war of the rebellion, a war destined to make him the most famous of living generals.

. . . . . Since the above was written, we have received a very long and interesting letter from a brother officer who served with Grant in the Fourth Infantry. We make the following extracts:

. . . . . "I cheerfully comply with your request to tell you what I know about Grant's early military life. My association with him began at Detroit, in 1848, at the time of his return from his bridal tour. I was then a second lieutenant in the Fourth Infantry, and I well remember the day Grant came to the post with his young bride and his sister. Grant was the regimental quartermaster, and, after his hard campaigns in Mexico, entitled to rest, but an officer, who, I have always believed, did it from purely selfish motives, got Grant ordered to the then bleak and undesirable post of Sackett's Harbor. Although Grant's proper place as quartermaster was at Detroit with the regimental head-quarters, he uncomplainingly obeyed the order. He, however, laid his grievances before Brevet Colonel Francis Lee, commanding the regiment, and, after due consultation, his case was forwarded to Washington for the decision of the General-in-Chief, Winfield Scott. The old General decided Grant should go back to Detroit, and, as soon as navigation on the lakes was open, he returned to head-quarters to the delight of many of us, and the complete discomfiture of his few, but selfish enemies. That Grant is a generous and magnanimous man, I think, is fully shown by the fact that, after his return to Detroit, he never kept spite against the officer who did him so great an injustice, but invited him to his ever hospitable quarters, and, during the late war, heaped upon him every honor he could.

. . . . . "It was while stationed at the City of the Straits, that Grant had a difficulty with Senator Chandler, then a merchant in that place. It was something about ice on Chandler's pavement, upon which Grant had fallen and hurt himself. He had Chandler brought before the city authorities, for violating the ordinances, and, I have always understood, came off first best in the affair.

. . . . . "I did not see Grant after leaving him at Detroit, until 1852, when I met him at Fort Columbus, New York, where the regiment had been concentrated, preparatory to embarking for California. He had to leave his wife and child behind; and, although this was a sad blow to him, he exhibited great energy, and did his best, as regimental quartermaster, to make the officers and men comfortable on their way out. At Panama Bay, the Asiatic cholera caught us, and here Grant lost his most intimate friend and companion, Brevet Major J. H. Gore, who died on the 1st of August, 1852. Grant remained fearlessly by the side of his stricken brother officers, and every day went among the men where the terrible disease was making great havoc, and did all he could to comfort and ease the poor fellows.

. . . . . "On arriving in California, we went for a short time to Benecia, from which place six companies, with the head-quarters, went to Fort Vancouver, Washington Territory. Grant and I went with them, and soon after our arrival there, Grant, who was always fond of horses, and a good judge, bought one of the finest animals in the Territory.

. . . . . "One morning, while sitting with some comrades in front of the officers' quarters, we observed Grant riding on his fine horse toward Major Hathaway's battery, which was in park about two hundred and fifty yards distant. As Grant drew near the guns, and we were observing the motions of his fine animal, we saw him gather the reins, take a tighter grip on his cigar, pull down his hat firmly on his head, and seat himself securely in the saddle. 'Grant is going to leap the battery,' cried two or three of the officers, and we all stood up to see him do it.

He ran his horse at the pieces, and put him one after another over the four guns as easily and gracefully as a circus rider.

"Speaking of Grant's excellent horsemanship, reminds me of a thing he did in Mexico, that is worth relating. One day he came to see Colonel Howard, who was in command of the Castle of Chepultepec. The colonel's quarters were inside of the fortress, which was surrounded by a high, broad earth-work. Grant rode up the slope outside, and, after riding around the castle two or three times and seeing no post to hitch his horse to, deliberately spurred the animal down the broad, but long and steep stone stairs that led into the fort. When Colonel Howard came out of the castle and saw Grant's horse tied at the door, where, perhaps, a horse had never before been, he said, in astonishment, 'Lieutenant, how in the world did you get your horse in here?' 'Rode him in, sir,' quietly replied Grant. 'And how do you expect to get him out?' 'Ride him up the steps instead of down,' answered Grant, and, mounting the animal, he rode him to the foot of the stairs, and, with Grant on his back, the intelligent brute climbed like a cat to the top, where Grant, waving his hat to Colonel Howard below, disappeared like a flash over the breastworks.

. . . . . "I did not now see Grant for some time, and the next place I met him was at Fort Humboldt, California, where he came to assume command of Company F, of the Fourth U. S. Infantry, to which he had been promoted captain by the death of General Taylor's son-in-law, Colonel Bliss. I remember soon after Grant's arrival we had a 'clam lunch,' and I asked Grant how he liked clams, when he drily replied, he thought them a very good substitute for 'gutta percha oysters.'

. . . . . "I have seen it stated that Grant resigned on account of trouble brought on by his drunkenness. There is not one word of truth in that.* The monotony of the small post of Humboldt was too much for him; he had been separated from his family for over two years, and wished to see them again. He applied for a leave of absence, which was refused him; and then, of his own free-will and accord, untrammeled by any outside circumstances, and from the sole desire to be with his family, he tendered his resignation, which was accepted.

. . . . . "The money you speak of was lost by Grant soon after the last battle was fought in Mexico. The amount was about six hundred dollars of quartermaster's funds, which Grant, for safe keeping, had given to his intimate friend and fellow-officer, the lamented Major John H. Gore. One day, while the officers where out of the tent, a soldier of the Fourth U. S. Infantry broke open Gore's trunk, took Grant's money and all the little valuables and trinkets Gore had. Neither the department, nor any one, ever blamed Grant for the loss of the money, and after the war began he was relieved from it by special act of Congress. Grant was really one of the best officers we ever had in the old Fourth Infantry, and esteemed and beloved by nearly every one."

---

* This officer is not a radical.

CHAPTER IV.

GRANT AS A COLONEL—IS ASSIGNED TO COMMAND OF A BRIGADE—IS APPOINTED BRIGADIER-GENERAL, AND ASSIGNED TO COMMAND AT CAIRO—GRANT'S ENEMIES—HE CUTS THE NEUTRALITY KNOT IN KENTUCKY—CAPTURE OF PADUCAH—THE BATTLE OF BELMONT—WHY THAT BATTLE WAS FOUGHT—THE EXPEDITION INTO KENTUCKY—PREPARATIONS TO ATTACK FORT HENRY—FALL OF FORT HENRY—PREPARATIONS TO ATTACK FORT DONELSON—CAPTURE OF FORT DONELSON—REJOICING OF THE PEOPLE—GRANT PROMOTED BY THE PRESIDENT TO MAJOR-GENERAL—NEW DISTRICT CREATED FOR HIM—HE GETS UNDER A CLOUD—IS RELIEVED FROM HIS DISGRACE—PREPARATIONS FOR THE BATTE OF SHILOH.

BEFORE going to Mexico, Missouri, Grant had marched with his regiment from Hannibal to Quincy, from thence to St. Joseph, and having obtained considerable knowledge by these movements, and inured his men to hardships, in coming in contact with other and greener regiments, although the youngest colonel, Grant's experience pointed him out as the fittest person to command the combined forces, and he was made acting brigadier-general. For a time his headquarters were at Mexico, and from there he marched to Pilot Knob, from thence to Ironton, thence to Jefferson City, to defend the river against the attacks of Jeff. Thompson. Grant fortified Marble Creek, and continued his military operations in Missouri until about the 23d of August, 1861, when he received his commission as brigadier-general. This commission was made August 7th, but appointed Grant to rank as brigadier from the 17th day of May, 1861. The first intimation Grant had of his appointment was through newspapers, and he knew little about it until he received his commission. But his promotion had not been obtained without a struggle. Hon. E. B. Washburn, who had never spoken to Grant until after the war began, had conceived a great liking for him, and urged his promotion with President Lincoln. The President sent in Grant's name with thirty-three others, and he stood No. 17, or in the middle of the list, about where he stood in the graduating class at West Point, in 1843. Again it is curious to trace the history of these men and see how the seventeenth general outstripped all the others in military renown. The roster stood at the beginning of 1864:

1. S. P. Heintzelman, not in active service.
2. E. D. Keys, not in active service.
3. Andrew Porter, not in active service.
4. Fitz John Porter, Cashiered.
5. William B. Franklin, commanding Nineteenth Army Corps.
6. William T. Sherman, commanding Department.
7. Charles P. Stone, Chief of Staff to General Banks.
8. Don Carlos Buell, not in active service.
9. Thomas W. Sherman, temporarily disabled.
10. James Oakes, not in service.
11. John Pope, commanding Department North-west.
12. George A. McCall, resigned.
13. William R. Montgomery, not in active service.
14. Philip Kearney, dead.
15. Joseph Hooker, commanding Grand Division.
16. John W. Phelps, resigned.
17. Ulysses S. Grant, Lieutenant-General.
18. J. J. Reynolds, commanding troops New Orleans.
19. Samuel R. Curtis, not in active service.
20. Charles S. Hamilton, not in active service.
21. D. N. Couch, commanding Department Susquehanna.
22. Rufus King, Foreign Minister.
23. J. D. Cox, commanding corps.
24. S. A. Hurlbut, commanding corps.
25. Franz Sigel, not in active service.
26. Robert C. Schenck, in Congress.
27. B. M. Prentiss, resigned.

28. F. W. Lander, dead.
29. B. F. Kelly, commanding Department West Virginia.
30. J. A. McClernand, not in active service.
31. A. S. Williams, commanding division.
32. J. B. Richardson, dead.
33. William Sprague, declined.
34. James Cooper, dead.

The President, at the request of Mr. Washburn, had sent in to the United States Senate the name of Colonel U. S. Grant for brigadier-general. At that time the Senators and the people knew no more who U. S. Grant was than they did about Bob Smith or Tom Jones. Some enemies of Grant had told several Senators he was a drunken, worthless fellow, and ought not to be confirmed. When his name came up two or three objected, and stated what they had heard, and the name of Grant was about to be rejected, when it so happened that Mr. Washburn, who was on his way home from the House, and who did not know the nominations were up, went by the Senate and called out Ben. Wade, of Ohio, to whom he said: "Mr. Wade, the President has sent in the name of Colonel U. S. Grant, of the Twenty-first Illinois Regiment, to be a brigadier-general; when it comes up, I wish you would remember the name and help him through."

"It is up now, and he is going to be rejected. They say he is a drunkard," replied Mr. Wade.

"He is no such thing, and I can prove it," answered Washburn.

Wade hurried into the Senate and asked that action on Grant's nomination might be postponed until the next day, which was done, and that night Washburn visited the Senators, explained away the ill-natured reports put in circulation about his friend, and next day Grant was confirmed.

Soon after his promotion, Grant was ordered to the Mississippi, given command of the District of South-east Missouri, and made his head-quarters at Cairo, the confluence of the Ohio and Mississippi Rivers.

He soon determined the strategic points in his district, and decided upon the seizure of Paducah, at the mouth of the Tennessee River. Kentucky was at this time playing the absurd role of neutrality, but while the Governor and his people were making loud professions of peace, the rebels were fortifying Columbus and Hickman, on the Mississippi, and Bowling Green, on the Big Barren. Without giving any heed to the armed neutrality parade, and silly State Rights doctrines of Kentucky, Grant hearing that the rebel troops were about to occupy Paducah in force, he advanced in the night with two regiments, drove out some rebel recruits, and seized the city. The *neutral* citizens had secession flags flying, and were in great glee, hourly expecting the arrival of some four thousand rebel troops, when Grant with his blue jackets tumbled into their streets.

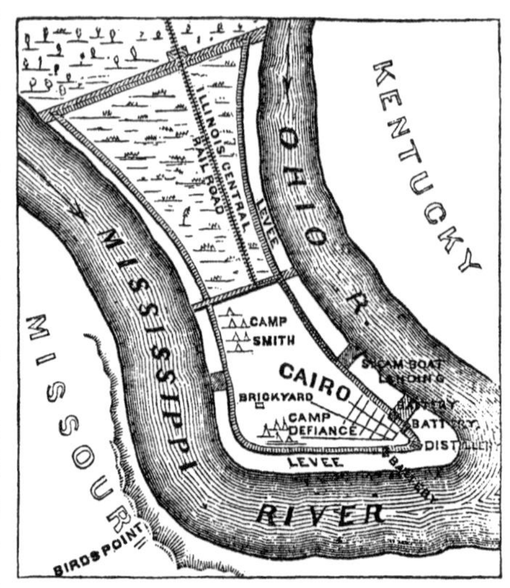

After fortifying Smithland, at the mouth of the Cumberland River, and leaving sufficient garrisons behind, he set out to return to his head-quarters at Cairo, but, before leaving Paducah, issued a proclamation to the citizens, which is a little curious, as being the first military paper issued by Grant in the war:

"PADUCAH, KY., September 6, 1861.

"*To the citizens of Paducah:*

"I am come among you, not as an enemy, but as your fellow-citizen. Not to maltreat you nor annoy you, but to respect and enforce the rights of all loyal citizens. An enemy, in rebellion against our common Government, has taken possession of, and planted its guns on the soil of Kentucky, and fired upon you. Columbus and Hickman are in his hands. He is moving upon your city. I am here to defend you against this enemy, to assist the authority and sovereignty of your Government. *I have nothing to do with opinions*, and shall deal only with armed rebellion and its aiders and abettors. You can pursue your usual avocations without fear. The strong arm of the Government is here to protect its friends, and punish its enemies. Whenever it is manifest that you are able to defend yourselves, and maintain the authority of the Government, and protect the rights of loyal citizens, I shall withdraw the forces under my command.

"U. S. GRANT,

"*Brigadier-General Commanding.*"

When it is remembered this paper was issued at a time when some of the ablest statesmen in the nation were puzzling their brains over the position of Kentucky, it will be seen how completely the blunt General cut the knot of neutrality, and exploded the fallacy of State Rights in time of war. Grant had marched upon the sacred soil of Kentucky without consulting any one, and as soon as the State authorities heard he had seized Paducah, they telegraphed General Fremont, Grant's superior officer, that a great outrage had been committed, and that Paducah, "*a city of Kentucky, was actually in the hands of United States troops.*" The State officials had first telegraphed Grant to know why he had presumed to advance with an armed force upon the soil of Kentucky, and the General gave the very sensible reply, that he had come to put down rebellion. His answer was sent to Fremont, and some sharp correspondence ensued between that General and Grant, not so much because Grant had advanced into Kentucky without orders, as because he "had corresponded with State and other high officials on matters of importance without the permission of his superiors," and he was peremptorily informed that the divine right of writing letters to governors, etc., lay only in the "head-quarters at St. Louis." Notwithstanding the exertions of the rebel governor, the legislature passed Union resolutions, and the loyal people of Kentucky, cheered by the knowledge of Grant's presence with an armed force in Paducah, began every-where to organize to sustain the old flag of the nation, and keep the State in the Union.

Larke, in his history, gives this picture of Grant in camp: "General Grant, when in camp at Cairo, presented little, in fact nothing, of the gewgaws and trappings which are generally attached to the attire of a general; and in this respect he showed a marked contrast between himself and some of his sub-lieutenants, whose bright buttons and glittering shoulder-straps were perfectly resplendent. The General, instead, would move about the camp with his attire carelessly thrown on, and left to fall as it pleased. In fact, he seemed to care nothing at all about his personal appearance, and in the place of the usual military hat and gold cord, he wore an old battered black hat, generally designated a "stove-pipe," an article that neither of his subordinates would have stooped to pick up. In his mouth he carried a black-looking cigar, which he was constantly puffing."

The situation in Grant's district, on the 23d of November, 1861, was as follows: Jeff. Thompson, at Indian Ford, on the St. Francois River, with three thousand men; Price, in South-western Missouri, awaiting reënforcements from Polk and Jeff. Thompson; Polk at Columbus. Hearing Polk was crossing troops from Columbus to Belmont, with a view to reënforce Price, Grant sent Col. Richard Oglesby against Jeff. Thompson, with instructions to attack him and break up his camps. On the night of the 7th, Grant, who had already sent C. F. Smith from Paducah to demonstrate against Columbus, hearing that Polk was about to move from Belmont with a force to cut off Oglesby, determined to attack that place. He at once moved, by boat, with three thousand men to Hunter's Point, three miles from Columbus, on the Missouri shore, where he debarked and marched for Belmont. The rebel Tappan's force was soon encountered and driven back, as was also Pillow, who came to his support with three regiments. Grant deployed his whole force as skirmishers, except one battalion held in reserve, and fighting from tree to tree, through sloughs and abattis, after a contest of four hours drove the rebels under the river bank and captured several hundred prisoners. Belmont is on low ground, and in range

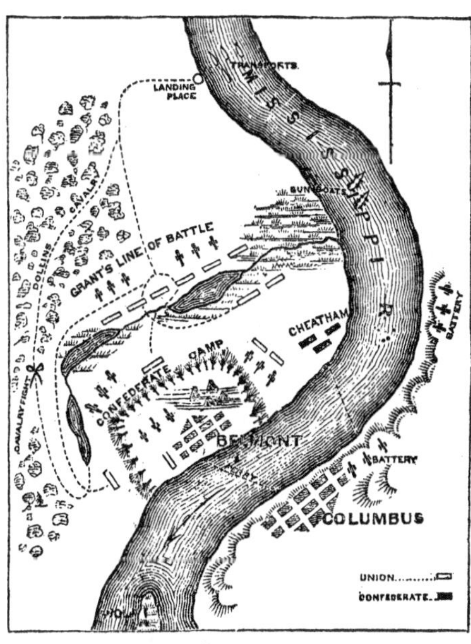

BELMONT.

of Columbus, from which place the rebel batteries kept up a plunging fire on the Union forces.

After whipping the rebels, our forces became disorganized and began plundering the rebel camps, while the colonels, instead of pursuing the rebels, went to making stump speeches. Meanwhile the rebels rallied; and Polk began to cross reënforcements from Columbus in transports. Grant attempted to call off his troops; but, being raw and green, and crazy with their victory, they would not obey him. To stop their pillaging, he ordered the rebel camps to be fired. Gathering what troops he could, he began his retreat toward his boats, but found the rebels had intercepted him. A staff officer galloped up to Grant, and excitedly cried out, "General, we are cut off and surrounded!" "*Silence, sir*," replied Grant," "*if that be so, we must cut our way out as we cut our way in.*" The General, who had already had one horse shot under him, behaved with great coolness and gallantry, going into the thickest of the fight and encouraging his men. He said, constantly, "*We have whipped them once and can do it again.*" The troops closed up, and, charging upon the enemy, cut their way to the transports, where they embarked under cover of the gunboats, and sailed up the river, while the rebels returned to their ruined and burning camps. We had eighty-five killed, three hundred and one wounded, and ninety-nine missing. The Confederate loss was six hundred and thirty-two.

Much has been said about the battle of Belmont, but we think nearly every one will now admit Grant acted wisely in fighting it. The reasons, in brief, for the battle seem to be: 1. The inordinate desire of our green troops to fight, they already began not only to call, but believe General Grant to be a coward. 2. The necessity of trying the spirit, endurance and power of the enemy, as well as giving our own men some experience in actual war before larger and more important movements began. 3. The necessity of preventing Polk from sending troops to cut off Oglesby. 4. By attacking, to show the rebel commander the importance of keeping his forces together, and thus prevent him from sending reënforcements to Price, in Missouri. All these objects were accomplished, and we respectfully submit that they were sufficient to justify the battle of Belmont.

INTERIOR OF FORT HENRY.

Halleck was now called to command the Department of Missouri, and one of his first acts was to enlarge Gen. Grant's district and give him additional troops. Having hastily organized his new command, Halleck, to prevent Polk from reënforcing Buckner at Bowling Green, ordered Grant to make a grand reconnoissance into Kentucky. General Payne moved from Cairo to Bird's Point, and thence to Fort Jefferson, where he remained, while General Smith with a column moved from Smithland through Blandville. The expeditionary forces marched to within one mile of the defenses of Columbus, when, having fully accomplished their object and obtained much valuable information, they returned. Smith, in his report of this expedition, represented the capture of Fort Henry as feasible, and Grant at once forwarded it to Halleck, "recommended," and the next day set out in person for St. Louis, to obtain, if possible, permission to attack Forts Henry and Donelson; but Halleck snubbed him, and sent him back to Cairo. Nothing daunted, Grant four days later telegraphed Halleck: "With permission, I will take and hold Fort Henry." To back him up, Grant got Commodore Foote to write Halleck and advise the attack on Fort Henry. On the 30th of January, Halleck gave his consent, and on the 2d of February Grant started from Cairo, with seventeen thousand men on transports. McClernand led the advance, and disembarked his troops eight miles from the fort; but Grant ordered them on board again, and continued up the river to Bailey's Ferry, where the dropping shells from the rebel guns admonishing him he was close enough, he rounded to and had his forces put on shore. The rebel General Tilghman commanded the fort, and had two thousand and seven hundred men. The works were strong, bastioned, embrasured, with sand bags on the parapets, and mounted seventeen heavy guns, twelve of which bore on the river and five inland. Outside of the works were intrenched camps, on heights defended by long lines of rifle-pits.

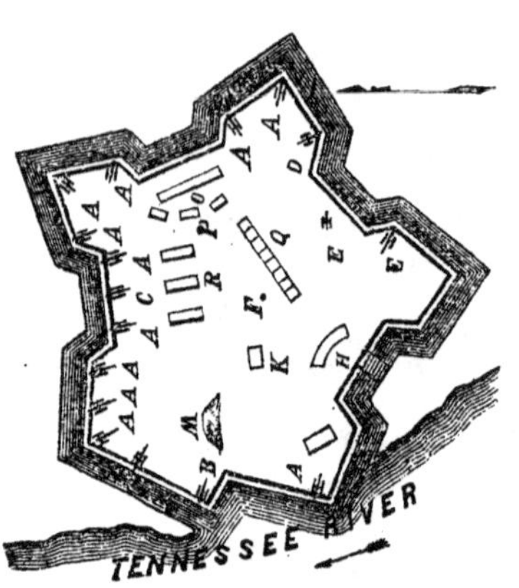

PLAN OF FORT HENRY.

The boats in the river began the battle at eleven o'clock

on the 6th day of February, while Grant was marching by land to invest the fort, having to march eight miles to get to the rear of the rebel works. While Grant was cutting roads through the woods and bridging the overflowed streams, the rebels made good use of the two or three hours thus afforded them, and ran away by the upper roads; but Gen. Tilghman, with his staff and about sixty men, remained, and surrendered to the navy before the land forces could get up. Grant, knowing Foote's modesty, and wishing to place the credit where it belonged, with the gallant tars, promptly telegraphed Halleck: "Fort Henry is ours; the gunboats silenced the batteries before the investment was completed." Next day Grant telegraphed Halleck: "I shall take and destroy Fort Donelson on the 8th." Grant's cavalry at once drove in the rebel outposts, and picketed to within one mile of the fort. On the 8th, according to prom-

A MORTAR-BOAT.

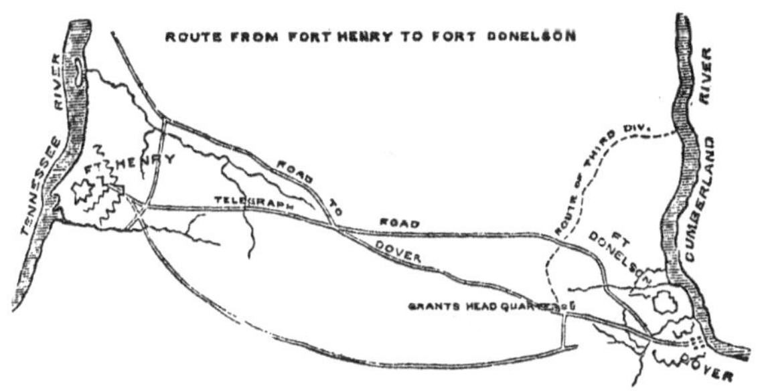

ise, the infantry and artillery began moving on Donelson, but the rain had so swollen the streams, the advance was delayed until the 11th. Meantime, Foote's gunboats, which had been up the Tennessee, returned, and advanced in conjunction with the land forces.

McClernand again led the advance, and, on the 12th, the

LOWER WATER-BATTERY, FORT DONELSON.

main column, under Grant, was well on the way, Generals Smith and Lewis Wallace commanding the divisions. Fort

Donelson was a strong work, built on precipitous heights, and surrounded by deep gorges and ravines. It covered a hundred acres of land and mounted fifteen heavy guns. The river was protected by heavy water-batteries, admirably located and well constructed. The rebel General Buckner was in the works, with twenty-one thousand men and sixty-five field pieces.

On the 12th, Grant began investing the works. McClernand, with his division, moved to the rear of the rebel forts, and constituted the right wing of the besieging forces. General Smith's division formed the left of the line, and Lew. Wallace's forces, under Grant in person, the center. On the 14th, the gunboats arrived and the skirmishing began. Friday, at three o'clock, six gunboats attacked the fort, and a terrific cannonade ensued. Foote was wounded, and all of his boats more or less injured, some of them being literally knocked to pieces—the flag-ship St. Louis having her wheel shot away, and receiving fifty-nine shots.

So shattered were the gunboats, that Commodore Foote said it would be necessary for him to return to Cairo and repair them, and he urged Grant to remain as quiet as possible until he returned; but, while Grant and Foote were still in conference, the rebels sallied from their works and attacked the extreme right of Grant's line. After a stubborn fight, McArthur's brigade was driven back, and all of McClernand's division for a time wavered; but Lew. Wallace came up promptly from the center to their support, and drove the rebels; but the attack was soon renewed on both McClernand and Wallace, and, after a close fight, their troops stubbornly fell back. The rebels did not follow far, and there was a lull in the battle, when Grant, who had just heard of the attack, and returned from the gunboats, rode up at full speed, and perceiving the condition of affairs, said to a staff officer: "Examine the rebel prisoners, and see if their haversacks are filled?" The staff officer did so, and found they contained three days' full rations. "Good," said Grant, in glee; "they are fighting to get out to Nashville; they have no idea of staying to fight us."* Then observing the wearied and disordered appearance of his men, and the quiet of the enemy, he said: "The contest has reached its height; whichever party first attacks now, will whip," and, putting spurs to his horse, he galloped furiously to the left, where Smith's division was drawn up, and ordered an attack to be at once made on the rebel right. Returning to his own right, he rode among the soldiers, assuring them the rebels were trying to cut out, and exhorting them to stand firm and hold the enemy fast, while the left assaulted. The dispirited men caught the idea and courage of their commander, and, with shouts, began to move to the front. Meantime Grant had sent word to the navy of what was going on, and brave old Foote run up his crippled boats, and again opened on the rebel forts. Smith's division, at the point of the bayonet, carried the heights and captured the key to the rebel position. That night Grant slept in a negro hut near the rebel works, and the weary troops bivouacked on the hard-frozen ground. The rebel generals held a council of war, and Floyd, who was the ranking officer, turned the command over to Pillow; Pillow, in turn, turned it over to Buckner, and then both he and Floyd ran away.

Next morning the Union troops began stirring early, and Grant was preparing to assault the rebel intrenchments, when a Confederate bugler brought him a note from Buckner asking him not to assault. Soon after it was light, another messenger from Buckner reached Grant, and a white flag was hoisted on Fort Donelson. The rebel commander proposed

---

* Grant was quite right, for Pillow says, in his official report: "We had fought the battle to open the way for our army, and relieve us from his (Grant's) investment.

an armistice until twelve o'clock, to settle the "terms of capitulation." Grant curtly replied: "No terms other than an

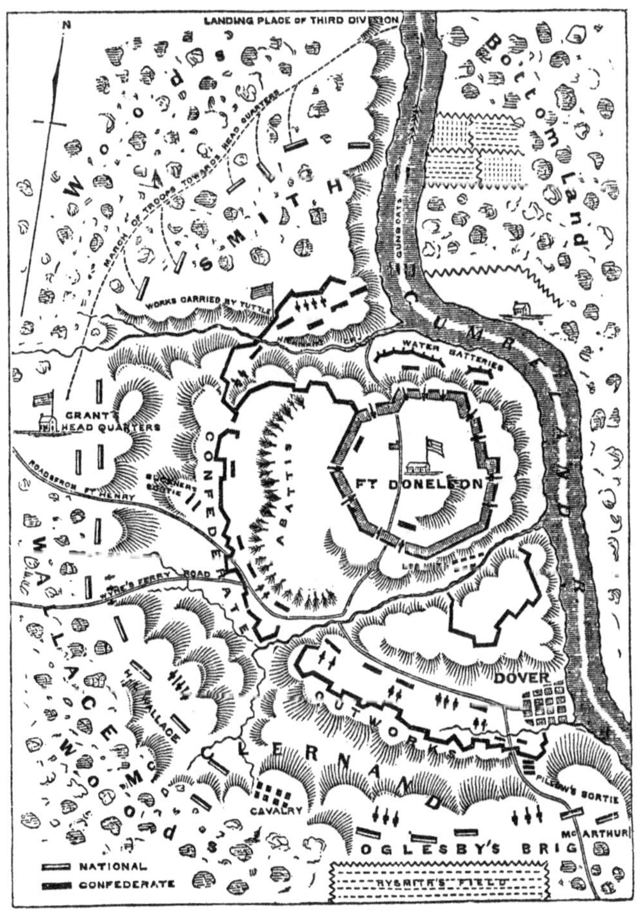

PLAN OF THE SIEGE OF FORT DONELSON.

unconditional and immediate surrender will be accepted. I propose to move immediately on your works." Buckner had already said, in his note to Grant, "Commissioners would be appointed to settle the terms of capitulation in accordance with the circumstances governing the present situation of affairs," and the object of Grant's reply was to relieve his Government of any complication. He was determined not to embarrass the authorities by recognizing in any doubtful way the Confederacy, its negroes, rights, or property. When we remember the confusion then existing in the public mind in regard to the Confederacy, we can not but admit the wisdom of General Grant's action.

GRANT'S HEAD-QUARTERS AT FORT DONELSON.

When he received Grant's terms he was not well pleased, but seeing no help for it, accepted "the ungenerous and unchivalrous conditions." Grant at once rode to Buckner's head-quarters and cordially shook hands with the rebel general, who had been his school-mate at West Point. "Ah," said Buckner, "if I had been in command yesterday, Grant, you could n't have reached Fort Donelson so easily." Grant, good-naturedly, replied, "Had you been in command, I should have waited for reënforcements before attacking, but I knew Pillow would not give me much of a fight."

Grant had twenty-seven thousand men in the battle of Donelson, and lost two thousand and forty-one killed, wounded, and missing; of these four hundred and twenty-five were killed. The rebels had about twenty-one thousand men; of these fourteen thousand six hundred and

VIEW AT FORT DONELSON IN 1866.*

* This is a view looking down the river, in which the remains of the upper water-battery are seen in the foreground. In the distance, on the left, near which is seen a steamboat, is the promontory behind which the Carondelet lay while bombarding the Confederate works on the 13th. The fort lay on the top of the hill on the extreme left. Across the river is seen the shore to which Pillow escaped when he stole out of the fort.—*Lossing's Civil War in America.*

twenty-three were captured; three thousand escaped with Floyd, one thousand with Forrest, and two thousand five hundred were killed and wounded. Sixty-five pieces of cannon, seventeen thousand six hundred stand of small arms, and a large quantity of ammunition also fell into the hands of the Union forces.

When the news of the capture of Fort Donelson reached Cairo, General Cullum telegraphed to the North: "The Union flag floats over Fort Donelson. Fifteen thousand prisoners taken." This news electrified the people, and the wildest rejoicing prevailed. While the names of Grant and Foote were in every body's mouth, the President sent Grant's name to the Senate as a major-general, and he was immediately confirmed, the whole country applauding.

The following amusing incident connected with Grant's victory is related by Larke:

"Several rumors had appeared in the newspaper press, and had otherwise been publicly proclaimed, that General Grant was in the habit of getting intoxicated. This idea may have arisen from his slovenly mode of attiring himself, or from some other equally unreliable cause. The friends of the Illinois troops under General Grant's command, being anxious for their safety, selected a delegation to visit General Halleck, and have Grant removed.

"'You see, General,' said the spokesman, 'we have a number of Illinois volunteers under General Grant, and it is not safe that their lives should be intrusted to the care of a man who so constantly indulges in intoxicating liquors. Who knows what blunders he may commit?'

"'Well, gentlemen,' said General Halleck, 'I am satisfied with General Grant, and I have no doubt you also soon will be.'

"While the deputation were staying at the hotel, the news arrived of the capture of Fort Donelson and thirteen thousand prisoners. General Halleck posted the intelligence himself on the hotel bulletin, and as he did so he remarked, loud enough for all to hear:

"'If General Grant is such a drunkard as he is reported to be, and can win such victories as these, I think it is my duty to issue an order that any man found sober in St. Louis to-night shall be punished with fine and imprisonment.'

"The people of St. Louis took the hint, and, nearly all that night, entered into the spirit of jollification. The temperance delegation from Illinois were not behind their neighbors in celebrating the occasion, and with whisky, too."

It is hardly worth while to refer further to General Grant's personal habits; but we can not forbear making the following quotation from the letter of an officer who has long served on Grant's staff. He says:

"I have seen him in every phase of his military life, and I can assert that the accusation of his being a drunkard is false. I have been in the same tent with him at all hours of the day and night, and I never *knew* him to be under the influence of liquor, or any thing even approaching it. I do not know what his former life may have been, but I do know that now he is a temperate man."

The capture of Fort Donelson penetrated the rebel line, and necessitated the evacuation of Nashville, Bowling Green, and Columbus. Kentucky, Tennessee, and Mississippi were thus freed from the rebel forces from St. Louis to Arkansas.

Our soldiers and people, who were not yet aware of the effect of strategic battles, were amazed as they saw city after city, and long lines of country, fall into our hands without a blow. The national spirit rose, and Grant's army was every-where praised as one that the rebels were afraid to meet. The increasing popularity of Grant was unfortunate for him, in that it excited the alarm of Halleck. This general, old, able, and experienced as he was, allowed a feeling of jealousy to spring up in his breast, and so thoroughly did it possess him, that it ultimately caused him to do Grant a great injustice.

Soon after the battle of Donelson, a new district, called the District of West Tennessee, was created, and Grant assigned the command of it, Brigadier-General W. T. Sherman succeeding him in command of the Cairo District.

Grant at once occupied Clarksville, fifty miles above Donelson, and sent Smith to take possession of Nashville. General Nelson, of Buell's army, had already taken the city, and Grant immediately repaired there in person. The enemy was now at Chattanooga, and Grant began fitting out expeditions against him.

On the 3d of March, 1862, Halleck telegraphed to McClellan: "Grant left his command without my authority, and went to Nashville. His army seems to be as much demoralized by the victory of Fort Donelson as was that of the Potomac by the defeat of Bull Run. It is hard to censure a successful general immediately after a victory, but I think he richly deserves it. I can get no returns, no reports, no information from him. Satisfied with his victory, he sits down and enjoys it, without any regard for the future."

Grant had been hard at work, preparing to move against the enemy, and the next day (March 4th) was surprised to receive from Halleck the following dispatch: "You will place Major-General C. F. Smith in command of expedition, and remain yourself at Fort Henry."

Grant was now a disgraced man, but bore his misfortunes as quietly as he had his victories.

On the 13th of March, Grant was relieved from his disgrace, and at once moved his head-quarters to Savanna, and began concentrating his troops for the great battle of Shiloh.

CHAPTER V.

GRANT RECEIVES A HANDSOME PRESENT—GRANT AT SAVANNAH—GENERAL C. F. SMITH AND GRANT—COMPOSITION OF THE TWO ARMIES—THE BATTLE-FIELD OF SHILOH—POSITION OF THE TROOPS—A. S. JOHNSTON'S ADDRESS TO HIS SOLDIERS—SKIRMISHING BEFORE THE BATTLE—THE BATTLE—CONDUCT OF LEWIS WALLACE AND NELSON—BUELL ARRIVES ON THE FIELD—WHAT HE SAID TO GRANT—THE SECOND DAY'S BATTLE—GRANT AND THE FIRST OHIO REGIMENT—THE NEW YORK HERALD'S ACCOUNT OF THE BATTLE—REJOICING OVER THE NEWS—COMPLIMENTARY ORDER TO GRANT AND BUELL—GRANT'S CONDUCT IN THE BATTLE.

BEFORE Grant started for his new head-quarters at Savannah, his fellow-officers presented him a handsome sword at Fort Henry, as an appreciation of his skill as a commander and their regard for him as a man. The sword had two scabbards—the service one being of fine gilt, while the parade scabbard was of rich gilt, mounted at the band. The handle was of ivory, mounted with gold, and the blade was of the finest tempered steel. The sword was enclosed in a fine rosewood case, and accompanied by an elegant sash and belt. On the scabbards were suitable inscriptions containing the names of his regimental commanders.

General C. F. Smith, who had been temporarily placed in command of the troops in the field, no sooner heard that his old commander was relieved from disgrace, than he made haste to write him: "I am glad to find that you are about to resume your old command, from which you were so unceremoniously and, as I think, so unjustly stricken down."

The relations between General Smith and Grant were of a peculiar character. When Smith was commandant at the Military Academy, Grant was a cadet. He often said he felt an awe when in the presence of his old commandant, and that it was very difficult at first for him to give Smith an order. General Smith soon perceived this, and one day said to Grant, with great frankness: "General, I appreciate your delicacy, but I am now a subordinate, and I know a soldier's duty; I hope you will feel no awkwardness about our new relations." Smith was sixty years old—a man of great military talent, and from the first understood Grant's worth as a soldier. The old veteran did all in his power to subordinate himself to his young chief, but, despite his efforts, Grant never could or would assume any great authority over him; and when, soon afterward, the gallant veteran sickened and died from disease brought on by exposure at Fort Donelson, Grant wept like a child.

Grant was now about to engage in the most important movement that had yet been made against the Confederacy; and that the rebels were thoroughly alive to the danger of his operations may be gathered from the speeches of their leading men and the publications in their journals at the time.

The Florence (Alabama) *Gazette*, of March 12, 1862, had the following very significant article:

"We learned yesterday that the Unionists had landed a very large force at Savannah, Tennessee. We suppose they are making preparations to get possession of the Memphis and Charleston Railroad. *They must never be allowed to get this great thoroughfare in their possession, for then we would indeed be crippled.* The labor and untiring industry of too many faithful and energetic men have been expended on this road to bring it up to its present state of usefulness to let it fall into the hands of the enemy to be used against us.

It must be protected. We, as a people, are able to protect and save it. If unavoidable, let them have our river; but we hope it is the united sentiment of our people *that we will have our railroad.*"

General Grant arrived at Savannah on the 17th of March, and established his head-quarters. From this point he could best oversee his whole force and assist in getting up the reënforcements. The rebel forces were estimated at over sixty thousand men, and were concentrated at Shiloh, General A. S. Johnston commanding, and General P. G. T. Beauregard second in command. The rebel army was divided into three corps, and the reserves as follows:

First Army Corps, Lieutenant-General L. Polk.
Second Army Corps, Lieutenant-General Braxton Bragg.
Third Army Corps, Lieutenant-General W. J. Hardee.
Reserves, Major-General G. B. Crittenden.

The organization of Grant's army was as follows:

Commanding General, Major-General U. S. Grant.
First Division, Major-General J. A. McClernand.
Second Division, Brigadier-General W. H. L. Wallace.
Third Division, Major-General Lewis Wallace.
Fourth Division, Brigadier-General S. A. Hurlbut.
Fifth Division, Brigadier-General W. T. Sherman.

The field on which the two armies were to contend was on the west bank of the Tennessee, and, for the most part, densely wooded with tall trees, and but little undergrowth. The landing is immediately flanked on the left by a short but precipitous ravine, along which runs the road to Corinth. On the right and left, forming a good, natural flanking arrangement, runs Snake and Lick Creeks, which would compel the attack of the enemy to be made in front. The distance between the mouths of these creeks is about two and a half miles. The battle-ground of Pittsburg Landing was selected by General C. F. Smith; and all writers agree that the position was admirably chosen. The locality where the fighting would take place was in easy range and protected by the gunboats Tyler and Lexington. Buell's Army of

PITTSBURG LANDING IN 1866.

the Ohio was coming up to reënforce Grant, and, although the river lay in rear of Grant's troops, that was also the direction of Buell's advance.

Grant had placed his five divisions as follows: Lewis Wallace's division—First Brigade at Crump's Landing; Second Brigade, two miles above it; Third Brigade at Adamsville —the whole division to be held in readiness to move down and join the main forces whenever circumstances should render it necessary. Prentiss held the extreme left of the line, with Stuart; McClernand was at some distance on his right, and facing south-west; Sherman was at Shiloh Church, on the right of McClernand, and in advance of him; Hurlbut and W. H. L. Wallace, a mile in rear of McClernand, in reserve—the former supporting the left, and the latter the right wing. Grant's whole force consisted of about thirty-eight thousand men.

SHILOH MEETING-HOUSE.

It was the evident design of the rebel commanders to attack and overwhelm Grant's forces before the Army of the Ohio, under Buell, could come up to his support. While Grant was anxiously awaiting the approach of Buell's army, a question of rank arose between McClernand and Smith, and to settle the matter, Grant had to move his head-quarters from Savannah to Pittsburg Landing, and personally assume command of the forces in the field.

It was now the 6th day of April, 1862, and the first day of the great battle of Shiloh, or, as it is more frequently called, Pittsburg Landing. Skirmishing had been going on since the 2d, and on the 3d the rebel commander had issued a stirring address to his army.

"*Soldiers of the Army of the Mississippi:*

"I have put you in motion to offer battle to the invaders of your country, with the resolution and discipline, and valor becoming men, fighting, as you are, for all worth living or dying for. You can but march to a decisive victory over agrarian mercenaries, sent to subjugate and despoil you of your liberties, property, and honor.

"Remember the precious stake involved; remember the dependence of your mothers, your wives, your sisters, and your children, on the result. Remember the fair, broad, abounding lands, the happy homes, that will be desolated by your defeat. The eyes and hopes of eight million people rest upon you. You are expected to show yourselves worthy of your valor and courage, worthy of the women of the South, whose noble devotion in this war has never been exceeded in any time. With such incentives to brave deeds, and with trust that God is with us, your general will lead you confidently to the combat, assured of success

"By order of

"General A. S. Johnston, *Commanding.*"

On the 4th of April the enemy felt Sherman's front with such force that many thought a battle imminent. Grant rode out to the front, and as he was returning after dark, through the rain, his horse, in crossing a log, slipped and fell on his rider, who received a severe contusion, and for over a week he suffered acute pains and was lame. It was this circumstance that originated the newspaper report that Grant was drunk and thrown from his horse at the battle of Shiloh.

On the evening of the 4th, General Lewis Wallace reported eight regiments of rebel infantry at Purdy, and an equal, if not a larger force, at Bethel. Grant ordered W. H. L. Wallace to support Lewis Wallace's division, if necessary, and then returned to Savannah, promising to come up to the front early next morning. On the 5th, the rebel cavalry had been very active, coming down boldly on Sherman's front, and driving in the Union vedettes. The same evening, the head of Nelson's column, belonging to

Buell's Army, arrived at Savannah, and reported Buell rapidly coming up. Grant at once ordered Nelson to take position south of Savannah, five miles from Pittsburg Landing, and hold himself in readiness to reënforce the army on the left bank.

The morning sun rose bright and clear on the 6th of April, and gayly shone on the tents of two great armies. The birds sang cheerily in the tree-tops, and there was nothing to indicate the terrible tragedy that was soon to be enacted in those quiet groves. Who could have believed, on that bright April morning, that the green sod beneath our feet would soon be slippery with human gore, and the firm earth trembling beneath the charge of enraged thousands? Yet it was so; the charge, the repulse, the calling to repeated action; the bearing of a thousand bosoms in a moment to whatever there is terrible in death and war; the groans of the wounded and dying—

"This is war that in a day
Can rob a nation of its peace;
Aye, rob a nation of itself,
And still it will not cease."

The rebels had breakfasted at three o'clock in the morning, and at early dawn laid aside their knapsacks and stripped for the bloody contest. Portions of the Union army were still wrapped in slumber when the battle began, and others were lazily preparing their breakfast.

Neither Grant nor Sherman had expected a battle on the 6th, and it was, therefore, with some surprise the next morning Grant, while eating an early breakfast with his staff, preparatory to riding out in search of Buell, heard such heavy firing in the direction of the landing as to convince him a severe action was in progress. Hastily dispatching Buell a note, informing him a battle had begun, and ordering Nelson to move his command to the river bank, Grant went on board a transport and hastened to the front. He stopped for a moment, on his way up the river, at Crump's Landing, to see Lewis Wallace, and instruct him in person as to what he would be expected to do in the battle.

The onset had begun by forty thousand rebels precipitating themselves suddenly on Prentiss' little division and completely doubling it up. Sherman's division was next attacked, and for a time held the rebels in check, but the troops being new and green, soon gave way and were forced back through their camp, which fell into the hands of the rebels. McClernand promptly moved up to support Sherman's wavering left, and Hurlbut marched forward to the support of Prentiss. W. H. L. Wallace had taken position in rear of Sherman, and was supporting the center and left of the line where the rebel attack was most furious.

Lewis Wallace had been sent for, and ordered to come up and connect with Sherman's right, but he never came. Early in the action, part of the brigade, composed of raw men, and stationed on Sherman's left, broke and fled to the rear in great confusion; this necessitated a change of position, and Sherman swung back his left, turning on the right as a pivot. Soon afterward Sherman's whole line was forced back, but he skillfully connected his left with McClernand's right, keeping his own right well out to prevent any flank movement of the enemy. The enemy never could get round Sherman's flank, and, despite their efforts, he held until night the important crossing of Snake Creek bridge. Sherman was unceasing in his efforts to keep his men up to the work and beat the enemy; although repeatedly wounded, he refused to leave the field for a moment, even to have his wounds dressed.

At ten A. M. the battle was raging fiercely, and Grant

rode to Sherman's front and commended him highly for his skill in opposing the enemy. The cartridges were now giving out; but Grant, with careful foresight, had started Colonel Pride, of his staff, to the front with an ammunition train, and this gallant officer, forcing his wagons over the narrow and crowded road, arrived just in time to supply the empty cartridge-boxes of the Union soldiers.

At intervals all day Grant was engaged in sending forward deserters to their commands, forming new lines out of those who straggled to the rear, and putting them into action again. He was on every part of the field constantly under fire, and making unwearied exertions to maintain his position until Nelson and Lewis Wallace should come up. As hour after hour wore on, and still Nelson and Wallace did not come, the Union forces fell suddenly back toward the landing, contracting their lines as they retreated. Nelson had been ordered to march at seven o'clock, but did not move out until after one, although, from the sound of the cannon, he must have known a fearful struggle was going on in his front. No sufficient excuse has ever been offered for this officer's conduct. Lewis Wallace, who had been personally instructed by General Grant to hold his forces in readiness to reënforce the troops on the left bank when he was sent for, set his column in motion and marched five miles the wrong direction, although he had been on the ground a month, and his men had helped to build a bridge over Snake Creek for just such an emergency as now occurred. When, finally, Colonel (afterward Major-General) McPherson reached him and set him right, it took him from one o'clock until seven at night to march five miles in the direction of the battle, the cannonading being heard at the same time more than fifty miles away.

On the evening of the 5th inst., Grant had gone down to Savannah to meet General Buell, but that officer having failed to come up, to the hour of the opening of the battle, at the landing on the morning of the 6th, Grant, before starting to the front, wrote and dispatched to Buell by courier the following note: "Heavy firing is heard up the river, indicating plainly that an attack has been made upon our most advanced positions. I have been looking for this, but did not believe that the attack could be made before Monday or Tuesday. This necessitates my forming the forces up the river, instead of meeting you to-day as I had contemplated." Buell had written General Grant on the 5th: "I shall be in Savannah myself to-morrow with, perhaps, two divisions. Can you meet me there?" To which Grant had at once replied: "Your dispatch just received. I will be at Savannah to meet you to-morrow. The enemy at and near Corinth are probably sixty to eighty thousand." This accounts for Grant being at Savannah, instead of with his command when the battle commenced, a matter about which some writers have made severe and unjust comments.

About ten o'clock on the morning of the battle, Grant, hearing that General Wood, with the Second Division of Buell's army, had arrived at Savannah, sent him the following order: "You will move your command with the utmost dispatch to the river at this point (landing), where steamers will be in readiness to transport you to Pittsburg." Still later in the day another dispatch was sent to the commanding officer of Buell's advance forces, urging him to hurry up, and closing by saying: "My head-quarters will be in the log building on the top of the hill, where you will be furnished a staff officer to conduct you to your place on the field." At three o'clock Buell arrived on the field in person. He had reached Savannah in the morning with another division of his command, and hearing a battle was raging at the front, had hastened on ahead of his troops. As he rode through the swarms of cravens who had run away from the front and crowded the landing, or cowered under the banks of the river, Buell no doubt made up his mind that Grant's army was whipped. Almost the first words he said to Grant when they met, were: "What preparations have you made for retreating, General?" "I have not despaired of whipping them yet," was Grant's quiet response.

RUINS OF SHILOH MEETING-HOUSE.

Hurlbut's command was now slowly falling back, but raked the rebels well each time they charged. On Hurlbut's right W. H. L. Wallace was gallantly fighting, and repelled four desperate assaults, but was finally forced to fall back toward the landing. About four o'clock the troops on his right and left having retired, Prentiss stubbornly continued the fight with his shattered division, until the rebels swept round his flanks and captured him and four regiments. The Union line now lay in a semicircle on the river, their flanks resting on Snake and Lick Creeks. With their backs to the river, the soldiers knew it would be death and destruction to give way, and they stood firm as a rock on their short line, hurling back the rebels like waves from the shore. The rebels came on again and again, but each time retired shattered and torn, only to be brought up again by their officers and launched against the invincible line of boys in blue. A battery of guns had been admirably posted by Colonel Webster, of Grant's staff, and mowed down the rebels; the gunboats Tyler and Lexington had also opened fire, and dropped their terrible missiles in the midst of the dense ranks of the enemy, where they exploded with fearful carnage. The rebels seeing they could not drive the Union line into the river, slackened their fire and sullenly retired as night crept over the hills, and put an end to the contest. When the battle began to wane, Grant was at Sherman's front, and at once gave him orders to advance and renew the battle early on the following morning. He said "the rebel fury is spent, the turning point has been reached; whoever renews the fight will win." He told to Sherman the story of Donelson; how at one time he saw that either side was ready to give way if the other showed a bold front; and he determined, in consequence, to do that very thing; how he had advanced his jaded troops, and the enemy had surrendered. The appearances on the field of Shiloh, he said, were the same, and the enemy would be beaten on the morrow.

During the night of the 6th, Buell busied himself in getting his troops up. Nelson's column, and nearly all of Crittenden's and McCook's divisions were ferried across the river, and put in position. All night long the gunboats dropped shells, at intervals, on the rebel lines, and the woods caught fire, lighting up the battle-field for miles away. But for a merciful shower of rain, thousands of helpless wounded would have been burned to death on that blazing battle-field. Grant had after dark visited every division, and encouraged, by his presence, the officers and men. To each he said: "As soon as it is light enough to see attack with a heavy skirmish line, and when you have found the enemy, throw upon him your whole force, leaving no reserve."

The new line of battle now stood in the following order: Lewis Wallace's division on the right; Sherman, McClernand, and Hurlbut, from right to left; McCook next, with Crittenden on his left, and Nelson on the extreme left.

EFFECTS OF A SHOT NEAR SHILOH MEETING-HOUSE.

The fighting began early, and, for a time, was obstinate; but the rebels were gradually pushed back until all the ground lost the day before had been regained. By two o'clock the Union victory was complete, and Beauregard in full retreat.

During the battle on the 7th, Grant met the First Ohio Regiment marching toward the northern part of the field, and immediately in front of a position which it was important should be taken. The regiment on the left was fighting hard, but about to yield, in fact, had given way, when Grant called upon the Ohio boys to change direction, and charge. The soldiers recognized their leader, and, with a cheer, obeyed, Grant riding along through the storm of lead cheering them on. The retreating troops seeing what was going on, took courage, and rallying, with loud shouts, drove the enemy from their strong position.

Grant rode along in the piece of woods toward the left of the line, where he met McCook and Crittenden. It was now late in the day, but Grant was anxious to push on after the beaten and retreating rebels. McCook and Crittenden said their troops were too much fatigued to continue the pursuit, and so the Union forces encamped.

BURNING HORSES ON THE FIELD OF SHILOH.

Grant's loss, including Buell's army, was twelve thousand two hundred and seventeen; of these, seventeen hundred were killed, seven thousand four hundred and ninety-five wounded, and three thousand and twenty-two missing. Two thousand one hundred and sixty-seven of the losses were in the Army of the Ohio. Beauregard reported a total loss of ten thousand six hundred and ninety-nine killed, wounded, and missing; but as our burying parties buried four thousand of his dead, his loss must have been much larger.

The New York *Herald*, which contained the first authentic account of the battle, said of General Grant and his staff:

"General Grant and staff, who had been recklessly riding along the lines during the entire day, amid the unceasing storm of bullets, grape, and shell, now rode from right to left, inciting the men to stand firm until our reënforcements could cross the river.

"About three o'clock in the afternoon, General Grant rode to the left where the fresh regiments had been ordered, and, finding the rebels wavering, sent a portion of his body-guard to the head of each of five regiments, *and then ordered a charge across the field, himself leading; and as he brandished his sword and waved them on to the crowning victory, the cannon-balls were falling like hail around him.*"

The *Herald* sums up its account as follows:

"There has never been a parallel to the gallantry and bearing of our officers, from the commanding general to the lowest officer.

"General Grant and staff were on the field, riding along the lines in the thickest of the enemy's fire during the entire two days of the battle, and all slept on the ground Sunday night, during a heavy rain. On several occasions General Grant got within range of the enemy's guns, and was discovered and fired upon.

"Lieutenant-Colonel McPherson had his horse shot from under him when along-side of General Grant.

"Captain Carson was near General Grant when a cannon-ball took off his head, and killed and wounded several others.

"General Sherman had two horses killed under him, and General McClernand shared like dangers; also General Hurlbut, each of whom received bullet holes through their clothes.

"The publication of the *Herald's* account so soon after the battle, created a great excitement among the citizens of New York, and during the day it was telegraphed to the National Capitol and to other parts of the Union."

Mr. Bennett telegraphed the account to the President and to both Houses of Congress, in which it was read aloud. In the lower House, Mr. Colfax, on asking leave to read the dispatch, was greeted on all sides of the House with cries of "To the Clerk's desk." The previous noise and excitement subsided, and as the House listened to the brief and pregnant details of the bloody struggle which preceded the glorious victory over the concentrated strength of rebeldom, all hearts were stilled, and the very breathing almost suppressed, till the last word of the dispatch was read. The rejoicing was great at the victory, though somewhat saddened at the price of blood with which it had been purchased.

On the 9th of April, the War Department issued the following complimentary order to all concerned:

"War Department, Washington, April 9th, 1862.

[Extract.]

. . . .

"The thanks of the department are hereby given to Generals Grant and Buell and their forces, for the glorious repulse of Beauregard, at Pittsburg, in Tennessee."

CHAPTER VI.

HALLECK ASSUMES COMMAND OF THE ARMY—GRANT'S ENEMIES AGAIN BUSY—WASHBURN'S DEFENSE OF HIM—ADVANCE ON CORINTH—DIGGING AND DITCHING—LETTERS FROM A UNION SOLDIER—ELLIOT'S RAID—PURSUIT OF THE ENEMY FROM CORINTH—GRANT'S POSITION—HE IS PLACED IN COMMAND OF THE DISTRICT OF TENNESSEE—HALLECK SUCCEEDS M'CLELLAN—GRANT AND THE REBELS—GRANT AND THE NEWSPAPERS—HOW HE TREATED GUERRILLAS—PRICE'S RAID—ADVANCE ON IUKA—THE BATTLE—DEFEAT AND ESCAPE OF THE REBELS—BATTLE OF CORINTH—DEFEAT AND RETREAT OF THE REBELS—GRANT'S CONGRATULATORY ORDER TO HIS ARMY—MR. LINCOLN'S DISPATCH.

IMMEDIATELY on hearing of the battle at Pittsburg Landing, General Halleck set out from St. Louis to assume command of the combined armies operating along the Tennessee. Before his arrival, however, Grant had sent Sherman up the river with some troops and gunboats to destroy the bridges over the Big Bear Creek, which he did, thus cutting Corinth off from Richmond. On the 22d of April General Pope came up from New Madrid with his army, twenty-five thousand strong, and on the 30th General Wallace was sent through Purdy and four miles beyond to destroy the bridge across the Mobile and Ohio Railroad, which was effectually done, cutting off the rebel reënforcements coming from Jackson, Tennessee. The "Grand Army," as it was now called, consisted of

The Army of the Ohio (center), under General Buell.
The Army of the Mississippi (left), under General Pope.
The Army of the Tennessee (right), under General Grant.

This grand army was composed of sixteen divisions, eight

of which formed the Army of the Tennessee, and were placed under the immediate command of General Grant; four under General Pope, and four under General Buell. General Grant's command was, therefore, as large as the two other armies combined, and was divided into the "right" or active wing, under General Thomas, and the "reserve" under General McClernand.

False reports had again been circulated against General Grant by his enemies, and the battle of Pittsburg Landing represented as a useless loss of human life. So busy were his detractors, and so general the outcry raised against him by the journals and the friends of the men who fell at Shiloh, that even Congressmen joined in and urged his removal. The governors from the Western States came down in a body to Pittsburg Landing and requested General Halleck to send General Grant away from the army. It was well known that General Halleck was not favorably-disposed toward General Grant; but he was a just man, and instead of yielding to the popular clamor against one whom he knew to be a good officer, he stood firmly by him, and on the 1st of May raised him to second in command of the combined armies. It was about this time the Hon. E. B. Washburn came to Grant's defense in the halls of Congress. Rising in his seat on the 2d of May, Mr. Washburn said:

"Mr. Speaker: I will only trouble the House for a few moments; but when justice claims to be heard, it is said that a nation should be silent. Lamartine, in his celebrated history of the Girondins, speaking of one of those incidents so characteristic of the French Revolution, says:

"'The news of the victory of Hondschoote filled Paris with joy. But even the joy of the people was cruel. The convention reproached as a treason the victory of a victorious general. Its commissioners to the army of the North, Hentz, Peyssard, and Duquesnoy, deposed Houchard, and sent him to the revolutionary tribunal.' . . . 'The unfortunate Houchard was condemned to death, and met his fate with the intrepidity of a soldier and the calmness of an innocent man.' . . . 'It was shown that even victory was not protection against the scaffold.'

"It may be inquired whether in this rebellion history is not repeating itself. I come before the House to do a great act of justice to a soldier in the field, and to vindicate him from the obloquy and misrepresentations so persistently and cruelly thrust before the country. I refer to a distinguished general who has recently fought the bloodiest and hardest battle ever fought on this continent, and won one of the most brilliant victories. I refer to the battle of Pittsburg Landing, and to Major-General Ulysses S. Grant. . . . . .

"Let no gentleman have any fears of General Grant. He is no candidate for the Presidency. He is no politician. Inspired by the noblest patriotism, he only desires to do his whole duty to his country. When the war shall be over he will return to his home, and sink the soldier in the simple citizen. Though living in the same town with myself, he has no political claims on me; for, so far as he is a politican, he belongs to a different party. He has no personal claims upon me more than any other constituent. But I came here to speak as an Illinoisian, proud of his noble and patriotic State; proud of its great history now being made up; proud, above all earthly things, of her brave soldiers, who are shedding their blood upon all the battle-fields of the Republic. If the laurels of Grant shall ever be withered, it will not be done by the Illinois soldiers who have followed his victorious banner.

"I see before me my friend from Pennsylvania [Mr. McPherson] which reminds me of a friend of us both—young Baugher, a lieutenant in the lead-mine regiment, who, wounded six times, refused to leave the field; and when finally carried off, waved his sword in defiance to the enemy. But who shall attempt to do justice to the bravery of the soldiers and the daring and skill of the officers; who shall describe all the valor exhibited on those days; who shall presume to speak of all the glory won on that blood-stained field? I have spoken of those more particularly from my own part of the State; but it is because I know them best, and not because I claim more credit for them than I know to be due to the troops from all parts of the State.. They all exhibited the same bravery, the same unbounded devotion, the same ardor in vindicating the honor and glory of the flag, and maintaining the prestige of our State.

"Sir, I have detained the House too long, but I have felt called upon to say this much. I came only to claim public justice; the battle of Pittsburg Landing, though a bloody one, yet it will make a bright page in our history. The final charge of General Grant at the head of his reserves will have a place, too, in history. While watching the progress of the battle on Monday afternoon, word came to him that the enemy was faltering on the left. With the genius that belongs only to the true military man, he saw that the time for the final blow had come. In quick words he said, 'Now is the time to drive them.' It was worthy the world-renowned order of Wellington, 'Up, Guards, and at them.'

"Word was sent by his body-guard to the different regiments to be ready to charge when the order was given; then, riding out in front, amid a storm of bullets, he led the charge in person, and Beauregard was driven howling to his intrenchments. His left was broken, and a retreat commenced which soon degenerated into a perfect rout. The loss of the enemy was three to our two in men, and in much greater proportion in the demoralization of an army which follows a defeat. That battle has laid the foundation for finally driving the rebels from the South-west. So much for the battle of Pittsburg Landing, which has evoked such unjust and cruel criticism, but which history will record as one of the most glorious victories that has ever illustrated the annals of a great nation."

The great Union army was now slowly moving up toward Corinth, so slowly, indeed, that it took it six weeks to march

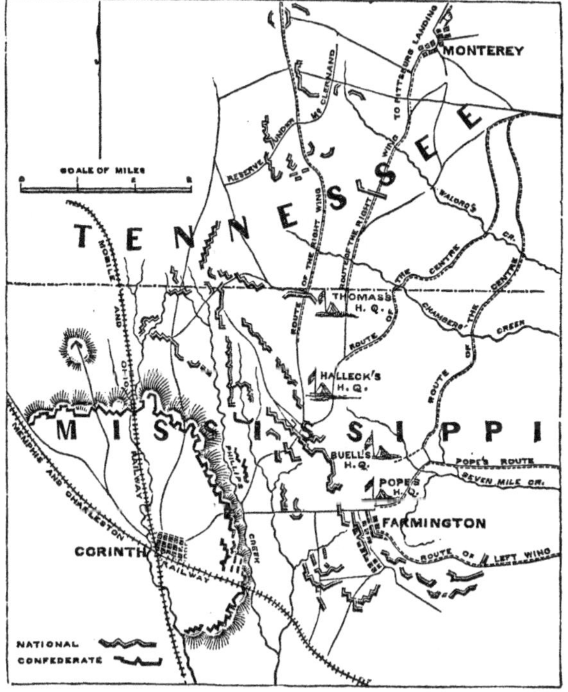

fifteen miles. Halleck, thoroughly alarmed by the outcry against Grant, intrenched every foot of the ground as he went, although the enemy made no offensive movement. On the 3d of May the Union advance was eight miles from

Corinth, and the same day Pope sent Paine's and Palmer's divisions to Farmington, where, on the 9th, they attacked and drove out four thousand rebels under Price, Van Dorn, and Marmaduke. The three armies were moving in echelon with great caution, and intrenching at every step.

Consultation and digging was now the occupation of the armies. If they advanced a mile or two, it was only to establish a new parallel and halt for a week. So time dragged along until the 17th of May, when Sherman, with his Fifth Division, got a lick at the enemy at Russel's house, and sent him flying toward Corinth. At length, on the 21st, the armies were fairly in line three miles from Corinth, and the soldiers in expectation of and anxious for the battle to begin. Halleck, having pronounced his funeral oration over the dead Confederacy, went out to look for the corpse, but found the body gone, Beauregard having retreated some days before. All the great Union armies got for their six weeks' digging and trenching, were a few old telegraph offices, some empty bottles and dirty linen that the rebels had left behind.

The following letter from a Union soldier describes so exactly the manner of conducting a gradual advance, that we quote it entire :

"First, the enemy must be driven back. Regiments and artillery are placed in position, and generally the cavalry is in advance, but when the opposing forces are in close proximity, the infantry does the work. The whole front is covered by a cloud of skirmishers, and then reserves formed, and then, in connection with the main line, they advance. For a moment all is still as the grave to those in the background. As the line moves on, the eye is strained in vain to follow the skirmishers as they creep silently forward; then, from some point of the line, a single rifle rings through the forest, sharp and clear, and, as if in echo, another answers it. In a moment more the whole line resounds with the din of arms. Here the fire is slow and steady, there it rattles with fearful rapidity, and this mingled with the great roar of the reserves as the skirmishers chance at any point to be driven in; and if, by reason of superior force, these reserves fall back to the main force, then every nook and corner seems full of sound. The batteries open their terrible voices, and their shells sing horribly while winging their flight, and their dull explosion speaks plainly of death. Their canister and grape go crashing through the trees, rifles ring, the muskets roar, and the din is terrific. Then the slackening of the fire denotes the withdrawing of the one party, and the more distant picket firing, that the work was accomplished. The silence becomes almost painful after such a scene as this, and no one can conceive of the effect who has not experienced it; it can not be described. The occasional firing of the pickets, which shows that the new lines are established, actually occasions a sense of relief. The movements of the mind, under such circumstances, are sudden and strong. It awaits with intense anxiety the opening of the contest, it rises with the din of battle, it sinks with the lull which follows it, and finds itself in fit condition to sympathize most deeply with the torn and bleeding ones that are fast being borne to the rear.

"When the ground is clear, then the time for working parties has arrived, and as this is the description of a real scene, let me premise that the works were to reach through the center of a large open farm of at least three hundred acres, surrounded by woods, one side of it being occupied by rebel pickets. These had been driven back, as I have described.

"The line of the works was selected, and at the word of command three thousand men, with axes, spades, and picks, stepped out into the open field from their cover in the woods. In almost as short a time as it takes to tell it, the fence-rails which surrounded and divided three hundred acres into convenient farm-lots were on the shoulders of the men, and on the way to the intended line of works. In a few moments more a long line of crib-work stretches over the slope of the hill, as if another anaconda fold had been twisted around the rebels. Then, as for a time, the ditches deepen, the cribs fill up, the dirt is packed on the outer side, the bushes and all points of concealment are cleared from the front, and the center divisions of our army had taken a long stride toward the rebel works. The siege-guns are brought up and placed in commanding positions. A log-house furnishes the hewn and seasoned timber for the platforms, and the plantation of a Southern lord has been thus speedily transferred into one of Uncle Sam's strongholds, where the stars and stripes float proudly."

On the 27th, Colonel Elliott, with the Second Michigan Cavalry, had been sent out along the Tuscumbia road to Cartersville and Boonesville, a distance of twenty-five miles from Corinth. His expedition was entirely successful, capturing and destroying at Boonesville five cars loaded with arms, five containing loose ammunition, six filled with officers' baggage, and five with subsistence stores. The rebels attempted to cut off and capture Elliott, but the bold raider skillfully eluded them, and returned in safety to Pope's army.

As soon as General Halleck found the rebels had escaped from Corinth, he ordered the pursuit. Gordon Granger, with a battery of artillery and a brigade of infantry, drove small bodies of the enemy through Boonesville and across Twenty-mile Creek to Baldwin and Guntown, where he halted, learning that Beauregard was in strong position at Tupelo, by Old Town Creek, a tributary of the Tombigbee. On the 9th of June, 1862, Halleck reported that the enemy had fallen back fifty miles from Corinth by the nearest railroad route, and seventy miles by wagon road, and that he was watching him.

CORINTH.

Grant was particularly active during the operations around Corinth, and had been constantly in the field making valuable suggestions, and aiding in every way he could to make the campaign a success. His position was a painful one, being nominally second in command, but virtually a figure-head to Halleck's staff; he, however, bore his misfortunes with resignation, and patiently waited for better days, which soon came, by Halleck being ordered to Washington and Grant placed in command of the army and district of Tennessee. Before starting for Washington to assume the position of Commander-in-Chief of all the armies of the Republic in place of McClellan, removed, Halleck called at the tent of Robert Allen, a quartermaster, with the rank of Colonel, and offered him command of the army at Corinth, but Colonel Allen declined, whereupon Halleck allowed Grant to retain the command. This curious piece of business has never been satisfactorily explained.

All the country from the Mississippi River to the western shores of the Tennessee, Cairo, Forts Henry and Donelson, the western shore of the Mississippi River, and the northern part of the State of Mississippi, was formed into the "Department of West Tennessee." Of this department General Grant was made the commander, with his head-quarters at Corinth.

Memphis, which had surrendered on June 6th, 1862, soon after the evacuation of Corinth, and had been occupied at once by the Union forces, now formed part of this department, and became, by this time, a very important post, both as a base of operations and of supplies.

The rebels gave General Grant great trouble by carrying on an illicit trade through the lines, and, after issuing various orders forbidding such trade, and cautioning persons not to engage in it, General Grant, finding his orders unheeded, on the 10th day of July summarily commanded that—

The families now residing in the city of Memphis, of the following persons, are required to move south, beyond the lines, within five days from the date hereof:

First. All persons holding commissions in the so-called Confederate army, or who have voluntarily enlisted in said army, or who accompany and are connected with the same.

Second. All persons holding office under or in the employ of the so-called Confederate Government.

Third. All persons holding State, county, or municipal offices, who claim allegiance to said so-called Confederate Government, and who have abandoned their families and gone South.

The rebel guerrillas now began to rob plantations, murder Union men, and commit all sorts of outrages, when General Grant ordered that wherever loss was sustained by the Government, collections should be made, by seizure of a sufficient amount, of personal property, from persons in the immediate neighborhood sympathizing with the rebellion, to remunerate the Government for all loss and expense of the same.

Persons acting as guerrillas, without organization, and without uniform to distinguish them from private citizens, were not entitled to the treatment of prisoners of war when caught, and would not receive such treatment.

As many of the guerrillas were the sons of rich rebel planters, this order suited their cases exactly; for however willing they were to aid the Confederacy, and have their sons rob, pillage, and murder, they were not quite willing to pay Union men for losses of property sustained at the hands of even such good rebels as their guerrilla sons. But, in addition to the expense of guerrilla warfare, it was found to be quite unsafe, when, the next few days after the issuing of General Grant's order, General Dodge telegraphed from Trenton, Tennessee, to Grant:

"GENERAL: The man who guided the rebels to the bridge that was burned was hung to-day. He had taken the oath. The houses of four others who aided have been burned to the ground."

The rebel newspapers which had been encouraging guerrilla outrages now became very abusive of General Grant and the Union cause, when the General summarily wound the matter up, in a three-line letter to the editor of the Memphis *Avalanche*, in the following words:

"You will suspend the further publication of your paper. The spirit with which it is conducted is regarded as both incendiary and treasonable, and its issue can not longer be tolerated.

U. S. GRANT, *Major-General*.

It was now the 19th of September, 1862. The rebel Price, with twelve thousand men, had marched to Iuka, driving before him the Union garrisons of Tuscumbia and

Jacinto, and capturing at Iuka a large quantity of supplies left behind by Colonel Murphy, who retreated precipitately, with his command, to Corinth. Grant had been quietly waiting to ascertain the exact position and whereabouts of Van Dorn and other rebel commanders, and, having obtained the desired information, he at once ordered Rosecrans to move, with nine thousand men, by way of Rienzi, and Ord, to move, from Bolivar and Jackson, with eight thousand soldiers—both forces to concentrate on Iuka as rapidly as possible, and simultaneously attack Price.

On the 18th of September Grant was at Burnsville, and Ord, with his forces, within four miles of Iuka. Rosecrans was still some twenty miles distant from Iuka, having been detained by the bad condition of the roads. At seven o'clock he sent a dispatch to General Grant, which Grant received at midnight, saying he could not possibly get up before two o'clock the next day. This gave Grant great uneasiness, as he had ordered General Ord to attack next day, and was in hourly expectation of hearing of the advance of Van Dorn on Corinth, which would necessitate the rapid withdrawal of Ord's forces from Iuka to defend Corinth. Trains of empty cars were brought up to Burnsville, to carry back Ord's troops if Van Dorn should advance, and the developments of the next few hours were awaited with the utmost anxiety.

VIEW ON IUKA BATTLE-FIELD.

Ord was instructed to wait until he heard the firing of

Rosecrans, and then attack. At four o'clock, having made a forced march, Rosecrans arrived at Barnett's farm, near Iuka, on the Jacinto road. A strong force of rebels suddenly attacked the head of his column, driving it in, and the battle began. The ground was exceedingly broken, covered with thickets, and full of ravines. The fighting was heavy, and done mostly by Hamilton's division, the nature of the ground being such that large bodies of troops could not be brought into action. Rosecrans held his own, but lost a battery, and seven hundred and thirty-six men, killed and wounded. At one o'clock at night, Rosecrans wrote Grant: "We have met the enemy, and had an engagement of several hours' duration. The firing was very heavy, and we lost two or three pieces of artillery. You must attack in the morning in force. The ground is horrid, unknown to us, and no room for development. We could not use our artillery at all, and fired but few shots. Push on to them until we can have time to do something. We will try to get a position on our right which will take Iuka.

Grant was astonished that Ord, in obedience to orders, had not attacked the rebels simultaneously with Rosecrans, and he at once wrote him: "Unless you can create a diversion in favor of Rosecrans, he may find his hands full." The wind had been blowing all day to the south and east, and no sound of the conflict raging so near had reached Ord. In the evening, however, some negroes brought word of the battle, and in the morning he moved promptly on Iuka before he received Grant's note. During the night, the rebels, who supposed themselves shut up in the town, were informed by Dr. Burton, a rebel, that Rosecrans' forces were all on one road, and that the Fulton road, to the south, was still open. Price hastily gathered his troops together, and, leaving his sick and wounded behind, beat a hasty retreat.

The following letter from a rebel soldier, published in the

Montgomery *Advertiser*, September, 1862, contains matter of interest in this connection:

"We held peaceable possession of Iuka for one day, and on the next were alarmed by the booming of cannon, and were called out to spend the evening in battle array in the woods. On the evening of the 19th, when we supposed we were going back to camp, to rest awhile, the sharp crack of musketry on the right of our former lines told us that the enemy was much nearer than we imagined. In fact, they had almost penetrated the town itself. How on earth, with the woods full of our cavalry, they could have approached so near our lines, is a mystery. They had planted a battery sufficiently near to shell General Price's head-quarters, and were cracking away at the Third Brigade, when the Fourth came up at double-quick, and then, for two hours and fifteen minutes, was kept up the most terrific fire of musketry that ever dinned my ears. There was one continuous roar of small arms, while grape and canister howled in fearful concert above our heads and through our ranks. General Little was shot dead early in the action. . . . It was a terrible struggle, and we lost heavily. All night could be heard the groans of the wounded and dying, forming a sequel of horror and agony to the deadly struggle, over which night had kindly thrown its mantle. *Saddest of all, our dead were left unburied and many of the wounded on the battle-field to be taken in charge by the enemy.*

"Finding that the enemy were being reënforced from the North, and as our strength would not justify us in trying another battle, a retreat was ordered, and we left the town during the night. The enemy pressed our rear the next day, and were only kept off by grape and canister.

"It grieves me to state that acts of vandalism, disgraceful to any army, were, however, perpetrated along the line of retreat, and makes me blush to own such men as my countrymen. Corn-fields were laid waste, potato patches robbed, barn-yards and smoke-houses despoiled, hogs killed, and all kinds of outrages perpetrated in broad daylight and in full view of the officers. The advance and retreat were alike disgraceful, and I have no doubt that women and children along the route will cry for the bread which has been rudely taken from them by those who should have protected and defended them." . . .

When Grant arrived at Iuka, at nine o'clock on the morning after the battle, he was deeply mortified at the escape of the rebels, having fully determined to capture Price. A vigorous pursuit was at once ordered, but the enemy had got so far on the road, he could not be overtaken, and, except some small skirmishes with the rear-guard, nothing more was seen of him. Rosecrans reported the rebel loss at Iuka, at fourteen hundred killed and wounded, among others, the rebel General Little killed, and Whitefield wounded.

Van Dorn, Lovell, and Price now concentrated their troops at and near Ripley, Tippah County, Mississippi, with the evident intention of attacking Corinth. On the 22d of September, Grant moved his head-quarters to Jackson, put Rosecrans in command at Corinth, and sent Ord to Bolivar. The rebel forces at La Grange and Ripley were threatening both Bolivar and Corinth, and it was impossible to tell which place they would attack. On the first of October, Grant telegraphed to Washington: "My position is precarious, but I hope to get out all right." On the 2d the rebels under Van Dorn, Price, Lovell, Villepigue, and Rust, appeared before Corinth in great array, and skirmishing continued for two days.

The morning of the 4th of October ushered in the battle. The rebels came on through the woods and across the fields, with heads averted like men striving to protect themselves from a driving storm of hail. They crossed the broad glacis, and, with a yell, rushed upon Davis' division on the right, scattering a part of it; but Rosecrans, sword in hand, dashed in and restored order, and hurled back the Confederates. They came on again and again, but each time the Union troops under Davis, Hamilton, Hackleman, Oglesby, and the batteries under Williams, Powell, Dillon, and Robinette, drove back the rebels with terrible slaughter. At noon the rebels retired, leaving in the hands of the Union soldiers fourteen hundred and twenty-three dead and wounded, and twenty-five hundred prisoners. The National loss was three hundred killed, eighteen hundred and twelve wounded, and two hundred and thirty-two prisoners and missing.

During the battle, Grant was in constant telegraphic communication with Rosecrans and Hurlbut from Grand Junction. Ord, from Bolivar, and McPherson, from Jackson, were marching down upon the rebel rear. McPherson came up during the fight, and being unable to get to the garrison, swept around the rebel flank, and made a brilliant charge on his rear.

Rosecrans had nineteen thousand men in the battle, and the rebels thirty-eight thousand.

The rebels retreated toward the Hatchie, closely pursued by the Union forces. On the morning of the 5th, Hurlbut's and Ord's troops formed a junction, and Ord assumed command. A severe fight took place at the crossing of Hatchie River, the rebel advance-guard suffering a heavy loss, and Ord capturing two batteries and two hundred prisoners.

On the 6th, Rosecrans telegraphed Grant: "The enemy is totally routed, throwing every thing away. We are following sharply."

And on the 7th, Grant telegraphed General Halleck: "Under previous instructions, General Hurlbut is also following. General McPherson is in the lead of General

Rosecrans' column. The rebel General Martin is said to be killed."

Grant issued, on the 7th of October, 1862, a congratulatory order to his troops, wherein, after returning his heartfelt thanks, for the victories vouchsafed the Republic on the 3d, 4th, and 5th instant, he says:

. . . .

"The enemy chose his own time and place of attack, and knowing the troops of the West as he does, and with great facilities for knowing their numbers, never would have made the attempt except with a superior force numerically. *But for the undaunted bravery of officers and soldiers, who have yet to learn defeat,* the efforts of the enemy must have proven successful.

"While one division of the army, under Major-General Rosecrans, was resisting and repelling the onslaught of the rebel hosts at Corinth, another, from Bolivar, under Major-General Hurlbut, was marching upon the enemy's rear, driving in their pickets and cavalry, and attracting the attention of a large force of infantry and artillery. On the following day, under Major-General Ord, these forces advanced with unsurpassed gallantry, driving the enemy back across the Hatchie, over ground where it is almost incredible that a superior force should be driven by an inferior, capturing two of the batteries (eight guns), many hundred small arms, and several hundred prisoners. . . . . .

"As in all great battles, so in this, it becomes our fate to mourn the loss of many brave and faithful officers and soldiers, who have given up their lives as a sacrifice for a great principle. The nation mourns for them."

President Lincoln, when he had received the intelligence from General Grant announcing the victories at Corinth and on the Hatchie, dispatched to him the following congratulations and inquiries:

"I congratulate you and all concerned in your recent battles and victories. How does it all sum up? I especially regret the death of General Hackleman, and am very anxious to know the condition of General Oglesby, who is an intimate personal friend. A. LINCOLN."

The disasters in the East were in part retrieved by these brilliant victories of General Grant in the West, but, as on former occasions, his enemies robbed him of the credit justly due him, and the honors were conferred on others. He did not complain, however, but was happy in the reflection of having done his duty, as a soldier, and been able to contribute something to the welfare of the Republic.

CHAPTER VII.

CHARACTER OF GRANT—HALLECK AND GRANT COMPARED—OPENING OF THE MISSISSIPPI—ADVANCE TO GRAND JUNCTION—COLONEL LEE'S RAID—GRANT'S ADMINISTRATIVE ABILITY—HE ESTABLISHES CONTRABAND CAMPS—SEVERITY OF HIS DISCIPLINE—THE COTTON TRADE—ANECDOTE OF GRANT—GRANT AND THE JEWS—HE REDUCES THE BAGGAGE OF HIS ARMY—ADVANCE ON VICKSBURG—SURRENDER OF HOLLY SPRINGS—GRANT FALLS BACK—ORGANIZATION OF HIS ARMY—SHERMAN'S EXPEDITION AGAINST VICKSBURG—REPULSE OF SHERMAN—FULL ACCOUNT OF THE FIRST ATTACK ON VICKSBURG—CAPTURE OF ARKANSAS POST—GRANT DETERMINED TO CAPTURE VICKSBURG—HIS TELEGRAM TO HALLECK.

THERE perhaps never was a person so little appreciated and more misunderstood than General Grant. Notwithstanding he has displayed talents second to no man since the days of Washington, yet there are hundreds of people who know him personally, and tens of thousands that know him by reputation, who do not believe that Grant is really a great man. It was so in the army, and Badeau has given us some little insight to the character of this truly remarkable soldier and citizen. "Grant's extreme simplicity of behavior and directness of expression imposed on various officers above and below him. They thought him a good, plain man, who had blundered into one or two successes, and who, therefore, could not be immediately removed; but they deemed it unnecessary to regard his judgment or count upon his ability. His superiors made their plans, invariably, without consulting him, and his subordinates sometimes sought to carry out their own campaigns in opposition or indifference to his orders, not doubting that, with their superior intelligence, they could conceive and execute triumphs which would excuse or even vindicate their cause. It is impossible to understand the early history of the war without taking into account that neither the Government nor its important commanders gave Grant credit for intellectual ability or military genius."

"His other qualities were rated low also. Because he was patient, some thought it impossible to provoke him, and because of his calmness it was supposed that he was stolid. In battle or in campaigning he did not seem to care or consider so much what the enemy was doing, as what he himself meant to do; and this trait to enthusiastic, and even brilliant, soldiers appeared inexplicable. A great commander, it was imagined, should be nervous, excitable, inspiring his men and captivating his officers; calling private soldiers by their names; making eloquent addresses in the field, and waving his drawn sword in the battle. Great commanders had done all these things and won, and many men who could do all these things fancied themselves, therefore, great commanders. Others imagined wisdom to consist in science alone; they sought success in learned and elaborate plans, requiring months to develop; and when the enemy was immediately before them, they maneuvered when it was time to fight; they intrenched when they should have attacked, and studied their books when the field should have been their only problem."

Grant was like none of these. If he possessed acquirements he seemed unconscious of them; he made no allusion to schools, and never hesitated to transgress their rules when occasion required or seemed to demand it. So he neither won men's hearts by blandishments, nor effected their imagination by brilliancy of behavior; nor did he seem profound to those who are impressed only by display of learning. He never looked wise nor pretended to know much about any subject that was brought before him. He listened to the theories of all who came to him, and each one went away proud of his superior judgment, and confident he had impressed and enlightened the stolid and stupid General. Men smiled when great civil questions pressed upon him, and wondered what he would do with them; and when, with easy and happy judgment, he disposed of them, all agreed that it was Grant's luck, and not his wisdom, that had found the solution. From the day when he cut the neutrality knot in Kentucky, by marching his troops to Paducah, down to the hour when he received the sword of Lee, at the Appottomax apple-tree, his military career was one of continued success and surprise to both his friends and foes. And, again, when the President placed him in the War Department, a position every one thought he had no particular ability for, he astonished the country by retrenching at once the expenses of the military establishment in one month, saving the people some millions of money, and so directing the affairs of his office that the nation saw in him one of the ablest war ministers it had ever had. When General Grant dies and his character and career come to be sifted and understood, it will be found that no such man has lived in America since the days of George Washington.

. . . .

On the 26th of October, 1862, General Grant, who had long been meditating the opening of the Mississippi to the Gulf, communicated what was on his mind to General Halleck, in the following words: "If you would give me some small reënforcements, I think I would be able to move down the Mississippi Central Railroad and cause the evacuation of Vicksburg." This is the first mention we find made in the military dispatches of the place destined afterward to become so famous in the history of the rebellion.

Halleck, who was essentially a defensive soldier, made haste to telegraph Grant: "Be prepared to concentrate your troops in case of an attack." The minds of the two soldiers were entirely of a different order. Halleck was a strategist, Grant a fighter; Halleck valued places, Grant only the winning of battle-fields; Halleck would risk nothing, Grant all; Halleck was always prepared for defeat, Grant always expected to win; Halleck counted his success by the number of towns and cities he could capture, Grant by the number of generals and armies he could defeat; the one reasoned that when the enemy had no soil or cities to defend he would surrender, the other said that when the enemy was beaten, the soil and cities would of necessity fall into the hands of the victor.

Grant receiving information that General Pemberton, who had succeeded Van Dorn, was strongly fortified on the Tallahatchie, with his advance out as far as La Grange and Grand Junction, determined to attack him; so, notwithstanding the caution about concentrating his troops for an attack, Grant, on the 2d of November, telegraphed Halleck: "I have commenced a movement on Grand Junction, with three divisions from Corinth and two from Bolivar." Taking command in person, he went to Holly Springs and Grenada, completing the telegraph and railroad as he went. Holly Springs is twenty-five miles from Grand Junction; Grenada one hundred miles from Grand Junction, and the Tallahatchie river about fifty miles from Grand Junction.

In the latter part of October, 1862, Grant had sent out an expedition, under Colonel A. L. Lee, of the Seventh Kansas Cavalry, who had gone as far as the towns of Orizaba and Ripley, both of which places he had captured and held for some time, and then returned in safety to Grand Junction. On the 4th of November, General Grant having removed his head-quarters to La Grange, he sent out

Colonel Lee again with fifteen hundred cavalry to Hudsonville, near which place Lee engaged a large body of rebel cavalry in flank with part of his force, while he sent the other half on to Hudsonville. Lee routed the cavalry opposed to him, capturing one hundred and thirty-four prisoners, with their horses, and killing sixteen. He also learned that Lovell had moved his rebel force from his camp north of Holly Springs, and was in the hills just beyond with two divisions; that Pemberton had come up from Jackson, and Price was seven miles from Holly Springs with twelve thousand men, while a large conscript camp was being formed at Abbeville. So ably had Colonel Lee conducted his expedition, and so valuable was the information he obtained, that General Grant, on his return to La Grange, at once recommended this gallant officer for promotion to brigadier-general.

Administrative duties again claimed the attention of General Grant, and he set to work with energy to correct the abuses and irregularities existing in his department. The negroes were escaping in large numbers and entering his camp, giving no little trouble. They had not yet been declared free, and their masters were continually reclaiming them and carrying them back into slavery. Grant was at heart an earnest abolitionist, but the laws and customs of the country were against him, and he could do but little toward aiding the slaves to obtain their freedom. He, however, as early as November 14, 1862, issued an order establishing contraband camps, and directed that all slaves entering the lines of the Union army should be sent to them fed, clothed, and given employment until the Government should adopt some definite policy regarding slavery. A number of Federal soldiers had been guilty of plundering, and upon these he assessed the value of the stores that had been taken, deducted the amount from their pay, and caused the money to be turned over to the people who had been robbed. Two officers who had permitted their men to rob a store at Jackson, Tennessee, Grant summarily dismissed from service, and so severely punished others, that plundering soon ceased almost entirely in his army. The cotton trade seriously disturbed the operations of the army, and Grant for a long time refused to grant any permits for it to be carried on.

An anecdote is told of General Grant, relative to his refusal to engage in or authorize any movements for the re-opening of trade with the rebellious States. On one occasion, especially, after his protests and orders suppressing such traffic, he was eagerly entreated by the agents of the Treasury Department to authorize some system of trade. He refused, for the reason that he could not successfully conduct his military operations while such persons were moving around him; but at last he conceded that a certain amount of trade in the recaptured districts of the South would be safe, proper, and even highly useful to the Union, provided it could be conducted through honest, umimpeachable Union hands. He was asked to name the persons whom he would be willing to trust.

"I will do no such thing," was Grant's reply; "for if I did, it would appear in less than a week that I was a partner of every one of the persons trading under my authority."

Some German Jews had, in their anxiety to trade, so often violated General Grant's orders, that at length his patience, completely exhausted, he excluded them from his department. This he did from no prejudice against their class, but because some of the Jews, then trading within his lines, were known to be aiding the enemy. He could not get hold of the guilty parties, and, although he feared some innocent persons might suffer with the guilty, such was the situation of affairs in his command that any aid or comfort, or, still worse, information given to the enemy would ruin him, and he was, therefore, compelled to issue the order against the Jews as a measure of safety to his military operations.

Halleck, before leaving for Washington, had set the example by reducing his baggage to a *tooth-brush*, and Grant, now finding his army was so loaded down with wagons, filled with the effects of officers and privates, that it would be impossible for him to move rapidly, he determined to remedy the evil at once. Taking away the large wall-tents, he caused small shelter tents to be issued in their stead, and the officers and men soon finding they had nothing to carry, of course needed no wagons, and so the teams were turned over to the quartermaster's department. Grant's personal baggage at this time is said to have consisted of a towel, two pieces of soap, a fine-tooth comb, and forty-one boxes of cigars.

His staff had been selected with great sagacity, and consisted of—

Brigadier-General J. D. Webster, superintendent military railroads.

Lieutenant-Colonel John A. Rawlins, assistant adjutant-general and chief of staff.

Colonel T. Lyle Dickey, chief of cavalry.

Colonel William S. Hillyer, aid-de-camp and provost marshal-general.

Colonel Clark B. Lagow, aid-de-camp and acting inspector-general.

Colonel George P. Ihrie, aid-de-camp and acting inspector-general.

Colonel John Riggin, Jr., aid-de-camp and superintendent of military telegraphs.

Colonel George G. Pride, chief engineer of military railroads.

Lieutenant-Colonel W. L. Duff, chief of artillery.

Lieutenant-Colonel J. P. Hawkins, chief of subsistence department.

Lieutenant-Colonel C. A. Reynold, chief of quartermaster's department.

Surgeon Horace R. Wirtz, chief of medical department.

Major William R. Rowley, aid-de-camp and mustering officer.

Captain T. S. Bowers, aid-de-camp.

Captain F. E. Prime, chief of engineers.

Lieutenant James H. Wilson, chief of topographical engineers.

Lieutenant S. C. Lyford, chief of ordinance department.

On the 28th of November, Grant, although he had not received all the reënforcements he expected, determined to begin his campaingn against Vicksburg, and the next day sent his cavalry across the Tallahatchie. Sherman was ordered to cross at Wyatt, and Grant moved his head-quarters to Holly Springs, telegraphing to Washington, "to-morrow we will be in Abbeville, or a battle will be fought."

Generals Hovey and Washburn had been directed to move with their troops from Helena, Arkansas, across the Mississippi, and cut the railroads in Pemberton's rear, which they did, thus hastening the evacuation of the rebel works on the Tallahatchie. December 1st the rebels were falling back, and Grant pursuing to Oxford. As the troops pushed forward, Grant found abundant evidence to justify his stringent order, on the 14th of November, against the Jews. Near Waterford one house in St. Louis had a branch clothing establishment for the supply of the rebels.

On the 3d Grant's head-quarters were at Oxford, and, so far, his expedition had been a perfect success; but now came the alarming intelligence that the enemy were in his rear on his communications, and that Colonel Murphy had surrendered Holly Springs to Van Dorn. Sufficient garrisons had been left at Columbus, Humboldt, Trenton, Jackson, Bolivar, Corinth, Holly Springs, Cold Water, Davis' Mills, Middleburg, and every precaution had been taken to secure his advance, still Grant felt that his communications might be cut, and was, therefore, not greatly suprised to hear of the enemy being in his rear. He was amazed, however, that Holly Springs should have been taken so easily; and finding he could not advance without supplies, he hastily gathered up his army and began to retrace his steps. On arriving at Holly Springs, and learning that Colonel Murphy had surrendered the post and all its stores without striking a blow, Grant issued an order dismissing him disgracefully from the service. The posts of Cold Water, Davis' Mills, and Middleburg had been attacked by the rebels, but were bravely defended and the enemy repulsed, and to the officers and men comprising the garrisons of these places, Grant issued a complimentary order.

The army now consisted of four corps, organized as follows: 1. The troops composing the Ninth Division, Brigadier-General G. W. Morgan commanding; the Tenth Division, Brigadier-General A. J. Smith commanding; and all other troops operating on the Mississippi River below Memphis, not included in the Fifteenth Army Corps, constituted the Thirteenth Army Corps, under the command of Major-General John A. McClernand.

2. The Fifth Division, Brigadier-General Morgan L. Smith commanding; the Division from Helena, Arkansas, commanded by Brigadier-General F. Steele, and the forces in the District of Memphis, constituted the Fifteenth Army Corps, and was commanded by Major-General William T. Sherman.

3. The Sixth Division, Brigadier-General J. McArthur commanding; the Seventh Division, Brigadier-General I. F. Quinby commanding; the Eighth Division, Brigadier-General

L. F. Ross commanding; the Second Brigade of Cavalry, Colonel A. L. Lee commanding, and the troops in the District of Columbus, commanded by Brigadier-General Davis, and those in the District of Jackson, commanded by Brigadier-General Sullivan, constituted the Sixteenth Army Corps, and was commanded by Major-General S. A. Hurlbut.

4. The First Division, Brigadier-General J. W. Denver commanding; the Third Division, Brigadier-General John A. Logan commanding; the Fourth Division, Brigadier-General J. G. Lauman commanding; the First Brigade of Cavalry, Colonel B. H. Grierson commanding, and the forces in the District of Corinth, commanded by Brigadier-General G. M. Dodge, constituted the Seventeenth Army Corps, and was commanded by Major-General J. B. McPherson.

Grant had determined to send General Sherman down the Mississippi with an expedition against Vicksburg, and for this purpose had ordered him to Memphis, General Morgan L. Smith's division being ordered to at once report to him to form part of the expedition. The navy, under Admiral Porter, was to coöperate with him, and on the 23d of December, Sherman embarked with four divisions, and immediately set sail down the river. On the 24th he arrived near Helena, with thirty thousand men, and that evening received a reënforcement from Helena of twelve thousand. Next morning he landed at Milliken's Bend, and spent three days in attempting to cut the Vicksburg and Shreveport Railroad, by which he was informed the rebels were sending reënforcements to Vicksburg. On the 26th, under convoy of Admiral Porter's gunboats, he advanced up the Yazoo River, which empties into the Mississippi nine miles from Vicksburg, and on the 27th landed near the mouth of Chickasaw Bayou. The expedition of General Sherman had been intended to coöperate with General Grant's movements by land on

Vicksburg. Sherman's forces were denominated the right wing, and Grant's the left wing. On reaching Chickasaw Bayou, Sherman expected to hear of Grant's advance, but could get no intelligence of his whereabouts. It was not until until several days afterward that Sherman heard of the surrender of Holly Springs, and Grant's retreat.

On the morning of the 28th, not being able to learn any thing of Grant, Sherman determined to move forward without waiting for him. A. J. Smith's division had the right, Morgan L. Smith's the right center, Morgan's the left center, and Steele's the left. The advance lay across bluffs covered with tangled undergrowth, and through swamps intersected by deep streams. The narrow causeways, along which the infantry had to advance, were under range of the rebel guns on the bluffs, and the hills were lined with rifle-pits, filled with sharp-shooters. Through these difficulties Sherman pushed his way, and on the 29th attacked the rebel lines. On the evening of that day he was at the foot of the bluffs and had effected a lodgment, but being unable, on account of the nature of the ground, to put but a part of his force into the action he was driven back with severe loss. He now determined to go higher up the Yazoo and attempt a landing under cover of the gunboats, but a rain setting in, and afterward a dense fog, so that the vessels could not move, nor the men see each other at ten paces distant, he gave up the movement and returned to the Mississippi, where he met his superior officer, General McClernand, to whom he turned over his command. Sherman lost in the expedition one hundred and seventy-five killed, nine hundred and thirty-seven wounded, and seven hundred and forty-three missing. His failure was entirely owing to the surrender of Holly Springs, and consequent non-coöperation of the left wing. No fault was found with him by General Grant or the department.

The following graphic description of the first attack on Vicksburg is given by an eye-witness:

"General Morgan, at eleven o'clock A. M., sent word to General Steele that he was about ready for the movement upon the hill, and wished the latter to support him with General Thayer's brigade. General Steele accordingly ordered General Thayer to move his brigade forward, and be ready for the assault. The order was promptly complied with, and General Blair received from General Morgan the order to assault the hill. The artillery had been silent for some time, but Hoffman's battery opened when the movement commenced. This was promptly replied to by the enemy, and taken up by Griffith's First Iowa Battery, and a vigorous shelling was the result. By the time General Blair's brigade emerged from its cover of cypress forest, the shell were dropping fast among the men. A field battery had been in position in front of Hoffman's battery; but it limbered up and moved away beyond the heavy batteries and the rifle-pits.

"In front of the timber where Blair's brigade had been lying was an abatis of young trees, cut off about three feet above the ground, and with the tops fallen promiscuously around. It took some minutes to pass this abatis, and by the time this was accomplished the enemy's fire had not been without effect. Beyond this abatis was a ditch fifteen or twenty feet deep, and with two or three feet water in the bottom. The bottom of the ditch was a quicksand, in which the feet of the men commenced sinking, the instant they touched it. By the time this ditch was passed the line was thrown into considerable confusion, and it took several minutes to put it in order. All the horses of the officers were mired in this ditch. Every one dismounted and moved up the hill on foot.

"Beyond this ditch was an abatis of heavy timber that

had been felled several months before, and, from being completely seasoned, was more difficult of passage than that constructed of greener and more flexible trees encountered at first. These obstacles were overcome under a tremendous fire from the enemy's batteries and the men in the rifle-pits. The line was recovered from the disorder into which it had been thrown by the passage of the abatis; and, with General Blair at their head, the regiments moved forward 'upon the enemy's works.' The first movement was over a sloping plateau, raked by direct and enfilading fires from heavy artillery, and swept by a perfect storm of bullets from the rifle-pits. Nothing daunted by the dozens of men that had already fallen, the brigade pressed on, and in a few moments had driven the enemy from the first range of rifle-pits at the base of the hill, and were in full possession.

"Halting but a moment to take breath, the brigade renewed the charge, and speedily occupied the second line of rifle-pits, about two hundred yards distant from the first. General Blair was the first man of his brigade to enter. All this time the murderous fire from the enemy's guns continued. The batteries were still above this line of rifle-pits. The regiments were not strong enough to attempt their capture without a prompt and powerful support. For them it had truly been a march

"'Into the jaws of death—
Into the mouth of hell.'

"Almost simultaneously with the movement of General Blair on the left, General Thayer received his command to go forward. He had previously given orders to all his regiments in column to follow each other whenever the first moved forward. He accordingly placed himself at the head of his advance regiment, the Fourth Iowa, and his order—'Forward, Second Brigade!'—rang out clear above the tumult. Colonel Williamson, commanding the Fourth Iowa, moved it off in splendid style. General Thayer supposed that all the other regiments of his brigade were following, in accordance with his instructions previously issued. He wound through the timber skirting the bayou, crossed at the same bridge where General Blair had passed but a few minutes before, made his way through the ditch and both lines of abatis, deflected the right and ascended the sloping plateau in the direction of the rifle-pits simultaneously with General Blair, and about two hundred yards to his right.

"When General Thayer reached the rifle-pits, after hard fighting and a heavy loss, he found, to his horror, that only the Fourth Iowa had followed him, the wooded nature of the place having prevented his ascertaining it before. Sadly disheartened, with little hope of success, he still pressed forward and fought his way to the second line, at the same time that General Blair reached it on the left. Colonel Williamson's regiment was fast falling before the concentrated fire of the rebels, and with an anxious heart General Thayer looked around for aid.

"The rebels were forming three full regiments of infantry to move down upon General Thayer, and were massing a proportionately formidable force against General Blair. The rebel infantry and artillery were constantly in full play, and two heavy guns were raking the rifle-pits in several places. With no hope of succor, General Thayer gave the order for a return down the hill and back to his original position. The Fourth Iowa, entering the fight five hundred strong, had lost a hundred and twenty men in less than thirty minutes. It fell back at a quick march, but with its ranks unbroken and without any thing of panic.

"It appears that just at the time General Thayer's brigade started up the hill, General Morgan sent for a portion of it to support him on the right. General Steele at once diverted the Second Regiment of Thayer's Brigade, which was passing at the time. The Second Regiment being thus diverted, the others followed, in accordance with the orders they had previously received from their commander. Notice of the movement was sent to General Thayer; but, in consequence of the death of the courier, the notification never reached him. This accounts for his being left with nothing save the Fourth Iowa Regiment. The occurrence was a sad one. The troops thus turned off were among the best that had yet been in action, and had they been permitted to charge the enemy they would have won for themselves a brilliant record.

"When General Blair entered the second line of rifle-pits, his brigade continued to pursue the enemy up the hill. The Thirteenth Illinois Infantry was in advance, and fought with desperation to win its way to the top of the crest. Fifty yards or more above the second line of rifle-pits is a small clump of willows, hardly deserving the name of trees. They stand in a corn-field, and from the banks of the bayou below presented the appearance of a green hillock. To this copse many of the rebels fled when they were driven from the rifle-pits, and they were promptly pursued by General Blair's men. The Thirteenth met and engaged the rebels hand to hand, and in the encounter bayonets were repeatedly crossed. It gained the place, driving out the enemy; but as soon as our men occupied it the fire of a field-battery was turned upon them and the place became too hot to be held.

"The road from Mrs. Lake's plantation to the top of the high ground and thence to Vicksburg, runs at an angle along the side of the hill, so as to obtain a slope easy of ascent. The lower side of this road was provided with a breastwork, so that a light battery could be taken anywhere along the road and fired over the embankment. From the nearest point of this embankment a battery opened on the Thirteenth Illinois, and was aided by a heavy battery on the hill. Several men were killed by the shell and grape that swept the copse.

"The other regiments of the brigade came to the support of the Thirteenth—the Twenty-ninth Missouri, Colonel Cavender, being in the advance. Meantime the rebels formed a large force of infantry to bring against them, and when the Twenty-ninth reached the copse, the rebels were already engaging the Union troops. The color-bearer of the Twelfth had been shot down, and some one picked up the standard and planted it in front of the copse. The force of the rebels was too great for our men to stand against them, and they slowly fell back, fighting step by step toward the rifle-pits, and taking their colors with them.

"In this charge upon the hill the regiments lost severely. In General Blair's brigade there were eighteen hundred and twenty-five men engaged in this assault, and of this number six hundred and forty-two were killed, wounded, and captured."

Sherman, who now took command under McClernand, at once proposed to go up Arkansas River and capture Arkansas Post, a strong work about fifty miles from the mouth of the river. As no orders had been or could be received from Grant for some time, McClernand agreed, and they advanced, accompanied by several gunboats. On the 11th of January, the land and naval forces made a combined attack on the enemy's works and captured them, with a loss of about one thousand men, killed, wounded, and missing. The fight lasted three hours, and the Union troops captured five thousand prisoners and seventeen pieces of cannon. As Sherman expected, this little victory greatly raised the spirits of our troops, and reconciled the country to the misfortunes of the army at Vicksburg.

The reporting of General McClernand to Grant necessitated a reorganization of the army, and, accordingly, on the 22d of December, an order was issued from army headquarters re-composing the corps, and assigning General McClernand to command the Thirteenth Army Corps, General Sherman to the Fifteenth Army Corps, General Hurlbut to the Sixteenth Corps, and General McPherson to the Seventeenth Corps.

Colonel Badeau, in his excellent life of Grant, has, for some reason or other, done great injustice to General McClernand; and, although it is not the intention of the author of this work to find fault with others, he could not omit to mention the fact that writers, whose province it is to discuss such matters, may set the gallant McClernand right before the country.

On the 17th of January, General Grant came down to Napoleon, where the transport fleet was then laying, with the troops on board, and on the 20th he announced his intention to again attack Vicksburg and reduce it, although he believed, as he wrote Halleck, "it will take time and men."

CHAPTER VIII.

THE PRESIDENT'S EMANCIPATION PROCLAMATION—GRANT ENFORCES THE POLICY OF THE GOVERNMENT—YOUNG'S POINT—THE WILLIAMS CANAL—ROUNDABOUT BAYOU EXPEDITION—MOON LAKE—YAZOO PASS EXPEDITION—ADMIRAL FARRAGUT—ADMIRAL PORTER—M'CLERNAND'S MARCH—RUNNING THE BATTERIES—GRIERSON AND HATCH'S RAID—BATTLE OF PORT GIBSON—GRANT'S FIGHTING APPEARANCE—EVACUATION OF GRAND GULF—PERPLEXING SITUATION OF GRANT—HIS PLANS DISAPPROVED BY THE PRESIDENT AND HALLECK—PEMBERTON AND JOHNSTON MARCH AGAINST HIM—BATTLE OF RAYMOND—ADVANCE ON JACKSON—PRELIMINARY MOVEMENTS—GRANT LEADS THE ADVANCE IN PERSON AND ON FOOT.

The President's emancipation proclamation, issued on the 22d of September, 1862, had caused great excitement in the country and army. Many gallant men declared if they had known they were to fight for the freedom of the negro, they would not have enlisted in the war. A large number of officers tendered their resignations, and so great was the dissatisfaction prevailing, that the department and army commanders felt compelled to put a stop to the matter. It having come to the ears of Grant that the surrender of Holly Springs, without striking a blow, was in consequence of the proclamation, he at once assembled a court of inquiry, and eight officers being found guilty, he dismissed them in disgrace from the army. Fully determined that the policy of the Government and the freedom of the slaves should be carried out, Grant issued a general order declaring that corps, division, and post commanders would afford all facilities for the completion of the negro regiments organizing in the department. Commissaries would issue supplies, and quartermasters furnish stores on the same requisitions and returns as were required from other troops. He said:

"It is expected that all commanders will especially exert themselves in carrying out the policy of the administration, not only in organizing colored regiments, and rendering them efficient, but also in removing prejudice against them." . . . . .

Grant's plan now was to find a base on the river, cross the country, and attack Vicksburg from the land side. With this view he ordered his army to rendezvous at Young's Point, and on the 29th of January proceeded to that place in person and assumed command. The navy, under Porter, was already at the Point; and the whole army, except Logan's division and some small garrisons, was expected in a few days.

At Vicksburg the Mississippi makes a great bend, or horseshoe, the distance across the neck being only about one mile. Proceeding to the neck of the bend, six miles below the city, Grant determined to cut a canal for his boats, and thus get below the city. The work on the Williams canal was immediately begun and vigorously continued until the 8th of March, when the dam, at the mouth, gave way, and the waters of the Mississippi rushed through, overflowing the land, and compelling the soldiers to seize their tents and implements and flee to the levees to keep from being drowned. The rebels laughed long and loud at Grant's failure, but he smiled good-naturedly, and at once showed them he had another plan for approaching their stronghold.

Proceeding with his engineers and some dredge-boats to Milliken's Bend, he began cleaning out Roundabout Bayou with a view of getting into Tensas River, but just as he had got the channel sufficiently dredged to allow the passage of some light steamers, the water in the river suddenly fell and put an end to the scheme. Again the rebels laughed at the Yankee general, but nothing discouraged, he began cutting a new canal from the Mississippi into Lake Providence. By this route he hoped to get into Baxter and Macon Bayous, and from them into Tensas, Washita, and White Rivers, down which he could sail to the Mississippi, communicate with Banks at Port Hudson, and thus flank Vicksburg and open communications with the Gulf. The route, however, was too long, and the project was soon abandoned.

The next effort was to get through Yazoo Pass, eight miles from Helena, into Moon Lake, and thence into Cold Water and Tallahatchie Rivers. One who was engaged in the expedition thus speaks of Yazoo Pass:

"I would like to describe the Yazoo Pass. I would like to compare it to something that would be intelligible. But I know of nothing in heaven or on earth, or in the waters under the earth, that will compare with it. Had the immortal bard desired a subject from which to draw a picture of the way that leads to the realms of darkness and despair, he had only to picture the Yazoo Pass. Let me try, in the feeble language I can command, to describe it. Perhaps the reader has passed through the Dismal Swamp of Virginia; or, if not, he has read accounts of travelers who have enjoyed that privilege. Then he has heard of the famous jungles of India. He has seen or read of the unbroken silence of the boundless tall forests of the John Brown tract in Western New York. Conceive the ugliest features of these three varieties of territory, and he will be able, by combining them, to form a tolerably correct idea of the region through which the Yazoo Pass runs. Those who have watched the course of a snake as he trails his way along the ground, winding this way and that, hither and yonder, going in all directions at the same time, and yet maintaining something of a regular course in the average, will, by exaggerating the picture in their own minds, understand something of the tortuous course of the Yazoo Pass. I have passed through it from one end to the other, and I assert candidly that there is not throughout its entire length a piece two hundred feet long of perfectly straight river."

Up this narrow and tortuous channel the gunboats were pushed, and the work continued until the 21st of March, when the expedition was given up, and the land and naval forces returned to Milliken's Bend.

Admiral Porter, of whom it was said he could run his gunboats wherever the ground was damp, had displayed the greatest energy in the operations along the Mississippi. On the 15th of March he had sailed up Steele's Bayou, and soon became so heavily engaged with the enemy, that he was obliged to send to General Grant for help. Grant promptly sent him General Sherman, with his Fifteenth Army Corps, and, after some hard fighting, the boats were got out of the bayous and into the Mississippi again. Of the timely arrival of Sherman and his troops, the following extract from an officer's letter will tell:

"While the adventure was of uncertain success—when the result seemed almost accomplished, and when our gunboats were surrounded with an enemy confident of victory, and their extrication seemed almost an impossibility—officers and men worked with equal alacrity, whether in building bridges or making forced marches, both by day and in the night. The whole time was used in labor—constant and severe. It seems almost a miracle that the boats were saved. If Generals Sherman and Stuart, by their utmost exertions and labor, had forwarded their troops a single half day later, if the second forced march under General Sherman had been retarded a single hour, in all human probability the whole force would have been lost."

An effort was now again made to remove Grant, but the President said: "I like the man, and will try him a little longer." The country, however, was clamoring at his delay, and Grant saw the necessity of promptly doing something to save himself from the disgrace of removal.

Admiral Farragut had run by the batteries at Port Hudson with his flag-ship, the Hartford, and her tender, the Albatross; and on March 17th was lying off Natchez, Miss. On March 21st the Hartford arrived off Vicksburg, and anchoring below the batteries, communicated with Admiral Porter and General Grant.

Porter was burning to eclipse his gallant rival by running the batteries of Vicksburg, and, on the 16th of April, was ready to make the attempt.

Grant had determined to move his forces below Vicksburg, on the Louisiana shore, so as to take the rebel works in rear. On the 29th of March McClernand, with the Thirteenth Army Corps, had started for New Carthage, but on arriving at Smith's plantation, two miles from Carthage, he found the levee broken and the town an island. It seemed as though the Mississippi was a rebel sympathizer. McClernand pushed on, however, going around Bayou Vidal and traversing the most horrible roads. At times it was found necessary to drag his wagons and cannon by hand, the men working in mud up to their knees. At length the Union troops reached the Mississippi, and established their camp on a rebel plantation just outside of New Carthage. McClernand now anxiously awaited the operations of the fleets up the river, and was soon gratified to learn of their success.

On the night of the 16th of April, Porter, with eight gunboats and the transports Forest Queen, Henry Clay, and Silver Wave, all well protected by cotton bales, steamed down the river. There was no moon, and the great city and bluffs lay shrouded in darkness. Porter led the way in the Benton, and was already close upon the hill-sides he knew to be bristling with rebel cannon. Slowly and noiselessly the great boats glided down the broad stream, the transports hugging the Louisiana shore. Suddenly the rebel sentries challenged, and receiving no reply, the batteries belched forth their contents, and the hills for miles lighted up with flames. The slumbering citizens of Vicksburg sprang from their beds in fright, and rushed wildly into the streets as the great iron shells of the gunboats went howling like demons over the city, or crashed through the houses and exploded with a noise like thunder. The rebel sharpshooters set fire to the buildings on the river bank to get light to see the boats by, and the shells soon setting fire to the houses further up in the city, the flames lighted up the hills for miles around. In the streets, toiling at their cannons, like red dragons, could be seen the rebel gunners, and, on the boats in the river, the sailors working their huge guns, looked like so many black devils. It was a scene such as has seldom been witnessed in this or any other country, and no one who was at Vicksburg on that eventful night will ever have his dreams entirely free from the horrible spectacle.

In one hour and a quarter the boats had all passed the batteries, and the firing ceased. The Henry Clay was lost, a shot from the rebel batteries having set her cotton on fire and demoralized her crew, who abandoned her. As she floated down the stream, ablaze with fire, she presented a beautiful sight with the stars and stripes streaming in the red light above her. The Forest Queen was disabled by a round shot, and every transport was struck, some of them being drawn into the eddy and compelled to run through the horrible fire of the batteries no less than three times. Surprising as it may seem, only one man was killed and eight wounded in all of Porter's boats that night. Grant had followed the fleet in a transport to just above the bend, where he remained and watched the operations, his boat being in close range of the rebel batteries, and the shot and shell falling thick around him.

The first intelligence McClernand and his troops had of what had taken place above, was communicated by the old rebel on whose plantation they were encamped. He rushed into McClernand's head-quarters, jubilantly exclaiming: "Where, now, are your gunboats? Burned to the water's edge, sir, and there they go floating down the stream charred and blackened hulks." When, however, the wrecks had passed, and one after another the black smokes of the gun-goats appeared in the bend of the river above, the old man became pallid with fear and rage as the Yankees pointed them out to him, and tauntingly asked: "Did Vicksburg put an end to them all?"

McPherson, with his corps, had closely followed McClernand to New Carthage, and the combined forces were now preparing to attack Grand Gulf from Hard Times. On the 26th of April, six other transports had run the batteries at Vicksburg, and Grant was now busily engaged in preparing his troops for the advance on Grand Gulf and Port Gibson.

Before leaving the north side of Vicksburg, General Grant had ordered Generals Grierson and Hatch, two of his most skillful cavalry officers, to take the First Cavalry Brigade, go south into the State of Mississippi, destroy the railroads, burn the bridges in the rear of Vicksburg, and then make their way to some point within the Union lines down the river. On the 17th of April, Grierson had started from La Grange, going to Ripley, where General Hatch, with his troops, left the main expedition, and made a flank movement, crossing the Tallahatchie five miles from New Albany. Grierson crossed at New Albany, and sending small bodies of troops to the right and left, to deceive the enemy as to his destination, pushed on with the main body to Peritotoc, where he attacked and dispersed a body of rebels. On the 20th, Grierson sent a small force back to La Grange, with some prisoners, directing them to make as much display as possible, and create the impression that the raid was over. The *ruse* was successful. Another force was detached under General Hatch, and sent to destroy the Mobile and Ohio railroad and attack Columbus. General Hatch was entirely successful, drawing off Chalmers' rebel troops after him, and leaving Grierson free to pursue his course with the main column to Starkville. The command united again at Louisville, Miss., and marched to Philadelphia, Decatur, Montrose, Raleigh, Westville, and finally emerged from rebeldom at Baton Rouge on the first of May. This was the greatest raid of the war, the troops having marched eight hundred miles through the heart of the enemy's country, cut off all communication with Vicksburg, captured one thousand prisoners, and made other captures as follows:

"Locomotives destroyed, 2; cars destroyed, nearly 200; bridges burned, etc., 9; telegraph wires cut, 2; railroad tracks destroyed and broken, 3; rebel camps destroyed, 3; important rebel mails destroyed, 3; tannery burned, 1; horses captured, over 1,200; value of property destroyed, over $4,000,000. Besides cutting off all railroad communication with the rebel strongholds on the Mississippi, as well as entirely destroying muskets, tents, stores, leather, boots, saddles, etc., of great value to the rebels in a military point of view."

Grierson and Hatch's loss was only three killed, seven wounded, and fourteen missing.

Meanwhile the navy had attacked the rebel batteries at Grand Gulf, and Grant had marched to Bruinsburg, and was now before Port Gibson. McClernand, who led the advance, divided his force, sending Osterhaus with a division to assault the place on the left, while, with Hovey's, Carr's, and A. J. Smith's brigades, he attacked on the right. The battle of Port Gibson was a hard one, General Grant being on the ground, and personally in command—for he well knew, if he suffered another defeat, or even check, his whole expedition against Vicksburg would be at an end. On the left, Osterhaus drove the enemy back all day, but on the right the fight was more stubborn. Logan's division had come up, and Grant sent a brigade to reënforce McClernand's right, where the fight was hottest; at the same time ordering Logan to take position on the left, with the other brigade. Charging with the bayonet, and working their way through the tangled cane-brake, Osterhaus' troops drove the rebels from their strongest positions on the left. The sight of fresh troops on the right, caused the enemy to fall back, and by night he was in full retreat. Darkness put an end to the conflict on the left, and next morning the rebels were gone, having crossed Bayou Pierre in the night, and destroyed the bridge behind them.

Grant determined to vigorously follow up the rebels, and compel them to fight or take refuge in their strong works at Vicksburg. Stripping his army of all surplus baggage, he put it on the roads, and pushed rapidly forward. Grant, at this time, was in admirable light marching order. In starting on the movement, the General had disincumbered himself of every thing, setting an example to his officers and men. He took neither a horse nor a servant, overcoat nor blanket, nor tent, nor camp-chest, nor even a clean shirt. *His only baggage consisted of a box of cigars and a toothbrush.* He always showed his teeth to the rebels. He shared all the hardships of the private soldier, sleeping in the front and in the open air, and eating hard-tack and salt pork. He wore no sword, had on a low-crowned, citizen's hat, and the only thing about him to mark him as a military man was his two stars on his undress military coat.

On the 3d of May, McPherson and Logan, who had been driving the enemy before them, about four o'clock in the afternoon came upon a strong force of rebels near Big Black River, and drove them precipitately across the stream. It was now evident that the rebels were evacuating Grand Gulf, and Grant hurried thither with one brigade of Logan's division, but arrived too late; not only was Grand Gulf deserted, but all the country between Big Black and Bayou Pierre open. On arriving at Grand Gulf, Grant, who had not been in bed, nor had his clothes off since leaving Bruinsburg, went on board a gunboat, took a good sleep, and then borrowed a change of linen from Admiral Porter, after which he wrote dispatches till midnight.

Grant now received information that Pemberton was marching out of Vicksburg to give him battle, while the rebel Joseph E. Johnston was coming down from Jackson, to fall upon his rear. The movement he contemplated presented most splendid advantages, but also difficulties and dangers that well might appall the heart of any commander. He must advance between two powerful armies, either of which was strong enough to be a formidable adversary, and both, by combining, could crush him. Badeau tells us that Grant's officers were seriously alarmed at the situation of affairs. His most trusted associates besought him to change his plans, while his superiors were astounded at his temerity, and strove to interfere.

Soldiers of reputation and civilians in high place condemned in advance a campaign that seemed to them as hopeless as it was unprecedented. If he failed, the country would concur with the government and the generals. Grant knew all this, and appreciated his danger, but was as invulnerable to the apprehensions of ambition as to the entreaties of friendship or the anxieties even of patriotism. That quiet confidence which never forsook him, and which amounted indeed almost to a feeling of fate, was uninterrupted. Having once determined in a matter that required irreversible decision, he never reversed, nor even misgave, but was steadily loyal to himself and his plans. This absolute and implicit faith was, however, as far as possible from conceit or enthusiasm. It was simply a consciousness—or conviction, rather—which brought the very strength it believed in—which was itself strength—and which inspired others with a trust in him, because he was able thus to trust himself.

General Howard also has alluded to this strong conviction, on the part of General Grant, that success would crown his endeavors. It is stated in a paragraph in the New York *Times*, of February 18th:

"General Howard says that General Grant is strictly a temperate man and religious. His marked characteristic is a wonderful faith in his success, amounting almost to the fatality in which Napoleon so strongly believed. General Howard can be relied on."

"My army," he wrote, "is composed of hardy and disciplined men, who know no defeat, and are not willing to learn what it is."

It is said, that, during all the fatigues of this campaign, General Grant practiced total abstinence from all intoxicating drinks. This is the testimony of those who were constantly with him.

An officer on his staff, who must have been acquainted with his daily habits, wrote some time after this:

"If you could see the General as he sits just over beyond me, with his wife and two children, looking more like a chaplain than a general, with that quiet air so impossible to describe, you would not ask me if he drinks. He rarely ever uses intoxicating liquors. He is more moderate in his habits and desires, and more pure and spotless in his private character, than almost any man I ever knew. He is more brave, has more power to command, and more ability to plan, than any man I ever served under; cool to excess when others lose nerve, always hopeful, always undisturbed, never failing to accomplish what he undertakes."

In this connection, the following extracts from the pen of Major Penniman will be read with interest:

"I have seen him in the familiarity and seclusion of camp life, and I know perfectly well what his personal habits are. He messes with his staff as he would with his own family. No intoxicating liquors are on the table at dinner or at any other time. It is not his habit to use them, nor does he encourage it in others. No man of all the hundreds of thousands he has commanded ever heard General Grant use profane language."

To add to his difficulties, Grant, who had been expecting assistance from Banks, received a letter from that general saying that he could not reach Port Hudson for two weeks, and, even after the reduction of that place, he could only reënforce Grant's army with about twelve thousand men. The President wrote Grant: "When you got below and took Port Gibson and Grand Gulf, I thought you should go down the river and join General Banks; and when you turned northward, east of the Big Black, I feared it was a mistake." Halleck wrote: "If possible, the forces of yourself and Banks should be united between Vicksburg and Port Hudson, so as to attack these places separately with combined forces." Turning a deaf ear to the arguments of his inferiors and imploring his superiors to grant him a few days respite from their orders, Grant turned his back on the Mississippi River and started for Hankinson's Ferry. Telegraphing his commissary, "Rush me forward rations with all dispatch," he set his army in motion, traveling with it on foot, riding borrowed horses, messing with any general near whose camp he happened to be, and sleeping at night in the porches of houses on the road. When he left Hard Times he took no baggage but a bunch of cigars, a towel and a tooth-brush, and his food consisted of a pound of boiled meat which he carried wrapped in the towel. Telegraphing to Washington, "You will probably not hear from me for several days," he cut loose from his communications and plunged into the wilderness of Black River.

Sending Sherman to make a feint on Haines' Bluff, and Logan to fall upon the enemy at Raymond, Grant quietly but anxiously awaited the result of his first move. Logan, on the 12th of May, about ten o'clock, came upon the rebel Gregg's brigade, which was soon reënforced by that of W. H. Walker. The fighting was severe, lasting two hours, when the rebels gave way and fled toward Jackson. Logan lost sixty-nine killed and three hundred and forty-one wounded. The loss of the enemy was much greater. Sherman made a dash toward Haines' Bluff, and then turned off and joined McPherson.

As soon as Grant heard of the victory at Raymond, he ordered McPherson and Sherman to move with all dispatch by parallel roads upon Jackson, where Joseph E. Johnston was reported to be with his rebel army. All the divisions were now concentrating on Jackson, and it was expected a great battle would soon be fought.

The following is a full account of the preliminary movements of the army, before the final advance on Raymond and Jackson:

"On Thursday, the 7th of May, General McPherson, commanding the Seventeenth Army Corps, moved his troops to Rocky Springs, and his camp was occupied next day by General Sherman, with the Fifteenth Army Corps. On

Saturday, the 9th, General McPherson again moved to the eastward, to the village of Utica, crossing the road occupied by the Thirteenth Army Corps, under General McClernand, and leaving the latter on his left. On Sunday morning, the 10th, General McClernand marched to Five Mile Creek, and encamped on the south bank at noon, on account of broken bridges, which were repaired the same day. On Monday morning, the 11th, General Sherman's corps came up, passed General McClernand's, and encamped that night at the village of Auburn, about ten miles south of Edwards' Station, which is on a portion of the railroad from Vicksburg to Jackson. As soon as it passed, General McClernand's corps followed a few miles, and then took a road going obliquely to the left, leading to Hall's Ferry, on the Big Black River. Thus, on Monday evening, May 11th, General McClernand was at Hall's Ferry; General Sherman was at Auburn, six or eight miles to the north-east, and General McPherson was about eight miles still further to the north-east, a few miles north of Utica. The whole formed an immense line of battle; Sherman's corps being in the center, with those of McPherson and McClernand forming the right and left wings. It will be observed, also, that a change of front had been effected. From Grand Gulf the army marched eastward; but, by these last movements, it had swung on the left as a pivot, and fronted nearly northward.

"Up to this the enemy had not appeared on our line of march. On Tuesday morning, May 12th, General McClernand's advance drove in the enemy's pickets near Hall's Ferry, and brisk skirmishing ensued for an hour or two, with little loss to either side. By noon the rebels had disappeared from his front, and seven wounded and none killed was the total Union loss. General Sherman put Steele's division in motion early in the morning, and came upon the enemy at the crossing of Fourteen Mile Creek, four miles from Auburn. The cavalry advance was fired into from the thick woods that skirt the stream, and was unable, owing to the nature of the ground, to make a charge or clear the rebels from their position. A battery was taken to the front, supported by two infantry regiments, and threw a few shell into the bushy undergrowth skirting the stream, which gave them cover. Skirmishers were thrown out and advanced to the creek, driving the enemy slowly. A brigade was thrown to the right and left flanks, when the rebel forces, mainly cavalry, withdrew toward Raymond. The bridge was burned during the skirmish, but a crossing was constructed in two hours, and the trains were passing before noon.

Grant was never behind his troops, but each day changed his head-quarters, keeping with the advance of the center of the three columns, the better to direct the movements of all."

CHAPTER IX.

PEMBERTON DECEIVED BY GRANT—DEFEAT OF JOHNSTON—CAPTURE OF JACKSON—DESTRUCTION OF REBEL PROPERTY—JOHNSTON DECEIVED BY GRANT—MEETING OF SHERMAN, GRANT AND M'PHERSON AT THE STATE CAPITAL—ADVANCE ON PEMBERTON—BATTLE OF CHAMPION HILLS—DETAILS OF THE BATTLE—RETREAT OF PEMBERTON—SHERMAN'S OPINION OF THE CAMPAIGN—GRANT'S REPLY—FIRST ASSAULT ON VICKSBURG—DETAILS OF THE ACTION—THE NAVAL OPERATIONS ON THE RIVER—COMMUNICATION WITH GRANT ESTABLISHED—HAINES' BLUFF SEIZED FOR A NEW BASE—PREPARATIONS FOR THE SIEGE.

To deceive Pemberton as to his destination, Grant sent McClernand to threaten Edwards' Station. Very skillfully McClernand deluded the foe, making him believe, until it was too late to help Johnston, that Edwards' Station was the objective point of attack. Sherman and McPherson were now nearing Jackson by different roads, and Johnston, alarmed at their approach, hastily sent an order to Pemberton to attack them in the rear at Clinton, but Pemberton had his hands full with McClernand, and was himself expecting an attack. Johnston marched out of Jackson and intrenched in battle array, hoping to check Grant in front until Pemberton could fall upon his rear.

On the 14th of May, Sherman and McPherson met before Jackson, and at once commenced the attack in the midst of a heavy rain. As the hostile batteries were exchanging shots, General Grant carefully examined the ground, and posted his troops for the decisive attack. We will not attempt to describe the tactics of the battle. For an hour it was delayed by a shower, in which the windows of heaven seemed to be opened, and both armies were drenched by the flood. No man could open his cartridge-box, lest it should be instantly filled with water.

As the rain abated, the battle commenced with the incessant rattle of musketry and the roar of artillery. Both parties fought with fierceness, with desperation. Sherman, early in the action, discovered the weakness of the enemy on his right, and pushing out a reconnoissance, he turned their defenses and caused a rapid evacuation of this part of their line. Meanwhile McPherson made a spirited assault on the left, Crocker's division charging with a yell, and completely breaking the rebel line. The enemy now fearing that Sherman, who was coming rapidly down the Mississippi Springs road, would get in their rear, fled in confusion, leaving seventeen cannon, the State capitol, and a vast quantity of valuable property in the hands of the Union troops. General Grant, with his staff, was the first to enter the enemy's works. His son, a lad of thirteen years, accompanied him upon this campaign. As they approached the town, the boy galloped ahead, and was the first to enter the capital of Mississippi.

General Grant allowed himself not a moment to repose upon his laurels. Indeed the rebels were all around him, and the utmost activity and vigilance were requisite to secure himself from disaster. The troops marched into the streets, and the national banner was proudly unfurled from the State House. The intrenchments and rifle-pits outside of the city were occupied by the Union troops. General Grant took possession of the house which General Johnston had the night before occupied. After destroying the railroads, bridges, arsenals, and every thing that could be of military use to the rebels, Grant gave immediate orders for the troops to wheel about, march with all rapidity to Edwards' Station and attack Pemberton. The soldiers, who had now begun to understand something about Grant's tactics, obeyed with alacrity, regardless of hunger or fatigue. In the evening Grant met his fighting generals, Sherman and McPherson, at the State House, and warm were the hand-shakings and congratulations.

Johnston, after his defeat at Jackson, had retreated about fifteen miles north by the Canton road, where he began fortifying, still expecting Pemberton to come up and attack Grant in the rear. Leaving him to enjoy his trenches, Grant, on the 15th, began his march on Pemberton. At five o'clock on the morning of the 16th, two railroad men, who were employés of the army, had passed through Pemberton's camps the evening before, were brought to Grant's head-quarters and reported that the rebel troops were advancing to attack him. Sherman, who had been left behind, was at once ordered up, and preparations made to meet him. Grant, who was always in the immediate vicinity of his fighting forces, and directing their movements, came up to Clinton and established his head-quarters. The troops were posted in the following order:

Extreme left, General Smith, supported by General Blair; on the right of General Smith, General Osterhaus, supported by General Carr; General Hovey in the center, with General McPherson's corps on the extreme right, with General Crocker as reserve. In this order the advance was made. General McClernand's corps, with the exception of General Hovey's division, reaching the position by way of the several roads leading from Raymond to Edwards' Station.

The first demonstration of the enemy was on our extreme left, which he attempted to turn. This attempt was most gallantly repulsed by General Smith, commanding the left wing. At seven o'clock the skirmishers were actively engaged; and as the enemy sought the cover of the forest our artillery fire was opened, which continued without intermission for two hours. At this time General Ransom's brigade marched on the field, and took up a position as reserve behind General Carr.

Now the battle raged fearfully along the entire line, the evident intention of the enemy being to mass his forces upon Hovey on the center. There the fight was most

CHAMPION HILLS BATTLE GROUND.

earnest; but General McPherson brought his forces into the field, and after four hours hard fighting the tide of battle was turned and the enemy forced to retire.

Disappointed in his movements upon our right, the rebels turned their attention to the left of Hovey's division, where Colonel Slack commanded a brigade of Indianians. Massing his forces here, the enemy hurled them against the opposing columns with irresistible impetuosity, and forced them to fall back; not, howewer, until at least one quarter of the troops comprising the brigade were either killed or wounded. Taking a new position, and receiving fresh reënforcements, our soldiers again attempted to stem the tide, this time with eminent success. The enemy was beaten back, and compelled to seek the cover of the forest in his rear. Following up their advantage, without waiting to reform, the soldiers of the Western army fixed their bayonets and charged into the woods after them. The rebels were seized with an uncontrollable panic, and thought only of escape. In this terrible charge men were slaughtered by hundreds. The ground was literally covered with the dead and dying. The enemy scattered in every direction, and rushed through the fields to reach the column now moving to the west along the Vicksburg road. At three o'clock in the afternoon, the battle was over and the victory won.

Of the part taken in this battle by McPherson's corps, it is only necessary to say that it rendered the most efficient and satisfactory assistance. To it belongs the credit of winning the fight on the extreme right.

The battle ended, the left wing was speedily advanced upon the Vicksburg road, driving the enemy rapidly before them, and picking up as they advanced numbers of prisoners and guns.

On the left of the road we could see large squads of rebel soldiers and commands cut off from the main column, and whom we engaged at intervals with artillery.

Thus we pushed the enemy until nearly dark, when we entered the little village, known by the name of Edwards' Station, the enemy was leaving it.

When, within rifle range of the station, we discovered, on the left, a large building in flames, and on the right a smaller one from which, just then, issued a series of magnificent explosions. The former contained commissary stores, and the latter shell and ammunition—five car-loads—brought down from Vicksburg on the morning of the day of the battle. In their hasty exit from Edwards' Station, the rebels could not take this ammunition with them, but consigned it to the flames rather than it should fall into our hands. We bivouacked in line of battle at night, and next day moved upon the bridge across Big Black River.

The following extracts from General McClernand's official report will also prove interesting, inasmuch as it sets forth the part taken by General Grant in this brilliant affair:

"The different divisions were started at different hours, in consequence of the different distances they had to march, which was designed to secure a parallel advance of the columns. Believing that General Hovey's division needed support, I sent a dispatch to General Grant, requesting that General McPherson's corps should also move forward. Assurances altogether satisfactory were given by the General, and I felt confident of our superiority."

After alluding to the demonstrations made in the early part of the contest, General McClernand continues:

"Early notifying Major-General Grant and Major-General McPherson of what had transpired on the left, I requested the latter to coöperate with my forces on the right, and directed General Hovey to advance promptly but carefully, and received a dispatch from General Hovey informing me that he had found the enemy strongly posted in front; that General McPherson's corps was behind him; that his right flank would probably encounter severe resistance; and inquiring whether he should bring on the impending battle. My command was now about four miles from Edwards' Station, and immediately informing Major-General Grant, *whom I understood to be on the field*, of the position of affairs, I inquired whether I should bring on a general engagement. A dispatch from the General, dated at thirty-five minutes past noon, came, directing me to throw forward skirmishers as soon as my forces were on hand, to feel and attack the enemy in force, if opportunity occurred, and *informing me that he was with Hovey and McPherson, and would see that they fully coöperated.* Meanwhile, a line of skirmishers had encountered Generals Osterhaus and Smith's divisions, closing up the narrow space between them. . . These measures had been taken in *compliance with General Grant's orders, based on information of which he had advised me, that the enemy was in greatest strength in front of my center and left, and might turn my left flank and gain my rear.* . . . Instantly upon the receipt of *General Grant's order to attack,* I hastened to do so."

The following is General Johnston's dispatch announcing the defeat of the rebel forces:

"CAMP BETWEEN LIVINGSTON AND BROWNSVILLE, MISS.,
"May 18, 1863.

"*To General S. Cooper:*

"Lieutenant-General Pemberton was attacked by the enemy on the morning of the 16th inst., near Edwards' Depot, and, after nine hours' fighting, was compelled to fall back behind the Big Black.

"J. E. JOHNSTON, *General Commanding.*"

The dispatch also shows the position of the forces that retreated from Jackson, and how, by General Grant's rapid movements, they had been cut off from forming a junction with Pemberton.

The Union forces lost about twenty-four hundred men, killed, wounded, and missing. The rebel loss was over three thousand.

Grant ordered the troops to push on with all haste, and attack Vicksburg. The bridge over Big Black was speedily built, and at nine o'clock on the 18th, Sherman's advance was within three miles and a half of the city. Sherman, at the beginning of the campaign, wrote to Grant, telling him he could not ration his command over the narrow and tortuous roads of Black River. Grant replied he did not intend to *haul* rations for his army. When Sherman read Grant's reply, he exclaimed, "Zounds, is the man mad; what can he mean?" The question had remained unanswered in Sherman's mind until the morning of the 18th of May, when he and Grant, who were riding together, ascended one of the high walnut hills, near Vicksburg,

GRANT'S HEAD-QUARTERS AT VICKSBURG.

overlooking Yazoo River and Haines' Bluff. As Uncle Billy's eye caught sight of the deep stream, and the rear of the bluffs, he had, in vain, sought to ascend a few months before, he turned abruptly to Grant and, with deep feeling, said, "Until this moment, General, I never thought your expedition a success. I never could see the end clearly, but I see it all now. This is indeed a campaign; a success if we never take the town."

Grant, in his quiet taciturn way, knocked the ashes off

his cigar and replied: "I guess it will do, and we shall take the place."

The troops now began to wind up the hills and encircle the doomed city. McClernand took the south side, McPherson the center, and Sherman on the right. The enemy fell back precipitately from Haines' Bluff, leaving fourteen guns in our hands. During the morning the rebels seemed to be giving away at all points, and a large number of prisoners were taken.

The fall of Vicksburg was now certain. The only question was, how many days it would be able to hold out.

But three weeks had passed since General Grant commenced his campaign. He had marched in that time over two hundred miles, had fought five battles, in which over twelve thousand rebels had been either killed, wounded, or taken prisoners. He had seized the capital of the State of Mississippi, and destroyed the railroads leading to it for a distance of more than thirty miles around. He had started upon this enterprise without baggage wagons, and with an average of but two days' rations in the soldiers' haversacks. His losses in all—killed, wounded, and missing—were but four thousand three hundred and thirty-five. As the crowning result of all this, he had invested the city and garrison of Vicksburg so that their fall was inevitable. The fall of Vicksburg insured the evacuation of Port Hudson. Thus the Mississippi would be open to the nation from Cairo to its mouths.

Anxious to conclude his brilliant campaign, and "relying," says General Grant, "upon the demoralization of the enemy in consequence of repeated defeats outside of Vicksburg, I ordered a general assault at two P. M. on this day."

The following account of the first attack on Vicksburg, written by an eye-witness, will be read with interest:

"The corps of General Sherman moved up on the Haines'

Bluff road, by a sort of poetic justice taking possession of the ground by the rear which he had once vainly attempted to gain from the front. McPherson advanced on the Jackson road, and covered the ground from the left of Sherman to the railroad, while McClernand's corps occupied the front from the railroad to the extreme left.

CAVES NEAR VICKSBURG.*

"The action began by a slow fire from our artillery along the whole line, our guns having a pretty long range, and eliciting but feeble response from the enemy.

"About noon, Osterhaus' division advanced on the left to within about six hundred yards of the enemy's works, to find themselves confronted by fifteen redoubts, with their rifle-pits, which opened fire upon us whenever we appeared on a crest or through a hollow.

*The streets of Vicksburg are cut through the hills, and houses are often seen far above the street passengers. In the perpendicular banks formed by these cuttings, and composed of clay, caves were dug at the beginning of the siege, some of them sufficiently large to accommodate whole families, and, in some instances, communicating with each other

Cave Life in Vicksburg.

"The guns of the rebels appeared to be of small caliber, throwing principally grape and canister. Our skirmishers were thrown further up; but little firing was done on either side.

"At two o'clock the order came for a general advance upon the rebel works, over ground which, on the left, at least, *was almost impassable under the most peaceful circumstances*. The order seemed a hard one; yet nothing is too hard for true soldiers to try.

---

by corridors. Such was the character of some made on Main Street, opposite the house of Colonel Lyman J. Strong, for the use of his family and others, and of which the writer made the accompanying sketch in April, 1866. The caves were then in a partially ruinous state, as were most of them in and around Vicksburg, for rains had washed the banks away, or had caused the filling of the caves. In this picture the appearance of the caves, in their best estate, is delineated, with furniture, in accordance with descriptions given to the writer by the inhabitants.

A graphic account of the events in these crypts is given in a little volume entitled, "*My Cave-Life in Vicksburg, by a Lady*," published in New York, in 1864. It was written by the wife of a Confederate officer who was in the besieged city, and lived in one of these caves with her children and servants.

The picture in the text above gives a good idea of the external appearance of these caves, in the suburbs of the city. It is from a

"General A. L. Lee, who commanded the First Brigade of Osterhaus' division, and was in the advance, determined to carry out his orders if their execution was possible. Addressing a few words of cheer to his men, he placed himself in front of the center of his brigade, led them forward in line of battle, and was the first man to gain the crest of the hill which he was attempting. He then found that it was only the first of several ridges which were to be crossed, the ravines between which were swept by the guns of the enemy's redoubt. Still he tried to press on, and his brigade of brave fellows to follow him, the air, in the meantime, thick with bullets and shells; but a ball from the rifle of a sharpshooter struck him in the face and he fell. His brigade withdrew a few feet only, behind the crest of the hill on which they had just raised, and held their position; one of the regiments getting so favorable a point, that they were able to remain within about two hundred yards of one of the redoubts, and to prevent the gunners from firing a single shot.

"I am glad to say that General Lee, though severely, was by no means dangerously wounded. His brigade sustained a much smaller loss than a distant observer could have believed possible.

"The same degree of success, or want of success, attended the movement along the whole line. Our forces moved very close to the works, and then remained waiting and watching for the nearer approach of our artillery. At night-fall our troops retired a short distance, and went into camp. During the night heavy siege-guns were planted by us for future

---

sketch made by the writer on the old Jackson road, where the Second Mississippi Regiment was stationed during a portion of the siege. In the view, the spectator is looking down toward Vicksburg. A plain, and the bluffs on the border of the Mississippi, are seen in the distance.—*Lossing's Civil War in America.*

use, our light artillery moved nearer, and a slight earth-work was thrown up to protect them.

"To-day (Wednesday, May 20th) the heavy guns on our left opened long before daylight. As heretofore, the enemy have failed to reply. Our skirmishers are pushed forward within a hundred and fifty yards of the whole line of the redoubts, and keep so sharp a lookout that the enemy finds it impossible to work his guns.

"On the center two heavy siege-guns are in position less than half a mile from a strong fort just in front of them—so near that the Minié-bullets were whistling merrily past the ears of the workmen. To-morrow they will open on the fort.

"On the right, Sherman still holds his line of skirmishers well up to the rebel forts on his front, and the artillerists are trying to level the rebel works, so far without success. During our operations to-day, thirty or forty men were wounded."

In the meantime, Admiral Porter, who was on the river just below Vicksburg, with his gunboats, hearing the firing on the 18th, had advanced to coöperate with the army. The Choctaw, Romeo, and Forest Rose, under Lieutenant Commander Breese, were ordered to the Yazoo, with instructions to push on until they opened communications with Grant or Sherman. This they did in a handsome manner. The De Kalb steamed up and took possession of Haines' Bluff, where Grant established his new base of supplies, and began preparations for the siege.

CHAPTER X.

SECOND ATTACK ON VICKSBURG—FULL ACCOUNT OF THE BATTLE—MISUNDERSTANDING BETWEEN GRANT AND M'CLERNAND—POSITION OF THE ARMY—PEMBERTON'S ADDRESS—SHERMAN'S EXPEDITION—THE MINES AT VICKSBURG—TERRIFIC EXPLOSION OF A MINE—FIGHT IN THE CRATER—PEMBERTON GIVES UP THE GHOST—HIS LETTERS TO GRANT—THEIR INTERVIEW—GRANT'S LETTERS TO PEMBERTON—SURRENDER OF THE REBEL GARRISON—ADVANCE OF THE UNION TROOPS INTO VICKSBURG—GRANT AT PEMBERTON'S HEAD-QUARTERS—IMPORTANCE OF THE SURRENDER OF VICKSBURG—LINCOLN'S LETTER TO GRANT.

AFTER the first attack on the works at Vicksburg, Grant withdrew his forces to a short distance from the rebel lines, and began throwing up intrenchments. Skirmishing continued lively, and Grant gave his rebel foes no rest by day or by night. Having completed his communications, established his depots, and supplied his hungry and weary army with an abundance of rations, the great General began to think of more fighting.

It was now near the end of May, and General Grant determined to at once assault the works, afterward giving his reasons, as follows:

"I believed an assault from the positions gained by this time could be made successfully. It was known that Johnston was at Canton with the force taken by him from Jackson, reënforced by other troops from the East, and that more were daily reaching him. With the force I had, a short time must have enabled him to attack me in the rear, and, possibly, succeed in raising the siege. Possession of Vicksburg at that time would have enabled me to have turned upon Johnston, and driven him from the State, and possess myself of all the railroads and practical military highways, thus effectually securing to ourselves all territory west of the Tombigbee, and this before the season was too far advanced for campaigning in this latitude. I would have saved the Government sending large reënforcements, much needed elsewhere; and, finally, the troops themselves were impatient to possess Vicksburg, and would not have worked in the trenches with the same zeal, believing it unnecessary, that they did after their failure to carry the enemy's works."

Feeling that it was best, for many reasons, to make the assault with as little delay as possible, he commenced his advance with General McClernand, with the Thirteenth Army Corps on the left, General McPherson, with the Seventeenth in the center, and General Sherman, with the Fifteenth, on the right.

On the night of the 21st and the morning of the 22d of May, Porter vigorously shelled the rebel forts, and at ten o'clock, the Union columns, under cover of a fierce artillery fire, were in motion. Grant stationed himself on the summit in McPherson's front, where he could see the operations of all the Seventeenth Corps and parts of the Thirteenth and Fifteenth, under McClernand and Sherman. Blair's division led Sherman's Corps, with Tuttle's in support, while Steele moved to the right, and made an attack. A correspondent, who witnessed the fight, gave this account of it:

"For two long hours did the cannonade continue, when a general charge was made. Winding through the valleys, clambering over the hills, every-where subjected to a murderous enfilading and cross-fire, the advance pressed up close to the rebel works—to find that a deep ditch, protected by sharp stakes along the outer edge, lay between them and the intrenchments. They planted their flag directly before the fort, and crouched down behind the embankment, out of range of the rebel fire, as calmly as possible, to await developments. The soldiers within the forts could not rise above the parapet to fire at them, for if they did, a hundred bullets came whizzing through the air, and the adventurers died.

"The rebels, however, adopted another plan. Taking a shell, they cut the fuse close off, lighted it, and rolled it over the outer slope of the embankment.

"Subsequently, with picks and shovels, a way was dug into one fort, and, through the breach, the boys walked bravely in. The first fort on the left of the railroad was stormed by a portion of General Carr's division, and gallantly taken. The colonel that led the charge was wounded.

"On the center the fire was persistent and terrible. Many brave officers were killed, and many more wounded. Colonel Dollins, of the Eighty-first Illinois, fell dead while leading his men to the charge.

"Later in the afternoon, Gen. Ransom's brigade charged the works opposite his position, with heavy loss.

"Steele and Tuttle, on the right, were also heavily engaged, and the former is reported to have lost nearly a thousand men."

A gentleman, who was present at General Grant's headquarters during the assault, writes as follows:

"At a given hour the troops were in motion, moving along the ravines, in which to assume the required formation and make the attack. The charges were most admirably executed. With perfect composure, the men moved up the hill, though not under fire, yet under the influence of a dreadful anticipation of a deadly volley at close quarters. When within forty yards of the works, of a sudden the parapet was alive with armed men, and in an instant more the flash of thousands of muskets hurled death and destruction most appalling into the ranks of our advancing columns. Five hundred men lay dead or bleeding on one part of the field at the first fire. Bravely, against all odds, this command fought, until its depleted ranks could no longer stand, when sullenly it withdrew, under cover of a hill near by. In addition to the heavy musketry fire which repelled the assault, artillery played, with dreadful havoc, upon the fading ranks, which, after every effort to win the goal, were obliged to give way—not to numbers, but impregnability of position.

"Upon the whole, as regards the designs of our movement, we were frustrated, but nothing more. Our troops, with but few exceptions, held their own. The loss of this day's engagement has been exceedingly heavy, according to first accounts, which are not the most reliable, and it is to be hoped the authenticated returns will greatly lessen the casualties."

Grant had, in his various assaulting columns, about thirty thousand men, while Pemberton opposed him with about eighteen thousand. The Union loss, in killed, wounded, and missing, was three thousand, and that of the rebels thirteen hundred.

On the field, during the action, a sharp correspondence took place between General Grant and General McClernand, the latter calling loudly and repeatedly for reënforcements when the former did not think he needed them. Grant, at length, reluctantly sent Quimby's division to McClernand, and ordered Sherman to make an assault in his favor, which greatly increased the mortality, without accomplishing any good result. McClernand's men, however, fought well, and, at one time, Benton's brigade, of Carr's division, and Burbridge's brigade, of Smith's division, had advanced so far as to plant their flags on the slopes of the enemy's forts.

The unfortunate misunderstanding between Generals Grant and McClernand during the battle subsequently led to the latter being relieved, and General Ord was placed in command of the Thirteenth Army Corps.

Grant, finding he could not carry the enemy's works by assault, withdrew on the evening of the 22d, and commenced a regular siege. The place had not been as yet completely invested; communications between Johnston, at Canton, and Pemberton, at Vicksburg, still existed. At several points on the extreme left, rebel troops could slip out, and supplies be got in, and Grant, knowing the place could not be reduced while these leaks remained, sent for Lauman's division, at Memphis, Smith's and Kimball's divisions, of the Sixteenth Army Corps, Herron's division, from Arkansas, and two divisions of the Ninth Corps, under Parke, and these having arrived, on the 14th of June the doomed city lay within a wall of Union steel.

Grant's army was now thus disposed: Sherman, with Fifteenth Corps, on the extreme right—from the river to the roads leading to the north-east bastion; McPherson, with the Seventeenth, on his left, extending to the railroad; Ord, with the Thirteenth Corps, on the left of McPherson, and extending to Lauman's; and Herron's division, at Stout's Bayou, and butting against the bluff, and resting on the swamp. Parke's troops, with Smith's and Kimball's divisions, were at Haines' Bluff, fortified; General Sherman, with parts of the Fifteenth and Seventeenth Corps, watching Johnston.

The siege was conducted with such vigor that, by the end of June, twelve miles of trenches had been dug, eighty-nine batteries reared, and two hundred and twenty guns put in position.

Pemberton's troops had become greatly dissatisfied, and were openly charging him with having sold the battles of Champion Hills and Black River Bridge, and with intending to surrender Vicksburg the first opportunity. To satisfy them, the rebel general issued the following pithy address to his soldiers:

"COMRADES: You have heard that I was incompetent and a traitor, and that it was my intention to sell Vicksburg. Follow me, and you will see the cost at which I will sell Vicksburg. *When the last pound of beef, bacon, and flour; the last grain of corn; the last cow, and hog, and horse, and dog shall have been consumed, and the last man shall have perished in the trenches, then, and only then, will I sell Vicksburg.*"

Seeing himself hopelessly bottled up, Pemberton, as early as the 27th of May, sent a courier to Johnston, with the following dispatch:

"I have fifteen thousand men in Vicksburg, and rations for thirty days—one meal a day. Come to my aid, with an army of thirty thousand men. Attack Grant in the rear. If you can not do this within ten days, you had better retreat. Ammunition is almost exhausted, particularly percussion caps."

This dispatch was sent by a young man named Douglas, whom Pemberton considered entirely trustworthy, but no sooner did he find himself outside of the rebel lines, than he went direct to the Union head-quarters, and delivered his dispatch to General Grant instead of Johnston, as he had been commanded to do.

Information reaching the ears of the commanding general that Johnston, in possession of a considerable force, was moving toward the Big Black River, with an intention of making a demonstration on our army in the rear of Vicksburg, induced the movement of a sufficient body of troops in that direction to meet the approaching enemy, if found, as reported, and engage him before he could effect a crossing, or, at every hazard, to repel any attempt he might make to secure a foothold on this side.

Sherman, who commanded this expedition, after a considerable march, returned, without finding Johnston, and brought the gratifying intelligence that the rear was all safe, bridges burned, trees felled to obstruct the roads, and that five hundred cattle and ten thousand pounds of bacon had been captured and brought in by the troops.

On the 25th of June the sappers and miners reported the mines ready to be sprung. The greatest possible secresy had been observed concerning these mines, and, except the general officers, none but the workmen knew where they were, or when they would be exploded. Approaching them through the deep ditches and zigzag trenches lined with our sharpshooters, one saw little holes in the earth, where men were crawling in and out on their hands and knees, pushing pans of dirt before them. These were the mines. Larke says of them:

"Looking around, one found himself in plain view and within five yards of the enemy's strongest work, the parapet of which was about twenty feet from the bottom of the ditch. This work was evidently of sod, almost perpendicular on its outer face, intended to mount four guns, and was supposed to be the keep of the rebel position. A few steps in advance, and the visitor was before the mine, which here had the appearance of a square shaft dug into the earth, with a gradual declivity as you penetrate. The entrance was made in the scarp of the enemy's fort, and presented an opening four feet square, well framed with timber to keep up the loose earth which the projectiles of the attacking party had broken from the face of the work. In order to protect the entrance, a number of gabions and boxes had been piled up before the mouth, and afforded ample security from hand grenades and shell thrown over by the rebel troops inside.

"The main gallery, from the mouth to the point of divergence of the other galleries, measured thirty-five feet. Here three smaller galleries set out, one ten feet deep, obliquely to the left; another eight feet, diverging to the right; and a third, eight feet in length, being a continuation of the main gallery. The chambers for the reception of the powder were let into the bottom of the shaft, and were about two feet in depth.

"Having completed one gallery, the powder was brought up and packed into the chambers in almost equal quantities, the entire quantity used being twenty-two hundred pounds, one thousand of which were placed at the end of the main gallery, the remainder being distributed in the extremities of the smaller galleries. From each of the chambers a fuse was run out to the mouth of the shaft, where the match was to be applied at the designated time.

"The working party, engaged on the mines, was formed of a detail from various regiments under General Grant, a call being made to forward to head-quarters all practical miners in the regiments. Accordingly, in a few hours fifty picked men, chiefly Welsh, Scotch, English, and Irish, of experience in the old country, were immediately organized into a corps, under the direct command of a miner of reputation. This party reported to the chief of the corps of engineers, and the work at once commenced, the entire time occupied for the excavation being forty hours.

"Another sap was also, on the last day, run off to the left, at an angle to the main one leading to the mine. This sap ran parallel to the enemy's breastwork, and just outside of where ran the exterior end of the ditch, which had been partly filled. The object of this new sap was to afford a secure place for the Union sharpshooters, and enable them to hold their ground on the right by keeping down a flank fire. The length of the sap was about fifty yards.

"It may be supposed by some that the running of mines

is the mere operation of the pick and shovel, without interference on the part of the enemy by means of the same instruments, as well as by his riflemen picking off the men as they approach, or by throwing hand grenades and shell over the parapet among the men. This idea is quite different from the reality. A few facts connected with the proceedings may enable the reader to form some notion of this dangerous operation. The work is generally performed after dark; and, on the night preceding the explosion of June 25, 1863, the working party returned to the mine, already a depth of thirty-five feet, which was the entire number of feet of the main gallery. The men had but fairly commenced when they heard, as they supposed, near by, the picking and shoveling of another party, which they knew to be the enemy, endeavoring to intercept the Union mine. The men of the attacking side at once desisted from their labors, and applied their ears to the walls of the gallery in order to detect the direction of approach, if possible, of the enemy's countermine. Soon, however, the enemy himself ceased his labors. The Unionists once more resumed operations, and worked until midnight, the enemy working at the same time, and seemingly approaching the outside shaft. 'At this juncture,' says a correspondent, 'an unexpected panic overcame the workers, and they hurried out of the mine with considerable dispatch. The cause of this excitement is said to have been a suspicion that the enemy was about to blow up his own mine, in view of counteracting our own. Accordingly, nothing was done until morning, when the party, re-assured, renewed their work.'"

The brilliant writer Keim, in his dispatches, thus describes the scene of the explosion:

"Every thing was finished. The vitalizing spark had quickened the hitherto passive agent, and the now harmless flashes went hurrying to the center. The troops had been withdrawn. The forlorn hope stood out in plain view, boldly awaiting the uncertainties of the precarious office. A chilling sensation ran through the frame as an observer looked down upon this devoted band about to hurl itself into the breach—perchance into the jaws of death. Thousands of men in arms flashed on every hill. Every one was speechless. Even men of tried valor—veterans insensible to the shouts of contending battalions, or nerved to the shrieks of comrades suffering under the torture of painful agonies—stood motionless as they directed their eyes upon the spot where soon the terror of a buried agency would discover itself in wild concussions and cortortions, carrying annihilation to all within the scope of its tremendous power. It was the seeming torpor which precedes the antagonism of powerful bodies. Five minutes had elapsed. It seemed like an existence. Five minutes more, and yet no signs of the expected exhibition. An indescribable sensation of impatience, blended with a still active anticipation, ran through the assembled spectators. A small pall of smoke now discovered itself; every one thought the crisis had come, and almost saw the terrific scene which the mind had depicted. But not yet. Every eye now centered upon the smoke, momentarily growing greater and greater. Thus another five minutes wore away, and curiosity was not satisfied. Another few minutes, then the explosion; and upon the horizon could be seen an enormous column of earth, dust, timbers, and projectiles lifted into the air at an altitude of at least eighty feet. Blackened and mangled forms of men, rocks, cannons, and trees rose toward the heavens, while the earth rocked as if rent with an earthquake. The siege-guns along a line of twelve miles of works burst forth with the fiercest blasts of war. The scene at this time was one of the utmost sublimity. The roar of artillery, rattle of small arms, the cheers of the men, flashes of light, wreaths of pale blue smoke over different parts of the field, the bursting of shells, the fierce whistle of solid shot, the deep boom of the mortars, the broadsides of the ships of war, and, added to all this, the vigorous replies of the enemy, set up a din which beggars all description.

"The troops rushed in at the gorge, which was large enough to hold two regiments. The rebel troops, with equal desperation, rushed forward to meet them; and thus the struggle continued, not only until the sun went down, not only until the twilight disappeared, but far into the hours of night. Volley after volley was fired, though with less carnage than would be supposed. The Forty-fifth Illinois charged immediately up to the crest of the parapet, and here suffered its heaviest, losing many officers in the assault.

"During the hottest of the action, General Leggett was in the fort in the midst of his troops, sharing their dangers and partaking of their glory. While here, a shell from one of the enemy's guns exploded in a timber lying on the parapet, distributing splinters in all directions, one of which struck the General on the breast, knocking him over. Though somewhat bruised and stunned, he soon recovered himself, and taking a chair, sat in one of the trenches near the fort, where he could be seen by his men."

When the mine exploded, six men of the Forty-third Mississippi Regiment, who were in the rebel shaft countermining, were buried alive, and their bones rest to this day in the grave their own hands had digged. Two other rebels, who were standing in the fort, were tossed into the air, and came down within the Union lines, sustaining no further injury than being badly shocked and frightened. One had his knapsack on his back, and seemed mightily astonished to see where he had landed.

Grant seemed well satisfied with the day's operations, and in the evening wrote to Ord:

"JUNE 25, 1863.

"GENERAL ORD:—McPherson occupies the crater made by the explosion. He will have guns in battery there by morning. He has been hard at work running rifle-pits right, and thinks he will hold all gained. *Keep Smith's Division sleeping under arms to-night, ready for an emergency.* Their services may be required, particularly about daylight. *There should be the greatest vigilance along the whole line.*

"U. S. GRANT, *Major-General.*"

In the meantime, the gunboat fleet off Warrenton commenced a bombardment of the enemy's forts. This was kept up without intermission until midnight, when it was slackened to desultory shots. The fuses of the shells as they ascended in the air were easily distinguishable, and looked in their course like shooting meteors. When they would strike, the shell would explode with a terrific report. Some of the shells exploded in the air, and the flashes which they emitted looked like an immense piece of pyrotechny.

Pemberton's spirit was now broken, and he saw before him nothing but defeat and surrender; yet he resisted with a bravery worthy of a better cause. Johnston had written to him to say, "I am too weak to save Vicksburg; can do no more than attempt to save you and your garrison. It will be impossible to extricate you unless you coöperate."

Flour was a thousand dollars a barrel in Vicksburg; beef two dollars and a half a pound; and molasses twelve dollars a gallon. The troops could not sleep at night for fear of being blown into the air before morning; and the citizens were burrowing into the earth, to escape the shells which were continually dropping in the streets or bursting in the houses. Pemberton had but seven days' full rations left, and plainly saw he must starve or surrender. The toils and cares of Grant were now overwhelming; he slept but little, and partook sparingly of food. His great mind seemed to be constantly studying the rebel works, and for hours at a time he gazed upon the high forts before him.

In the admirable "Military History of General Grant," by General Adam Badeau, we have the following extracts from dispatches sent by General Grant to his subordinate officers, which will give the reader some idea of the multiplicity of cares which must have engrossed his mind:

To Parke he wrote: "I want the work of intrenching your position pushed with all dispatch. Be ready to receive an attack, if one should be made; and to leave the troops free to move out, should the enemy remain where he is."

To Ord: "Get batteries as well advanced as possible, during the day and night."

To Parke, directing him to join Sherman: "An attack is contemplated, evidently by way of Bear Creek, and that within two days. Move out four brigades of your command, to support your cavalry; and obstruct their advance, as near Black River as possible, until all the forces to spare can be brought against them. Travel with as little baggage as possible, and use your teams as an ordnance and supply train, to get out all you may want from the river."

To Dennis: "An attack upon you is not at all impossible. You will therefore exercise unusual vigilance in your preparations to receive an attack. Keep your cavalry out as far as possible, to report any movement of the enemy; and confer with Admiral Porter, that there may be unanimity in action."

To Parke: "Certainly use the negroes, and every thing within your command, to the best advantage."

To Herron: "Be ready to move with your division at the shortest notice, with two days' cooked rations in their haversacks."

To McPherson: "There is indication that the enemy will attack within forty-eight hours. Notify McArthur to be ready to move at a moment's notice on Sherman's order. The greatest vigilance will be required on the line, as the Vicksburg garrison may take the same occasion for an attack also."

By the 1st of July, Grant's works, at ten different points, were within a few hundred feet of the rebel defenses. The time for final assault had now come. It was understood in both armies that it would take place on the 4th of July. On the morning of the 3d, two rebel officers were seen approaching the Union lines with a flag of truce, and bearing an official communication for General Grant. These officers, General Bowen and Colonel Montgomery, were halted at the picket-line, while the letter they bore was sent with all haste by a courier to General Grant's head-quarters. On opening it, the General found it was from Pemberton, and read as follows:

"HEAD-QUARTERS, VICKSBURG, July 3, 1863.

"*Major-General Grant, commanding United States forces:*

"GENERAL: I have the honor to propose to you an armistice for — hours, with a view to arranging terms for the capitulation of Vicksburg. To this end, if agreeable to you, I will appoint three commissioners, to meet a like number to be named by yourself, at such place and hour as you may find convenient. I make this proposition to save the further effusion of blood, which must otherwise be shed to a frightful extent, feeling myself fully able to maintain my position for a yet indefinite period. This communication will be handed you, under flag of truce, by Major-General James Bowen.

"Very respectfully, your obedient servant,

"J. C. PEMBERTON."

Great was the joy of Grant, for he saw in this brief epistle the end of all his toils and labors; yet those who looked in that calm, quiet face saw no indication of the great joy that was swelling his heart nigh to bursting. Turning to his desk, Grant wrote :

"HEAD-QUARTERS DEPARTMENT OF TENNESSEE,
"IN THE FIELD, NEAR VICKSBURG, July 3, 1863.

"*Lieutenant-General J. C. Pemberton, commanding Confederate forces, etc.:*

"GENERAL: Your note of this date, just received, proposes an armistice of several hours, for the purpose of arranging terms of capitulation through commissioners to be appointed, etc. The effusion of blood you propose stopping by this course, can be ended at any time you may choose, *by an unconditional surrender of the city and garrison.* Men who have shown so much endurance and courage as those now in Vicksburg, will always challenge the respect of an adversary, and I can assure you will be treated with all the respect due them as prisoners of war. I do not favor the proposition of appointing commissioners to arrange terms of capitulation, *because I have no other terms than those indicated above.* I am, General, very respectfully, your obedient servant,

"U. S. GRANT, *Major-General.*"

Folding up the letter, he handed it to an officer, with the instructions that the rebel soldiers should bear it to their chief. General Bowen, who was anxious to put an end to the slaughter and suffering of the garrison, requested permission to speak with General Grant about the surrender, but Grant declined to hold any converse with him on that subject. Blindfolded, the rebel officers were conducted from the Union camp, where they were set at liberty, and were speedily within their own camp and in the presence of their brave but disconsolate General. Before leaving Grant, the rebel officers had made a proposition that the two Generals should meet between the lines and personally arrange the terms of capitulation. To this Grant had promptly agreed, and said "If Pemberton wished to surrender, he would see him that afternoon, at three o'clock, in front of McPherson's works."

Pemberton immediately sent word to Grant to be at the front of McPherson's works at the time named, and he would meet him there. Keim thus describes the meeting between the two army commanders:

"At three o'clock precisely, one gun, the prearranged signal, was fired, and immediately replied to by the enemy. General Pemberton then made his appearance on the works in McPherson's front, under a white flag, considerably on the left of what is known as Fort Hill. General Grant rode through our trenches until he come to an outlet, leading to a small green space, which had not been trod by either army. Here he dismounted, and advanced to meet General Pemberton, with whom he shook hands, and greeted familiarly.

"It was beneath the outspreading branches of a gigantic oak that the conference of the generals took place. Here presented the only space which had not been used for some purpose or other by the contending armies. The ground was covered with a fresh, luxuriant verdure; here and there a shrub or clump of bushes could be seen standing out from the green growth on the surface, while several oaks filled up the scene, and gave it character. Some of the trees in their tops exhibited the effects of flying projectiles, by the loss of limbs or torn foliage, and in their trunks the indentations of smaller missiles plainly marked the occurrences to which they had been silent witnesses."

The party made up to take part in the conference was composed as follows:

UNITED STATES OFFICERS.

Major-General U. S. Grant.
Major-General James B. McPherson.
Brigadier-General A. J. Smith.

REBEL OFFICERS.

Lieutenant-General John C. Pemberton.
Major-General Bowen.
Colonel Montgomery, A. A. G. to General Pemberton.

When Generals Grant and Pemberton met they shook hands, Colonel Montgomery introducing the party. A short silence ensued, at the expiration of which General Pemberton remarked:

"General Grant, I meet you in order to arrange terms for the capitulation of the city of Vicksburg and its garrison. What terms do you demand?"

"*Unconditional surrender*," replied General Grant.

"Unconditional surrender?" said Pemberton. "Never, so long as I have a man left me! I will fight rather."

"*Then, sir, you can continue the defense*," coolly said General Grant. "*My army has never been in a better condition for the prosecution of the siege*."

During the passing of these few preliminaries, General Pemberton was greatly agitated, quaking from head to foot, while General Grant experienced all his natural self-possession, and evinced not the least sign of embarrassment.

After a short conversation standing, by a kind of mutual tendency, the two Generals wandered off from the rest of the party and seated themselves on the grass, in a cluster of bushes, where they talked over the important events then pending. General Grant could be seen, even at that distance, talking coolly, occasionally giving a few puffs at his favorite companion—his black cigar. General McPherson, General A. J. Smith, General Bowen, and Colonel Montgomery, imitating the example of the commanding generals, seated themselves at some distance off, while the respective staffs of the generals formed another and larger group in the rear.

After a lengthy conversation the generals separated. General Pemberton did not come to any conclusion on the matter, but stated his intention to submit the matter to a council of general officers of his command; and, in the event of their assent, the surrender of the city should be made in the morning. Until morning was given him to consider, to determine upon the matter, and send in his final reply. The generals now rode to their respective quarters.

During this memorable interview, the characters of the two men were plainly indicated by their personal conduct. Pemberton was restless, impulsive, and bitter, his stormy and irascible spirit at times breaking forth in angry words. Grant was calm, cool, and deliberative, puffing his cigar, and talking as casually as if Pemberton were an acquaintance he had chanced to meet on the road-side, and had only stopped to pass the time of day and compliments of the season. The great oak tree under which the two generals sat during this interview has long ago disappeared, (having been cut up into canes,) and on the spot stands a beautiful monument, with this inscription on its base: "To the memory of the surrender of Vicksburg, by Lieutenant-General J. C. Pemberton to Major-General U. S. Grant, U. S. A., on the 3d of July, 1863."

General Grant, having conferred at his head-quarters with his corps and division commanders, sent the following letter to General Pemberton, by the hands of General Logan and Lieutenant-Colonel Wilson:

"HEAD-QUARTERS DEPARTMENT OF TENNESSEE,
"NEAR VICKSBURG, July 3, 1863.

"*Lieutenant-General J. C. Pemberton, commanding Confederate forces, Vicksburg, Miss.:*

"GENERAL: In conformity with the agreement of this afternoon, I will submit the following proposition for the surrender of the city of Vicksburg, public stores, etc. On your accepting the terms proposed, I will march in one division, as a guard, and take possession at eight o'clock to-morrow morning. As soon as paroles can be made out and signed by the officers and men, you will be allowed to march out of our lines, the officers taking with them their regimental clothing, and staff, field and cavalry officers one horse each. The rank and file will be allowed all their clothing, but no other property.

"If these conditions are accepted, any amount of rations you may deem necessary can be taken from the stores you now have, and also the necessary cooking utensils for preparing them; thirty wagons also, counting two two-horse or mule teams as one. You will be allowed to transport such articles as can not be carried along. The same conditions will be allowed to all sick and wounded officers and privates as fast as they become able to travel. The paroles for these latter must be signed, however, while officers are present, authorized to sign the roll of the prisoners.

"I am, General, very respectfully,

"Your obedient servant,

"U. S. GRANT, *Major-General.*"

This communication was sent by Grant late in the evening, but before daylight a rebel messenger brought him the following reply:

"HEAD-QUARTERS, VICKSBURG, July 3, 1863.

"*Major-General Grant, commanding United States forces:*

"GENERAL: I have the honor to acknowledge the receipt of your communication of this date proposing terms for the surrender of this garrison and post. In the main, your terms are accepted; but, in justice both to the honor and spirit of my troops, manifested in the defense of Vicksburg, I have the honor to submit the following amendments, which, if acceded to by you, will perfect the agreement between us. At ten o'clock to-morrow, I propose to evacuate the works in and around Vicksburg, and to surrender the city and garrison, under my command, by *marching out with colors and arms and stacking them in front of my present limits*, after which you will take possession; officers to retain their side-arms and personal property, and the rights and property of citizens to be respected.

"I am, General, yours, very respectfully,

"J. C. PEMBERTON, *Lieutenant-General.*"

Grant, willing to gratify tho vanity of his rebel foes, in not getting up a scene of surrender, at once replied:

"HEAD-QUARTERS DEPARTMENT OF TENNESSEE,
"BEFORE VICKSBURG, July 4, 1863.

"*Lieutenant-General Pemberton, commanding forces in Vicksburg:*

"GENERAL: I have the honor to acknowledge your communication, of the 3d of July. The amendments proposed by you can not be acceded to in full. It will be necessary to furnish every officer and man with a parole signed by himself, which, with the completion of the rolls of prisoners, will necessarily take some time. Again: I can make no stipulation with regard to the treatment of citizens and their private property. *While I do not propose to cause any of them any undue annoyance or loss, I can not consent to leave myself under restraint by stipulations.* The property which officers can be allowed to take with them will be as stated in the proposition of last evening—that is, *that officers will be allowed their private baggage and side-arms, and mounted officers one horse each. If you mean, by your proposition, for each brigade to march to the front of the lines now occupied by it and stack their arms, at ten o'clock A. M., and then return to the inside and remain as prisoners until properly paroled, I will make no objection to it.* Should no modifications be made of your acceptance of my terms by nine o'clock A. M., I shall regard them as having been rejected, and act accordingly. Should these terms be accepted, white flags will be displayed along your lines, to prevent such of my troops as may not have been notified from firing on your men.

"I am, General, very respectfully,

"Your obedient servant,

"U. S. GRANT, *Major-General U. S. A.*"

Pemberton hastily sent the following brief dispatch, and the preliminaries of one of the greatest surrenders the world ever witnessed was completed:

"HEAD-QUARTERS, VICKSBURG, July 4, 1863.

"*Major-General U. S. Grant, commanding United States forces, etc.:*

"GENERAL: I have the honor to acknowledge the receipt of your communication of this date, and, in reply, to say that the terms proposed by you are accepted.

"Very respectfully, your obedient servant,

"J. C. PEMBERTON, *Lieutenant-General.*"

According to agreement, the last of the rebel regiments, having marched out, stacked their arms, and returned within the fortifications. There was nothing now to do but for the Union forces to march in and take possession of the city, men, and property. It is said that some of the old rebel veterans, as they gave up their arms and colors, shed tears of regret, and that Grant's men, who were looking on, were silent and respectful, having great admiration for the bravery with which these misguided men had defended their city.

Keim thus describes the entrance of the Union troops into Vicksburg:

"It was about one o'clock P. M., before matters had assumed such a stage of completion as would admit of the entrance of the city by our troops. A slight further detention was also occasioned awaiting the pioneer corps, thrown out in advance, to open a passage through the breastworks and across the ditches and rifle-pits of the enemy. After this was finished, no further obstructions presented themselves, and the column moved forward. The order of march was by a seniority of brigade commanders, with an exception in the case of the Forty-fifth Illinois Infantry, Colonel J. A. Maltby, *which was specially ordered to lead the column, in consequence of heroic conduct during the siege and operations in the campaign against Vicksburg.*"

At the head of the troops rode General U. S. Grant, puffing the always-present black cigar, and then followed his numerous and brilliant staff. Next came—

Major-General J. B. McPherson and staff.

Major-General J. A. Logan and staff.

Brigadier-General M. D. Leggett, First Brigade, Third Division, led by the Forty-fifth Illinois Infantry.

Brigadier-General Z. E. G. Ransom, First Brigade, Seventh Division, temporarily assigned to Logan.

Brigadier-General John Stevenson, Second Brigade, Third Division; and with each brigade its batteries, baggage-train, etc.

The division of General John E. Smith, though part of

the Seventeenth Army Corps which was designated by General Grant to occupy the city, was held outside of the works, as a kind of outer line of guards, to prevent the escape of prisoners.

After passing through several inner lines of the rifle-pits and breastworks, the column of occupation penetrated the suburbs of the city, and marched through its principal streets to the court-house. As might be expected, from the long schooling the city had received under the influence of the secession conspirators, no demonstrations of satisfaction at our arrival were made along the line of march; but on the contrary, houses were closed, the citizens within doors, and the city was wrapped in gloom. It seems as if the population anticipated their next step would be into the grave.

Upon arriving at the court-house, the troops were drawn up in line, facing the building. This done, the ceremony of possession was completed by the display of the flags of the Forty-fifth Illinois Infantry, and of the head-quarters of the Seventeenth Corps, from the dome of the court-house.

Upon the appearance of the flags, the troops cheered vociferously, making the city ring to its very suburbs with shouts of the votaries of liberty. It was an occasion which few ever have the opportunity of witnessing, and one which will secure a life-long remembrance in the minds of all present.

In consideration of the active part taken by the Seventeenth Corps in the campaign which consummated in the capture of Vicksburg, that command was designated by General Grant to take possession of the city. General Logan's division occupied within the works, while General John E. Smith held the Union works without. General McArthur continued with General Sherman's army in its operations against Johnston.

In view of General Grant's plans, Major-General McPherson was appointed to the command of the new district about to be formed, and having Vicksburg for its center.

Major-General Logan commanded the city and its environs.

The provost-marshal's department was placed in charge of Lieutenant-Colonel James Wilson, provost-marshal of the corps—provost-guard, Forty-fifth Illinois Infantry.

The vessels in the river were soon in motion, and but an hour or two elapsed ere seventy steamers or barges lined the levee, and the city suddenly emerged from the death of rebellion to life and activity.

Grant, making his way through the rebel soldiers, who gazed in silence and wonder at their conqueror, rode at once to the head-quarters of General Pemberton. There was no one to receive him. He dismounted, and entered the porch. General Pemberton sat there with his staff. These men then very conspicuously developed their novel ideas of "chivalry." Though each one wore his sword, through the generosity of General Grant, not one rose, in courteous greeting of the valiant and magnanimous soldier. Pemberton was especially sullen and discourteous.

The day was hot, and the trampling of the armies had filled the air with clouds of dust. General Grant, heated and thirsty, asked for a glass of water. He was brusquely told that he could find it inside. He groped his way through the passages till he found a negro who gave him a cup of water. Returning, he found no seat, and remained standing in the presence of his vanquished foes, who were seated, during an interview of half an hour.

It is said that this surrender was the most important recorded in the annals of war. At the capitulation of Ulm, hitherto considered without a parallel, thirty thousand prisoners were surrendered, and sixty pieces of cannon. Thirty-four thousand six hundred men surrendered at Vicksburg, with two hundred and eighteen cannon.

The following table will give the reader a more definite idea of the value of the surrender of Vicksburg: Lieutenant-General J. C. Pemberton, Major-General Bowen, Major-General Martin L. Smith, Major-General Forney, Brigadier-Generals Barton, Cochran, Lee, Vaughn, Reynolds, Baldwin, Harris, Taylor, Cummings, Stevenson, Hebart, Wall, Moore, Schopf, Buford, and Cockrell.

Total generals	20
Field, staff, and line officers	4,600
Non-commissioned officers and privates	30,000
Total, without regard to rank	34,620

KILLED, WOUNDED, AND STRAGGLERS.

Killed in battles and skirmishes	1,000
Wounded in battles and skirmishes	4,000
Captured in hospitals in Vicksburg and elsewhere	6,000
Stragglers, including men cut off and unable to rejoin their commands	800
Total	11,800

RECAPITULATION.

Total prisoners	34,620
Killed, wounded, and in hospital	11,000
Stragglers, etc	800
Making a loss to the enemy, in sixty-five days, of	46,420

The following table also shows the losses of material sustained by the enemy during the same length of time:

FIELD ARTILLERY.	PIECES.
Captured in battle	83
At Vicksburg	128
Total	211

SIEGE ARTILLERY.

At Vicksburg	90

CAPTURED SMALL ARMS.

In battle	10,000
At Vicksburg	35,000
Total	45,000

RECAPITULATION.

Artillery captured	301
Muskets and rifles	45,000

Besides this, a number of field-pieces and siege-guns were destroyed at Jackson, Haines' and Snyder's Bluffs, which are not included in the above estimate, and, also, immense quantities of powder, ball, shells, tools, machinery, and great numbers of wagons, wood-wheels, and castings.

General Grant, in his official report, sums up the Union losses, during the series of battles of the Vicksburg campaign, as follows:

	KILLED.	WOUNDED.	MISSING.	TOTAL.
Port Gibson	130	718	5	853
Fourteen-Mile Creek (skirmish)	4	24	—	28
Raymond	69	341	32	442
Jackson	40	240	6	286
Champion's Hill	426	1,842	189	2,457
Big Black Railroad Bridge	29	242	2	273
Vicksburg	245	3,688	302	4,236
Grand total	943	7,095	537	8,575

GENERAL RECAPITULATION.

Rebel losses in killed, wounded, and prisoners	46,420
Union losses in killed, wounded, and prisoners	8,575
Balance in favor of Grant	37,845

The President, who had long been importuned to relieve General Grant, at length agreed to do so, and had sent out Adjutant-General Thomas with instructions to investigate certain charges made against Grant at the national capitol, and if he found them as alleged, to remove him at once. General Thomas, however, on reaching Milliken's Bend, with great good sense and judgment, kept the President's order in his pocket, and sustained Grant fully in his report.

Several gentlemen were near the President at the time he received the news of Grant's success, some of whom had been complaining of the rumors of his habit of using intoxicating drinks to excess.

"So I understand Grant drinks whisky to excess?" interrogatively remarked the President.

"Yes," was the reply.

"What whisky does he drink?" inquired Mr. Lincoln.

"What whisky?" doubtfully queried his hearers.

"Yes. Is it Bourbon or Monongahela?"

"Why do you ask, Mr. President?"

"Because, if it makes him win victories like this at Vicksburg, I will send a demijohn of the same kind to every general in the army."

His visitors saw the point, although at their own cost.

The good-hearted President, conscious he had unintentionally done Grant great injustice, then sat down and wrote him the following frank and manly letter:

"EXECUTIVE MANSION, WASHINGTON, July 13, 1863.

"*To Major-General Grant:*

"MY DEAR GENERAL: I do not remember that you and I ever met personally. I write this now as a grateful acknowledgment for *the almost inestimable service you have done the country.* I wish to say a word further. When you first reached the vicinity of Vicksburg, I thought you should do what you finally did—march the troops across the neck, run the batteries with the transports, and thus go below; and I never had any faith, except a general hope that you knew better than I, that the Yazoo Pass expedition, and the like, could succeed. When you got below and took Port Gibson, Grand Gulf, and vicinity, I thought you should go down the river and join General Banks; and when you turned northward, east of the Big Black, I feared it was a mistake. I now wish to make a personal acknowledgment *that you were right and I was wrong.*

"Yours, very truly,

"A. LINCOLN."

CHAPTER XI.

PREPARATIONS TO ATTACK JOHNSTON—SURRENDER OF PORT HUDSON—INVESTMENT OF JACKSON—JEFF. DAVIS' LIBRARY—JOHNSTON'S ADDRESS TO HIS ARMY—RETREAT OF THE REBELS—GRANT AND THE REBEL MAJOR—HIS TREATMENT OF SUBORDINATE OFFICERS—FRIENDSHIP BETWEEN GRANT AND SHERMAN—MRS. GRANT VISITS HER HUSBAND—ANECDOTE OF MRS. GRANT—GRANT AND HIS SOLDIERS—ADMINISTRATIVE ABILITY OF GRANT—HONORS TO GRANT AT MEMPHIS—REVIEW AT NEW ORLEANS—TERRIBLE ACCIDENT TO GRANT—HE IS APPOINTED TO A NEW COMMAND—VISITS LOUISVILLE—HIS NEW ARMY AND GENERALS—BRAGG'S FORCES—THE CHATTANOOGA CAMPAIGN.

No sooner had General Pemberton signified his intention of surrendering Vicksburg, than General Grant began preparations for new military movements. He wrote at once to Sherman:

"There is little doubt but that the enemy will surrender to-night or in the morning. Make your calculations to attack Johnston, and destroy the road north of Jackson."

He also wrote to Steele and Ord:

"I want Johnston broken up as effectually as possible. You can make your own arrangements, and have all the troops of my command, except one corps."

In another letter, on the 4th of July, written to his generals, Grant said:

"Drive Johnston from the Mississippi Central Railroad. Destroy the bridges as far north as Grenada, with your cavalry, and do the enemy all the harm possible. I will support you to the last man that can be spared."

One of the good results of the fall of Vicksburg was the immediate surrender of Port Hudson. The news was first communicated to the rebels by our troops, who shouted across the lines: "Vicksburg is taken, Johnny, and Grant is coming down the river." No sooner did the startling intelligence reach the rebel commander in his head-quarters, than he addressed the following letter to General Banks, who commanded the besieging forces:

"HEAD-QUARTERS PORT HUDSON, LA., July 7, 1863.

"*To Major-General Banks, commanding U. S. forces near Port Hudson:*

"GENERAL: Having received information from your troops that *Vicksburg has been surrendered*, I make this communication to ask you to give me the official assurance whether this is true or not, *and, if true, I ask for a cessation of hostilities*, with a view to the consideration of terms for surrendering this position.

"I am, General, very respectfully, your obedient servant,

"FRANK GARDNER,

"*Major-General commanding Confederate States forces.*"

General Banks, early the next morning, replied as follows:

"HEAD-QUARTERS DEPARTMENT OF THE GULF,
"BEFORE PORT HUDSON, July 8, 1863.

"*To Major-General Frank Gardner, commanding Confederate States forces, Port Hudson:*

"GENERAL: In reply to your communication, dated the 7th instant, by flag of truce received a few moments since, I have the honor to inform you that I received yesterday morning, July 7th, at forty-five minutes past ten o'clock, by the gunboat General Price, an official dispatch from Major-General Ulysses S. Grant, United States Army, whereof the following is a true extract:

"I regret to say that, under present circumstances, I can not, consistently with my duty, consent to a cessation of hostilities for the purpose you indicate.

"Very respectfully, your obedient servant,

"N. P. BANKS, *Major-General commanding.*

"'HEAD-QUARTERS DEPARTMENT OF THE TENNESSEE,
"'NEAR VICKSBURG, July 4, 1863.

"'*Major-General N. P. Banks, commanding Department of the Gulf:*

"'GENERAL: The garrison of Vicksburg surrendered this morning. The number of prisoners, as given by the officers, is twenty-seven thousand; field artillery, one hundred and twenty-eight pieces; and a large number of siege-guns, probably not less than eighty. Your obedient servant,

"'U. S. GRANT, *Major-General.*'"

The rebel commandant immediately dispatched the following communication to General Banks:

"PORT HUDSON, July 8, 1863.

"*To Major-General Banks, commanding United States forces:*

"GENERAL: I have the honor to acknowledge the receipt of your communication of this date, giving a copy of an official communication from Major-General U. S. Grant, United States Army, *announcing the surrender of the garrison of Vicksburg.*

"*Having defended this position as long as I deem my duty requires, I am willing to surrender to you,* and will appoint a commission of three officers, to meet a similar commission appointed by yourself, *at nine o'clock this morning,* for the purpose of agreeing upon and drawing up the terms of surrender, and for that purpose I ask a cessation of hostilities. Will you please designate a point outside of my breastworks, where the meeting shall be held for this purpose?

"I am, very respectfully, your obedient servant,

"FRANK GARDNER,

"*Commanding Confederate States forces.*"

General Banks replied at once in the following language:

"HEAD-QUARTERS UNITED STATES FORCES,
"BEFORE PORT HUDSON, July 8, 1863.

"*To Major-Cencral Frank Gardner, commanding Confederate States forces, Port Hudson:*

"GENERAL: I have the honor to acknowledge the receipt of your communication of this date, stating that you are willing to surrender the garrison under your command to the forces under my command, and that you will appoint a commission of three officers, to meet a similar commission appointed by me, at nine o'clock this morning, for the purpose of agreeing upon and drawing up the terms of surrender.

"In reply, I have the honor to state that I have designated Brigadier-General Charles P. Stone, Colonel Henry W. Birge, and Lieutenant-Colonel Richard B. Irwin, as the officers to meet the commission appointed by you.

"They will meet your officers, at the hour designated, at a point where the flag of truce was received this morning. I will direct that active hostilities shall entirely cease on my part, until further notice, for the purpose stated.

"Very respectfully, your obedient servant,

"N. P. BANKS, *Major-General commanding.*"

With the surrender of Port Hudson, there fell into the hands of the Union troops one major-general, one brigadier-general, twenty pieces of heavy artillery, five field batteries, numbering thirty-one pieces, five thousand stand of small arms, two steamers, and an immense quantity of powder, shells, and rifle-balls.

The glad news from Vicksburg and Port Hudson coming at the same time the nation was rejoicing over the great victory won by the Union arms at Gettysburg, completely electrified the North, and the people were filled with great joy.

Meantime, General Grant was marching against Johnston at Jackson. On the 12th of July, General Sherman had invested the city, from Pearl River, on the north, to the same stream, on the south side. Pearl River runs through the city, and Sherman, by his investment, had cut the railroad, and shut off hundreds of cars from the Confederacy.

The rebel President's library, one of the largest in the United States, was also captured. Among other valuable documents found in this library, were many letters on the subject of secession. Some of these letters dated back as far as 1852. Many of the more prominent writers accepted the separation of the North and South as a foregone conclusion, but only disagreed how and when it should be done. Davis is alluded to as the political Moses in this measure, and the allusions to him would seem as if he were looked upon in the light of a demi-god.

Johnston, finding Sherman was about to attack him, issued the following blatant proclamation to his troops:

"FELLOW-SOLDIERS: An insolent foe, *flushed with hope by his recent success at Vicksburg, confronts you,* threatening the people, whose homes and liberty you are here to protect, with plunder and conquest. Their guns may even now be heard as they advance.

"*The enemy it is at once the duty and the mission of you, brave men, to chastise and expel from the soil of Mississippi. The commanding general confidently relies on you to sustain his pledge, which he makes in advance,* and he will be with you in the good work, even unto the end.

"The vice of 'straggling' he begs you to shun and to frown on. If needs be, it will be checked by even the most summary remedies.

"The telegraph has already announced a glorious victory over the foe, won by your noble comrades of the Virginia army on Federal soil; may he not, with redoubled hopes, count on you, while defending your firesides and household gods, to emulate the proud example of your brothers in the East?

"The country expects in this, the great crisis of its destiny, that every man will do his duty.

"JOSEPH E. JOHNSTON, *Gen. Com'ding.*"

Having said this much, the boasting rebel General decamped, retreating in the direction of Meridian, Sherman closely following "fighting Joe Johnston" and his army. The army of Johnston, according to the testimony of rebel prisoners, was numerically as strong as ours. It was composed of a portion of Pemberton's old army, and reënforcements from Bragg's army, and detachments from Mobile and Charleston, S. C. In it were the divisions of Generals Breckinridge, Loring, Walker, and Gist, besides thousands of home-guards from the interior of Mississippi and Alabama. General Gist brought ten regiments with him from South Carolina, many of them of the "best blood," as a prisoner stated, of the Palmetto State, whose motto was, "No surrender." What a sorry failure they made of it.

From May 1st up to the capture of Jackson, General Grant's army had been unremittingly at work. They had fought, within that time, seven hotly-contested battles, at the cost of many a gallant life, but with twofold victory to our arms. The trophies of these battles, in arms and prisoners, were counted by thousands; but the crowning event of the campaign *was the opening of the Mississippi River.* The rebel army of the West had been scattered to the winds, and those not killed or captured were fleeing with fright from before our army of veterans.

Grant was now at Vicksburg, actively engaged in organizing negro regiments and setting his department in order.

Finding that Yazoo City was being fortified, he sent General Herron there with his division. He captured several hundred prisoners and one steamboat. Five pieces of heavy artillery and all the public stores fell into our hands. The enemy burned three steamboats on the approach of the gunboats. The De Kalb was blown up and sunk in fifteen feet of water by the explosion of a torpedo. Finding that the enemy were crossing cattle for the rebel army at Natchez, and were said to have several thousand there, *he sent steamboats and troops to collect them and destroy all boats and means for making more.*

Among the incidents of General Grant's occupation of Vicksburg is the following: "A major in the rebel army had formerly served in the same regiment of the United States army with Grant, but was then his prisoner. Grant treated him kindly, invited him to his private apartment, and after he left, gave a sketch of the rebel's former life to the members of his staff. He said, that when the rebel major was in his room and he was talking to him about being in the Confederate service, the latter replied, "Grant, I tell you, I ain't much of a rebel, after all, and when I am paroled, I will let the d—d service go to the mischief."

One of Grant's first acts after a great victory was always to acknowledge the services of his troops, and the aid he had received from subordinate officers. He never said anything about himself, but was loud in the praises of others. Thus he wrote the department, after the fall of Vicksburg, asking that Sherman and McPherson should be made brigadier-generals in the regular army. "The first reason for this," he said, "is their great fitness for any command that it may ever become necessary to intrust to them. Second, their great purity of character, and disinterestedness in any thing except the faithful performance of their duty, and the success of every one engaged in the great battle for the preservation of the Union. Third, they have honorably won this distinction upon many well-fought battle-fields. The promotion of such men as Sherman and McPherson always adds strength to our army."

The warm personal friendship existing between Sherman and Grant during the latter part of the war became a matter of national notoriety. Few persons knew, however, that from their earliest acquaintance, these two great commanders appreciated and liked each other. The following personal letter, written by Grant to Sherman at the time when Sherman was marching against Johnston, will, in this connection, be read with interest:

"I hope you will be in time to aid in giving the rebels the worst, or best, thrashing they have had in this war. I have constantly had the feeling that I shall lose you from this command entirely. Of course, I do not object to seeing your sphere of usefulness enlarged; and I think it should have been enlarged long ago, having an eye to the public good alone. But it needs no assurance from me, General, that, taking a more selfish view, while I would heartily approve such a change, I would deeply regret it on my own account. "U. S. GRANT."

In this letter, Grant seems to have foreseen the future career of his brilliant fellow-soldier, and while he wished him joy and success, he could not but regret to lose, in his command, the services of so valuable an officer.

Grant has ever displayed greatness of soul that never yet went with littleness of mind. Who has said as much as he in praise of Sheridan, Sherman, McPherson, Thomas, Meade? Remember how he lay with his gallant army before Petersburg, in the fall of 1864, when popular impatience in vain goaded him to attack, when the press and the people began to demand his dismissal, and to stigmatize him as "the butcher;" how, then, when Sheridan won his great victories in the Valley, and every cap went up for "Little Phil," Grant capped the whole by telegraphing that he regarded him as among the first of living generals; how, then, when Hood invaded Tennessee, the lieutenant-general gave Thomas all the men he could, and all the means, and contributed in every way to the splendid success at Nashville, yet scrupulously refrained from doing any thing to take the glory from Thomas, as he might have done by simply going on in person; how, then, when Sherman had gone

"From the center all round to the sea,"

Grant gave him a brother's welcome, tenderly covered his sad mistake at diplomacy, and presented him to the nation as the great strategist of the war.

As a mark of their affection, and an appreciation of his services at Vicksburg, General Grant's brother officers presented him with a magnificent sword. The scabbard was of solid silver, appropriately and most beautifully finished. The handle of the sword represented a carved figure of a young giant, crushing the rebellion, and was most elaborately designed. The box in which it was placed was made of rosewood, bound with ivory, and lined with velvet and white satin. On the interior of the lid the name of General Grant was marked with crimson silk. The whole, in design, execution, and intrinsic value, displayed great taste on the part of those selected to carry out the presentation.

President Lincoln also honored the victor by appointing him to the vacant major-generalship in the regular army of the United States, with a commission dating from the occupation of Vicksburg, July 4, 1863.

General Grant's wife, who had been an anxious watcher of his military movements and success, now, that victory and peace were secured in his department, left her home for a time to visit her husband, at the noted place which had caused him so much labor and anxiety to gain the possession of, and the reduction of which had made his name forever famous in history. While at St. Louis, she was, in honor of her husband, serenaded by a fine band, attended by an immense throng of civilians. After the music had ceased, three rousing cheers were given by the crowd for General Grant, and three more for Mrs. Grant, when that lady appeared at the window, with Brigadier-General Strong standing by her side, and on repeated calls for a speech, the General, in behalf of Mrs. Grant, responded:

"GENTLEMEN: I am requested by Mrs. Grant to express her acknowledgment for the honor you have done her on this occasion. I know well that, in tendering her thanks, I express your sentiments, when I say the compliment through her to her noble husband is one *merited by a brave and great man, who has made his name forever honored and immortal, in the history of America's illustrious patriots, living or dead.* Mrs. Grant does not desire, in the testimony you have offered, that you should forget *the brave and gallant officers and soldiers, who have so largely assisted in bringing about the glorious result*, which has recently caused the big heart of our nation to leap with joy. She asks you also to stop and *drop a tear over the graves of the noble dead who have fallen in the struggle*, that you and I, and all of us, might enjoy the fruits of their patriotic devotion to a country second to none on the earth. We trust that the Mississippi forever will be under the control of our glorious country. Mrs. Grant is now on the way to join her husband, *who, since the commencement of the war, has not asked for one day's absence. He has not found time to be sick.* With these remarks she bids you good-night, and begs that you accept her thousand thanks."

An amusing anecdote is told of Mrs. Grant about this time. One day, while riding in the cars, a young officer, in all the glory of a span new second lieutenant's uniform, entered the train, and seeing no other place vacant, seated himself by the side of Mrs. Grant. He at once began talking about the war, and presently said:

"Madam, this war is a sad calamity, indeed, and I hope we may all live through it."

"I hope so," replied the lady.

"As you perceive, madam, I am an officer, and going to the front. Pray, have you any friends in the army?"

"Yes," replied the lady, "my husband is a soldier."

"Indeed, madam," said the lieutenant. "I hope then to meet him. Perhaps, being an officer, I may be able to do him a service, as I shall likely have some influence with my brother officers, and, indeed, with the affairs of the army, for I am well connected. What is your husband's name?"

"Thank you," replied the lady, "but I doubt if you can be of much help to my husband," and then she modestly added, "his name is Ulysses Grant."

At the mention of that name, then ringing throughout the land, the young soldier sprang up, and hastily excusing himself, retired to another part of the car. The good woman did not intend, however, to drive the lieutenant away, and the youthful soldier may readily be pardoned for his vanity, when one recollects the exhilarating effects of a first commission in the army, and a blue and gold uniform.

General Grant, who had been a most rigid disciplinarian as long as the danger lasted, now, that the enemy was beaten and his department safe, became a most liberal and patronizing commander. All his sick soldiers, who could stand the journey, were sent home to their friends on furlough, and five per cent. of the whole army was furloughed for thirty days. The men, by order of Grant, were paid before they started, so as, the boys said, "to have money for a good time up North, and to drink the General's health with occasionally." In their anxiety to get home, the soldiers would submit to any imposition rather than be detained, and the steamboat men knowing they had plenty of money, charged enormous fares. One day it came to the ears of the General that a boat, then in port, was charging as much as twenty-five dollars to carry soldiers from Vicksburg to Cairo. Putting on his hat, the General said: "I will let these fellows know that the men who have periled their lives to open the Mississippi River for their benefit, can not be imposed upon with impunity." Going on the boat, he ordered the captain to pay back the men their money, and then told him he could carry the soldiers to Cairo, or go to prison and have his boat confiscated. The steamboat man, anxious to escape from the presence of the terrible general, steamed out of port, while the soldiers crowded upon the decks and cheered again and again for their general, who stood upon the shore watching their departure and puffing his black cigar.

Can it be wondered at, with such evidence of their General's care, the soldiers of the Army of the Tennessee should fairly worship him?

The severity of General Grant's orders may be inferred from the following extract:

"*Conduct disgraceful to the American name* has been frequently reported to the Major-General commanding, particularly on the part of portions of the cavalry. *Hereafter, if the guilty parties can not be reached, the commanders of regiments and detachments will be held responsible*, and those who prove themselves unequal to the task of preserving discipline in their commands will be promptly reported to the War Department for "muster out." *Summary punishment must be inflicted upon all officers and soldiers apprehended in acts of violence or lawlessness.*

"By order of Major-General U. S. GRANT.

"T. S. BOWERS, *Acting A. A. G.*"

If General Grant was kind to his soldiers, and willing to defend them against all persons who would do them injustice, he was equally determined they should not do wrong to others. His army was always in a fine state of discipline, and his orders promptly obeyed, because his soldiers knew the General was watching them and would know how they behaved, and whether they were good soldiers or not.

Much has been said about the administrative ability of General Grant, and a good many people have feared that, able a soldier as he has been, he might not make a good administrator of the laws. It is probably not generally known that the first paper defining and fixing the status of the black people, after they were set free by the proclamation, was written by General Grant. So just, so clear and comprehensive were the provisions of this document, that the Government adopted its doctrines as the right policy to be pursued toward the negroes, and it has never been changed. From General Grant's order also grew the Freedmen's Bureau, and an examination of the order will show that every provision and power of the bureau to-day is contained in that order, so clearly did the illustrious general, at the very beginning, comprehend the wants and necessities of the black people. The following brief extracts are made from the order referred to above:

"At all military posts in States within this department where slavery has been abolished by the proclamation of the President of the United States, *camps will be established for such freed people of color as are out of employment.*

"Commanders of posts or districts will detail suitable

officers from the army as superintendents of such camps. It will be the duty of such superintendents to see that suitable rations are drawn from the Subsistence Department for such people as are confided to their care.

"*All such persons supported by the Government will be employed in every practicable way, so as to avoid, as far as possible, their becoming a burden upon the Government.* They may be hired to planters or other citizens, on proper assurance that the negroes so hired will not be run off beyond the military jurisdiction of the United States; they may be employed on any public works, in gathering crops from abandoned plantations, and generally in any manner local commanders may deem for the best interests of the Government, in compliance with law and the policy of the administration.

"It will be the duty of the provost-marshal at evey military post to see that every negro within the jurisdiction of the military authority is employed by some white person, or is sent to the camps provided for freed people.

"*Citizens may make contracts with freed persons of oolor for their labor, giving wages per month in money, or employ families of them by the year upon plantations, etc., feeding, clothing, and supporting the infirm as well as able-bodied, and giving a portion, not less than one-twentieth of the commercial part of their crops, in payment for such services.*

"*Where negroes are employed under this authority, the parties employing will register with the provost-marshal their names, occupation, and residence, and the number of negroes so employed. They will enter into such bonds as the provost-marshal, with the approval of the local commander, may require, for the kind treatment and proper care of those employed, and as security against their being carried beyond the employé's jurisdiction.*

"Nothing of this order is to be construed to embarrass

the employment of such colored persons as may be required by the Government.

"Major-General U. S. GRANT."

In August, 1863, General Grant, having occasion to visit Memphis, he was received with great honor. An address was presented him by the loyal citizens, and a public dinner tendered him.

The dinner was a grand affair, and is thus described by one who was present:

"At precisely nine o'clock, the band struck up one of the national airs, the doors of the reception room flew open, and General Geant made his appearance. There was a great rush, on the part of the enthusiastic and impatient to grasp the hero by the hand. An hour at least, though it seemed less, was thus consumed in hand-shaking and congratulations. After the lapse of this time, the band again sent forth its melody in the shape of a march. The whole assemblage then formed in two ranks, headed by General Grant. This being done, the entire party marched into the dining-room, made the complete round of the tables, examining the preparations, and then seated themselves. As would be expected, no sooner had each individual fastened himself to his seat than commenced a grand, simultaneous, and destructive assault upon the various dishes before him. Under the withering gastronomic abilities of the assemblage the victory was complete, and wound up by the total wreck and dissipation of the scene which, but a few moments before, shone refulgent in all its beauty. There suddenly appeared a masked battery of champagne on our rear, which opened upon the guests a vigorous champagne cannonade. Soon the engagement became general, and, like all general engagements, every body did pretty much as he pleased, so that he kept in the ranks and did not shirk, or leave the field.

"Next followed the regular toasts of the evening.

"The assemblage being called to order, the chairman arose and stated the fact.

"The toasts were then read.

"'The United States of America—They have one constitution and government: may they have one grand destiny while human institutions endure.' Responded to by Hon. Charles Kortrecht.

"'The Army and Navy—Their deeds and heroism in this war will be the noble theme of poet and historian in all future time.' Responded to by Adjutant-General Lorenzo Thomas.

"'General Grant—the guest of the city.'

"This was the signal for the wildest applause, and it was some minutes before order could be restored. It was expected that General Grant would be brought to his feet by this; but the company were disappointed upon perceiving that, instead, his place was taken by his staff surgeon, Dr. Hewitt, who remarked:

"'I am instructed by General Grant to say that, as he has never been given to public speaking, you will have to excuse him on this occasion, and, as I am the only member of his staff present, I therefore feel it my duty to thank you for this manifestation of your good-will, as also tho numerous other kindnesses of which he has been the recipient ever since his arrival among you. *General Grant believes that, in all he has done, he has no more than accomplished a duty, and one, too, for which no particular honor is due.* But the world, as you do, will accord otherwise.'

"The doctor then proposed, at General Grant's request—

"'The officers of the different staffs and non-commissioned officers and privates of the Army of the Tennessee.'

"'The Federal Union—It must and will be preserved!' Responded to by Major-General L. A. Hurlbut.

"'The Old Flag!—May its extinguished stars, rekindled by the sacred flame of human liberty, continue to shine forever, undiminished in number, and undimmed in splendor.' Responded to by General Veatch.

"'General Grant—Your Grant and my Grant. Having granted us victories, grant us the restoration of the "Old Flag;" grant us supplies, so that we may grant to our friends the grant to us.'

"'Abraham Lincoln—He must be sustained.' Colonel J. W. Fuller.

"The Star-spangled Banner was here sung, the whole party joining in the chorus.

"'The Loyal Men of Tennessee—Their devotion to the Union, the cause of republican government, and constitutional liberty, is like gold tried seven times by fire.' Mr. J. M. Tomeny."

A poem was then read, combining the name of Grant with De Soto, who discovered the Mississippi River, and Fulton, who made it alive with steamers. The poem closes with the following verses:

"Then spoke an enemy—and on his banks
Armed men appeared, and cannon-shot proclaimed
The Mississippi closed—that mighty stream!
Found by De Soto, and by Fulton won!
One thought to chain him—ignominious thought!
But then the grand old monarch shook his locks
And burst his fetters, like a Samson freed!
The heights were crowned with ramparts, sheltering those
Whose treason knew no bounds; the frowning forts
Belched lightnings, and the morning gun
A thousand miles told mournfully the tale—
The Mississippi closed.

"Not long; from the Lord God of Hosts was sent
A leader, who with patient vigil planned
A great deliverance: height by height was gained,

Island and hill, and woody bank and cliff.
Month followed month, till on our natal day
The last great barrier fell—and never more
The sire of waters shall obstruction know!
Now with De Soto's name and Fulton's, see
The greater name of Grant!
Our children's children, noble Grant, shall sing
That great deliverance! On the floods of spring
Thy name shall sparkle; smiling commerce tell
Thy great achievement which restores the chain,
Never again to break, which makes us one."

In order that the people of Memphis might fully understand his sentiments and feelings, General Grant sent them the following excellent letter of thanks:

"In accepting your attentions, which I do at great sacrifice to my personal feelings, I simply desire to pay a tribute to the first public exhibition in Memphis of loyalty to the Government which I represent in the Department of the Tennessee. I should dislike to refuse, for considerations of personal convenience, to acknowledge, anywhere or in any form, the existence of sentiments which I have so long and so ardently desired to see manifested in this department. The stability of this Government, and the unity of this nation, depend solely on the cordial support and the earnest loyalty of the people. While, therefore, I thank you sincerely for the kind expressions you have used toward myself, I am profoundly gratified at this public recognition, in the city of Memphis, of the power and authority of the Government of the United States."

Proceeding down the river, and stopping to inspect his posts, Grant, in due time, arrived at New Orleans, where a review had been arranged for him on the 4th of September.

General Banks, accompanied by a numerous staff, was at

the St. Charles Hotel as early as eight o'clock, and, at nine o'clock, both generals left for Carrolton, where the review took place. The street was crowded to witness the departure of these officers, all present being desirous of seeing General Grant. *He was in undress uniform, without sword, sash, or belt; coat unbuttoned, a low-crowned black felt hat, without any mark upon it of military rank; a pair of kid gloves, and a cigar in his mouth.* It must be known, however, that he is never without the latter, except when asleep.

Mounted on a magnificent charger, placed at his disposal by General Banks, Grant dashed at full gallop along the lines, and was with difficulty followed by his brilliant cortege. At length he drew up under a fine old oak for the troops to march by in review. He lifted his hat with a more formal courtesy, and bowed his head lower as the shot-pierced colors of his old regiments passed by, and when the soiled and torn standard of the old Thirteenth Corps came up, Grant's eye brightened with a tear as memory rushed back to the days of Belmont, Donelson, Pittsburg Landing, and Shiloh.

But a sad accident happened to Grant as he was returning home from the review. The shrill scream of a railroad whistle frightened his horse, and the terror-stricken animal dashed madly off, crushing a carriage that was in its way, and throwing Grant upon the street. Grant's injuries were of such a serious nature, that it was feared he would never be able to take the field again. He was carried from Carrolton on a litter to the steamer "Franklin," which took him up the river; his breast-bone was said to have been crushed, three ribs broken, and one side paralyzed; and his brain was thought to be affected from the concussion of the fall from his horse. Fortunately for the country, by the aid of a good surgeon, he was enabled, after over a month's illness, to take the position destined for him, as Chief Commander in the West.

As soon as he was able to travel, Grant moved on up the Mississippi, stopping to rest and visit the military posts along the bank. When he arrived at Indianapolis, he found that a telegram was there awaiting him at the depot, requesting him to delay his further journey until the arrival of that official. It was not long before they met, and, as soon as the Secretary of War and General Grant had passed the usual compliments between gentlemen on their first personal acquaintance, the former handed the latter the following order:

"War Department, Adjutant-General's Office,
"Washington, October 16, 1863.

"[*General Orders, No.* 337.]

"By direction of the President of the United States, the Departments of the Ohio, of the Cumberland, and of the Tennessee, will constitute the Military Division of the Mississippi. Major-General U. S. Grant, United States army, is placed in command of the Military Division of the Mississippi, with his head-quarters in the field.

"Major-General W. S. Rosecrans, U. S. Vols., is relieved from the command of the Department and Army of the Cumberland. Major-General G. H. Thomas is hereby assigned to that command.

"By order of the Secretary of War.

"E. D. Townsend, *A. A. G.*"

The party then proceeded, with their special attendants, to Louisville, where their arrival created intense excitement. They found a wondering crowd gathered in the hall of the Galt House to catch a glimpse of the hero of Vicksburg. Numerous were the exclamations of wonder as General Grant made his appearance. There seemed to have been an impression that the General was above the ordinary stature of men.

"I thought he was a large man," said a native. "He would be considered a small chance of a fighter if he lived in Kentucky."

The medium-sized frame of the General formed a strange contrast to the huge figures of the Kentuckians who swarmed to behold him.

In the afternoon, General Grant rode out and visited the principal places of interest about the city, and that same night issued an order accepting and assuming charge of his new command, which was the largest that had ever been intrusted to a subordinate in this or any other country. He had under his direction four of the largest armies in the field. His own army, with which he won the victories in and around Vicksburg and throughout Mississippi; the "Army of the Cumberland;" the "Army of the Ohio," and General Hooker's grand division. Under him were a perfect galaxy of marshals. His army commanders were Generals Sherman, Thomas, Burnside, and Hooker. (General Foster's column was afterward added.) His corps commanders were as follows:

The Fourth Army Corps, General Granger; the Ninth Army Corps, General Potter; the Eleventh Army Corps, General Howard; the Twelfth Army Corps, General Slocum; the Fourteenth Army Corps, General Palmer; the Fifteenth Army Corps, General J. A. Logan; the Sixteenth Army Corps, General Hurlbut; the Seventeenth Army Corps, General McPherson; and the Twenty-third Army Corps, General Manson.

His division and brigade leaders were not inferior, while the regiments were of the best fighting material in the world.

The country embraced within the limits of this new

command included the States of Michigan, Illinois, Indiana, Ohio, Kentucky, Tennessee, Mississippi, Northern Alabama, and North-western Georgia. One glance at the map will therefore show what comprised General Grant's Military Division of the Mississippi.

To meet this grand combination, Bragg had his own army, Longstreet's and Hill's Corps, Pemberton's army, which was reported exchanged, Johnston with thirty thousand men, S. D. Lee's division of five thousand men, and two small brigades in Mississippi. Perhaps never before were such masses of men scattered over such a vast area, under the command of men other than generals-in-chief.

Grant never rested a moment when there was work to be done. Although still suffering intensely from his wounds, he had received notice of his assignment to a new command one day, had accepted it the next, was at Nashville the day following, and arrived at Chattanooga on the 23d of October, where he immediately began his short but brilliant Chattanooga campaign.

CHAPTER XII.

CHATTANOOGA—THE UNION ARMY—THE REBEL ARMY—BRAGG'S BLUNDER—WHAT JEFF DAVIS SAID—HOOKER'S BATTLE ON THE 28TH OF OCTOBER—BURNSIDE SHUT UP IN KNOXVILLE—HOOKER'S BATTLE ABOVE THE CLOUDS—FULL ACCOUNT OF SHERMAN'S ADVANCE—THRILLING BATTLE SCENES—GENERAL GRANT IN BATTLE—DEFEAT OF BRAGG—GRANT'S PURSUIT—FIGHT AT RINGGOLD—HEROIC CONDUCT OF GRANT—WHAT HIS STAFF OFFICERS SAY OF HIM—SHERMAN REACHES KNOXVILLE—DEFEAT AND RETREAT OF LONGSTREET—END OF THE CHATTANOOGA CAMPAIGN—CONGRATULATIONS AND REJOICING.

GRANT found the Union army at Chattanooga in a strong position, with its flanks resting on the Tennessee river. The enemy was drawn up on Mission Ridge, across Chattanooga Valley, and on Lookout Mountain. The long lines of communications over which the supplies for the Union forces had to be brought were infested with bands of guerrillas, who so annoyed and delayed the trains that the army was often on the point of starvation.

Having improved his means of supplies as best he could, Grant, with restless activity, began preparations for battle.

He sent General W. F. Smith, with four thousand men, to Brown's Ferry, six miles below, to cross the river and seize the steep hills at the mouth of Lookout Valley. On the night of the 27th of October, General Hazen, a dashing young soldier, with a body of picked men, quietly dropped down the stream in boats, landed unobserved, seized the rebel pickets, and occupied the spurs of the mountain near the river. Hooker was now marching up from Nashville, by way of

Bridgeport, and on the 28th, brought his forces into Lookout Valley, at Wauhatchie. Sherman was also on the march to Chattanooga, coming from Corinth, by way of Florence, and driving the enemy before him.

Bragg, maddened by the clamor of rebel citizens, and goaded on by an unfriendly rebel press, committed the fatal blunder of detaching a large body of his troops, under Longstreet, and sending them to attack Burnside at Knoxville. When Grant heard of what Bragg had done, he gravely said, "I approve of his action," and at once telegraphed to Sherman: "Drop every thing east of Bear Creek and hurry up with your whole force." On the 23d of November, the head of Sherman's column arrived at Brown's Ferry, Hooker was well up, and Thomas threatening the enemy beyond Orchard Knob. Affairs looked decidedly interesting, and a great battle seemed impending. Davis had been telegraphed to, and about this time the rebel President paid a visit to Bragg's army, to ascertain the true condition of affairs, and it is reported that the following scene occurred on the summit of Lookout Mountain:

Looking down one bright day from the lofty eminence commanding a clear view into four States, and a very distant view into a fifth, Davis saw Grant's army almost beneath his feet, across the valley, working like beavers on their fortifications.

"I have them now," said he, "in just the trap I set for them."

To which Lieutenant-General Pemberton, who was sitting on horseback beside him, replied, "Mr. Davis, you are commander-in-chief, and you are here. You think the enemy are in a trap, and can be captured by a vigorous assault. I have been blamed for not ordering a general attack on the enemy when they were drawing around me their lines of circumvallation at Vicksburg. Do you now order an attack upon those troops down there below us, and I will set you my life that not one G—d d—d man of the attacking column will ever come back across that valley except as a prisoner."

Hooker had pushed well up Lookout Valley, and his troops now covered the two excellent parallel roads leading from Bridgeport to Brown's and Kelly's Ferries. The difficulties in the way of Hooker's advance can only be properly estimated by reading the following account of his fighting on the 28th of October, written by an eye-witness:

"The morning of the 28th opened with a clear, bright, beautiful moonlight, the scenery on every side traced in dark somber hues on the background of the sky. High, towering mountains—the Raccoon Mountain on one side and the Lookout Mountain on the other—and the valley diversified by open fields and small clumps of woods, formed a curious picture. On Lookout Mountain bright fires burned, and told us too plainly where to look for the enemy and his signal officers. Our camp-fires burned brightly, and our line lay on a parallel with what was the enemy's on the day previous. Two divisions were encamped on the left or front of our line. Another division, General Geary's, was in bivouac, about one mile and a half from the other two divisions. Between the two sections of the command the enemy held a position on the Chattanooga road proper, as also on the railroad. In brief, the enemy had a force, in a gap between the base of the point of Lookout Mountain, along the river on the flats and some hills, partially situated in our rear. Suddenly the Union troops were aroused by the heavy firing in the direction of General Geary's division. At once preparation was made for a general engagement. The troops were soon in column, and the trains and ambulances got in readiness for the emergency. As they pressed forward on the road to join General Geary, the enemy opened a heavy fire of musketry from a high hill close to their line of advance. At once our commanding generals comprehended the state of affairs. The enemy had intended their movement to be a surprise, and one with a view to the probable surrounding and possible capture of Geary's force. From prisoners taken during the fight that ensued, we learned that General Longstreet, on beholding our column move up the Lookout Valley toward Chattanooga, quietly massed two divisions on Lookout Mountain, and moved them up to and across Lookout Creek, with a view to the carrying out of the plan of his surprise movement. About eight P. M. he moved his division across the creek. One division passed on to the Chattanooga road and occupied two hills commanding the road, on a parallel, leading to Brown's Ferry. The other division passed down the railroad, and from there on to the Chattanooga road, below the fork. The rebels had intrenched themselves on the hill, and from their works had opened fire upon the Union command; but this did not delay the advance of the reënforcements, which pushed along under fire through an open space or field to the right of the front of the hills.

"While this command was pressing forward, a second division was moved up on the road, and a courier sent to inform General Geary of the near approach of assistance.

"An order was now given to take the hill, and the second division was assigned to the task. The advance was commenced and the enemy poured down a heavy fire of musketry. Slowly the men went up the hill, the ascent of which was so steep that it was as much as a man could do to get to the top in peaceful times, and with the help of daylight. This hill was covered with briar-bushes, fallen trees, and tangling masses of various descriptions, but our boys pressed forward in spite of all obstructions. The whole division at last gave a sudden start forward and gained the crest of the hill. The enemy's line wavered and broke, and the rebels composing it went down the other side of the hill with broken, flying, and disordered ranks. On gaining the crest our men found that they had not only driven the enemy off, but had taken some tolerably well-constructed earth-works, behind which the rebels had posted themselves. It was then ascertained, too, that the hill had been occupied by about two thousand rebels. The success and gallantry with which the height was taken elicited general commendation to the skill and bravery of the troops and their commanding officers."

Soon after this a detachment from another division took the next hill to the right without much resistance.

The enemy continued a scattering fire for some time after the hills were taken, but finally ceased troubling us. In the meantime, General Geary had bravely resisted the rebel attack, and, after two hours hard fighting, the enemy had retreated, without making Geary's line waver or fall back one foot. Almost every horse, in one section of artillery, was shot dead. The enemy retired across the railroad, and from there to the other side of the creek.

"Fighting Joe Hooker" bravely overcame every obstacle, and pushed on until, in the language of Grant, "he reached the proper place."

On the 14th of November, Longstreet was reported crossing the Little Tennessee River with a strong force, and the same evening Burnside's Union troops attacked the rebel advance and drove it back. At Lenoir the rebels were again brought to a halt, and a severe action, lasting from noon until night, was fought at Campbell's Station.

The detention of the rebels enabled the Unionists to withdraw their garrisons and get off their trains, which they sent within the defenses at Knoxville. The holding of the rebels in check also enabled Grant to complete his operations in front of Chattanooga.

On the 19th of November, Burnside notified Grant that the Union forces, trains, and supplies, were all safely housed within the strong works of Knoxville, and that the rebels were before the city beginning a siege. Grant, who had feared all along that Longstreet might be recalled to the aid of Bragg, when he heard that the rebel general was besieging Knoxville, drew forth a long cigar, and lighting it, exclaimed, with evident satisfaction: "Good! we have them now where we want them. I will move on the enemy's works."

It was now the morning of the 23d of November, and the first act in the great drama of Chattanooga was about to begin. Grant, Thomas, Howard, and Wood stood on the ramparts of Fort Wood watching the long lines of soldiers debouching from their camps and forming on the plains.

The rebels watched the formation and movement from their picket-lines and rifle-pits, and from the summits of Missionary Ridge, five hundred feet above, and *thought it was a review and drill, so openly and deliberately, so regular, was it all done.*

The line advanced, preceded by skirmishers, and at two o'clock P. M. reached our picket-lines, and opened a rattling volley upon the rebel pickets, who replied and ran into their advanced line of rifle-pits. After them went our skirmishers and into them, along the center of the line of twenty-five thousand troops which General Thomas had so quickly displayed, until we opened fire. Prisoners assert that they thought the whole movement was a review and general drill, and that it was too late to send to their camps for reënforcements, and that they were overwhelmed by force of numbers. *It was a surprise in open daylight.*

At three P. M., the important advanced position of Orchard Knob and the lines right and left were in our possession, and arrangements were ordered for holding them during the night.

The next day, at daylight, General Sherman had five thousand men across the Tennessee, and established on its south bank, and commenced the construction of a pontoon bridge about six miles above Chattanooga. The rebel steamer Dunbar was repaired at the right moment, and rendered effective aid in this crossing, carrying over six thousand men.

By night-fall General Sherman had seized the extremity of Missionary Ridge nearest the river, and was intrenching himself. General Howard, with a brigade, opened communication with him from Chattanooga on the south side of the river. Skirmishing and cannonading continued all day on the left and center. General Hooker scaled the slopes of Lookout Mountain, and from the valley of Lookout Creek drove the rebels around the point. He captured some two thousand prisoners, and established himself high up the mountain side, in full view of Chattanooga. This raised the blockade, and now steamers were ordered from Bridgeport to Chattanooga. They had run only to Kelley's Ferry, whence ten miles of hauling over mountain roads and twice across the Tennessee on pontoon bridges brought us our supplies.

The day had been one of dense mists and rains, and *much of General Hooker's battle was fought above the clouds*, which concealed him from our view, but from which his musketry was heard.

The fighting in Hooker's front had been desperate in the extreme. Shanks, who witnessed it, gives the following account:

"Now began the heavy struggle of the day. Sending two regiments to hold the road which crosses the spur of the mountain from the east, he advanced the rest of his forces to the front line. An advance was immediately ordered, and for an hour and a half (it was now two o'clock P. M.) a very heavy sharpshooters' fight was kept up. I can not expect to give any clear idea of this engagement. It was no place to maneuver columns. Each man and company fought upon his and its 'own hook.' From Chattanooga nothing was visible save the misty smoke which enveloped and hid the mountain. But beneath this the combatants saw each other, and here they continued to fight with desperation until four o'clock, when there came a tide in Hooker's fortune, which he did not fail to take at the flood.

"The skirmish line was enabled, under cover of the trees which grew along that part of the ridge, to advance much nearer the rebel line than those in the immediate front of the enemy and the open field. It was also upon the flank of the position; and the weakness of the enemy having compelled him to contract his left, a lodgment was found very near their rifle-pits. General Hooker, upon being informed of this, at four o'clock ordered a charge of the line, and through a heavy and rapid fire, kept up for five long minutes—and minutes are sometimes very long—the men dashed forward upon, over, and into the abandoned pits. The enemy had seen the long line of steel that glittered even amid the rain which was pouring upon them, and they could n't stand that. They also saw troops upon their left flank, and, filled with that holy horror which old soldiers have for 'flank movements,' they could n't stand that. They fell back, abandoning works, artillery, and position, but still holding the important Summertown road.

"But the enemy, though flanked and overpowered, did not appear disposed to leave us in quiet possession of his works and guns. He hastily reformed his lines, and prepared to assault in turn. The Unionists had hardly occupied the captured position, or been able to remove the captured guns, before the enemy returned to the attack. He pressed forward with great vigor, and gained ground very rapidly at first, but found in his way the same obstacle of the open field, while he did not have the advantage of superior numbers. As soon as it came to close work, his rapidly advancing lines were halted very suddenly by the terrible fire which was now poured in upon him. He continued, however, to fire rapidly, and with some execution upon our line, but would have been ultimately repulsed without other assistance, had not a very serious obstacle presented itself.

"Men in line of battle very soon expend their ammunition. In a skirmishing engagement, like that they were then having, they dispose of it even more rapidly. We were nearly out of ammunition, and the commanding officer had serious fears he would have to relinquish possession of the works, if his cartridge-boxes were not soon replenished. General Hooker, anticipating this, had sent for ammunition at an early hour after getting possession of the road across the spur of the mountain; but the difficulties of the uncertain pontoon bridges had prevented his getting any. He again asked for it, and this time it came, and at the opportune moment. The men were beginning to fall out of line occasionally, entirely out of ammunition; for when a man puts his hand behind him and into his cartridge-box, to find no cartridges there, a good deal of his confidence, if not courage, oozes out at the ends of his fingers, with which he thought to grasp the death-dealing messenger. The line was beginning to be thinned by men who had fired their sixty rounds, when the ammunition which General Thomas had sent sprang across Chattanooga Creek. The enemy had begun to perceive his advantage and to push forward, when this ammunition marched up the hill. The enemy had even ventured upon a shout of assured victory, when this ammunition deployed into line and double-quicked across the open field, and sprang into the vacated places. There were one hundred and twenty thousand rounds of it, strapped upon the backs of as good men as had stayed with Thomas at Chickamauga, and in ten minutes after it reached the works it had repulsed the enemy! The reënforcements which so opportunely arrived, consisted of a brigade of the Fourteenth Corps, and upon it devolved the remainder of the labor of the day. It was dark by the time the enemy were repulsed, and those who stayed in Chattanooga describe the fight as the most magnificent view of the grand panorama of war which we have just witnessed. It was just beginning to be dark enough to see the flash of the muskets, and still light enough to distinguish the general outline of the contending masses. The mountain was lit up by the fires of the men in the second line, and the flash of musketry and artillery. An unearthly noise rose from the mountain, as if the old monster was groaning with the punishment the pigmy combatants inflicted upon him as well as upon each other. And during it all, the great guns upon the summit continued, as in rage, to bellow defiance at the smaller guns of Moccasin Point, which, with lighter tone, and more rapidly, as if mocking the imbecility of its giant enemy, continued to fire till the day roared itself into darkness.

"The enemy fell back, after his repulse, to a point covering the Summertown ascent to the summit of the mountain, and for the remainder of the night confined himself to the defense of that defile, and to the evacuation of the mountain.

"Subsequently, about midnight, the enemy, to cover his retreat, made an assault upon the Union lines, but though they did some execution, they were handsomely repulsed.

"General Hooker made a great reputation, by this attack, with the men of the Army of the Cumberland. As his lines would advance after night, the men could see his fires springing up and locating his new line. As each line became developed by these fires, those on the mountain could plainly distinguish the cheers of their comrades below. One of the expressions used by a private who was watching the fires from Orchard Knob, has already grown into the dignity of a camp proverb. On seeing the line of camp-fires advanced to Carlin's house, and beyond the rifle-pits of the enemy, a soldier in General Wood's command sprang up from his reclining position on Orchard Knob, and exclaimed:

"'Look at old Hooker! Do n't he fight for keeps?'"

The sequel of the fight—the morning's handsome epilogue to the night's drama—is already known. Hooker found the enemy gone, and the assault of Lookout Mountain had not been in vain.

The following is General Grant's modest dispatch with regard to the operations of the second day:

"CHATTANOOGA, Nov. 24—6 P. M.

"*Major-General H. W. Halleck, General-in-Chief, Washington, D. C.:*

"The fighting to-day progressed favorably.

"General Sherman carried the end of Missionary Ridge, and his right is now at the tunnel, and his left at Chickamauga Creek.

"The troops from Lookout Valley carried the point of the mountain, and now hold the eastern slope and point high up.

"I can not yet tell the amount of casualties, but our loss is not heavy.

"General Hooker reports two thousand prisoners taken, besides which a small number have fallen into our hands from Missionary Ridge.

"U. S. GRANT, *Major-General.*"

In the above dispatch General Grant says nothing about

himself, or in what manner he had participated in the struggle, although, notwithstanding his crippled condition, he anxiously watched the movements of the troops at a position within cannon shot of the enemy.

At night, after the battle, the clouds broke away, and the full moon shone bright and clear upon the terrible scene. At one o'clock A. M., the twinkling sparks upon the mountain side showed that the skirmishing had already begun, and continued until the light broke and ushered in another day of battle.

The rebel troops were seen, as soon as it was light enough, streaming regiments and brigades along the narrow summit of Missionary Ridge, either concentrating on the right to overwhelm Sherman, or marching for the railroad to raise the siege.

They had evacuated the valley of Chattanooga. Would they abandon that of Chickamauga?

The twenty-pounders and four-and-a-quarter-inch rifles of Wood's redoubt opened on Missionary Ridge. Orchard Knob sent its compliments to the ridge, which, with rifled Parrots, answered, and the cannonade thus commenced, continued all day. Shot and shell screamed from Orchard Knob to Missionary Ridge, and from Missionary Ridge to Orchard Knob, and from Wood's redoubt, over the heads of Generals Grant and Thomas and their staffs, who were with us in this favorable position, from whence the whole battle could be seen as in an amphitheater. The head-quarters were under fire all day long.

Cannonading and musketry were heard from General Sherman, and General Howard marched the Eleventh Corps to join him.

General Thomas sent out skirmishers, who drove in the rebel pickets and chased them into their intrenchments; and at the foot of Missionary Ridge, Sherman made an assault against Bragg's right, intrenched on a high knob next to that on which Sherman himself lay fortified. The assault was gallantly made.

The following thrilling account of Sherman's advance is from the pen of the accomplished writer, B. F. Taylor:

"The iron heart of Sherman's column began to be audible, like the fall of great trees in the depth of the forest, as it beat beyond the woods on the extreme left. Over roads indescribable, and conquering lions of difficulties that met him all the way, he at length arrived with his command of the Army of the Tennessee. The roar of his guns was like the striking of a great clock, and grew nearer and louder as the morning wore away. Along the center all was still. Our men lay as they *had* lain since Tuesday night, motionless behind the works. *Generals Grant, Thomas, Granger, Meigs, Hunter, Reynolds, were grouped at Orchard Knob, here;* Bragg, Breckinridge, Hardee, Stevens, Cleburne, Bates, Walker, were waiting on Mission Ridge, yonder. And the northern clock tolled on! At noon, a pair of steamers, screaming in the river across the town, telling over, in their own wild way, our mountain triumph on the right, pierced the hushed breath of air between two lines of battle with a note or two of the music of peaceful life.

"At one o'clock the signal flag at Fort Wood was a flutter. Scanning the horizon, another flag, glancing like a lady's handkerchief, showed white across a field lying high and dry upon the ridge three miles to the north-east, and answered back. The center and Sherman's corps had spoken. As the hour went by, all semblance to falling tree and tolling clock had vanished; it was a rattling roar; the ring of Sherman's panting artillery, and the fiery gust from the rebel guns on Tunnel Hill, the point of Mission Ridge. The enemy had massed there the corps of Hardee and Buckner, as upon a battlement, utterly inaccessible save by one steep, narrow way, commanded by their guns. A thousand men could hold it against a host. And right in front of this bold abutment of the ridge, is a broad, clear field, skirted by woods. Across this tremendous threshold up to death's door moved Sherman's column. Twice it advanced, and twice I saw it swept back in bleeding lines before the furnace blast, until that russet field seemed some strange page ruled thick with blue and red. Bright valor was in vain; they lacked the ground to *stand* on; they wanted, like the giant of old story, a touch of earth to make them strong. It was the devil's own corner. Before them was a lane, whose upper end the rebel cannon swallowed. Moving by the right flank, nature opposed them with precipitous heights. There was nothing for it but straight across the field, swept by an enfilading fire, and up to the lane, down which drove the storm. They could unfold no broad front, and so the losses were less than seven hundred, that must otherwise have swelled to thousands. The musketry fire was delivered with terrible emphasis; two dwellings, in one of which Federal wounded men were lying, set on fire by the rebels, began to send up tall columns of smoke, streaked red with fire; the grand and the terrible were blended.

. . . .

"At half-past three, a group of generals, whose names will need no 'Old Mortality' to chisel them anew, stood upon Orchard Knob. The hero of Vicksburg was there, calm, clear, persistent, far-seeing. Thomas, the sterling and sturdy; Meigs, Hunter, Granger, Reynolds. Clusters of humbler mortals were there, too, but it was any thing but a turbulent crowd; the voice naturally fell into a subdued tone, and even young faces took on the gravity of later years. *Generals Grant, Thomas, and Granger conferred, an order was given, and in an instant the knob was cleared like a ship's deck for action.* At twenty minutes of four, Granger stood upon the parapet; the bugle swung idle at the bugler's side, the warbling fife and the grumbling drum unheard:—there was to be *louder* talk—six guns at intervals of two seconds, the signal to advance. Strong and steady his voice rang out: 'Number one, fire! Number two, fire! Number three, fire!' it seemed to me the tolling of the clock of destiny; and when at 'Number six, fire!' the roar throbbed out with the flash, you should have seen the dead line that had been lying behind the works all day, all night, all day again, come to resurrection in the twinkling of an eye—leap like a blade from its scabbard, and sweep with a two-mile stroke toward the ridge. From divisions to brigades, from brigades to regiments, the order ran. A minute, and the skirmishers deploy; a minute, and the first great drops begin to patter along the line; a minute, and the musketry is in full play like the crackling whips of a hemlock fire; men go down here and there, before your eyes; the wind lifts the smoke and drifts it away over the top of the ridge; every thing is too distinct; it is fairly *palpable;* you can touch it with your hand. The divisions of Wood and Sheridan are wading breast deep in the valley of death.

. . . .

"'Take the ridge if you can'—'Take the ridge if you can'—and so it went along the line. But the advance had already set forth without it. Stout-hearted Wood, the iron-gray veteran, is rallying on his men; stormy Turchin is delivering brave words in bad English; Sheridan—'little Phil'—you may easily look down upon him without climbing a tree, and see one of the most gallant leaders of the age if you do—is riding to and fro along the first line of rifle-pits, as calmly as a chess-player. An aid rides up with the order. 'Avery, that flask,' said the General. Quietly filling the pewter cup, Sheridan looks up at the battery that frowns above him, by Bragg's head-quarters, shakes *his* cap amid that storm of every thing that kills, when you could hardly hold your hand without catching a bullet in it, and with a 'How are you?' tosses off the cup. The blue battle-flag of the rebels fluttered a response to the cool salute, and the next instant the battery let fly its six guns, showering Sheridan with earth. Alluding to that compliment with any thing but a blank cartridge, the General said to me in his quiet way, 'I thought it —— ungenerous!' The recording angel will drop a tear upon the word for the part he played that day. Wheeling toward the men, he cheered them to the charge, and made at the hill like a bold-riding hunter; they were out of the rifle-pits and into the tempest and struggling up the steep, before you could get breath to tell it, and so they were throughout the inspired line.

"And now you have before you one of the most startling episodes of the war; I can not render it in words; dictionaries are beggarly things. But I *may* tell you they did not storm that mountain as you would think. They dash out a little way, and then slacken; they creep up, hand over hand, loading and firing, and wavering and halting, from the first line of works to the second; they burst into a charge with a cheer, and go over it. Sheets of flame baptize them; plunging shot tear away comrades on left and right; it is no longer shoulder to shoulder; it is God for us all! Under the tree-trunks, among rocks, stumbling over the dead, struggling with the living, facing the steady fire of eight thousand infantry poured down on their heads as if it were the old historic curse from heaven, they wrestle with the ridge. Ten, fifteen, twenty minutes go by like a reluctant century. The batteries roll like a drum; between the second and last lines of rebel works is the torrid zone of the battle; the hill sways up like a wall before them at an angle of forty-five degrees, but our brave mountaineers are clambering steadily on—up—upward still! You may think it strange, but I would not have recalled them if I could. They would have lifted you, as they did me, in full view of the heroic grandeur: they seemed to be spurning the dull earth under their feet, and going up to do Homeric battle with the greater gods.

"The race of the flags is growing every moment more terrible. There at the right, a strange thing catches the eye; one of the inverted V's is turning right side up. The men struggling along the converging lines to overtake the flag have distanced it, and there the colors are, sinking down in the center between the rising flanks. The line wavers like a great billow and up comes the banner again, as if heaved on a surge's shoulder. The iron sledges beat on. Hearts, loyal and brave, are on the anvil, all the way from base to summit of Mission Ridge, but those dreadful hammers never intermit. Swarms of bullets sweeps the hill; you can count twenty-eight balls in one little tree. Things are growing desperate up aloft; the rebels tumble rocks upon the rising line; they light fuses and roll shells down the steep; they load the guns with handfuls of cartridges in their haste; and as if there were powder in the word, they shout 'Chickamauga!' down upon the mountaineers. But it would not all do, and just as the sun, weary of the scene, was sinking out of sight, with magnificent bursts all along the line, exactly as you have seen the crested seas leap up at the breakwater, the advance surged over the crest, and in a minute those flags fluttered along the fringe where fifty rebel guns were kenneled. God bless the flag! God save the Union!

. . . .

"As Sheridan rode up to the guns, the heels of Breckinridge's horse glittered in the last rays of sunshine. That crest was hardly 'well off with the old love before it was cn with the new.'

"But the scene on the narrow plateau can never be painted. As the blue coats surged over its edge, cheer on cheer rang like bells through the valley of the Chickamauga. Men flung themselves exhausted upon the ground. They laughed and wept, shook hands, embraced; turned round and did all four over again. It was as wild as a carnival. Granger was received with a shout. 'Soldiers,' said he, 'you ought to be court-martialed every man of you. I ordered you to take the rifle-pits and you scaled the mountain!' but it was not Mars' horrid front exactly with which he said it, for his cheeks were wet with tears as honest as the blood that reddened all the route. Wood uttered words that rang like 'Napoleon's,' and Sheridan, the rowels at his horse's flanks, was ready for a dash down the ridge with a 'view halloo,' for a fox hunt.

"But you must not think that this was all there was of the scene on the crest, for fight and frolic was strangely mingled. Not a rebel had dreamed a man of us all would live to reach the summit, and when a little wave of the Federal cheer rolled up and broke over the crest, they defiantly cried, 'Hurrah, and be damned!' the next minute a Union regiment followed the voice, the rebels delivered their fire, and tumbled down in their rifle-pits, their faces distorted with fear. No sooner had the soldiers scrambled to the ridge and straightened themselves, than up muskets and away they blazed. One of them, fairly beside himself between laughing and crying, seemed puzzled at which end of his piece he should load, and so abandoning the gun and the problem together, he made a catapult of himself and fell to hurling stones after the enemy. And he said as he threw—Well, you know our 'army swore terribly in Flanders.' Bayonets glinted and muskets rattled. General Sheridan's horse was killed under him; Richard was not in his role, and so he leaped upon a rebel gun for want of another. Rebel artillerists are driven from their batteries at the edge of the sword and the point of the bayonet; two rebel guns are swung round upon their old masters. But there is nobody to load them. Light and heavy artillery do not belong to the winged kingdom. Two infantry men claiming to be old artillerists, volunteer. Granger turns captain of the guns, and—right about wheel!—in a moment they are growling after the flying enemy. I say 'flying,' but that is figurative. The many run like Spanish merinos, but the few fight like gray wolves at bay; they load and fire as they retreat; they are fairly scorched out of position.

"A sharpshooter, fancying Granger to be worth the powder, coolly tries his hand at him. The general hears the *zip* of a ball at one ear, but does n't mind it. In a minute away it sings at the other. He takes the hint, sweeps with his glass the direction whence the couple came, and brings up the marksman, just drawing a bead upon him again. At that instant a Federal argument persuades the cool hunter, and down he goes. That long range gun of his was captured, weighed twenty-four pounds, was telescope-mounted, a sort of mongrel howitzer.

"A colonel is slashing away with his saber in a ring of rebels. Down goes his horse under him; they have him on the hip; one of them is taking deliberate aim, when up rushes a lieutenant, claps a pistol to one ear and roars in at the other, 'Who the h—l are you shooting at?' The fellow drops his piece, gasps out, 'I surrender,' and the next instant the gallant lieutenant falls sharply wounded. He is a 'roll of honor' officer, straight up from the ranks, and he honors the roll.

"A little German, in Wood's division, is pierced like the lid of a pepper-box, but he is neither dead nor wounded. 'See here,' he says, rushing up to a comrade, 'a pullet hit te preach of mine gun—a pullet in mine pocket-book—a pullet in mine coat tail; they shoots me tree, five times, and py tam I gives dem h—l yet!'

"But I can render you no idea of the battle caldron that boiled on the plateau. An incident here and there I have given you, and you must fill out the picture for yourself. Dead rebels lay thick around Bragg's head-quarters and along the ridge. Scabbards, broken arms, artillery horses, wrecks of gun carriages, and bloody garments, strewed the scene; and, tread lightly, oh! loyal-hearted, the boys in blue are lying there; no more the sounding charge, no more the brave, wild cheer, and never for them, sweet as the breath of the the new-mown hay in the old home fields, 'The Soldier's Return from the War.' A little waif of a drummer-boy, somehow drifted up the mountain in the surge, lies there; his pale face upward, a blue spot on his breast. Muffle his drum for the poor child and his mother.

"Our troops met one loyal welcome on the height. How the old Tennesseean that gave it managed to get there, nobody knows; but there he was, grasping a colonel's hand, and saying, while the tears ran down his face, 'GOD be thanked! I *knew* the Yankees would fight!' With the receding flight and swift pursuit the battle died away in murmurs, far down the valley of the Chickamauga; Sheridan was again in the saddle, and with his command spurring on after the enemy. Tall columns of smoke were rising at the left. The rebels were burning a train of stores a mile long. In the exploding rebel caissons we had 'the cloud by day,' and now we are having 'the pillar of fire by night.' The sun, the golden dish of the scales that balance day and night, had hardly gone down, when up, beyond Mission Ridge, rose the *silver* side, for that night it was full moon. The troubled day was done. A Federal general sat in the seat of the man who, on the very Saturday before the battle, had sent a flag to the Federal lines with the words:

'Humanity would dictate the removal of all non-combatants from Chattanooga, as I am about to shell the city!'"

Bragg left the house in which he had held his head-quarters, and rode to the rear, as our troops crowded the hill on either side of him. General Grant proceeded to the summit, and then only did we know its height. At the sight of their beloved chieftain, who was now to inscribe "Chattanooga" upon the banner already blazoned with the glorious names of "Donelson" and of "Vicksburg," the soldiers raised a shout which reached the ears of the rejoicing thousands in the city below, and which added new speed to the footsteps of the fugitives, who in the most rapid flight alone could hope for safety. "There is nothing in this world," said the Duke of Wellington, "more dreadful than a great victory, except a great defeat." This victory cost four thousand Union men, in killed and wounded.

Grant captured at Chattanooga six thousand prisoners, forty guns, seven thousand stand of small arms, and a great quantity of ammunition.

General Meigs, writing to the Secretary of War from the battle-field, says: "Probably not so well directed, so well ordered a battle has taken place during the war. But one assault was repulsed; but that assault, by calling to that point the rebel reserves, prevented them repulsing any of the others." The strength of the rebellion in the center is broken. Burnside is relieved from danger in East Tennessee. Kentucky and Tennessee are rescued. Georgia and the south-east are threatened in the rear, *and another victory is added to the chapter of "Unconditional Surrender Grant."* Without waiting to rest for a moment, Grant ordered the pursuit of the enemy to begin, and early the next morning sent Sherman with his corps to the relief of Burnside at Knoxville.

Hooker and Palmer marched on the Rossville road to

White Oak Ridge and Taylor's Ridge, where they found a strong rebel force under Cleburne posted in ambush. A severe action ensued, in which the rebels were badly beaten.

Sherman's column marched to Ringgold, where Davis' division came upon the enemy. Our advance was driven back, but Osterhaus and Geary were ordered up, and soon turned the tide of battle in favor of the Union arms. The rebels lost one hundred and thirty killed. Two pieces of artillery and two hundred and thirty prisoners, mostly wounded, were taken by the Union troops. Our loss was sixty killed and three hundred and seventy wounded. This brilliant little fight was the last one in which General Grant was personally engaged in the West, and he signalized it by the most heroic conduct. From the beginning to the close of the action he was under fire, and in person directed the movement of the troops. One of his staff officers, writing soon after the battle to a friend, says in his letter:

"It has been a matter of universal wonder in this army that General Grant himself was not killed, and that no more accidents occurred to his staff; for the General was always in the front (his staff with him, of course), and perfectly heedless of the storm of hissing bullets and screaming shell flying around him. His apparent want of sensibility does not arise from heedlessness, heartlessness, or vain military affectation, but from a sense of the responsibility resting upon him when in battle. When at Ringgold, we rode for half a mile in the face of the enemy, under an incessant fire of cannon and musketry; nor did we ride fast, but upon an ordinary trot; and not once do I believe did it enter the General's mind that he was in danger. I was by his side, and watched him closely. In riding that distance we were going to the front, and I could see that he was studying the positions of the two armies, and of course, planning how to defeat the enemy, who was here making a most desperate stand, and was slaughtering our men fearfully."

Grant was naturally very anxious about Burnside. That General had sent Grant word that his supplies would only last until the 3d day of December, and that Knoxville could not be abandoned. It was now near the end of November, and Grant sent Granger word to hasten to Knoxville; but Granger not going fast enough for the sleepless anxiety of Grant, Sherman was ordered to supersede him and push on day and night until he reached the beleaguered city.

It was now a race between the Union troops and famine, which should get to Knoxville first, and the Union troops won.

Longstreet, hearing that Sherman was coming down upon him with the speed of a race-horse, ordered the bayonets to be fixed and the works assaulted at once. The attack was gallantly repulsed, and Sherman sent a note to Burnside to hold on, that he was coming by forced marches with twenty-five thousand men and would fall upon Longstreet's rear. Longstreet did not wait for him, however, but raised the siege and precipitately retreated toward Virginia.

On the 5th of December, just two days after Burnside had declared his rations would give out, Sherman arrived at Marysville, one day's march from Knoxville, and sent Burnside the following note:

"I am here, and can bring twenty-five thousand men into Knoxville to-morrow. But, Longstreet having retreated, I feel disposed to stop, for a stern chase is a long one. But I will do all that is possible. Without you specify that you want troops, I will let mine rest to-morrow, and ride to see you." On the morning of the 7th, the commands of Potter and Manson started in pursuit of the enemy, but failed to come up with any but small parties; and thus ended the most brilliant campaign since the days of Napoleon. On the 8th, President Lincoln sent the following dispatch to General Grant:

"Understanding that your lodgment at Chattanooga and at Knoxville is now secure, I wish to tender you, and all under your command, my more than thanks, my profoundest gratitude, for the skill, courage, and perseverance with which you and they, over so great difficulties, have effected that important object. God bless you all!"

On the 10th of December, General Grant, having returned to his head-quarters at Chattanooga, issued to his troops the following congratulatory order:

"HEAD-QUARTERS MILITARY DIVISION OF THE
"MISSISSIPPI, IN THE FIELD,
"CHATTANOOGA, TENNESSEE, Dec. 10, 1863.

"[*General Orders, No.* 9.]

"The General commanding takes this opportunity of returning his sincere thanks and congratulations to the brave armies of the Cumberland, the Ohio, the Tennessee, and their comrades from the Potomac, for the recent splendid and decisive successes achieved over the enemy. In a short time you have recovered from him the control of the Tennessee River from Bridgeport to Knoxville. You dislodged him from his great stronghold upon Lookout Mountain, drove him from Chattanooga Valley, wrested from his determined grasp the possession of Mission Ridge, repelled with heavy loss to him his repeated assaults upon Knoxville, forcing him to raise the siege there, driving him at all points, utterly routed and discomfited, beyond the limits of the State. By your noble heroism and determined courage, you have most effectually defeated the plans of the enemy for regaining possession of the States of Kentucky and Tennessee. You have secured positions from which no rebellious power can drive or dislodge you. For all this the General commanding thanks you collectively and individually. The loyal people of the United States thank and bless you. Their hopes and prayers for your success against this unholy rebellion are with you daily. Their faith in you will not be in vain. Their hopes will not be blasted. Their prayers to Almighty God will be answered. You will yet go to other fields of strife; and with the invincible bravery and unflinching loyalty to justice and right which have characterized you in the past, you will prove that no enemy can withstand you, and that no defenses, however formidable, can check your onward march.

"By order of Major-General U. S. GRANT."

"T. S. BOWERS, A. A. G."

We seldom have a more striking exemplification of the power of the mind triumphing over the body, than General Grant presented during these hours of exhausting care and toil. He was then in feeble health, still severely suffering from his fall at New Orleans. He was so emaciated, and walked so feebly, that many feared he would never recover. Still, with all this bodily languor and suffering, his mind retained its accustomed energies, and he worked as indefatigably as if in the enjoyment of vigorous health.

A woman, who resided upon the plateau of Missionary Ridge, said to one of our generals: "Before you all came up here, I asked General Bragg, 'What are you going to do with me, general?' He said to me, 'Lord! madam, the Yankees will never dare to come up here.' And it was not fifteen minutes till you were all around here."

During the dark days of the siege, when food and forage were scarce, and the ghastly corpses and bleached skeletons of starved mules lined the thoroughfares thereabouts, General Grant and Quartermaster-General Meigs arrived in Chattanooga. Taking an airing on horseback one afternoon, they passed the carcass of a huge mule lying by the roadside, whose "ill-savor went up" before and around them. The hero of Vicksburg removed his brier-root from his lips, and remarked sorrowfully, "Ah, General! there lies a dead soldier of the Quartermaster's Department." "Yes, General," replied the Quartermaster-General, in subdued tones, "in him you see the 'ruling passion strong in death' exemplified, for the old veteran has already assumed the offensive."

General Grant, unlike most of our great Generals, never made a show of himself. A correspondent, writing about his personal habits in the army, says:

"Another feature in General Grant's personal movements is that he requires no escort beyond his staff, so regardless of danger is he. Roads are almost useless to him, for he takes short cuts through fields and woods, and will swim his horse through almost any stream that obstructs his way. Nor does it make any difference to him whether he has daylight for his movements, for he will ride from breakfast until two o'clock in the morning, and that too without eating. The next day he will repeat the dose, until he finishes his work. Now such things come hard upon the staff, but they have learned how to bear it."

CHAPTER XIII.

GRANT'S VICTORIES—VOTE OF THANKS BY CONGRESS—BILL TO REVIVE THE GRADE OF LIEUTENANT-GENERAL—A MEDAL GIVEN HIM—APPOINTED LIEUTENANT-GENERAL AND ASSUMES COMMAND OF THE ARMY—HONORS TO GENERAL GRANT—HE RECEIVES VALUABLE PRESENTS—THE OLD SOLDIER'S GIFT—GRANT VISITS NASHVILLE AND KNOXVILLE—CROSSES THE CUMBERLAND MOUNTAINS ON HORSEBACK—HIS RECEPTION AT LEXINGTON, KENTUCKY—VISIT TO LOUISVILLE—HONORS AT MEMPHIS—A GRAND DINNER—SERENADE TO GRANT, AND HIS SPEECHES—GRANT LEAVES THE WEST—HIS LETTER TO SHERMAN, AND SHERMAN'S REPLY—HIS VISIT TO WASHINGTON—THE PRESIDENT PRESENTS HIM HIS COMMISSION AS LIEUTENANT-GENERAL.

When the news of General Grant's great victories reached the country, there was general rejoicing, and President Lincoln recommended the people to assemble in their places of worship and give thanks to Almighty God for the great advancement vouchsafed the Union cause. Grant was every-where praised for his skill as a commander, and Mr. Washburn, yielding to the national wish, as soon as Congress assembled, rose and offered a bill "to revive the grade of Lieutenant-General of the army," and another "to provide that a medal be struck for General Grant, and that a vote of thanks be given him and the officers of his army." Both bills passed, and were signed by the President, the first on the 17th of December, 1863, and the second on the 1st of March, 1864.

The medal, the tribute of a nation's admiration, was designed by Leutze. On one side there was a profile likeness of General Grant, surrounded by a laurel wreath. His name, and the year of his victories, were inscribed upon it; and the whole was surrounded by a galaxy of stars. On the opposite side was the figure of Fame, gracefully seated on the American Eagle, which, with outspread wings, seemed preparing for flight. In her right hand she held the symbolical trumpet. With her left hand she presented a scroll, on which were inscribed the names of Corinth, Vicksburg, Mississippi River, and Chattanooga. On her head there was a helmet, ornamented in Indian fashion, with feathers radiating from it. In front of the eagle, its breast resting against it, was the emblematical shield of the United States; beneath were sprigs of pine and palm twined together, indicative of the union of the North and South. Over all, in a curved line, were the words, "Proclaim liberty throughout all the land."

The medal was accompanied by the resolution of thanks passed by Congress, beautifully engrossed on parchment. In accordance with the design of the bill passed by Congress, President Lincoln, on the 10th day of March, issued the following executive order:

"Executive Mansion, Washington, March 10, 1864.

"Under the authority of the act of Congress to appoint to the grade of lieutenant general in the army, of March 1, 1864, Lieutenant-General Ulysses S. Grant, United States Army, is appointed to the command of the armies of the United States. Abraham Lincoln."

This order was forwarded by a courier to Nashville, where General Grant then was, and on the 17th of March, he issued the following brief response:

"Head-quarters Armies of the United States,
"Nashville, Tenn., March 17, 1864.

"In pursuance of the order of the President, I assume

command of the armies of the United States. Head-quarters will be in the field, and until further orders, will be with the Army of the Potomac. There will be an office head-quarters in Washington, to which all official communications will be sent, except those from the army where the head-quarters are at the date of their address.

"U. S. GRANT, *Lieutenant-General.*"

In the meantime, General Grant had been enjoying great honors and hospitalities at the hands of his fellow-citizens. Colleges, religious and literary societies had hastened to elect him an honorary member, and tenders of dinners, receptions, and ovations were pouring in upon him from all quarters. The Rev. F. Marlay, Secretary of the Missionary Society of Cincinnati, wrote him he had been elected an honorary member of that body, and Grant replied:

"CHATTANOOGA, Dec. 7, 1863.

"*Rev. F. Marlay, Secretary Society:*

"DEAR SIR: Through you permit me to express my thanks to the society of which you are the honored secretary, for the compliment they have seen fit to pay me by electing me one of its members.

"I accept the election as a token of earnest support, by members of the Methodist Missionary Society of the Cincinnati Conference, to the cause of our country in this hour of trial.

"I have the honor to be, very truly,

"Your obedient servant,

"U. S. GRANT, Major-General U. S. A."

Rev. Dr. Dunn, of Norristown, New Jersey, wrote Grant:

"*To Major-General U. S. Grant:*

"DEAR SIR: I have the pleasure of informing you that

the church of which I am pastor, the Methodist Episcopal Church of this town, highly appreciating your services for your country, and rejoicing in the victories which God has wrought out through you and your noble army, and praying that you may be spared to see the end of this accursed rebellion, have contributed one hundred and fifty dollars ($150) to constitute you a life director of the Missionary Society of the M. E. Church. Will you please direct where we shall send your certificate? May God Almighty bless and keep you, and continue to crown your arms with victory and triumph!"

Grant promptly replied through a staff officer:

"In reply to your letter of December 19th, to Major-General U. S. Grant, he directs me to express his gratitude to the people of Norristown for their prayerful remembrance of him before the throne of the Most High, and to thank them, through you, for the honor conferred upon him. Be good enough to send his certificate of membership to Mrs. U. S. Grant, Louisville, Kentucky.

"J. H. Wilson."

A beautiful pair of revolvers were made for him by Colt's manufactory. The handles were of black horn, beautifully polished, and the barrels, magazines, and other steel parts elaborately inlaid with pure gold, which was beaten into a design previously cut out of the steel. The other ornaments, guard, etc., were of a solid gold. The pair were enclosed in a handsome rosewood-box, lined with velvet, and accompanied by all the tools, etc., belonging to them—the cartridge-boxes, etc., being manufactured of silver.

The Legislature of Ohio passed and forwarded to him the following resolution:

"*Resolved*, That the thanks of the people of this State be tendered to General Grant and his army for their glorious victories in the Valley of the Mississippi, and the still more glorious victory of Missionary Ridge and Lookout Mountain, and that a certified copy of this resolution be forwarded to General Grant."

New York, Pennsylvania, and other States passed him votes of thanks. Grant hats, coats, vests, cigars, pipes, and knives were made in abundance, and mothers every-where began to call their male children Grant. Of all the presents and honors he received, there is one that he refers to with more pleasure than the rest. It is a fine brier-wood cigar-case, made for him with a pocket-knife, and presented by a poor soldier, who said he gave it "because he loved his old gineral, and wanted him to sometimes think of him." The old soldier is remembered.

General Grant, before leaving the Army of the West, determined to make a tour of inspection. Every-where he was received with the wildest enthusiasm by both citizens and soldiers. He visited Nashville and Knoxville, and from there passed over the Cumberland Mountains on horseback. It was the severest days in midwinter, and often he was compelled to walk on foot. His object was to test the passability of the roads for troops. Traveling through Barboursville, London, and Danville, he reached Lexington in safety. Notwithstanding the deep snow and bitter cold weather, crowds every-where turned out to see the hero pass by, and, at Lexington, he was met with a spontaneous reception from the citizens.

The town was crowded with the country visitors, and nothing would satisfy them but a speech. The General, however, contented himself with making his appearance. The people insisted on his getting upon a chair, that he might be seen to better advantage, and, half pushed by General Leslie Coombs, General Grant mounted the improvised rostrum. General Coombs then introduced him in a neat little speech, in which he said that "General Grant had told him in confidence—and he would not repeat it—that he never had made a speech, knew nothing about speech-making, and had no disposition to learn." After satisfying the curiosity of the people, but without ever having opened his mouth, General Grant dismounted from his chair and retired, amid the cheers of the assemblage.

From Lexington he went to Louisville. His arrival at the Galt House was not generally known, and few who had not looked at the books suspected that the little man in faded blue overcoat, with heavy red whiskers and keen, bright eyes, the hero of the two rebel Gibraltars of Vicksburg and Chattanooga, stood before them. The people had been so used to brilliantly-dressed and cleanly-shaven staff-officers, with star or double star, that they never dreamed of recognizing in the blue overcoated men who figured in the scene with him, the admirable and hard-working staff-officers who have aided in no little degree to General Grant's success.

On the 26th of January General Grant visited St. Louis to see a sick child. He went quietly to the hotel and recorded his name *U. S. Grant, Chattanooga.* Visitors to the hotel, on looking over the register, as their eyes fell on those significant initials, were startled, and it was considered by many a joke. It soon became noised about, however, that the great General was indeed in the city, and a large crowd assembled in and about the house. A letter tendering a public dinner was sent him, and Grant immediately replied:

"St. Louis, Mo., January 27, 1864.

"*Colonel John O'Fallan, Hon. John Howe, and citizens of St. Louis:*

"Gentlemen: Your highly complimentary invitation 'to meet old acquaintances and make new ones,' at a dinner to be given by citizens of St. Louis is just received. *I will state that I have only visited St. Louis on this occasion to see a sick child.* Finding, however, that he has passed the crisis of his disease, and is pronounced out of danger by his physicians, I accept the invitation. My stay in this city will be short—probably not beyond the 1st proximo. On to-morrow I shall be engaged. Any other day of my stay here, and any place selected by the citizens of St. Louis, it will be agreeable for me to meet them.

"I have the honor to be, very respectfully, your obedient servant,

"U. S. GRANT, *Major-General U. S. A.*"

The same evening he attended the St. Louis theater with his family, and was the cynosure of the eyes of all around him during the whole of the performance. After the fall of the curtain upon the play of Richelieu, cheers were proposed and heartily given for the "famous military chieftain." The General rose from his box bowing his acknowledgments, and, in response to calls, was understood to say that he had never made a speech in his life, and never expected to. Asking to be excused, he resumed his seat amid a shower of cheers. The orchestra struck up "Hail Columbia," followed by "Yankee Doodle."

Next day the City Council passed him a vote of thanks, and the mayor, by order of the municipal departments, tendered him the hospitalities of the city.

At his hotel Grant was overwhelmed by the cordial greetings tendered him.

The lady inmates of the house took possession of an adjoining parlor, through the open door of which they could see the General, and several of his most ardent admirers among the fair spectators took the opportunity of his near proximity to the door in question to obtain an introduction.

The dinner was a splendid affair.

Over two hundred guests met in the spacious hall at the Lindell Hotel, to confer honor upon the distinguished visitor. The room was richly decorated, and General Grant was not a little embarrassed by the attentions which were lavished upon him. There were three elegant tables spread lengthwise in the hall, provided abundantly from the larder of the hotel. In the center of the one on the north side were seated the President of the Committee of Citizens, Judge Samuel Treat, with General Grant next on his right, followed by General Schofield, Colonel Leighton, Colonel Marcy, and Lieutenant-Governor Hall. Next on his left sat General Rosecrans, General Osterhaus, and Mr. F. Dent, father-in-law of the guest of the evening. Mr. Dent is a white-haired, florid, fine-looking gentleman, about sixty-five years old. He resided in St. Louis County, on the Gravois road. Immediately opposite Judge Treat, at the same table, sat Judge Lord, of the Land Court, flanked on the left by Major Dunn, C. B. Hubbell, Colonel Merrill, and G. Hoeber; and on the right by Colonel Callender, Colonol Myers, Colonel Haines, and Major C. P. E. Johnson.

At the center of the south table were seated Honorable Wayman Crow, with General McNeil, General Fisk, General Brown, General Totten, and General Gray. The remaining guests, to the number of two hundred, occupied the other seats at the tables. The hall, superb in the ceiling and wall colorings which embellished it, was further decorated by the spirited drapings of the national flag from each of the arched windows, and presented a magnificent appearance.

When the toast, "Our distinguished guest, Major-General U. S. Grant," was given, the band struck up "Hail to the Chief," and General Grant rose, amid a storm of applause, and said:

"Gentlemen, in response it will be impossible for me to do more than to thank you."

In the evening he was serenaded; and an immense crowd surrounded the hotel, anxious to catch a sight of the hero, and clamorous for a speech. After some delay, General Grant stepped upon the balcony, and taking off his hat, in the midst of profoundest silence, said:

"Gentlemen, I thank you for this honor. I can not make a speech. It is something I have never done, and never intend to do; and I beg you will excuse me."

Loud cheers followed this brief address, at the conclusion of which the General replaced his hat, took a cigar from his pocket, lit it, and stood on the balcony in the presence of the crowd, puffing his Havana and watching the rockets as they ascended and burst in the air.

"Speech! speech!" vociferated the multitude, and several gentlemen near him urged the General to say something to satisfy the people, but he declined. Judge Lord, of the Land Court, appeared very enthusiastic, and, placing his hand on General Grant's shoulder, said: "Tell them you can fight for them, but can 't talk to them—do tell them that!"

"I must get some one else to say that for me," replied the General; but the multitude continuing to cry out "Speech! speech!" he leaned over the railing, blew a wreath of smoke from his lips, and said:

"Gentlemen, making speeches is not my business. I never did it in my life, and never will. I thank you, however, for your attendance here," and with that the General retired.

General Grant, after visiting the places of public interest, the universities and ladies' fair, left St. Louis much pleased with his visit, and taking with him the good wishes of all loyal citizens.

General Grant's work was now done in the West, and he found it his sad duty to take leave of his officers and soldiers. To Sherman he wrote:

"DEAR SHERMAN: The bill reviving the grade of lieutenant-general has become a law, and my name has been sent to the Senate for the place. I now receive orders to report to Washington immediately in person, which indicates a confirmation, or a likelihood of confirmation. I start in the morning to comply with the order.

"While I have been eminently successful in this war, in at least gaining the confidence of the public, no one feels more than I how much of this success is due to the energy, skill, and the harmonious putting forth of that energy and skill, of those whom it has been my good fortune to have occupying subordinate positions under me.

"There are many officers to whom these remarks are applicable to a greater or less degree, proportionate to their ability as soldiers; but what I want is to express my thanks to you and McPherson, as the men to whom, above all others, I feel indebted for whatever I have had of success.

"How far your advice and assistance have been of help to me, you know. How far your execution of whatever has been given you to do, entitles you to the reward I am receiving, you can not know as well as I.

"I feel all the gratitude this letter would express, giving it the most flattering construction. The word *you* I use in the plural, intending it for McPherson also. I would write to him, and will some day; but, starting in the morning, I do not know that I will find time just now.

"Your friend,

"U. S. GRANT."

This letter was forwarded to General Sherman, at Memphis. His reply, on the 10th of March, is so noble, and so beautifully reflects the friendship existing between these illustrious men, that we can not refrain from giving it entire:

"DEAR GENERAL: I have your more than kind and characteristic letter of the 4th instant. I will send a copy to General McPherson at once.

"You do yourself injustice, and us too much honor, in assigning to us too large a share of the merits which have led to your high advancement. I know you approve the friendship I have ever proffered to you, and will permit me to continue, as heretofore, to manifest it on all proper occasions.

"You are now Washington's legitimate successor, and occupy a position of almost dangerous elevation; but if you can continue, as heretofore, to be yourself—simple, honest, and unpretending—you will enjoy through life the respect and love of friends, and the homage of millions of human beings, who will award you a large share in securing to them and their descendants a government of law and stability.

"I repeat, you do General McPherson and myself too much honor. At Belmont you manifested your traits, neither of us being near. At Donelson, also, you illustrated your whole character. I was not near, and General McPherson was in too subordinate a capacity to influence you.

"Until you had won Donelson, I confess I was almost cowed by the terrible array of anarchical elements that presented themselves at every point; but that admitted a ray of light I have followed since. I believe you are as brave, patriotic, and just as the great prototype, Washington; as unselfish, kind-hearted, and honest as a man should be; but the chief characteristic is the simple faith in success you have always manifested, which I can liken to nothing else than the faith a Christian has in the Savior.

"This faith gave you the victory at Shiloh and at Vicksburg. Also, when you have completed your best preparations, you go into battle without hesitation, as at Chattanooga—no doubts, no reserves; and, I tell you, it was this which made us act with confidence.

"My only point of doubt was in your knowledge of grand strategy, and of books of science and of history; but I confess your common sense seems to have supplied all these.

"Now, as to the future. Don't stay in Washington. Come West; take to yourself the whole Mississippi Valley. Let us make it dead sure; and, I tell you, the Atlantic slopes and Pacific shores will follow its destiny as surely as the limbs of a tree live or die with the main trunk. We have done much, but still much remains. Time, and time's influence, are with us. We could almost afford to sit still, and let these influences work.

"Here lies the seat of the coming empire; and from the West, when our task is done, we will make short work of Charleston and Richmond, and the impoverished coast of the Atlantic. "Your sincere friend,

"W. T. Sherman."

On the 3d of March, General Grant received a dispatch from Washington urging him to hasten his arrival there, and assume charge of his new duties. Abbott, in his pleasant book, thus records the hero's passage to the National Capitol:

"At every depot crowds were gathered to catch a glimpse of one whose achievements were so illustrious, and whose name was on all lips. Wherever he appeared, enthusiastic cheers greeted him. Upon his arrival in Washington, he quietly repaired to Willard's Hotel, and, unobserved, took a seat at a table in the dining-room, with his son by his side. A gentleman recognized him, and, rising, informed the guests that General Ulysses S. Grant sat at the table. Simultaneously, and as by an instinctive impulse, all rose; and cheer upon cheer rang through the hall. Many pressed around him to take him by the hand; and the crowd immediately became so great that it was with difficulty he could make his way to his private apartment.

"In the evening he attended the President's levee at the White House. Here the enthusiasm which his presence created was very great. He engrossed the attention of the whole company. The crowd pressed him to an adjacent sofa, and lifted him from his feet, until he was compelled to stand where all could see him. Such a scene of enthusiasm was never before witnessed in the presidential mansion. President Lincoln, magnanimous, generous, unselfish, whose soul was never sullied with a jealous thought, stood by the side of Grant, and joined as heartily as any of the company with cheer after cheer in tribute to the merits of this great and good man.

"But these ovations were only painful to General Grant. He had no taste for pageantry, and his modest nature shrank from these displays of admiration and homage. Though by no means insensible to manifestations of confidence and affection, he still wished to avoid them. Upon retiring that night from the levee, he said to a friend:

"'I hope to get away from Washington as soon as possible, for I am tired of the show-business already.'

"The next day, March the 9th, was the time appointed by President Lincoln for presenting him his commission as lieutenant-general. The impressive scene took place in the executive chamber, with true republican simplicity. All the cabinet were present, and also several other distinguished invited guests. President Lincoln rose from his chair, and thus addressed him:

"'GENERAL GRANT: The nation's approbation of what you

have already done, and its reliance on you for what remains to do in the existing great struggle, is now presented with this commission, constituting you *Lieutenant-General* of the Army of the United States. With this high honor devolves on you a corresponding responsibility. As the country here intrusts you, so under God it will sustain you. I scarcely need add, that with what I here speak for the nation, goes my own hearty personal concurrence.'

"General Grant, taking the commission in his hand, replied:

"'MR. PRESIDENT: I accept this commission with gratitude for the high honor conferred. With the aid of the noble armies who have fought on so many fields for our common country, it will be my earnest endeavor not to disappoint your expectations. I feel the full weight of the responsibility now devolving upon me. I know that, if it is properly met, it will be due to these armies, and, above all, to the favor of that Providence which leads both nations and men.'"

CHAPTER XIV.

GRANT IN HIS NEW COMMAND—THE REBEL CHIEFTAIN LEE—GRANT'S COMBINATIONS—ALL READY TO ADVANCE—BATTLES OF THE WILDERNESS—GALLANTRY OF CRAWFORD—DEATH OF WADSWORTH—HANCOCK'S FIGHTING—DEATH OF SEDGWICK—BATTLE OF SPOTTSYLVANIA COURT-HOUSE—CAPTURE OF A REBEL DIVISION AND TWO REBEL GENERALS—BURNSIDE'S BATTLES—FORWARD ALONG THE WHOLE LINE—ANECDOTES OF GRANT—BATTLE OF COLD HARBOR—ORDER OF BATTLE—TERRIBLE FIGHTING—CROSSING THE JAMES—ASSAULTS ON PETERSBURG—INVESTMENT OF THE CITY—THE SIEGE BEGUN—PRESIDENT LINCOLN'S LETTER TO GRANT—GRANT'S REPLY.

GRANT was now to measure swords with the great man of the rebellion, Robert E. Lee. McClellan, Pope, Burnside, Hooker, and Meade had all been unable to conquer the rebel chief, and thousands feared that even the great soldier of the West would fail.

Quietly looking over the situation, Grant began his combinations for the final campaign in the East. Sending orders to Steele and Banks to drive the rebels in Louisiana and Arkansas into Texas and capture Shreveport, he wrote Butler to move up the James and intrench at City Point, at the same time he instructed Sigel to send ten thousand men under Crook into the Kanawha Valley, and go himself, with seven thousand more, up the Shenandoah. This done, he consulted with Sherman, and the great campaign in the West was organized that resulted in the brilliant "march to the sea."

Already the ponderous machinery of war was in motion,

under the direction of the master-mind of Grant, and the coil of iron was tightening around the doomed Confederacy. Hastening to the army of the Potomac, he reorganized it. The number of army corps were reduced to three: the Second, under command of Major-General Winfield S. Hancock; the Fifth, under command of Major-General G. W. Warren; and the Sixth, under command of General Sedgwick. On the fourth of April, 1864, Major-General Sheridan was placed in command of the cavalry corps. Division officers were also re-assigned.

All was now prepared, and the great General stood on the banks of the Rapidan, bugle in hand, ready to sound the "onward" into the bowels of the Confederacy. When at length, on the 3d of May, the advance was blown and the army crossed the Rubicon, the whole nation stood still, and with breathless anxiety awaited the result. Nor had they long to wait, for soon the terrible news that three hundred thousand men were fighting came up from the Wilderness and blanched every cheek in the nation.

The contest began on the 5th and extended for five miles, over hills, through forests, and down deep and dark ravines. Warren, with Wadsworth's and Griffin's divisions, drove Ewell steadily back, until exhausted and bleeding, the troops halted and waited for the Sixth Corps to come up. But the tangled wilderness and impassable roads delayed the relief, and the rebels in turn assaulted. Wadsworth was forced back, and for a time the gallant Crawford, on Wadsworth's left, was isolated. Bravely he held his position, fighting against all odds, until the ground was strewn with his dead and dying; still he would not yield, but fought his way out, although with fearful loss. Getty, rapid and brave, attacked Hill on the Orange plank road, and poured volley after volley into the enemy, declaring he would hold his position until Hancock could come up to his relief. The rebels Johnson, Jones, Stuart, Rhodes, Daniel, and Gordon now in turn attack Warren, and the Union troops yield ground stubbornly, covering every foot given up with their dead. The battle is spreading, and over there the guns of the Sixth Corps can be heard beating through the tangled thicket. Hancock, too, is coming up on the left, and Hill and Longstreet are marching to meet him. The rebels Heth, Wilcox, and Anderson are already in action, and soon the battle rages furiously. Men are shot down by unseen enemies, and the lines reel backward and forward like drunken men. The rebel Jones lies dead with his aids, and our gallant General Hays falls, pierced by a ball while leading his men in the thickest of the fight. The sun goes down in the west, and as darkness creeps over the earth, the noise of the combat dies way in the groans of the wounded and dying. Six thousand men, struck down by the missiles of war are stretched upon that battle-field. The grim chieftain sits upon his horse, surveying the scene, and as the knives of the surgeons begin to reek with the blood of the wounded, he says, "It is well; to-morrow we shall renew the attack," and then rides away to prepare for another day of blood. Yet his heart is heavy and sad, and while the tired soldiers sleep, he sits all night long in front of his tent awake, thinking of the morrow.

Slowly the gray mists are rising, and the red streamers in the east proclaim the morning. Already the cracking noise, like the breaking of dry sticks, tells us the skirmishers are at work in the woods, and at 5 o'clock loud crashes of musketry are heard. The smoke curls over the tree-tops in Getty's and Wadsworth's front, and now it spreads away to the right and left. The sun comes up in an unclouded sky, and a hundred thousand rebels are again on the move. Instantly the roar of battle runs along the lines. Assault after assault is made by the rebels, now upon this point and now upon that; but each is unavailing. Though the Union line at times bends before the storm and sways to and fro, and the ravines and hill-sides are crimsoned with blood and strewed with the dead, the Stars and Stripes gradually advance upon the infuriated foe. General Hancock drives a portion of the rebels more than two miles before him. On this day the noble General Wadsworth fell, and the whole nation mourned his loss. A bullet struck him on the head, and he dropped senseless, mortally wounded. There are few names which can stand so high upon the American roll of honor as that of James S. Wadsworth. Accursed be that rebellion which has thus robbed our nation of so many of the noblest of her sons!

Twice Hancock was driven back to his breastworks, and once the rebels had so far succeeded as to plant their colors on his field-works, but the stay was short. The conflict was now terrific. Such fighting as Hancock did that day, for bravery, could never have been surpassed. Back and forth —first charged and then charging—until hundreds of the dead bodies of Union and rebel soldiers lay side by side in their last sleep.

At last Burnside, with the Ninth Corps, came to his relief, when he was allowed a breathing spell. Later in the day, Sedgwick's hour of trial came. In the forenoon they made a desperate effort to turn Grant's left, and now, in the afternoon, they revived the effort on the extreme right. A. P. Hill was commanding the enemy, and two of the Union brigades, on the extreme right, commanded by Seymour and Staler, were swallowed up by the impetuous charge of the yelling rebels. They almost caused a route in this part of the army, but Sedgwick, bold and ever brave, took advantage of the reflux, which always follows the first impetus of a charge, and formed the corps and drove the enemy beyond his breastworks, and plucked safety, if not victory, out of danger.

The teamsters and straggling soldiers who had been watching this fearful conflict from a safe distance, just as night set in, commenced a stampede. This wild scene lasted about one hour and a half, when it was checked by the iron hand of military law.

All the day long the battle raged until darkness came. Our loss in killed, wounded, and missing was estimated at over ten thousand men. The rebel loss probably was not less. What imagination can gauge the dimensions of such a woe! The wail of agony or the cry of death which rose from that bloody field was reëchoed and intensified in twenty thousand distant homes.

In the morning the rebels were gone. Lee, in the night had retreated toward Spottsylvania Court-house. Grant, during the whole of the two days' fighting, had been on the battle-field. Most of the time he was on a piny knoll, with Meade, just in rear of Warren. Those who observed him during the actions were struck with his unpretending appearance and his imperturbable manner. Neither danger nor responsibility seemed to affect him; but he seemed, at times, lost in thought, and occasionally, on the receipt of information, would mount his horse and gallop off to the point where he was needed, to return with equal speed to his post of observation.

The pursuit was at once ordered, and Burnside and Sedgwick marched for Spottsylvania. On the morning of the 7th of May the fighting was renewed, and continued until the 13th. Friday, Warren's Fifth Corps was marching Southward, by the Brock road, followed by Hancock's second, through Todd's Tavern, and Burnside's ninth, by way of Piny Branch Church. The cavalry, under dashing Phil. Sheridan, had been fighting near Todd's Tavern, and was now riding on the heels of the beaten enemy.

It was Sunday, and the troops were drawn up in battle

array two miles north of Spottsylvania Court-house. They had marched fifteen miles since Saturday noon. The rebels had taken possession of intrenchments previously prepared, and were every moment adding to the strength of these earth-works. General Grant commenced a furious onset upon them, that they might not have time to add to their defenses, and to recover from the confusion of their retreat.

All the day long the roar of battle continued, until darkness enveloped the scene. Both parties fought with equal desperation. The Union soldiers, however, though with very severe loss, drove the rebels out of their first line of intrenchments, and took twenty-five hundred prisoners.

Another night came; and again these panting, bleeding armies threw themselves upon the ground for such repose as could be found amidst the dying and the dead. Both parties were in the extreme of exhaustion. For five days and nights they had been almost incessantly engaged in fighting or marching. But General Grant, the tireless leader of the patriot host, allowed his guilty foe no repose.

With the early light he opened upon the rebels a harassing fire from his batteries, while his skirmishers and sharpshooters annoyed them at every available point. General Sedgwick was in the front of the extreme right of his corps, with a few of his staff, superintending the posting of some guns. An occasional shot from a sharpshooter whistled, with elongated sound, about the group, causing some of the men to wince. The General joked them about their nervousness, saying, "Pooh, men, they can't hit an elephant at that distance." The words had scarcely passed his lips, when a ball pierced his face, just below the left eye, and with a serene smile, as if connected with his last words, he fell, the blood streaming from his nostrils. He died immediately, as he would have asked to die if he could have chosen the manner of his death.

It was now the afternoon of the 10th day of May, and the fifth day of the fighting. Colonel Upton, with the Second Brigade of the Sixth Corps, First Division, and D. A. Russell, with the Third Division had just made a memorable charge upon the enemy at Spottsylvania Court-house. The men sprang over the enemy's works, took upward of a thousand prisoners and several cannon, and only retired, being obliged to abandon the captured artillery, because they were so far in advance as to make the position perilous, and were not supported by Mott on their left. Mott, however, succeeded in forming connection with the Ninth Corps, which had now moved to the left from the Fredericksburg road.

Although the carnage had been so great as to make the losses on our side not far from ten thousand, and the rebels not much less, the battle was indecisive. Again had the rival generals divided each other's purposes, and terrible shocks had been the result. Thus ended the first day of the battle of Spottsylvania Court-house, and the troops rested on their arms, feeling sure that a struggle as desperate awaited them on the morrow, or, at least, at a very early time.

The morning of Wednesday, the 11th, rose bright and clear, and the closeness of contact of the two armies caused desultory fighting at many points, but no general engagement. We had lost very heavily, probably at least thirty-five thousand men, since the beginning of the campaign; but we had taken many prisoners, had inflicted terrible losses upon the enemy, and reënforcements were rapidly pushing forward to us—among the material of which, it is a significant fact that there were heavy artillery trains, designed for siege service at Richmond.

It was on the 11th that Grant sent to the War Department his celebrated dispatch:

"HEAD-QUARTERS IN THE FIELD, May 11, 1864—8 A. M.

"We have now ended the sixth day of very heavy fighting. The result, to this time, is much in our favor.

"Our losses have been heavy, as well as those of the enemy. I think the loss of the enemy must be greater.

"We have taken over five thousand prisoners by battle, while he has taken from us but few, except stragglers.

"I PROPOSE TO FIGHT IT OUT ON THIS LINE, IF IT TAKES ALL SUMMER.

"U. S. GRANT, *Lieutenant-General,*
"*Commanding the Armies of the United States.*"

Lee had sent a flag of truce, asking forty-eight hours' cessation of hostilities, that he might bury his dead. Grant had replied: "I have no time to bury my own dead, but propose an immediate advance." With this reply he pushed forward, his advanced lines shelling the woods, but no response was met from where the enemy's center had been a few hours before.

Certain now that victory was within his grasp, he ordered General Hancock to move during the night close up to the intrenchments, held by the rebel General Ewell's corps. Slowly and surely Hancock's men crept forward, and at dawn they were close upon the sleeping and unsuspecting enemy. At the proper moment the order to charge was given, and with a loud yell Hancock's men leaped over the rebel intrenchments, and with the butts of their muskets (the quarters were too close to fire) commenced to slay the enemy right and left. They were surrounded, cornered, and dumbfounded, and when they were commanded to surrender, they dropped their arms and became prisoners of war. Even the artillery had not time to limber up, get away, or fire one single volley. The General—E. Johnson

—whose head-quarters was somewhat to the rear, had no time to escape. In making this memorable and brilliant charge, the Union troops moved over a rugged and densely wooded space, but so silent and swift had been their advance that the rebels, who were at breakfast, knew nothing of their approach until they heard the cheers of the blue jackets, and rushed out only in time to see them climbing over their breastworks. The captures were Edward Johnson's entire division, with its general; two brigades of other troops, with their commander, Brigadier-General George H. Stuart; and thirty guns. The number of prisoners taken was between three and four thousand. It was the most decided success yet achieved during the campaign. When Hancock heard that these generals were taken, he directed that they should be brought to him. Offering his hand to Johnson, that officer was so affected as to shed tears, declaring that he would have preferred death to captivity. He then extended his hand to Stuart, whom he had known before, saying, "How are you Stuart?" but the rebel, with great haughtiness, replied, "I am General Stuart, of the Confederate army; and, under present circumstances, I decline to take your hand." Hancock's cool and dignified reply was: "And under any other circumstances, general, I should not have offered it."

Hancock dispatched Grant:

"I have captured from thirty to forty guns. I have finished up Johnson, and am now going into Early."

The great machinery of war, in Grant's hands, was now fairly at work. News came that Sherman was moving by the flank around Johnston at Dalton, and that the place was being evacuated. Butler was defeating the rebels on the south side of the James, and Sheridan, with his cavalry, was destroying the railroad bridge over the Chickahominy River, fighting battles with the rebel cavalry at Yellow

Tavern, and charging down Brock road to the enemy's works on that side of Richmond.

On the 13th of May, Burnside, with the Ninth Corps, lay across the pike leading from Spottsylvania Court-house to Fredericksburg, about two miles from the former place; here he had a severe engagement with A. P. Hill. Although Burnside moved early to the attack, he found the rebels over a mile in front of their works waiting for him; the fight commenced, and the rebels were soon pushed back into their first line of fortifications, and then forced to take refuge in their main line of intrenchments. Burnside renewed the attack in the afternoon, but a flanking brigade of rebels captured a portion of the Fifty-fifth Pennsylvania, One Hundred and Ninth New York, and the Seventeenth Michigan regiments. Burnside gained a better position than he had at the commencement of the fight, but with a loss of near three thousand men. The roads were very bad, and it was difficult to move, and little was done until Lee, weary and disheartened, showed signs of attempting a retreat. On the 18th, Grant renewed the attack; the assault was commenced early, but the rebels were not again to be found napping; by this move Grant soon discovered the enemy strongly posted behind breastworks. On the 19th, Ewell's corps made an attempt to turn Grant's right, but was severely punished by Birney and Tyler's divisions. Grant had now received about twenty-five thousand splendid fresh troops, forwarded to him to make up for his losses during the terrific battles on the Rapidan. On the 20th of May, he, by the flanking process, compelled Lee to abandon his strong works at Spottsylvania Court-house, the rebels retreating toward Richmond, Grant's army in pursuit. Falling behind the North Anna River, Lee took up another strong position; by marching the Fifth and Sixth Corps by way of Harris' Store to Jericho Ford, the Sixth Corps crossing, Lee was again flanked, and compelled to abandon his strong position on the North Anna, and fell back to the South Anna River. Here Lee's position was discovered to be one of great strength, and Grant deeming it only a waste of life to make an assault, recrossed the North Anna River, moving his army in the direction of Hanover Junction. Thus outgeneraling and flanking Lee's position on the South Anna, he forced him again to abandon his elaborately constructed fortifications. By these master strategic movements, it became evident to all the corps and division commanders in Grant's army that he had outmaneuvered Lee, and drove him from all his positions, using him merely as his mouth-piece, as he had previously used Bragg at Chattanooga. It could be seen by all that it was Grant, and not Lee, that was commanding the rebel army. General Sheridan, with his cavalry, had taken possession of the Hanover Ferry, and all points designated for bringing the army over the Pamunkey River, and by the 29th, Grant's entire force was across and encamped in a fertile country only fifteen miles from Richmond. By this great move he turned all Lee's works on the Little River and the South Anna, avoiding the hazard of crossing these strongly defended streams; by this strategy he became master of the situation with regard to his new base of supplies, and he was now left to choose his own route to the rebel capitol, and all this had been accomplished in twenty-four days from the day he struck tents at Culpepper Court-house, without leaving, as previous commanders did, one-fourth of his army behind for the defense of the capitol—he was now master of the peninsula without having uncovered Washington for a single hour.

During Grant's advance, a gentleman, who was a warm friend of the General, called upon him one morning, and found him in his tent talking to one of his staff officers.

"General," said the friend, "if you flank Lee, and get between him and Richmond, will you not uncover Washington, and leave it exposed to the enemy?" "Yes, I reckon so," was General Grant's taciturn and quiet reply. "Do you not think, General," the friend continued, "that Lee can detach sufficient force to reënforce Beauregard at Richmond, and overwhelm Butler?" "I have not a doubt of it," Grant replied. "And is there not danger," the friend added, "that Johnston may come up and reënforce Lee, so that the latter will swing round and cut off your communications and seize your supplies?" "Very likely," was the unconcerned reply. His friend looked at him in surprise, and anxiously inquired: "What, then, are you going to do?" "Beat them," was Grant's quiet response.

While conversing with several officers on the subject of the capture of Richmond, the question was asked: "Can it be taken?" "With ease," General Grant replied. "By the Peninsula?" the inquirer asked. "No," said the General. "I shall want two large armies—one to move directly on Lee; and the other to land at City Point, and cut communications to the southward. Lee would be then compelled to fall back; and the army from the north could press, and, if possible, defeat him.

"If he would open up communications again with the Cotton States, he must fight the army south of the James; and, to do this, he must cross his whole force—otherwise he would be defeated in detail. If he did so cross, the Northern army could take Richmond. If he did not, that from the south could move up to the heights south of the James, and shell and destroy the city."

Our losses, in the battles of the Wilderness, were about fifteen thousand men. Our losses from the 12th of May to the 21st, were as follows: Killed, one hundred and fourteen officers and two thousand and thirty-two enlisted men; wounded, two hundred and fifty-nine officers and seven thousand six hundred and ninety-seven men; missing, thirty-one officers and two hundred and forty-eight men; total, ten thousand three hundred and eighty-one. Our losses from the 21st to the 31st of May, were: Killed, twelve officers and one hundred and thirty-three enlisted men; wounded, sixty-seven officers and one thousand and sixty-three men; missing, three officers and three hundred and twenty-four men; total, one thousand six hundred and seven.

The month of June opened with the battle at Cold Harbor. On Thursday, June 2d, our line of battle extended from Cold Harbor to Bethesda Church. Hancock, on the left, occupied Cold Harbor; the Sixth Corps was on his right, and then, in order, the Eighteenth and Fifth, while Burnside, with the Ninth, had the extreme right at Bethesda Church.

On Friday, June 3d, a new movement was begun, at four o'clock in the morning, and resulted in one of the most terrible and hardly-contested battles of the war. Before making a new advance by the left flank, Grant determined again to try the strength of the enemy, and had issued orders that an assault should be made upon him along the whole line. At the specified time, all moved forward with varying fortune. Hancock, on our left, advanced, with the divisions of Gibbon and Barlow, up the slope in his front, which was swept by a terrible artillery fire. So vigorous was this attack, that the enemy was pushed out of his works, and thrown back upon his second line. But here he rallied, threw in a fearful enfilading fire upon our advance, and in turn drove it out in hot haste to seek shelter from the iron storm; but not so rapidly as not to take with it three hundred prisoners and one color. Not content with this, however, the enemy attacked our lines furiously again and again, but were repulsed.

Quite similar to this was the fortune of the attack made by our center, under Smith and Wright. They also carried the works in their front by a splendid charge, but were driven out by the enemy, and forced to throw up intrenchments near his works. As the enemy had massed heavily on our left and left center, the principal fighting was in front of these corps, and when it was found that we could not drive him from his intrenchments, offensive operations ceased at about eleven o'clock.

The fighting in front of Warren and Burnside was unimportant; but Burnside reported that he had carried an advanced line in his front. During the entire day the enemy made wild charges against our lines, which were never successful in breaking them.

On our extreme right, Wilson had been posted with the Third Cavalry Division, and there he came in contact with the cavalry of Wade Hampton, which he drove away. There, too, he fell upon an infantry brigade of Heth's division, which had been sent to envelop Burnside. He drove this force back, and took from it a number of prisoners.

It would require a volume faithfully to describe the varied events of this one battle, or rather this series of battles, in which three hundred thousand men, along a line several miles in extent, struggled in the deadly conflict, all day long, with almost superhuman energies. Clouds of cavalry swept over the plain. Batteries were lost and batteries were won. There were successful charges, and the cheer of victory rose over the thunderings of war's tempest. And there was the repulse when the shout of the victors faded away into the wail of death. Night came, and the battle ceased. The carnage on both sides had been severe. In counting up our losses, it appeared that seven thousand were numbered among the killed, the wounded, and the missing. Though we gained several important positions, and made a decided advance, it was evident that the rebels were so firmly intrenched that they could not be driven from their works, except at too great a sacrifice of the lives of our brave soldiers.

On Sunday morning, June 12th, Grant began to withdraw his army, and prepare to cross the James River, at Wilcox Wharf and Powhattan Point. By Sunday night, the troops were in position for crossing the James River in thirty hours, and in six hours more the entire army, with scarcely the loss of a man, was landed on the south side of the James River. On Wednesday, General Smith commenced an attack on Petersburg. Several efforts were made to carry the place by assault, but Grant was convinced that the Cockade City could only be captured by a protracted siege. General Wilson, with six thousand picked troops, was sent to destroy the Weldon and Southside railroads; the former was struck at Ream's Station, and the latter at Ford's Station, and some sixty miles of track, together with bridges, cars, and locomotives were destroyed. General Wright, with the Sixth Corps, coöperated with Wilson, by moving on the Weldon road below Petersburg, and destroying about five miles of track. Lee, becoming worried and disheartened, thought to divert Grant from his well-settled purpose, sent Breckinridge on a raid against Washington; but Grant could not be induced to withdraw his army from the James. Breckinridge went and made the feint, and was defeated, leaving 500 of his men killed and wounded under the guns of Fort Stephen.

Grant had begun the investment of Petersburg in earnest, and his wearied troops, for the first time in two months, got some rest. The fighting had been almost continuous, and over seventy thousand men and officers had been lost. Of officers alone, six hundred had been killed, more than two thousand wounded, and three hundred and fifty were missing. Brigades were commanded by majors and regiments by captains, all the senior officers having been killed, wounded, or captured. Reënforcements were pouring in upon him, but Grant felt he had reached that point where the siege should take the place of battles in the field.

The President had written General Grant to say:

"LIEUTENANT-GENERAL GRANT: Not expecting to see you before the spring campaign opens, I wish to express, in this, my entire satisfaction with what you have done up to this time, so far as I understand it. The particulars of your plans I neither know nor seek to know. You are vigilant and self-reliant; and, pleased with this, I wish not to obtrude any restraints or constraints upon you. While I am very anxious that any great disaster or capture of our men in great numbers shall be avoided, I know that these points are less likely to escape your attention than they would be mine. If there be any thing wanting which it is within my power to give, do not fail to let me know it.

"And now, with a brave army and a just cause, may God sustain you.

"Yours very truly,

"A. LINCOLN."

General Grant had immediately replied:

"THE PRESIDENT: Your very kind letter of yesterday is just received. The confidence you express for the future, and satisfaction for the past, in my military administration, is acknowledged with pride. It shall be my earnest endeavor that you and the country shall not be disappointed. From my first entrance into the volunteer service of the country to the present day, I have never had cause of complaint, have never expressed or implied complaint against the administration, or the Secretary of War, for throwing any embarrassment in the way of my vigorously prosecuting what appeared to be my duty.

"Indeed, since the promotion which placed me in command of all the armies, and in view of the great responsibility and importance of success, I have been astonished at the readiness with which every thing asked for has been yielded, without even an explanation being asked. Should my success be less than I desire and expect, the least I can say is, the fault is not with you.

"Very truly your obedient servant,

"U. S. Grant."

CHAPTER XV.

SIGEL RELIEVED—HUNTER IN THE VALLEY—BATTLE ON NORTH RIVER—BRILLIANT SUCCESS OF HUNTER—HIS DEFEAT NEAR LYNCHBURG—SHERIDAN AT DEEP BOTTOM—HE MARCHES TO WITHIN TWELVE MILES OF RICHMOND—COLONEL PLEASANTS' MINE—THE EXPLOSION—SUCCESS OF THE MINE—FAILURE OF THE TROOPS—FIGHTING IN THE CRATER—EARLY'S ADVANCE ON WASHINGTON—GREGG'S ATTACK ON THE WELDON RAILROAD—HEAVY FIGHTING—SHERIDAN IN THE VALLEY—BATTLE OF OPEQUAN—DEFEAT OF SHERIDAN'S FORCES BY EARLY—SHERIDAN'S RIDE—HE REGAINS THE BATTLE—GRANT'S PRAISE OF SHERIDAN—THE PRESIDENT'S LETTER TO HIM—HE IS MADE A MAJOR-GENERAL IN THE REGULAR ARMY—SHERMAN'S MARCH TO THE SEA.

GRANT was now drawing his lines around Petersburg. Sigel had been relieved in the Shenandoah Valley, and Hunter, who had been assigned in his place, was beating up the enemy's quarters at Piedmont. Grant wrote Halleck, May 20th:

"The enemy are evidently relying for supplies greatly on such as are brought over the branch road running through Staunton. On the whole, therefore, I think it would be better for General Hunter to move in that direction; reach *Staunton and Gordonsville*, if he does not meet too much opposition. If he can hold in it a force equal to his own, he will be doing good service."

Again, on the 25th, he writes Halleck: "If Hunter can possibly get to *Charlottesville and Lynchburg*, he should do so—living on the country. The railroads and canals should be destroyed beyond the possibility of repair for weeks. Completing this, he could find his way back to his original base, or, from about Gordonsville, join this army."

Hunter fought a battle with the rebel Jones on North River, in which he defeated Jones, and captured fifteen hundred prisoners, three cannon, and three hundred stand of arms. The battle lasted ten hours, and the rebel commander was left dead on the field. He pushed on through White Sulphur Springs to Gaston Depot, on the Virginia Railroad, which he destroyed. He then marched to Lynchburg, near which place he was defeated, and compelled to retreat to the Kanawha.

Meantime, Grant was pushing forward his works at Petersburg. On the 26th of June, he made a diversion by sending Sheridan, with part of the Second Corps, and two divisions of cavalry, across the James to Deep Bottom, to operate in conjunction with Butler's army and threaten the enemy. On the 28th, he extended his lines across to New Market and Long Bridge road. Lee, alarmed at these movements, sent large bodies of troops to meet Grant's detached forces, and some hard fighting took place.

On the 26th of July, Sheridan, who had crossed the Appottomax at Point of Rocks, pushed forward to the James, and crossed it at Jones' Neck. He then marched to within twelve miles of Richmond, where he found a rebel camp which he charged, scattering the rebels right and left, and capturing their intrenchments and cannon.

Colonel Pleasants, of the Forty-eighth Pennsylvania, had been at work for a month on a mine, which he completed on the 23d of July. This gallant and skillful officer had, without mining tools, in the face of all opposition and discouragements, persevered until he brought his mine to a successful conclusion. On the 30th, the troops were drawn up to see the mine explode. Burnside was in front of the work with orders to assault. Warren was on his left, and Ord on the right.

At half-past three o'clock in the morning, the match was applied, but the mine did not explode. Pleasants knew in a moment the difficulty. He had been obliged to use a spliced fuse, instead of a whole one, or, indeed, two or three fuses, and it had stopped burning at the splice. Two brave men of the regiment, who believed in the mine, and who had toiled at it night and day under Pleasants, volunteered for the dangerous service to go in and relight it. These were Lieutenant Jacob Douty, and Sergeant Harry Reese. They go along the gallery one hundred feet before they reach the point where the fire stopped. Again, at ten minutes before five, the insidious flame travels to its destined goal. Generals Grant and Meade are at the front. "It lacks a minute," said Pleasants. "Not a second," said Douty, "for there she goes!" A quiver, which becomes an earthquake tremor—and then, with a tremendous burst, a conical mountain rises in the air, streaked and seamed with lightning flashes. The vast mass is momentarily poised; and as it thus hangs in air, discloses timber, planking, earth, bodies, and limbs of men, and even one or two of the sixteen guns in the work. It is known that the work was occupied by portions of the Seventeenth, Eighteenth, and Twenty-second South Carolina regiments, under Colonel Fleming. Except the guard, the garrison was asleep. One instant of awakening, and then the crashing death. Rocks, timbers, earth, guns, and men were thrown, in a vast spreading column, one hundred and fifty feet into the air. These were all enveloped in heavy folds of billowy smoke, which, wrapped in its funeral pall, blended with the *débris*, the mangled forms of two hundred men.

For a moment there was a pause, as all eyes regarded the gigantic apparition. The next moment a hundred guns opened their roar, and in rapid fire hurled round-shot and shell in and upon the rebel works. For miles upon miles the resounding thunder rolled. As the vast column thrown into the air fell in wide-spread and indescribable ruin, an immense chasm appeared, several hundred feet long, fifty feet wide, and twenty feet deep.

Thus far the mine had been a triumphant success. For some cause, not easily explained, the charging column, after a delay of ten minutes—when seconds were of priceless value—rushed into the gap, and there halted, and commenced throwing up intrenchments. The important point to be gained was the crest of Cemetery Hill, four hundred yards beyond.

Ledlie still halted in the excavation. Wilcox and Potter soon followed him, and the three divisions became intermixed, and general confusion prevailed. An hour of precious time was lost. Ledlie made no attempt to move in or out, and Potter and Wilcox could not go forward while he blocked the way.

The delay was fatal. The rebels concentrated their fire on the crater where the troops were massed, and the place became a slaughter pen. The troops retreated as best they could, but our loss was very heavy. Killed, forty-seven officers, and three hundred and seventy-two enlisted men; wounded, one hundred and twenty-four officers, one thousand five hundred and fifty-five men; missing, ninety-one officers, one thousand eight hundred and nineteen men; total, four thousand and three.

Grant was greatly disappointed at the failure of the mine, but continued to push the siege with renewed vigor.

Lee had sent Early, with a corps to threaten Washington, and on the 10th of July, Early's cavalry advance was reported at Rockville. Grant had detached Wright, with a part of the Sixth Corps, and dispatched him to the defense of the National Capitol. On the 18th of August, Grant sent Gregg, with a division of cavalry, to seize and destroy the Weldon Railroad, in Lee's rear. Lee, hearing of the move, sent an overwhelming force to protect the road, which, coming to the ears of Grant, he in turn sent down the Fifth Corps to the support of Gregg. A desperate action took place, and the rebels were on the point of obtaining a victory, when the Ninth Corps came up and turned the tide in favor of the Union arms.

The battle was fought on Friday, and the next day, Saturday, the rebels were so exhausted they could not renew the contest, but having received large reënforcements, on Sunday morning they fiercely attacked our troops, but were repulsed. On Monday, the battle was begun again. Speaking of this day's action, Abbott says:

"Again their charging lines melted away before the awful storm of grape and canister belched from our ramparts. Tuesday, these desperate men, with renovated numbers, marched forth again to the assault; and again, torn and broken, they retreated, leaving the ground covered with their slain. We had gained the Weldon road, two and a half miles from Petersburg, and all the powers of rebeldom could not force General Grant to relinquish his hold. The loss of the road was a terrible calamity to General Lee. It cut off so important a line for supplies and recruits as to forebode the destruction of his army, Lee therefore resolved to make another attempt, with all his available strength, to regain the road. He concentrated an immense force, gathered from every point of his encampment from which troops could be spared, and massed them in heavy columns concealed in the forest.

"At a given signal they all rushed upon our lines, leaped over our breastworks, and engaged in a hand-to-hand fight.

The struggle on both sides was marked with a desperation which had not been surpassed during the war.

"The carnage was dreadful. Our troops fought desperately against these overpowering numbers. Though they lost two thousand prisoners, and a thousand in killed and wounded, they still held their position during the day. When night came, they fell back a few miles along the railroad to a still stronger position, where they could defy all the efforts of the enemy to dislodge them."

The loss of the Weldon Railroad was indeed a severe blow to Lee, but despite his efforts to regain it, our troops continued to hold it.

SHERIDAN IN THE VALLEY.

Grant, with that sagacity which always enabled him to put the right man in the right place, after the many failures in the Shenandoah, determined to send Sheridan to the command there. Grant himself says he never gave Sheridan any instructions but two words, "Go in." He asked Sheridan if he could go on Tuesday; Phil. replied, "yes, on Monday," and in fact was off before daylight.

On the 19th, he attacked Early at Opequan, and defeating him, drove him through Winchester. Sheridan wrote: "Fought Early all day, whipped him at five o'clock, and took five guns and about five thousand prisoners. Early is whirling up the Valley, leaving three thousand killed and wounded on the field. Fitzhugh Lee and two other of Early's generals killed and four reported wounded. Pushing vigorously." What a volume is contained in those six lines. Glorious, great, gallant little Phil. Sheridan, the Murat of America.

Early having failed, Lee sent Rosser to try his hand on Sheridan, but in the first fight, Rosser was attacked in front, flank, and rear, lost all his ambulances, caissons, supplies, and wagons, and went flying back to Richmond, while "the mad Union General" eat up Rosser's preserves and good things, and then marched to Cedar Creek, to devour Longstreet, who had been sent out to reënforce Early.

Rapidly crossing the mountains, Longstreet forded the North Fork, and creeping along the front of Crook's corps, aided by the darkness and fog, he drew up, unobserved, in battle array within a few hundred yards of our lines. Sheridan was absent and the rebels knew it.

Springing upon our lines with the yells of demons, our sleeping troops were cut to pieces, and, bewildered, fled, leaving guns, tents, and wagons in the hands of the enemy. It was a brilliant feat, skillfully conceived and daringly executed. But the master mind was not there, else it had been different. Sheridan was at Winchester, twenty miles away, but hearing the faint booming of his cannon, he sprang upon his horse and rode away like the wind in the direction of the ominous sound. A courier met him to tell him all was lost, but burying the rowels in the flanks of his panting steed, and lashing his withers with the reins, he rode madly on. Presently he met a mass of defeated soldiers, coatless, hatless, shoeless, running down the road. "Halt!" shouted Sheridan; "face the other way, boys, we are going back." The sight of that horseman, swinging his hat around his head, put new courage into the defeated men. Long and loud rose the cry, "Sheridan is here! Sheridan has come!" and as the thousands heard that magic name, they halted, loaded their guns, and faced to the foe. The army was in confusion. It had lost confidence in itself. But the presence of Sheridan inspired all with a new hope. The change was like magic.

Pushing forward past the stragglers, who at once began to rally, he reached the main body, repeating his fiery words. "Boys," he added, "if I had been here, this never should have happened; we are going back." Arranging and strengthening his lines while the enemy had, most of them, stopped for a time to plunder our camps, he was just in readiness to move forward, when the rebels came in for a new and overwhelming assault. Resisting this manfully, he caught its surge, and hurled it back; assumed the offensive; attacked again in two columns; employed his cavalry in vigorous charges on both flanks; succeeded, with Custer's division, in turning their left and rolling it up, and again routed them. Thus he snatched victory out of the jaws of defeat. And all this—no one can gainsay it—was due to the brilliant genius and personal *élan* of Sheridan himself. The slaughter of the enemy was great. We captured almost every thing they had, including the guns and camps which we had lost in the morning. Sheridan was every-where to be seen urging his men to press on after the retreating foe, which had become a rout. The rebels being chased through the streets of Middletown, and on to Mount Jackson, over two thousand broke and ran down the mountain, throwing away arms, knapsacks, and blankets to aid in securing safety. The rebel loss was about three thousand killed, seven thousand prisoners, many of them wounded, fifty-five cannon, a great number of small arms, ten battle-flags, and over three hundred wagons and ambulances. The Union officers suffered severely, in one of General Grover's brigades, every field officer being killed or disabled; in another only three were left. The Union loss in killed, wounded, and missing was four thousand and eighty-six.

No one was more gratified than Grant, who, as soon as he heard the news, telegraphed to the Secretary of War these words:

"I had a salute of one hundred guns fired from each of the armies here, in honor of Sheridan's last victory.

Turning what bid fair to be a disaster into a glorious victory, *stamps Sheridan, what I have always thought him, one of the ablest of generals.*

"U. S. GRANT, *Lieutenant-General.*"

The President wrote to Sheridan:

"EXECUTIVE MANSION, WASHINGTON, Oct. 22, 1864.

"MAJOR-GENERAL SHERIDAN: With great pleasure I tender to you and your brave army the thanks of the nation, and my own personal admiration and gratitude for the month's operations in the Shenandoah Valley, and especially for the splendid work of October 19th.

"Your obedient servant,

"ABRAHAM LINCOLN."

The resignation of George B. McClellan having been accepted, the President ordered:

"That for personal gallantry, military skill, and just confidence in the courage and patriotism of his troops, displayed by Philip H. Sheridan on the 19th of October, at Cedar Run, whereby, under the blessing of Providence, his routed army was reorganized, a great national disaster averted, and a brilliant victory achieved over the rebels for the third time in pitched battle within thirty days, Philip H. Sheridan is appointed major-general in the United States Army, to rank as such from the 8th day of November, 1864."

The enemy now abandoned the Shenandoah Valley, and Grant withdrew the Sixth Corps. It is a pleasure to linger over the deeds of Sheridan, for of all the brilliant men produced by this war, none can compete in personal daring with glorious Phil. Sheridan.

Sherman, with sixty thousand men and three thousand

wagons, had swept across the Confederacy. His trail was sixty miles wide and three hundred long.

The destruction was awful. The army marched the whole distance in twenty-four days. In the entire command, but five hundred and sixty-seven men of all ranks were either killed or wounded. Ten thousand negroes, liberating themselves, entered Savannah in the train of the army. Thirteen hundred and thirty-eight of the Confederate army were made prisoners. Twenty thousand bales of cotton were burned, beside twenty-five thousand captured at Savannah. Thirteen thousand head of beef-cattle, nine million five hundred thousand pounds of corn, and ten million five hundred thousand pounds of fodder were taken from the country. Foragers were every day sent out, along the whole line of route, to gather all the sheep, hogs, turkeys, geese, chickens, sweet potatoes, and rice from the plantations. Five thousand horses and four thousand mules were impressed for the cavalry and trains. Three hundred and twenty miles of railway were destroyed, by burning every tie, twisting every rail while heated red hot over the flaming piles of the ties, and laying in ruins every depot, engine-house, repair-tank, water-tank, and turn-table. Thus the communication between the Confederate armies in Virginia and in the West was effectually severed. General Sherman estimated the damage done to the State of Georgia at a hundred million dollars. Of this, twenty million dollars inured to our advantage. The remainder was simple waste and destruction. Such is war.

Grant, who knew all about Sherman's campaign, was only waiting for him to reach the right place, and then the order to assault Lee would be given. A good many have claimed the exclusive honor of the march to the sea for Sherman, but it was only a part of the great whole of which Grant was the head.

Sherman himself said, in a speech made after the close of the war at Louisville:

"While we are here together to-night, let me tell you, as a point of historical interest, that here, upon this spot, in this very hotel, and, I think, almost in the room through which I reached this balcony, General Grant and I laid down our maps and studied the campaign which ended the war. I had been away down in Mississippi, finishing up an unfinished job I had done there, when General Grant called for me, by telegraph, to meet him in Nashville. But we were bothered so much there that we came up here, and in this hotel sat down with our maps, and talked over the lines and the operations by means of which we were to reach the heart of our enemy. He went to Richmond, and I to Atlanta. The result was just as we laid it out in this hotel, in March, 1864."

CHAPTER XVI.

THE SITUATION—BEGINNING OF THE END—ANECDOTES OF GRANT—SHERIDAN LOOSE AGAIN—INTERVIEW BETWEEN LINCOLN, GRANT, MEADE, SHERIDAN, AND SHERMAN—ADVANCE OF THE FIFTH CORPS—SHERIDAN AT FIVE FORKS—CAPTURE OF PETERSBURG—ADVANCE OF THE ARMY—THE FIGHTING—FALL OF RICHMOND—THE REBEL RAMS BLOWN UP—CORRESPONDENCE BETWEEN GRANT AND LEE—SHERIDAN AT THE APPOMATTOX—INTERVIEW BETWEEN GRANT AND LEE—TERMS OF SURRENDER PROPOSED—LEE SURRENDERS HIS ARMY—SCENES OF THE SURRENDER—FORM OF PAROLE—NUMBER OF PRISONERS TAKEN BY GRANT—SHERMAN'S MOVEMENTS—THE END—THE MARCH HOMEWARD—REVIEW AT WASHINGTON—GRANT TAKES LEAVE OF HIS ARMY—GRANT AT HOME.

THE sagacious Grant now saw the rebellion drawing to a close, and was doubling for his final spring upon it. This was the situation: Sherman at Savannah, Hood's army defeated, and General Price driven out of Missouri, Early used up by Sheridan in the Shenandoah, Breckinridge checkmated in East Tennessee, Canby operating effectually in Louisiana, and preparing to capture Mobile, and Grant at Richmond holding Lee in a vice from which there was no escape.

Grant was drawing his lines close about Petersburg, but the public, thrilled with the brilliant operations of Sherman and Sheridan, were impatient for him to attack Lee. Even some of Grant's generals were grumbling at his delay. An anecdote is told of Grant, which is worth relating in this connection. When General Grant went to the army of the Potomac, he knew that a good deal of jealousy existed between the different generals, and that one cause of the repeated failures of that army was the jealousy of subordinates toward former commanding generals. Determined to obviate this, if possible, he gave each general his orders without consulting the others. One day, having occasion to make an important move, he called several of the generals together at his head-quarters. Of course each one came prepared to debate the several propositions submitted, but imagine their surprise when the general did not ask their opinion on a single point. After talking pleasantly to them for some time about the weather, the crops, troops, and other common-place matters, the general took from his table a well-marked map and said, "Gentlemen, I wish to make an important movement, and will show you the route you are to march." He then pointed out and explained minutely what he wanted done. Folding up the map, Grant drew from a drawer in his desk several sealed envelopes, and handing one to each of the generals said, "Here are your orders, and maps of your route as explained to you; be sure, gentlemen, and be on time." Then getting up, he lit his cigar and put on his hat, as much as to say, "it is unnecessary to talk further about the matter." The generals departed, and as two of them were mounting their horses to ride away, one said, laughingly to the other, "Egad, we have got our master at last, and there is nothing left for us to do but obey orders."

One day during the Petersburg campaign, as Grant was walking along the river bank, he saw several private soldiers who were engaged in unloading from a transport what they called "salt horse." The soldiers were in charge of a lieutenant of a New York regiment, who took every occasion to show his authority. To one of his abusive remarks one of the privates made reply, whereupon the lieutenant administered severe kicks to the offender, who offered no resistance, but continued on with his work. Grant, who was a short, thick set man, and wore a slouched hat and rather seedy officer's cloak, had been standing for some time watching the operations going on, and when he saw the officer strike the soldier, he threw off his cloak and coat, and proceeded to help unload the transport. After the task was accomplished, he donned his coat and cloak, and asked the lieutenant, in very civil terms, his name and regiment. "Lieutenant — of the — New York Volunteers. By what authority do you dare ask such a question?" "Report yourself immediately to your colonel under arrest, by order of General Grant, for cruelty to your men; and remember that abuse of privates by officers is not tolerated by the present commander of this army," replied the "thick-set" officer, lighting a cigar, and walking slowly away.

The end had now come. Sherman's columns had united at Goldsboro', and he was moving majestically on, driving the rebels before him. Hood, crippled and bleeding, was creeping away from Thomas, and Canby was marching on Mobile. Grant, sending orders to Thomas to push out his cavalry after the rebels, and sending another expedition into the Confederacy from Vicksburg, ordered Sheridan to cut through the Confederacy in Virginia, while he himself prepared to assault Lee.

Like a thunderbolt Sheridan fell upon Early in his fortified camp at Waynesboro', overturned him, capturing sixteen hundred prisoners, eleven guns, and two hundred wagons, with seventeen battle-flags, after which he marched to Charlottesville, New Market, and from thence to White House, where he communicated with Grant.

On the 29th of March, 1865, Ord was at Hatcher's Run, with two divisions under Gibbon, one under Burney, and McKenzie's cavalry.

On the 28th Sheridan had marched for Dinwiddie Court-house with five thousand men under Merritt, and three thousand under Crook. On the 29th, at 5 o'clock, he arrived at the Court-house and received the following instructions from Grant:

"GRAVELLY RUN, March 29, 1865.

"GENERAL: Our line is now unbroken from the Appomattox to Dinwiddie. We are all ready, however, to give up all from the Jerusalem plank road to Hatcher's Run, whenever the forces can be used advantageously. After getting into line south of Hatcher's, we pushed forward to find the enemy's position. General Griffin was attacked near where the Quaker road intersects the Boydton road, but repulsed it easily, capturing about one hundred men. Humphreys reached Dabney's mill, and was pushing on when last heard from.

"I now feel like ending the matter, if it is possible to do so, before going back. I do not want you, therefore, to cut loose and go after the enemy's roads at present. In the morning, push round the enemy if you can, and get on to his right rear. The movements of the enemy's cavalry may, of course, modify your action. We will act all together as one army here, until it is seen what can be done with the enemy. The signal officer at Cobb's Hill reported at 11:30 A. M., that a cavalry column had passed that point from Richmond toward Petersburg, taking forty minutes to pass.

"U. S. GRANT, *Lieutenant-General.*

"MAJOR-GENERAL P. H. SHERIDAN."

On the day before, General Sherman had arrived at Grant's head-quarters, where Mr. Lincoln also was. An eye-witness gives the following account of the interview between the illustrious men there assembled:

"I was sitting in the office of General Grant's adjutant-general, on the morning of the 28th of March, and saw

President Lincoln, with Generals Grant, Sherman, Meade, and Sheridan, coming up the walk. Look at the men whose names are to have a conspicuous place in the annals of America: Lincoln—tall, round-shouldered, loose-jointed, large-featured, deep-eyed, with a smile upon his face; he is dressed in deep black, and wears a fashionable silk hat. Grant is at Lincoln's right, shorter, stouter, more compact; wears a military hat, with a stiff, broad brim; has his hands in his pantaloons pocket, and is puffing away at a cigar, while listening to Sherman. Sherman—tall, with high, commanding forehead, is almost as loosely built as Lincoln; has sandy whiskers, closely cropped, and sharp, twinkling eyes, long arms and legs, shabby coat, slouch hat, his pants tucked into his boots. He is talking hurriedly, gesticulating now to Lincoln, now to Grant, his eyes wandering everywhere. Meade—also tall, with thin, sharp features, a gray beard, and spectacles; is a little stooping in his gait. Sheridan—the shortest of all, quick and energetic in all his movements, with a face bronzed by sun and wind; courteous, affable, a thorough soldier. The plan of the lieutenant-general was then made known to his subordinates, and each departed, during the day, to carry into execution the respective parts assigned them."

"Meantime the Second Corps had left their intrenchments near Hatcher's Run, and advanced out along the Vaughn road. The Fifth Corps, which had been stationed in the rear of the Second, at three and a half o'clock A. M., started, going over by-roads across the country, so as to reach the Vaughn road at a point beyond where the Second Corps was to march. Up to this time, General Ayer's division taking the lead, one brigade under General Gwin was posted at Scott's House to cover the Vaughn road, while the remainder of the division was held in reserve. Griffin's division was then placed in advance.

The column now left the Vaughn road, at a point distant about four miles from Dinwiddie Court-house, and advanced up the Quaker road in the direction of Boydton plank road, some three miles distant. A short distance from here the troops found a line of abandoned rebel breastworks, from which their pickets had just retired. Skirmishers were now thrown forward, and sharp firing commenced; the skirmishers crossing an open plateau, the further side of which Bushrod Johnson's rebel divisions were posted. The first brigade of Griffin's division was now ordered forward to support the skirmishers, and when within rifle-shot of the woods, a tremendous volley of musketry greeted their advance, causing them to waver and fall back. The Second Brigade now came up to the support of the first, which caused the latter to rally and stand firm. In the meantime, battery B, of the First United States, was got into position and commenced firing with effect. While the fight was in progress, General Warren was engaged in forming his line of battle on the right and left of the Quaker road. The enemy, seeing that a large force was being moved against them, retired to a point further back. Sheridan was on the extreme left at Dinwiddie Court-house; Mead's head-quarters were on the Vaughn road, three miles beyond Hatcher's Run, and General Grant's about a mile further out.

With an impetuosity that could not be resisted, Sheridan rushed forward and seized the Five Forks, but the enemy had made head against Warren, and were now driving back the Fifth Corps. Sheridan's position was perilous in the extreme, but he fought desperately, retiring slowly toward Dinwiddie Court-house. Humphreys now advanced, driving the enemy before him to Burgess' Mill, and Ord and Wright were preparing to go in. Grant, anxious for Sheridan's safety, sent the Fifth Corps to report to him, but it came up so slowly, the impatient soldier censured its commander, General Warren.

Sunday, April 2d, at four o'clock, A. M., the time for action had now come. General Parke, in front of Petersburg, was pressing close up to the town. His divisions were: Wilcox on the right, resting on the Appomattox; Hartranft in the center; Potter, with the Second Division, was on the left, joining Wheaton, of the Sixth Corps. The plan was for Wilcox to make a feint upon the rebel front on the Appomattox. It was promptly and vigorously made, the men creeping up to within a few feet of the rebel fort. At the word of command, the gallant First Division sprang to its feet, and, with a yell, rushed on the work. At a quarter past four o'clock they were in the fort, having captured the garrison of fifty men and four guns. This was the feint of Wilcox. Hartranft and Potter advanced about the same time, and in the same manner, stealing up under cover of darkness, they, without firing a gun, sprang forward, capturing four forts, twenty-seven guns, and hundreds of prisoners. Thus at daylight Parke, without loss, had gained possession of the rebel lines in his front. The Sixth Corps had simultaneously begun their work. Wheaton on the right, Seymour in the center, and Getty on the left, joining at Fort Sampson the new line of the Twenty-fourth Corps, with Foster's division on the right. Wright's corps had to sustain a volley in their advance, but they carried the rebel line, and not five minutes elapsed from the time Wright gave the signal to storm, before Generals Seymour, Wheaton, and Getty were over the line and in possession of all the rebel guns. All the regiments did their duty. In the first charge Wheaton took twelve pieces of artillery, and nearly the entire Mississippi brigade of Heth's division; thus, by five o'clock, the rebels were driven from all their outer works on the south and west of

Petersburg. At seven o'clock, the Second and Twenty-fourth Corps began the work assigned them. Turner and Foster, of the Twenty-fourth Corps, made the assault and carried the rifle lines with little loss, while the Second Corps advanced immediately on the opposite side of Hatcher's Run. The advance of this corps was a gradual ascent all the way. Colonel Olmstead and Colonel McIvor, of the First and Second Brigades, rushed into the two forts before them, capturing five guns and a large number of prisoners, with the loss of only ten men. The Nineteenth Massachusetts and the Seventh Michigan, the far East and far West, join hands this Sunday morning in the "last ditch" of the rebellion. Other forts were taken by New York, Pennsylvania, and New Jersey troops. Thus, by eight o'clock, the entire rebel line, from the Appomattox to Burgess' Mill, had every-where been broken, and the Sixth Corps had swung round and was facing Petersburg from the west. The Twenty-fourth Corps was marching from Hatcher's Run east inside the rebel line, and the Second Corps in the same direction on the Boydton road. Every soldier looked as if he understood the mighty events taking place. The smile of triumph was on every lip, the sparkle of joy in every eye.

General Grant, having left his head-quarters at Dabney Mills to overlook the work yet to be done, came riding along the lines on a trot, cheer upon cheer every-where saluted him, and nothing ever equaled the enthusiasm. The military genius of Napoleon in his Italian campaigns was growing dim before the splendor of the great American general. Few things in the annals of war can compete with the genius displayed by Grant in his final operations around Richmond. Sheridan had done splendid work in front of Dinwiddie Court-house. As soon as the Fifth Corps got up, he assaulted the enemy again in front of

Ayres', Crawford's, and Griffin's divisions, while Merritt and McKenzie, with their cavalry, fell upon the rebel's right flank.

The enemy were driven from their strong line of works and completely routed, the Fifth Corps doubling up their left flank in confusion, and the cavalry of General Merritt dashing on to the White Oak road, capturing their artillery and turning it upon them, and riding into their broken ranks, so demoralized them, that they made no serious stand after their line was carried, but took to flight in disorder.

Between five thousand and six thousand prisoners fell into our hands, and the fugitives were driven westward, and were pursued till long after dark by Merritt's and McKenzie's cavalry, for a distance of six miles.

During the fighting of the Fifth Corps, the Second and Third Divisions were driven back in confusion. General Griffin rode up to General J. Lawrence Chamberlain, and said:

"General, the Fifth Corps is disgraced. I have told General Warren that you can retake that field. Will you save the honor of the corps?"

It was an appalling undertaking. With one brigade, already exhausted by hard fighting, and weakened by severe loss, General Chamberlain was to attack the foe flushed with victory. He formed his lines, dashed through the stream, and drove the enemy back for more than a mile to the edge of a hill. Here, as the enemy appeared in greater force, he was ordered to halt, that the strength and position of the foe might be ascertained. But he begged permission to press on, asking only for several regiments to support his flanks *en èchelon.* He then, upon the double-quick, swept the field, and gained a lodgment on the White Oak road, which enabled the Fifth Corps to render essential service in cutting off the retreat of Lee.

The night of the 2d of April was one of consternation and terror in Richmond. The people had been lulled by the long years of security, and deceived by their leaders. No intelligent man doubted the result, but the hoodwinked populace still believed that Richmond was impregnable, and would never be evacuated. Their eyes were now suddenly opened. Without warning, it was now announced, while Jeff. Davis was in church (for it was Sunday), that the army was evacuating the city, and that the "Federals" would enter at once. Lee, who had long before seen the folly of continuing the struggle, had been overruled by Jeff. Davis; but now there was no choice. The army left that night, in frantic haste, to move by the Danville road, and form a junction with Johnston. But it was too late.

On the 3d, Sheridan followed with cavalry, striking for Danville, to head off Lee's retreat. On the same day, General Weitzel entered Richmond at eight and a quarter o'clock in the morning.

Thus the great capital of treason and rebellion, which had defied the Union army for four years, fell. Richmond and Petersburg were now captured, hundreds of guns and thousands of prisoners taken, Lee's army demoralized, shattered, broken, and driven to the four winds. This is the history of the day. How can it be told? what pen can write it? or who comprehend the magnitude of the issues decided by this mighty event? Two hundred and forty-five years ago, on this very spot, our traffic in human flesh began. During this long period the earnest prayers and agonizing groans of an outraged people had been ascending to the throne of God. They have not been in vain. Let it forever be remembered that Washington gave us a country, but this day's victory made it free.

On the night of the 2d, the rebel rams Virginia and Rappahannock, which were lying in the James River near

Howlett House, had been blown up about midnight, shaking the earth like a volcano, and strewing the river for miles with the wrecks.

On the 5th, Grant, feeling that the war in Virginia was nearly over, wrote Sherman:

"WILSON'S STATION, April 5, 1865.

"GENERAL: All indications now are that Lee will attempt to reach Danville with the remnant of his force. Sheridan, who was up with him last night, reports all that is left—horse, foot, and dragoons—at twenty thousand, much demoralized. We hope to reduce this number one-half. I shall push on to Burkesville, and if a stand is made at Danville, will in a few days go there. If you can possibly do so, push on from where you are, and let us see if we can not finish the job with Lee's and Johnston's armies. Whether it will be better for you to strike for Greensboro', or nearer to Danville, you will be better able to judge when you receive this. Rebel armies now are the only strategic points to strike at.

"U. S. GRANT, *Lieutenant-General.*

"MAJOR-GENERAL W. T. SHERMAN."

On the 6th, Sheridan struck the rebels south of Sailors' Creek, near the Appomattox, and fought a battle, capturing sixteen guns, four hundred wagons, and delaying the enemy until the Sixth Corps could come up, when a combined attack was made, and seven thousand prisoners, including several generals, were taken. On the 7th, the pursuit was continued by both infantry and cavalry, and so close were our forces on the heels of the rebels, that they were unable to destroy the bridges behind them. In the evening of this day, Grant being prepared to strike, and feeling confident it would be useless for Lee to further resist, sent him the following note:

"April 7th, 1865.

"The result of the last week must convince you of the hopelessness of further resistance, on the part of the Army of Northern Virginia in this struggle. I feel that it is so, and regard it as my duty to shift from myself the responsibility of any further effusion of blood, by asking of you the surrender of that portion of the Confederate States Army known as the Army of Northern Virginia.

"U. S. Grant, *Lieutenant-General.*

"General R. E. Lee."

On the 8th, Grant, who was then at Farmville, received the following reply from General Lee:

"April 7th, 1865.

"General: I have just received your note of this date. Though not entertaining the opinion you express of the hopelessness of further resistance on the part of the Army of Northern Virginia, I reciprocate your desire to avoid useless effusion of blood; and, therefore, before considering your proposition, ask the terms you will offer on condition of its surrender.

"R. E. Lee, *General.*

"Lieutenant-General U. S. Grant."

To this, Grant replied:

"April 8th, 1865.

"General: Your note of last evening in reply to mine of the same date, asking the condition on which I will accept the surrender of the Army of Northern Virginia is just received. In reply I would say, that, peace being my first desire, there is but one condition I insist upon; namely, that the men surrendered shall be disqualified for taking up arms against the Government of the United States, until properly exchanged. I will meet you, or will designate officers to meet any officers you may name for the same purpose, at any point agreeable to you, for the purpose of arranging definitely the terms upon which the surrender of the Army of Northern Virginia will be received.

"U. S. GRANT, *Lieutenant-General.*

"GENERAL R. E. LEE."

Meanwhile, the pursuit was being continued. The infantry were pushing with all haste for Appomattox Station, and on the afternoon of the 8th, Sheridan struck the Appomattox Railroad, whipped the enemy, and captured twenty-five guns and four trains of cars.

The same day, Lee wrote to Grant:

"APRIL 8th, 1865.

"GENERAL: I received, at a late hour, your note of to-day. In mine of yesterday, I did not intend to propose the surrender of the Army of Northern Virginia, but to ask the terms of your proposition. To be frank, I do not think the emergency has arisen to call for the surrender of this army; but as the restoration of peace should be the sole object of all, I desired to know whether your proposals would lead to that end. I can not, therefore, meet you with a view to surrender the Army of Northern Virginia; but so far as your proposal may affect the Confederate State forces under my command, and tend to the restoration of peace, I should be pleased to meet you at 10 A. M. to-morrow, on the old stage road to Richmond, between the picket lines of the two armies.

"R. E. LEE, *General.*

"LIEUTENANT-GENERAL U. S. GRANT."

Grant next day replied:

"April 9th, 1865.

"General: Your note of yesterday is received. I have no authority to treat on the subject of peace; the meeting proposed for 10 A. M. to-day, could lead to no good. I will state, however, General, that I am equally anxious for peace with yourself, and the whole North entertains the same feeling. The terms upon which peace can be had are well understood. By the South laying down their arms they will hasten that most desirable event, save thousands of human lives, and hundreds of millions of property not yet destroyed. Sincerely hoping that all our difficulties may be settled without the loss of another life,

"I subscribe myself, etc.,

"U. S. Grant, *Lieutenant-General.*

"General R. E. Lee."

Lee at once wrote Grant:

"April 9th, 1865.

"General: I received your note of this morning, on the picket line, whither I had come to meet you, and ascertain definitely what terms were embraced in your proposal of yesterday, with reference to the surrender of this army. I now ask an interview in accordance with the offer contained in your letter of yesterday, for that purpose.

"R. E. Lee, *General.*

"Lieutenant-General U. S. Grant."

The two great captains, accompanied each by three officers, met in the road between the lines near the house of Mr. W. McLean. After shaking hands, the two Generals entered the house and the following terms of surrender were agreed upon. Grant wrote:

"I propose to receive the surrender of the Army of

Northern Virginia on the following terms—to wit: Rolls of all the officers and men to be made in duplicate, one copy to be given to an officer to be designated by me, the other to be retained by such officer or officers as you may designate. The officers to give their individual paroles not to take up arms against the Government of the United States until properly exchanged; and each company, or regimental commander, to sign a like parole for the men of their commands. The arms, artillery, and public property, to be packed and turned over to the officers appointed by me to receive them. This will not embrace the side-arms of the officers, nor their private horses or baggage. This done, each officer and man will be allowed to return to his home, not to be disturbed by the United States authority, so long as they observe their paroles, and the laws in force where they may reside.

[SIGNED.] "U. S. GRANT, *Lieutenant-General.*"

To this, Lee wrote: "The terms are accepted. I will proceed to designate the proper officers to carry the stipulations into effect.

"R. E. LEE, *General.*"

It was over. Nothing could exceed the joy of the troops and chagrin of the rebels. A rebel gives the following account of the scenes then transpiring in the rebel army:

"As General Lee was seen riding to the rear, dressed more gayly than usual, and begirt with his sword, the rumor of immediate surrender flew like wildfire through the Confederates. It might be imagined that an army, which had drawn its last regular rations on the first of April, and harassed incessantly by night and day, had been marching and fighting until the morning of the 9th, would have welcomed any thing like a termination of its sufferings, let it come in what form it might. Let those who idly imagine that the finer feelings are the prerogative of what are called the 'upper classes,' learn from this and similar scenes to appreciate 'common men.' As the great Confederate captain rode back from his interview with General Grant, the news of the surrender acquired shape and consistency, and could no longer be denied. The effect on the worn and battered troops—some of whom had fought since April, 1861, and (sparse survivors of hecatombs of fallen comrades) had passed unscathed through such hurricanes of shot, as within four years no other men had ever experienced—passes mortal description.

"Whole lines of battle rushed up to their beloved old chief, and choking with emotion, broke ranks and struggled with each other to wring him once more by the hand. Men who had fought throughout the war, and knew what the agony and humility of that moment must be to him, strove, with a refinement of unselfishness and tenderness which he alone could fully appreciate, to lighten his burden and mitigate his pain. With tears pouring down both cheeks, General Lee at length commanded voice enough to say, 'Men, we have fought through the war together. I have done the best that I could for you.' Not an eye that looked on that scene was dry. Nor was this the emotion of sickly sentimentalists, but of rough and rugged men, familiar with hardships, danger, and death in a thousand shapes, mastered by sympathy and feeling for another which they never experienced on their own account. I know of no other passage of military history so touching, unless, in spite of the melo-dramatic coloring which French historians have loved to shed over the scene, it can be found in the Adieu de Fontainebleau.

"It remains for me briefly to notice the last parade of an army, whereof the exploits will be read with pride so long as the English tongue is spoken. In pursuance of an arrangement of the six commissioners, the Confederate army marched by divisions, on the morning of April the 12th, to a spot at the Appomattox Court-house, where they stacked arms and deposited accouterments. Upon this solemn occasion Major-General Gibbon represented the United States authorities. With the same exalted and conspicuous delicacy which he had exhibited throughout the closing scenes, General Grant was not again visible after his final interview with General Lee. About seven thousand eight hundred Confederates marched with their muskets in their hands, and were followed by about eighteen thousand unarmed stragglers, who claimed to be included in the capitulation. Each Confederate soldier was furnished with printed form of parole, which was filled up for him by his own officer, and a duplicate handed to a distinguished Federal officer. By the evening of the 12th, the paroles were generally distributed, and the disbanded men began to scatter throughout the country. Hardly one of them had a farthing of money. Some of them had from fifteen hundred to two thousand miles to travel, over a country of which the scanty railroads were utterly annihilated."

When the first moments of their grief were over, and the rebels remembered that they would now soon be enabled to revisit their homes and friends, they rejoiced that the end had come. The main body of Lee's army was drawn up in a plain, surrounded by hills which were held by our troops, and from which there was no escape. The Union troops were ready to open fire on the rebels, when they were astounded by the outbursts of cheer upon cheer from the exhausted, bleeding, despairing enemy. They had first received the tidings of the capitulation, and their joyful shouts conveyed the glad news to our army. The cheer was echoed back, and the voices of friend and foe blended in that joyful cry. The Union troops, who were pressing along in the rear, caught the shout, learned its significance, and passed it along their ranks in thunder roar. For miles the hills and forests rang with the acclaim of that grand patriot army, rejoicing that the spirit of rebellion was now trampled down forever.

In the battles around Petersburg and in the pursuit, Lee lost over ten thousand men killed and wounded, and twenty thousand men in prisoners and deserters, including those taken in battle, and those picked up in pursuit; embracing all arms of the service—teamsters, hospital force, and every thing—from sixteen to eighteen thousand men were surrendered by Lee. As only fifteen thousand muskets and about thirty pieces of artillery were surrendered, the available fighting force could hardly have exceeded fifteen or twenty thousand men. Our total captures of artillery during the battles and pursuit, and at the surrender, amounted to about one hundred and seventy guns. Three or four hundred wagons were handed over.

In the terms of surrender, the officers gave their own paroles, and each officer gave his parole for the men within his command. The following is the form of the personal parole of officers:

"We, the undersigned prisoners of war belonging to the Army of Northern Virginia, having been this day surrendered by General R. E. Lee, commanding said army, to Lieutenant-General U. S. Grant, commanding the armies of the United States, do hereby give our solemn parole of honor that we will not hereafter serve in the armies of the Confederate States, or in any military capacity whatever, against the United States of America, or render aid to the enemies of the latter until properly exchanged in such manner as shall be mutually approved by the respective authorities.

"R. E. Lee, General.

"W. H. Taylor, Lieutenant-Colonel and A. A. G.

"Chas. S. Venable, Lieutenant-Colonel and A. A. G.

"Chas. Marshall, Lieutenant-Colonel and A. A. G.

"H. E. Praton, Lieutenant-Colonel and Inspector-General.

"Giles Brooke, Major and A. A. Surgeon-General.

"H. S. Young, A. A. General.

"Done at Appomattox Court-house, Va., this ninth (9th) day of April, 1865."

[COUNTERSIGNED.]

"The above-named officers will not be disturbed by United States authorities as long as they observe their parole, and the laws in force where they reside.

"GEORGE H. SHARPE,
"*General Assistant Provost Marshal.*"

The paroles for the men were in the same form, except commencing with the words "I, the undersigned commanding officer of —— belonging to the Army of Northern Virginia," etc. These were signed by the officers commanding the men, and countersigned by the provost marshal or his assistants.

As soon as the terms of surrender were signed, General Grant had designated the command of Major-General Gibbon, the Fifth Army Corps under Griffin, and McKenzie's cavalry, to remain at Appomattox Court-house until the paroling of the surrendered army was completed, and to take charge of the public property. The remainder of the army immediately returned to the vicinity of Burkesville.

On receipt of General Grant's letter of the 5th of April, General Sherman had moved directly against General Johnston, who retreated rapidly on and through Raleigh, which place General Sherman occupied on the morning of the 13th. On the day preceding, news of the surrender of General Lee reached him at Smithfield.

On the 14th, a correspondence was opened between General Sherman and General Johnston, which resulted on the

18th in an agreement for the suspension of hostilities, and a memorandum or basis for peace, subject to the approval of the President. This agreement was disapproved by the President on the 21st, which disapproval, together with the instructions of the Secretary of War, were communicated by General Grant in person to General Sherman, at Raleigh, North Carolina, on the morning of the 24th. Notice was at once given by him to General Johnston for the termination of the truce that had been entered into. On the 25th another meeting between them was agreed upon, to take place on the 26th, which terminated in the surrender and disbandonment of Johnston's army upon substantially the same terms as were given to General Lee.

An expedition, under General Geo. Stoneman, had moved on the 20th of March, from East Tennessee, and going by way of Boone, North Carolina, had struck the railroad at Wytheville, Chambersburg, and Big Lick. The force striking it at Big Lick pushed on to within a few miles of Lynchburg, destroying the important bridges, while with the main force he effectually destroyed it between New River and Big Lick, and then turned for Greensboro', on the North Carolina Railroad; struck that road and destroyed the bridges between Danville and Greensboro', and between Greensboro' and the Yadkin, together with the depots and supplies along it, and captured four hundred prisoners. At Salisbury he attacked and defeated a force of the enemy under General Gardiner, capturing fourteen pieces of artillery and one thousand three hundred and sixty-four prisoners, and destroyed large amounts of army stores. At this place he destroyed fifteen miles of railroad and the bridges toward Charlotte. Thence he moved to Slatersville.

General Canby, who had been directed in January to make preparations for a movement from Mobile Bay against Mobile and the interior of Alabama, commenced his movement on the 20th of March. The Sixteenth Corps, Major-General A. J. Smith commanding, moved from Fort Gaines by water to Fish River; the Thirteenth Corps, under Major-General Gordon Granger, moved from Fort Morgan and joined the Sixteenth Corps on Fish River, both moving thence on Spanish Fort and investing it on the 27th; while Major-General Steele's command moved from Pensacola, cut the railroad leading from Tensas to Montgomery, effected a junction with them, and partially invested Fort Blakely. After a severe bombardment of Spanish Fort, a part of its line was carried on the 8th of April. During the night the enemy evacuated the fort. Fort Blakely was carried by assault on the 9th, and many prisoners captured; our loss was considerable. These successes practically opened to us the Alabama River, and enabled us to approach Mobile from the north. On the night of the 11th the city was evacuated, and was taken possession of by our forces on the morning of the 12th.

The expedition under the command of Brevet Major-General Wilson, consisting of twelve thousand five hundred mounted men, was delayed by rains until March 22d, when it moved from Chickasaw, Alabama. On the 1st of April, General Wilson encountered the enemy in force under Forrest near Ebenezer Church, drove him in confusion, captured three hundred prisoners and three guns, and destroyed the central bridge over the Cahawba River. On the 2d he attacked and captured the fortified city of Selma, defended by Forrest with seven thousand men and thirty-two guns, destroyed the arsenal, armory, naval foundry, machine shops, vast quantities of stores, and captured three thousand prisoners. On the 4th he captured and destroyed Tuscaloosa. On the 10th he crossed the Alabama River, and after sending information of his operations to General Canby, marched on Montgomery, which place he occupied on the 14th, the enemy having abandoned it. At this place many stores and five steamboats fell into our hands. Thence a force marched direct on Columbus, and another on West Point, both of which places were assaulted and captured on the 16th. At the former place we got one thousand five hundred prisoners and fifty-two field-guns, destroyed two gunboats, the navy-yard, foundries, arsenal, many factories, and much other public property. At the latter place we got three hundred prisoners, four guns, and destroyed nineteen locomotives and three hundred cars. On the 20th he took possession of Macon, Georgia, with sixty field-guns, one thousand two hundred militia, and five generals, surrendered by General Howell Cobb. General Wilson, hearing that Jeff. Davis was trying to make his escape, sent forces in pursuit and succeeded in capturing him on the morning of May 11th.

On the 4th day of May, General Dick Taylor surrendered to General Canby all the remaining rebel forces east of the Mississippi.

A force sufficient to insure an easy triumph over the enemy under Kirby Smith, west of the Mississippi, was immediately put in motion for Texas, and Major-General Sheridan designated for its immediate command; but on the 26th day of May, and before they reached their destination, General Kirby Smith surrendered his entire command to Major-General Canby. This surrender did not take place, however, until after the capture of the rebel President and Vice-President; and the bad faith was exhibited of first disbanding most of his army, and permitting an indiscriminate plunder of public property.

The scattered rebel bands, upon hearing of the surrender of the great armies, surrendered or disbanded, and went to their homes. The whole number of rebel soldiers surrendered to the Union forces was one hundred and seventy-four thousand two hundred and twenty-three. The number of rebel prisoners then on hand was ninety-eight thousand eight hundred and two. The whole number of the Union forces, May 11, 1865, was one million five hundred and sixteen men.

Early in May the armies of Grant and Sherman were ordered to Washington, and on the 22d the Army of the Potomac led by Meade, and Sherman's bronzed heroes led by the old chief in person, were reviewed on Pennsylvania Avenue by General Grant, the President, Secretary of War, and members of the cabinet. The splendid pageant and ceremonies lasted for two days, and were witnessed by thousands of citizens from all parts of the republic.

On the 14th of April, 1865, President Lincoln was assassinated at Ford's Theater, in Washington city, by Wilkes Booth, and General Grant narrowly escaped sharing his fate. In the early part of the evening it was the intention of the General to accompany the President to the theater, but business calling him away, he went north that night.

Grant made tours of pleasure and inspection through the North, South, and Canada, and every-where throngs of people pressed to see him, bid him welcome, and take by the hand the quiet, unpretending, and sturdy man who had saved his country, and won a military fame second to no general in the world. When he visited West Point he was received with great honor, and the humble cadet of 1844, now generalissimo of all the armies of the United States, did honor to his alma mater.

Harvard College, and many other institutions and associations of learning, conferred upon him their most honorable degrees, and made him Doctor of Laws.

On the 7th of January, 1865, a number of the principal citizens of Philadelphia presented him with a handsome house, thoroughly furnished, in Chestnut Street, above Twentieth. To tell of his honors, and the gifts he has received, would fill a volume such as this.

Among all the ovations given him, none perhaps was more grateful to him than that at his old home, Galena, Illinois, on the 28th of August, 1865. There were arches decorated with the long scroll of his victories, enthusiastic plaudits from his old friends and fellow-citizens; and over the street where he lived, and the sidewalk which he had calumniated, was the motto: "General, the sidewalk is built." The fond thought which had prompted such an expression of his ambition—to be Mayor of Galena, and build the sidewalk—thus treasured by his old friends, would touch the heart of Grant, when "the applause of listening senates" would have little power to move him.

The soldiers longed to revisit their homes, from which some of them had been constantly separated for four years; and General Grant, anxious to gratify a desire so natural to all men, caused them to be mustered out of service as rapidly as possible. On the 2d of June, 1865, he closed his official relations with the great volunteer armies of the Union, and issued to the soldiers he had commanded so long and well the following address:

"Soldiers of the Armies of the United States: By your patriotic devotion to your country in the hour of danger and alarm, your magnificent fighting, bravery, and endurance, you have maintained the supremacy of the Union and the Constitution; overthrown all armed opposition to the enforcement of the laws, and of the proclamations forever abolishing slavery—the cause and pretext of the rebellion; and opened the way to the rightful authorities to restore order and inaugurate peace, on a permanent and enduring basis, on every foot of American soil.

"Your marches, sieges, and battles, in distance, duration, resolution, and brilliancy of results, dim the luster of the world's past military achievements, and will be the patriot's precedent in defense of liberty and right in all time to come. In obedience to your country's call, you left your homes and families, and volunteered in its defense. Victory has crowned your valor, and secured the purpose of your patriotic hearts. And with the gratitude of your countrymen, and the highest honors a great and free nation can accord, you will soon be permitted to return to your homes and your families, conscious of having discharged the highest duties of American citizens.

"To achieve these glorious triumphs, and secure to yourselves, your fellow-countrymen, and posterity the blessings of free institutions, tens of thousands of your gallant comrades have fallen, and sealed the priceless legacy with their lives. The graves of these a grateful nation bedews with tears, honors their memories, and will ever cherish and support their stricken families."

CHAPTER XVII.

THE GRADE OF GENERAL—GRANT COMMISSIONED A GENERAL—HIS PERSONAL APPEARANCE, HABITS, MANNERS, CONDUCT, AND DRESS—GRANT IN BATTLE—HIS MILITARY FAME—HIS KINDNESS OF HEART—DEATH OF COLONEL O'MEARA—A PLEASANT LETTER—THE OLD SOLDIER AND GRANT—ANECDOTE OF STANTON AND LINCOLN—GRANT'S RELIANCE UPON DIVINE PROVIDENCE—HIS TREATMENT OF SUBORDINATE OFFICERS—WHAT HE SAID OF SHERMAN, THOMAS, SHERIDAN, AND OTHERS—ANECDOTE OF GRANT—HIS JUSTICE—A CANDIDATE FOR THE PRESIDENCY.

In the summer of 1866, the grade of general was revived in the army, and on the 25th of July, 1866, the President commissioned Grant to the office, General Sherman on the same day succeeding him as lieutenant-general. In 1798, Congress conferred on Washington the grade of lieutenant-general, and had he lived another year, he would have been a full general. Upon the death of Washington the grade was discontinued.

In the long years from February, 1849, to December, 1852, earnest efforts were made to confer the grade of lieutenant-general, by brevet, on General Winfield Scott, for his long and illustrious services to the country; but his enemies were ingenious and malignant, and among them the most pertinacious was the then Honorable Jefferson Davis.

When General McClellan succeeded to the command of the armies, General Scott was retired as a lieutenant-general; but no officers, except Washington and Grant, ever held the full rank. Grant is the first full *General* of the armies, and is now a little over forty-six years of age.

General Grant is not such a man as an idealist would picture for a great hero. He is small of stature, and neither striking in appearance, nor eloquent in speech. Though strong and compactly built, he is what might emphatically be termed, a "plain little man." At first sight, the beholder wonders how such a man ever became great, and at once feels a personal superiority over this dull little personage; but after being in his society for an hour or two, the stranger, with all his smartness, finds out he can make nothing out of the quiet General, and begins to suspect he is the smartest of the two. A close observer can now and then detect a merry twinkle in the General's eye, as the pompous politician, with learned and particular phrase assumes to instruct his dull auditor, and sometimes a word escapes him which shows Grant knows more of the subject on hand than he chooses to let on. "You must talk plainly with Grant," said a distinguished statesman to a friend, as they were entering the General's head-quarters, "for he is about the dullest fellow on politics I ever saw." When they came out the friend to whom this caution had been given said: "That man, Grant, is as smart as a whip. Did you not observe how shrewd he was in finding out our opinions, and yet, when we came back at him for his, he talked round us, and said—just nothing; and withal, was so frank and polite, we had to put up with what he did say? He got our opinions, but I can't say we got his; yet I am sure he has one, if he don't tell it."

The truth is, Grant is a good listener, and always knows just what he is going to do, but he seldom tells of it beforehand. When he doubts, he selects his adviser, sends for him, and after laying the whole case before him asks for an opinion, which, when given, the General weighs carefully, and then acts. He is strictly honest, and a strong believer in human instinct. When a man's heart is pure, and prompts him to do a thing, the General thinks he should follow the leadings of that better nature. Grant's brow is contracted, but the forehead is smooth and of the ordinary height; his teeth are small and firmly set in a square and compact jaw, that says plainly enough, "my will must be carried out." His nose is aquiline, but not much of a nose; and his mouth, broad and firm, with full red lips. The eyes are sad and dreamy in their expression, blue in color, and light up when he talks or smiles. When Grant laughs, his eyes begin to laugh first, and then it spreads over his face, and terminates in shaking his whole body, but he never roars. The whole of the lower part of the face is covered with a closely cropped reddish beard, and on the upper lip he wears a moustache, cut to match the beard. His hair is abundant; brown, worn short, and parted on the left side. When he was young, it is said he wore his hair parted in the middle; but this is utterly unworthy of belief.

In his private life, Grant is irreproachable. Humane, generous, and pure, whether we consider him as a citizen, a son, a husband, a father, he is blameless. Some years ago, he occasionally took a glass of whisky, but after they began to censure him for it in public he quit entirely, and does not at the present time even taste wine.

In manners, he is the gentlest of gentlemen, and his mildness is proverbial. No one ever was rebuffed or insulted by General Grant, and his whole deportment invites confidence. The humblest drummer boy in the army can approach him and have an interview if he desires it, and even the beggars on the street feel that "the kind-looking gentleman" will surely give them something. "If I can only see General Grant for a minute, I shall be all right," said a poor, sick soldier who wanted to go home; and he was quite right, for when he got into the head-quarters the kind-hearted General gave him a furlough.

In his dress, General Grant is plain but neat. He is seldom seen in uniform, and when he is, wears no gaudy plumes nor trappings. In the field, he was careless of his personal appearance; indeed, his mind was so much engaged he could give little thought to his body. A person who saw Grant in battle, thus writes about him:

"Those who had never seen General Grant would scarcely be likely to have singled him out from the hundred others on the ground around Chattanooga as the man whom the country recognizes as having done the most, and of whom so much is expected, to crush the rebellion by hard blows, and of the exercise of those qualities which enter into a character of true greatness. He was there to be seen, enveloped in a rather huge military coat, wearing a slouched hat, which seemed to have a predisposition to turn up before, and down behind, with a gait slightly limping from his accident at New Orleans, giving his orders with as few words as possible, in a low tone, and with an accent which partook of the slight nervousness, intensity of feeling, yet perfect self-command, seen in all his movements. General Grant might be described best as a little old man—yet not really old—who, with a keen eye did not intend that any thing should escape his observation. At that battle he was not in his usual physical condition, his recent illness, added to his arduous labors, having made him lean in flesh, and given a sharpness to his features which he did not formerly have. Those features, however, go far to define the man of will and self-control that he is. At the critical moment of the day's operations, the muscles appeared to gather tighter and harder over his slightly projecting chin, which seemed to have an involuntary way of working, and the lips to contract. There is in what he does or says nothing that has the slightest approach to ostentation or show, but the palpable evidence of a plain man of sense, will, and purpose, who has little idea that more eyes are turned on him than on any other man on the continent. From his first struggle at Belmont to his last at Chattanooga, the men led by him have fought more steadily, fiercely, and successfully than those of any other portion of our army. In looking back over the history of the war, the eye rests upon no more glorious pages than those whereon are written Fort Donelson, Vicksburg, and Chattanooga."

The prestige of Grant is entirely impersonal. Reticent and impassive, he has not the temperament which inspires spontaneous individual enthusiasm. You see him, and find it difficult to associate his personality with his deeds, and make them one, but you always feel you are in the presence of an honest, kind-hearted man, and if you want him to do you a favor, you will not hesitate one moment to ask him.

Grant is an inveterate smoker, and is seldom seen without his cigar. He loves horses and always keeps two or three good ones. He is entirely without ostentation in his house and table, and is exceedingly hospitable. Every body and every thing about him is for use, and his servants and attendants are never permitted to put on airs. His duties are all attended to with the utmost regularity, and his subordinates are required to be prompt and industrious. He is scrupulously polite in his business intercourse with his officers, and endeavors to have every one treated kindly who comes to his head-quarters.

There are many instances of Grant's kindness of heart, but two or three must here suffice: When he heard of the death of Colonel O'Meara, one of the officers under his command at Chattanooga, he hastened to see the daring and brave man's remains, which were at the landing in a coffin, waiting for transportation. The General ordered the coffin to be opened, that he might take "a last look at the gallant colonel of the Irish Legion." When the coffin was opened, the General was touched at the sight of one whom he had honored and publicly thanked before he had been two months in the Army of the Tennessee. O'Meara's defense of the trestlework, a few miles north of Holly Springs, Miss., when Van Dorn made a raid there in December, 1862, and which saved Grant's army from starvation, was never forgotten by the General. The spectators were moved at the touching farewell of the commander of the Department of the Mississippi from the corpse of the young Irish soldier, who had forfeited his life in the belief that the highest and best duty of all native or foreign born citizens was to stand by the flag which is the hope of the exile, the emblem of philanthropy, and the ensign of the American people.

General Quimby, one of Grant's generals, wrote him for a lock of his hair for his wife, who was prominent in a ladies' fair. Although in the midst of his Chattanooga campaign, Grant found time to write the following kind letter:

"My Dear Madam: The letter of my old friend and former class-mate, your husband, requesting a lock of my hair, if the article is not growing scarce from age—I presume he means it to be put in an ornament, (by the most delicate of hands, no doubt,) and sold at the bazaar for the benefit of disabled soldiers and their families—is just received.

"I am glad to say that the stock is yet abundant as ever, though time or other cause is beginning to intersperse here and there a reminder that winters have passed.

"The object for which this little requisite is made is so praiseworthy that I can not refuse it, even though I do, by granting it, expose the fact to the ladies of Rochester, that I am no longer a boy. Hoping that the citizens of your city may spend a happy week, commencing to-morrow, and that this fair may remunerate most abundantly,

"I remain, truly your friend,

"U. S. GRANT."

A political committee at Philadelphia called at the arsenal to inquire how certain workmen were going to vote. One man, an old soldier, named Owens, told the committee it was none of their business how he would vote, and was so saucy that on the recommendation of the committee he was forthwith discharged. "I will go and see General Grant about this," said the old man. "Do," replied the chairman, "and be sure and let the committee know what he says."

Filled with wrath, the old soldier trudged off, amid the laughter of the by-standers, and went directly to the city, where General Grant was temporarily residing. Going up to the door-bell he boldly rang it, and a moment afterward stepped into the hall, where he met a servant coming to answer the bell. Seeing a coarse and rusty looking old man, the servant said sharply, "What do you want, sir?"

"I want to see General Grant and have an interview," replied the old man.

"The General is busy just now and can't see you, but I'll take your card up."

Just then a little girl appeared on the stairs, and the old soldier, turning from the servant, said to her, "Sissy, run up stairs and tell your Pap an old Fourth Infantry man is down here and wants to see him." The child bounded away, and a moment afterward the little voice was heard at the head of the stairs shouting down, "Papa says come up, old soldier man."

The old man went up, and conducted by the child, entered a room where the General was seated, with his cigar, at a desk, writing. Shaking the General by the hand he said, "You do n't remember me, General, do you?"

"No," said Grant, looking at him, "I see so many people nowadays you know, I can't remember them all."

"Well, I'm Lem Owens, one of your old soldiers; you commanded me when you was a lieutenant in the old regiment. I'm in trouble, General, and I come down here to get you to help me out, if you will. I have a large family, and they have discharged me from the arsenal, 'cause why them politiciner fellows wanted to know, and I would n't tell them, how I was going to vote."

Grant turned to his desk and wrote:

"To—— The bearer of this, Lem Owens, an old soldier of mine, who has a large family to support, tells me he has been discharged. I particularly desire that he shall be reëmployed. U. S. GRANT, *General.*"

Reading it to the soldier, he said, "I guess that will fix you all right." "Let me have that ere dociment," said the old soldier. "Lord, Gineral, how them political chaps' eyes will bulge out when they see it, for they all thought so great a man as you would not bother with the troubles of a poor old soldier, but I knew better, Gineral, and I told them so, when they laughed at me."

Armed with his paper, the old soldier went back to the arsenal and was immediately rëemployed.

Lincoln loved Grant, and took every opportunity to honor and reward him for his great services. These truly great men had none of that petty jealousy in their natures which so often manifests itself in the public men of our day. Often Lincoln and Grant wrote each other privately, and each entered largely into the thoughts of the other.

At a celebration, on the 22d of February, before the surrender of Vicksburg, while all around were drinking toasts in sparkling champagne, General Grant, pushing aside a glass of wine, and taking up a glass of Mississippi water, remarked: "This suits the matter in hand," drink to the toast, "God gave us Lincoln and Liberty; let us fight for both."

One day when Grant was before Petersburg with his army, Secretary Stanton, who felt uneasy about the safety of Washington, went to the President, and said: "Had we not better order Grant to send more troops to cover Washington?" "Look here, Stanton," replied Lincoln, in his simple way; "you and I have been issuing orders to the Army of the Potomac for about four years, and I do n't see as we have accomplished much by it; now, suppose we let Grant alone and see how he will make out with the matter."

And Grant was left alone, for be it said to the credit of Mr. Lincoln's good sense and judgment, he would never interfere with Grant's plans, or allow any one else to do so.

In many of his orders and dispatches, Grant devoutly recognized the providence of God, and his reliance upon it, as being the chief strength of nations and men; and if he ever swears, the religious world may be certified that his oaths are in the same category with those of my Uncle Toby and of Washington at Monmouth. He is phlegmatic, but not insensible; cool, but not without enthusiasm; habitually grave, with a simple dignity, but easily approachable by all, even to the poorest private; in speech, laconic, but unaffected; no official non-committal about him; clear-headed, forgetting nothing, arranging details easily in his capacious brain, without much reliance upon red tape; blushing when praised, and bearing both praise and blame with silent magnanimity. Above all, he combines what Guizot has called the "genius of common sense" with a determination to "go ahead."

His justice to his subordinate officers has always been a matter of comment in Grant's military career, even of those who divided with him the national esteem. He never seemed in the least jealous, but rejoiced as heartily as any one over their success. Thus he was the first to congratulate Sheridan on his brilliant victories in the Valley; and not only thanked, but praised Thomas for defeating Hood at Nashville. So, too, when Sherman fell under the national displeasure for his treaty with Johnston, Grant kindly took him by the hand, corrected his mistake, and presented his great fellow-soldier to the nation as worthy of their greatest confidence. Of Sherman, Grant wrote to the President:

"To General Sherman I was greatly indebted for his promptness in forwarding to me, during the siege of Fort Donelson, rëenforcements and supplies from Paducah. At the battle of Shiloh, on the first day, he held with raw troops the key-point to the landing. *To his individual efforts I am indebted for the success of that battle.* Twice hit, and several (I think three) horses shot under him on that day, he maintained his position with raw troops. It is no disparagement to any other officer to say that I do not believe there was another division commander on the field who had the skill and experience to have done it. His services as division commander in the advance on Corinth, I will venture to say, were appreciated by the new General-in-Chief beyond those of any other division commander.

"General Sherman's arrangement as commander of troops in the attack on Chickasaw Bluffs, last December, was admirable. Seeing the ground from the opposite side from the attack, I saw the impossibility of making it successful. *The conception of the attack on Arkansas Post was General Sherman's.* His part of the execution, no one denies, was as good as it possibly could have been. His demonstration at Haines' Bluff, in April, to hold the enemy about Vicksburg, while the army was securing a foothold east of the Mississippi; his rapid marches to join the army afterward; his management at Jackson, Mississippi, in the first attack; his almost unequaled march from Jackson to Bridgeport, and passage of Black River; his securing Walnut Hills on the 18th of May, and thus opening communications with our supplies, *all attest his great merit as a soldier.* The siege of Vicksburg and last capture of Jackson and dispersion of Johnston's army, entitle General Sherman to more credit than usually falls to the lot of one man to earn. The promotion of such men as Sherman always adds strength to our arms."

Grant wrote equally strong recommendations of McPherson, Sheridan, and other officers; always securing them promotions whenever he could, and doing all in his power to have full justice done to every officer according to his merits and the services he rendered the nation.

Such is the great American soldier and patriot; such—Ulysses Grant, who now offers himself to the people, and asks their suffrages for the highest and most honorable office in their gift. Who more worthy? Who so deserving? What citizen can refuse him?

CHAPTER XVIII.

SOLDIERS' AND SAILORS' NATIONAL CONVENTION AT CHICAGO—THE PROCESSION—THE EAGLE "OLD ABE"—THE HALL—THE SCENES—CONVENTION CALLED TO ORDER—GOVERNOR FAIRCHILD TEMPORARY CHAIRMAN—HIS SPEECH—THE COMMITTEES—GOVERNOR HAWLEY'S SPEECH—REMARKS OF GENERALS SICKLES, HALSTEAD, AND OTHERS—PERMANENT ORGANIZATION—GENERAL LOGAN'S REMARKS—GRANT'S FATHER—HIS SPEECH—ADDRESSES BY GENERAL COCHRANE, MAJOR HAGGERTY, AND O'CONNER—COLONEL STOKES, OF TENNESSEE—THE RESOLUTIONS—GRANT UNANIMOUSLY NOMINATED BY HIS COMRADES FOR PRESIDENT—GREAT ENTHUSIASM—THE LARGEST DELEGATED CONVENTION EVER ASSEMBLED—ADJOURNMENT OF THE CONVENTION.

On the 19th of May, 1868, a convention, composed of General Grant's comrades from all parts of the Union, assembled at Chicago, for the purpose of nominating him for the high office of President. They marched through the streets, headed by brass bands and carrying the famous war eagle "Old Abe," a bird that had been carried through the war by a Wisconsin regiment. Many of the delegations were led by the Governors of their States, and scores of the most distinguished generals in the late war marched in the procession. Over one thousand delegates, representing all the States and Territories in the Union, sat down in the immense Turners' Hall, which was beautifully decorated with flags and mottoes. As the well-known generals of the war stepped upon the platform, and the soldiers recognized their old leaders, cheer after cheer broke forth, and a scene of the wildest enthusiasm ensued, such as had never before been witnessed in this country. There were hand-shakings and meetings after years of separation, such as can only take place between men who have shared together the dangers of the battle-field.

At noon, Major William S. Morse, Chairman of the Soldiers' and Sailors' National Executive Committee, called the Convention to order, and the Rev. John Fellows, of Wisconsin, offered up an eloquent and fervent prayer. Governor Fairchild, of Wisconsin, a one-armed soldier, was chosen temporary chairman, and on taking the chair said:

"GENTLEMEN OF THE CONVENTION: In behalf of the State of Wisconsin, whose soldiers you have honored to-day in the selection of myself as temporary chairman, I thank you. I shall receive it as an honor to the State and to the soldiers of Wisconsin. I do not take it as personal. I am very glad, indeed, my friends, to meet so many of the old soldiers of the Union army. I was glad last night, at a little meeting of a few delegates to know why we came here. I understand we came here representing nearly a million of loyal hearts. We came here to muster in for three years or the war; we came to swear by the love we bore those men that we will never—we can swear by the good old flag we fought for—we came here to swear by the widows and orphans of our comrades—that we will never give up the fight until this country is reconstructed upon the basis of equal and exact justice to all men. Do you swear it for your comrades? No man in this land, my friends—no one could have fought better than our soldiers did. And, as we say upon our great Wisconsin banner, thus it will again be with them in every State of the Union. The Union soldiers will fight as they fought when the Union men of the South demanded a certain plan of reconstruction with a plainly written constitution, and the rebels South demanded another plan of reconstruction. I say the Union soldiers North—

all good friends of the Union—the soldiers of the North will give to the Union men of each State that plan of reconstruction which they asked, until, in every section of the South, in every school district—I hope they will have school districts in the South—a Union man can stand up before God and declare his life for the Union, the flag, and the country. The fight will continue, and we will be at the front."

Lieutenant Thomas C. Donelson, of Ohio; Major A. C. Tates, of New York; Capt. H. H. Thomas, of Tennessee; W. A. Short, D. C.; Major O. M. Wilson, of Indiana, and Lieutenant Samuel Reeves, of New Jersey were chosen temporary Secretaries of the Convention.

A committee, consisting of Dr. J. Y. Cantwell, of Alabama; J. W. Fuller, of Arkansas; Captain J. T. Litbald, of California; Captain W. H. Tubbs, of Connecticut; General Loveland, of Delaware; General Ranboum, of Florida; General Watson, of Georgia; General J. L. Beveridge, of Illinois; General Kimball, of Indiana; E. W. Rice, of Iowa; J. P. Blunt, of Kansas; R. B. Harris, of Kentucky; E. P. Dowe, of Maine; Major Ben Perley Poore, of Massachusetts; C. G. Lowdney, of Minnesota; Colonel M. L. Demott, of Missouri; Colonel Geo. F. Burnham, of Maryland; General Henry Baxter, of Michigan; Colonel J. M. Clarrington, of Nebraska; Captain R. H. Lee, of New Jersey; Captain G. F. Lee, of North Carolina; Major E. W. Farr, of New Hampshire; General Pleasanton and General Samuel A. Yoman, of Ohio; J. H. Stewart, of Pennsylvania; B. F. Whittemore, of South Carolina; General W. W. J. Smith, and Colonel J. H. Lockwood, of Virginia; Lieutenant-Colonel W. W. Grant, of Vermont, and General J. S. Allen, of Wisconsin, was appointed on permanent organization.

A Committee on Resolutions was appointed, as follows:

Colonel R. M. Reynolds, of Alabama; Colonel J. E. Cowen, of California; Colonel A. H. Grimshaw, of Delaware; General John A. Logan, of Illinois; General W. M. Stone, of Iowa; Colonel B. H. Bristow, of Kentucky; General George F. Shepley, of Maine; Colonel Edwin F. Stone, of Massachusetts; Colonel Aiken, of Minnesota; Colonel W. Grosvens, of Mississippi; General Titus, of New Hampshire; General Dennis T. Burke, of New York; General F. Sawyer, of Ohio; General Charles H. Hopkins, of Rhode Island; Lieutenant-Colonel Robert K. Smith, of Texas; W. S. McCullough, of Arkansas; Colonel J. H. Lockwood, of West Virginia; General Charles Crow, of Indiana; General E. M. Lee, of Connecticut; B. R. Anthony, of Kansas; Captain E. Pinchbloss, of Louisiana; General R. H. Richardson, of Maryland; General W. Stoughton, of Michigan; H. T. Fisher, of Mississippi; Captain B. Hall, of Nebraska; W. S. Davenport, of New Jersey, and J. C. Mann, of North Carolina.

While the committees were out, General Hawley, of Connecticut was loudly called for, and, in response, delivered an eloquent speech. Among other things he said:

"General Grant was undoubtedly the people's choice, and next November will see him elected President of the United States. So far as the Southern people are concerned, he would say that whenever they manifest a desire to return to the good old Union, and act like good citizens, he was in favor of throwing around them the protection of the Government. It made no difference whether that citizen was white or black, he was a citizen still. He believed that, if necessary, two million 'Boys in Blue' would come again and protect him in his rights."

General Halsted, of New Jersey; Major O'Conner, of New York, and the hero, General Daniel E. Sickles, of New York, next made stirring speeches, saying the Convention had assembled to choose a successor to the lamented Lincoln, favoring the nomination of General Grant, and counseling the soldiers throughout the land to stand firmly by their chieftain in the coming political campaign as they stood by him during the war.

The Committee on Permanent Organization, reported:

For President, *General John A. Logan*, of Illinois.

	Vice-Presidents.	*Secretaries.*
Alabama	Col. R. T. Smith.	Capt. B. F. Williams.
Arkansas	Gen. H. B. Morse.	Col. S. H. Root.
California	Gen. P. S. Conner.	Col. James Cary.
Connecticut	Col. Charles Warren.	Lieut. J. M. Knowlscn
Delaware	A. F. A. Torbett.	Col. W. Lamott.
Florida	Capt. Rowlan Rombanes.	Lieut. T. B. Carroll.
Georgia	Capt. W. H. Watson.	Capt. E. B. McTimony.
Illinois	Gen. Julius White.	Gen. E. S. Solomon.
Indiana	Gen. R. S. Foster.	Major O. Wilson.
Iowa	Gen. C. L. Mathias.	Capt. C. F. Gardner.
Kansas	Capt. W. G. Karimer.	Col. G. W. Veal.
Kentucky	Gen. John P. Croxton.	Capt. Jas. M. Fidler.
Louisiana	Gen. W. L. McMillan.	Capt. P.B.S.Phinchback.
Maine	Gen. G. L. Beall.	Geo. H. M. Plaister.
Maryland	Gen. A. W. Dennison.	Capt. H. Parison.
Massachusetts	Gen. J. S. Cunningham.	Col R. G Asher.
Michigan	Gen. O. L. Spalding.	Capt. E. Weeks.
Minnesota	Gen. C. C. Andrews.	Col. J. G. Gee.
Missouri	Gen. H. W. Barry.	Col. A Warner.
Missouri	Gen. John McNeill.	Gen. Draper.
Nebraska	Col. A. J. Harding.	Major John Gillespie.
New Hampshire	Capt. J. B. Clark.	Chaplain Lovering.
New Jersey	Col. W. Ward.	Lieut. L. C. Reeves.
New York	Gen. C. K. Graham.	Major A. C. Tate.
North Carolina	Gen. S. G. Eslis.	Major S. C. Mann.
Ohio.	Gen. Oliver Wood.	Gen. J. M. Marsh.
Pennsylvania	Gen. H. L. Cape.	Col. H. C. Alleman.
Rhode Island	Gen. C. H. Tompkins.	Capt. G. B. Beck.
South Carolina	Chap. B. F. Whittemore.	Sergt. H. E. Hayne.
Tennessee	Gen. John B. Rodgers.	Capt. H. E. Hudson.
Texas	Major A. H. Longley.	Dr. R. K. Smith.

	Vice-Presidents.	Secretaries.
Vermont	Gen. Stephen Thomas.	Private Henry Conglon.
Virginia	Gen. H. A. Pierce.	Capt. George Tucker.
West Virginia	Col. P. H. Lockwood.	Capt. W. J. Purdy.
Wisconsin	Gen. C. S. Hamilton.	Capt. Henry Harshan.
Dist. of Columbia	Gen. N. P. Chipman.	Private Wm. A. Short.

Governor Fairchild having announced that the father of General Grant was in the house, loud calls were made for him, and, amid great cheering he was led forward. The convention received him standing, and called for a speech. He is a very old man, and, on that occasion, carried a blue cotton umbrella under his arm, which, as the day was bright and clear, amused the boys very much. Adjusting his spectacles and depositing his umbrella with the President for safe keeping, the venerable man said with deep emotion: "Soldiers! I thank you for asking me to speak to you. Oh! it fills my heart with gratitude when I think that one of my children led this great band of brave men through a successful war for the Union. I was too old to do much in the war, and I don't know why I should be called upon to speak to so many distinguished and brave men." Here a soldier rose up in the convention and said: "Never mind, father Grant, you gave us a boy to lead us—that was enough." The house shook with applause, and Mr. Grant continued for some time speaking in an eloquent and appropriate manner.

General Logan, on being conducted to the chair, made an able speech, thanking the soldiers for the honor conferred upon him, but said he could not take the chair from one so eminently worthy to preside as Governor Fairchild. He then retired amid a storm of applause, and the one-armed governor resumed his duties as President of the Convention. He was deeply affected by the delicate mark of respect paid him, and again thanked the gallant general and the soldiers for the honor of presiding over their deliberations.

General Cochrane and Major Haggerty next made amusing and interesting speeches, and were followed by Colonel Stokes, of Tennessee.

General Logan, Chairman of the Committee on Resolutions, reported as follows:

"*Resolved*, That the soldiers and sailors, steadfast now as ever to the Union and the flag, fully recognize the claims of General Ulysses Grant to the confidence of the American people; and believing that the victories achieved under his guidance in war, will be now illustrated by him in times of peace by such measures as shall secure the fruits of our exertions, and the restoration of the Union upon a loyal basis, we declare it as our deliberate conviction, that he is the choice of the soldiers and sailors of the Union for the office of President of the United States.

"*Resolved*, That in the maintenance of those principles which underlie our Government, and for which we fought during four years of war, we pledge our earnest and active support to the Republican party, as the only political organization which, in our judgment, is true to the principles of loyalty, liberty, and equality before the law.

"*Resolved*, That, speaking for ourselves and the soldiers and sailors who imperiled their lives to preserve the Union, we believe that the impeachment of Andrew Johnson by the House of Representatives, for high crimes and misdemeanors in office, and his trial before the United States Senate, have presented unmistakable proofs of his guilt, and that whatever may be the judgment of the tribunal before which he is arraigned, *the verdict of the people is 'guilty;'* and we regard any Senator who has voted for acquittal as falling short of the proper discharge of his duty in this hour of the nation s trial, and as unworthy of the confidence of a brave and loyal people.

"*Resolved*, That the soldiers and sailors recognize no difference between native and adopted citizens, and they demand that the Government protect the naturalized citizen abroad as well as those of native birth."

On motion of General W. M. Gregg, of New York, the resolutions were unanimously adopted, amid cheers for Grant.

The following additional resolutions were unanimously passed.

On motion of Colonel Alleman, of Pennsylvania, it was

"*Resolved*, That a committee of nine be appointed to wait upon General U. S. Grant, and present him a copy of the resolutions of the Soldiers' and Sailors' National Convention."

The chairman announced the committee of nine, provided for in Colonel Alleman's resolution, as follows: Colonel H. C. Alleman, General W. M. Gregg, General D. E. Sickles, General John A. Logan, General A. Pleasanton, General J. T. Hartcauft, Colonel W. B. Stokes, Captain A. Grant, and Governor James W. Hawley.

On motion of W. S. Andrews, it was—

"*Resolved*, That we, the soldiers of the republic, extend to the loyal men of the South our sympathy, and the promise of our support in the struggles yet in store for them under the present administration, before they can enjoy the liberties of American citizens, without fear of prosecution and assassination, and that, if necessary, we stand ready to aid them with our strength in the future as we have in the past."

On motion of Colonel Hempstead, the following preamble and resolutions were adopted:

"WHEREAS, Many of the late defenders of the Union being now out of employment, and they and their families suffering privation by reason of sacrifices during the war; therefore,

"*Resolved*, By us, the soldiers and sailors of the republic in the late war, in national convention assembled on the 19th day of May, 1868, that we hold it to be the duty of the administrators of the national and state governments to carry into practical effect a substantial gratitude to the defenders of the nation, in bestowing upon those of our comrades who are needy, employment in the offices of manual and clerical labor.

Resolved, That the Chairman of the Convention send a copy of these resolutions to the Chairman of the National Republican Convention."

On motion of General Daniel E. Sickles, of New York, the Convention adjourned, subject to the call of the President, and thus ended the first Soldiers' and Sailors' Political National Convention, it having been the largest delegate body ever assembled in the United States.

CHAPTER XIX.

NATIONAL REPUBLICAN CONVENTION AT CHICAGO—GENERAL SCHURTZ MADE TEMPORARY CHAIRMAN—HIS SPEECH—PROCEEDINGS OF THE CONVENTION—THE COMMITTEES—PERMANENT ORGANIZATION—SPEECH OF GOVERNOR HAWLEY—SOLDIERS RECEIVED—ELOQUENT SPEECH BY GOVERNOR FAIRCHILD—SECOND DAY'S PROCEEDINGS—THE PLATFORM—ADDITIONAL RESOLUTIONS—LOGAN'S SPEECH—GENERAL GRANT UNANIMOUSLY NOMINATED—THE VOTE BY STATES—THE ANNOUNCEMENT—WILD SCENES IN THE CONVENTION—THE EFFECT OF THE NOMINATION UPON THE PEOPLE—NOMINATION OF A VICE-PRESIDENT.

In obedience to the call of the National Republican Committee, a convention assembled at Chicago, on the 20th day of May, 1868, to nominate for the Republican party candidates for the Presidency and Vice-Presidency of the United States.

The body was called to order at twelve o'clock by Governor Ward, of New Jersey, and Bishop Simpson offered up an earnest prayer. By direction of the National Committee, Governor Ward nominated General Carl Schurtz for temporary chairman, and that gentleman, having been unanimously elected, was conducted to the platform by Lyman Tremaine, of New York, and Richard W. Thompson, of Indiana. On taking the chair, General Schurtz made an eloquent speech, and closed by declaring:

"The Republican party will not be ended until the great truth proclaimed in the Declaration of Independence, in the fullest meaning of the term, shall have become a living reality. [Applause.] Yes, let us be true to our history, be true to ourselves, and fear nothing. No step backward—'Onward!' is the watchword. Let us see again the banner of progress, of liberty, of equal rights, of national faith nailed to the very top of the mast, and I say to you I spurn the idea that the American people could ever so far forget themselves as to throw their destinies into the hands of men who, but yesterday, sought to destroy the republic, and who, to-day, stand ready to dishonor it." [Loud and continued applause.]

After settling the cases of contested seats, and deciding to admit the delegates from the Territories and Southern States, the Convention proceeded to appoint the following important committees:

Committee on Organization.—California, W. E. Lovett; Colorado, John Evans; Connecticut, A. H. Byington; Delaware, Wilson L. Sumner; Florida, B. C. Chamberlain; Georgia, W. H. Watson; Illinois, Amos C. Babcock; Indiana, George A. Buskirk; Iowa, Seth H. Crane; Kansas, John A. Bartlett; Kentucky, Oscar H. Burbridge; Louisiana, George C. Penance; Maine, Walz Hubbard; Massachusetts, Alfred R. Field; Michigan, Hampton Briggs; Minnesota, P. C. Amberly; Nebraska, E. C. Stevens; Nevada, H. H. Beck; New Hampshire, John H. Bailey; New Jersey, Thomas H. Bartlett; New York, Hamilton Harris; North Carolina, Wm. R. Myers; Ohio, Israel Green; Pennsylvania, James Orne; Rhode Island, Lysander Flagg; South Carolina, B. F. Whittemore; Tennessee, L. C. Blank; Texas, A. H. Longley; Vermont, William H. Grout; Virginia, F. A. Kimble; West Virginia (name not understood).

E. Scott Sloan, of Maryland, declined to name a committee-man until her contested State should be settled.

Committee on Resolutions.—Alabama, David C. Upton; Arkansas, W. D. Morse; Connecticut, J. N. Woodman; Delaware, D. S. Taylor; Illinois, Herman Paston; Indiana, Richard W. Thompson; Iowa, George W. Dodge; Kansas, B. F. Simpson; Kentucky, Charles Eggleston; Louisiana, L. W. Eugene; Massachusetts, Francis W. Bird; Maryland, John L. Holmes, Jr.; Michigan, R. R. Beecher; Minnesota, R. McClarin; Mississippi, R. L. Van Horn; Nebraska, R. W. Turner; Nevada, C. E. Dedong; New Hampshire, James T. Briggs; New Jersey, John Davidson; New York, Charles Andrews; North Carolina, L. D. Hess; Ohio, John C. Lee; Oregon, H. R. Kinkaid; Pennsylvania, S. E. Dimmick; Rhode Island, R. G. Hazard; South Carolina, S. O. Duncan; Texas, George W. Pascall; Vermont, W. H. Johnson; Virginia, Lysander Hill; West Virginia, R. S. Brown; Wisconsin, H. Ruble.

Committee on Business.—Alabama, George M. Reynolds; Arkansas, H. Gardsell; California, R. P. Chapin; Connecticut, D. L. Sayler; Delaware, J. J. Jenkins; Florida, B. P. Chamberlain; Georgia, David G. Coffing; Illinois, Emory A. Stout; Indiana, G. K. Steele; Iowa, K. M. Holt; Kansas, W. B. ——; Kentucky, T. J. Pickett; Louisiana, A. J. Sypher; Maine, W. E. Harriman; Massachusetts, T. Howe; Michigan, W. B. Williams; Minnesota, A. H. Butler; Mississippi, D. M. Williams; Missouri, J. O. Bullins; Nevada, O. R. Leonard; New Hampshire, Edwin Farr; New Jersey, Chas. Hildreth; New York, G. Barker; North Carolina, F. F. French; Ohio, Thos. L. Young; Pennsylvania, Thos. E. Corcoran; Rhode Island, W. H. Reynolds; South Carolina, J. C. Ebbingham; Tennessee, Blank Lewis; Texas, J. P. Keating; Vermont, G. C. Shepard; Virginia, John Oxford; West Virginia, H. C. McWard; Wisconsin, A. J. Turner.

The Convention then adjourned until five o'clock, when it

re-assembled and proceeded to business. The Committee on Organization reported the name of General James R. Hawley, of Connecticut, for permanent chairman, and he was unanimously elected. The new president, amid great cheering, was conducted to the chair by Ex-Governor Solomon, of Wisconsin, and Ex-Governor Brown, of Georgia. On taking his seat, Governor Hawley made an eloquent speech, and closed by saying:

"Every bond, in letter and spirit, must be as sacred as a soldier's grave. We must win, and we shall win. It is the old fight of liberty, equality, and fraternity, against oppression, caste, and aristocracy. It is the old fight to make the world better, 'with malice toward none, and with charity for all.' We may halt for a moment or change direction, but the good cause always goes steadily forward. It is related, and whether true or not, the incident is well invented, that on the evening of that awful battle of the Wilderness, when the legions of the Union army had fought all day by faith rather than by sight in the tangled brush, that some man asked General Grant to step back and organize, and he replied, 'We have done very well, gentlemen. At half-past three in the morning we move forward.' We accept his spirit and his words, and perhaps I am not anticipating in saying we shall accept him in person as our leader. Thanking you again, heartily, for the honor conferred, I await the further pleasure of the Convention."

The Convention completed its organization by appointing the following Vice-Presidents and Secretaries:

Vice-Presidents—Alabama, General Warner; Arkansas, A. McDonald; California, James Cory; Colorado, J. B. Chaffee; Connecticut, W. S. Pearson; Delaware, L. Thompson; Florida, H. H. Moody; Georgia, Foster Blodgett; Illinois, Jesse K. Dubuois; Indiana, W. Q. Gresham; Iowa,

J. M. Hedrick; Kansas, S. Proutty; Kentucky, Joshua J. Speed; Louisiana, W. P. Kellogg; Maine, A. D. Fessenden; Maryland, H. Stockbridge; Massachusetts, D. W. Gooch; Michigan, H. Waldron; Minnesota, H. P. Van Cleve; Mississippi, Thomas L. White, Missouri, A. J. Harlan; Nebraska, A. Landers, and J. M. Walker; New Hampshire, E. Gould; New Jersey, John S. Irick; New York, Chauncey N. Deprew; North Carolina, A. Dockery; Ohio, N. O. McFarland; Oregon, J. Failing; Pennsylvania, J. K. Moorehead; Rhode Island, G. Green; South Carolina, C. J. Stodbrand; Tennessee, T. A. Hamilton; Texas, S. D. Wood; Vermont, George N. Standard; Virginia, John Burch; West Virginia, S. D. Cares; Wisconsin, Edward Solomon.

Secretaries—Thomas D. Foster, V. Del, C. B. Higby, F. B. Solomon, Joshua T. Heald, J. Rombeaur, G. W. Wilbur, John P. Rust, J. H. Easton, Lewis Weil, William Goodloe, Colonel C. W. Lowell, Stephen D. Lindsay, E. S. Waters, W. W. Scott, A. Worley Patterson, J. C. S. Colby, Samuel Maxwell, G. N. Collins, F. Ayer, R. C. Bellville, L. Caldwell, J. W. Holden, C. Kinney, Max Ramsey, A. C. Harmer, M. R. Parther, M. Kinley, William Horne, Colonel R. D. Ringer, Joshua T. Hoke, Charles Seymour, John H. Longnecker.

A committee from the Soldiers' and Sailors' Convention was announced by the chair, and conducted to the platform by General Cochrane, of New York, General Schurtz, of Missouri, Colonel Craig, of Iowa, Mr. Cripple, of West Virginia, and Mr. Sweet, of Illinois.

SPEECH OF GENERAL COCHRANE.

Mr. President: I have the honor in behalf of the committee recently appointed by yourself to announce that they have discharged the duty to which they were appointed, and I introduce to the Convention, through yourself, Governor Fairchild, chairman of the committee to which I referred.

SPEECH OF GOVERNOR FAIRCHILD.

Governor Fairchild—Mr. President and gentlemen of the Convention: As instructed by the members of the Soldiers' and Sailors' Convention, I appear before you in their behalf to present to you a resolution passed unanimously by them yesterday P. M., as follows:

Resolved, That we, the soldiers and sailors, steadfast now as ever to the Union and flag, fully recognize the claims of General U. S. Grant to the confidence of the American people, and believing that victories won under his guidance in war will be illustrated by him in peace by such measures as will secure the fruits of our exertions, and restore the Union on a loyal basis, we declare our deliberate conviction that he is the choice of the soldiers and sailors of the Union, for the office of President of the United States.

Gentlemen: The soldiers of the United States ask the nomination of General Grant for President because they love him, and they love him because he is loyal to the Union, loyal to justice, loyal to freedom, and loyal to right; and if you will give them their comrade as a leader in the campaign of 1868, they will bear upon the enemy's works as they did in the field in 1864.

REPLY OF GENERAL HAWLEY.

President Hawley—It is hardly necessary that I should say such a communication is received with the warmest interest from Republican soldiers and by a Republican Convention.

The committee then withdrew, and after speeches by Governor Brown, of Georgia, and others, the Convention adjourned until the next day.

SECOND DAY'S PROCEEDINGS.

On Thursday morning, May 21st, the Convention reassembled at ten o'clock. An immense throng was present, including hundreds of ladies. The six hundred delegates, representing every State and Territory in the Union, occupied the lower floor and part of the dress circle. The galleries were packed with people from all parts of the Union, and although it was a bright day, the gas was lighted up and greatly added to the brilliancy of the scene. The President, Vice-President, Secretaries and distinguished men, to the number of five hundred, occupied the stage, and a full band discoursed delicious music from the orchestra in front of the foot-lights.

After prayer by the Rev. Dr. John P. Gulliver, of Chicago, the Convention proceeded to business. A debate sprung up on entering upon the records of the Convention the resolutions of the Union League, when, on motion of Judge Jones, of Ohio, the whole matter was laid on the table.

By invitation of the Convention the distinguished German orator, Fred. Hassaurek, of Cincinnati, addressed the immense assemblage, and was followed in an eloquent speech by General John M. Palmer, of Illinois. Generals Logan, Schurtz, Cochrane and Colonel Forney, were loudly called for, but declined to speak.

The Committee on Resolutions being announced, reported through their Chairman, Col. R. W. Thompson, of Indiana, the following as a platform for the Republican party:

The National Republican Party of the United States, assembled in National Convention, in the City of Chicago, on the 21st day of May, 1868, make the following Declaration of Principles:

1. We congratulate the country on the assured success of the reconstruction policy of Congress, as evinced by the adoption, in the majority of the States lately in rebellion,

of constitutions securing equal civil and political rights to all, and it is the duty of the Government to sustain those institutions, and to prevent the people of such States from being remitted to a state of anarchy.

2. The guarantee by Congress of equal suffrage to all loyal men at the South was demanded by every consideration of public safety, of gratitude, and of justice, and must be maintained; while the question of suffrage in all the loyal States properly belongs to the people of those States.

3. We denounce all forms of repudiation as a national crime; and the national honor requires the payment of the public indebtedness in the uttermost good faith to all creditors at home and abroad, not only according to the letter but the spirit of the laws under which it was contracted.

4. It is due to the labor of the nation that taxation should be equalized, and reduced as rapidly as the national faith will permit.

5. The national debt, contracted as it has been for the preservation of the Union for all time to come, should be extended over a fair period for redemption; and it is the duty of Congress to reduce the rate of interest thereon, whenever it can be honestly done.

6. That the best policy to diminish our burden of debt is to so improve our credit that capitalists will seek to loan us money at lower rates of interest than we now pay, and must continue to pay so long as repudiation, partial or total, open or covert, is threatened or suspected.

7. The Government of the United States should be administered with the strictest economy, and the corruptions which have been shamefully nursed and fostered by Andrew Johnson, call loudly for radical reform.

8. We profoundly deplore the untimely and tragic death of Abraham Lincoln, and the accession to the Presidency of Andrew Johnson, who has acted treacherously to the people

who elected him and the cause he was pledged to support; who has usurped the legislative and judicial functions; who has refused to execute the laws; who has used his high office to induce other officers to oppose and violate the laws; who has employed his executive powers to render insecure the property, the peace, liberty, and life of the people; who has abused the pardoning power, and has denounced the national legislature as unconstitutional; who has persistently and corruptly resisted, by every means in his power, every proper attempt at the recnostruction of the States lately in rebellion; who has perverted the public patronage into an engine of wholesale corruption; and who has been justly impeached for high crimes and misdemeanors, and properly pronounced guilty thereof by the vote of thirty-five Senators.

9. The doctrine of Great Britain and other European powers, that because a man is once a subject he is always so, must be resisted at every hazard by the United States, as a relic of feudal times, not authorized by the laws of nations, and at war with our national honor and independence. Naturalized citizens are entitled to protection in all their rights of citizenship, as though they were native-born, and no citizen of the United States, native or naturalized, must be liable to arrest and imprisonment by any foreign power for acts done or words spoken in this country, and, if so arrested and imprisoned, it is the duty of the government to interfere in his behalf.

10. Of all who were faithful in the trials of the late war, there were none entitled to more especial honor than the brave soldiers and seamen who endured the hardships of campaign and cruise, and imperiled their lives in the service of their country; the bounties and pensions provided by the laws for these brave defenders of the nation, are obligations never to be forgotten; the widows and orphans of the gal-

lant dead are the wards of the people—a sacred legacy bequeathed to the nation's protecting care.

11. Foreign emigration, which in the past has added so much to the wealth, development, and resources, and increase of power to this republic, the asylum of the oppressed of all nations, should be fostered and encouraged by a liberal and just policy.

12. This Convention declares itself in sympathy with all oppressed people struggling for their rights.

Unanimously added, on motion of General Schurtz:

Resolved, That we highly commend the spirit of magnanimity and forbearance with which men who have served in the rebellion, but who now frankly and honestly coöperate with us in restoring the peace of the country and reconstructing the Southern State governments upon the basis of impartial justice and equal rights, are received back into the communion of the loyal people; and we favor the removal of the disqualifications and restrictions imposed upon the late rebels in the same measure as their spirit of loyalty will direct, and as may be consistent with the safety of the loyal people.

Resolved, That we recognize the great principles laid down in the immortal Declaration of Independence as the true foundation of democratic government, and we hail with gladness every effort toward making these principles a living reality on every inch of American soil.

The resolutions were unanimously adopted, amid great cheering, swinging of hats and waving of handkerchiefs. The following resolution was adopted, on motion of Colonel Thompson:

Resolved, That the adjournment of this Convention shall not work a dissolution of the same, but it shall remain as organized, subject to be called together again at any time and place that the National Republican Executive Committee shall designate.

GENERAL GRANT NOMINATED.

Mr. French, of North Carolina. I move, sir, that we now proceed to ballot for a candidate for President. [Great applause and cries of "Vote."]

General Logan, of Illinois. I rise to propound a question to the Chair. According to the order of business, it is not necessary for a vote in reference to the nomination of a candidate for President. Is it not the question to be announced by the Chair, under the rules, is the nomination of a President now in order?

The President. The order of business does not prescribe any specific time when it shall go into order of business. It may delay it until after the nomination of Vice-President if it chooses.

General Logan. Is it the decision of the Chair that nominations are now in order?

The President. Yes.

Cries of "bully," etc.

General Logan. Mr. President: Then, sir, in the name of the loyal citizens, soldiers, and sailors of this great Republic of the United States of America; in the name of loyalty, of liberty, of humanity, and of justice; in the name of the National Union Republican party, I nominate, as the candidate for the Chief Magistracy of this nation, Ulysses S. Grant. [Here there was a storm of applause. The mass of the people rose to their feet, and in all the hall there was the waving of hats and handkerchiefs. A lady in the gallery of the house, at this point of time, let loose a tri-colored pigeon, which flew through the room to the stage. Three lusty cheers were given, upon motion of a delegate, for General Grant, and the band played "Hail to the Chief."]

Mr. Bright, of South Carolina. I move, sir, that the vote

be taken by acclamation. [Cries of "No, it can't be done," etc.]

The President. The rules provide the manner of taking the vote. Give your attention to the call of the States, and as the call be made, let each delegation announce the choice of the State for the office of President.

The Secretary then called the roll.

THE VOTING.

The following remarks were made by the several chairmen of delegates when delivering the votes of the States:

Alabama—Through our delegation we cast eighteen votes for General Ulysses S. Grant.

Arkansas—The State of Arkansas casts ten votes for U. S. Grant.

California—Mr. President: We come, ten of us, some six thousand miles to cast her vote for General U. S. Grant. [Applause.]

Colorado—Mr. President: The delegates from Colorado say, U. S. Grant, six votes.

Connecticut—Mr. Chairman: Connecticut unconditionally surrenders her twelve votes for U. S. Grant. [Applause.]

Dakotah—U. S. Grant, two votes.

Delaware—The State of Delaware gives six votes for U. S. Grant.

District of Columbia—The District of Columbia casts her two votes for U. S. Grant.

Florida—Florida, the land of flowers, gives six votes for Ulysses S. Grant.

Georgia (ex-Governor Brown)—Mr. President, the Republicans of Georgia, many of whom were original secessionists, recognizing the wisdom of the maxim, "Enemies in war, in peace friends," and ardently desiring the speedy restoration of union, harmony, peace, and good government, instruct me through their representatives now here, to cast eighteen votes for General Ulysses S. Grant.

Idaho—The Territory of Idaho casts two votes for U. S. Grant.

Illinois—(General Logan)—Mr. President, Illinois casts thirty-two votes for U. S. Grant.

Indiana—(Mr. Lane)—Indiana casts twenty-six votes for U. S. Grant.

Iowa—Mr. President, Iowa casts sixteen votes for General U. S. Grant, and promises to back it up with forty thousand majority.

Kansas—Mr. President, Kansas, the John Brown State, gives six votes for U. S. Grant.

Kentucky—Mr. President, the State of Kentucky has directed my delegation to cast the vote of Kentucky, twenty-two votes, for Ulysses S. Grant.

Louisiana—(General A. L. Lee)—Mr. President, the State of Louisiana casts fourteen votes for General U. S. Grant, and we propose "to fight it out on this line if it takes all summer."

Maine—Maine gives fourteen votes for General U. S. Grant.

Maryland—Mr. Chairman, believing that our great Captain will crush treason in the Cabinet as he has crushed it in the field, Maryland, "My Maryland," gives fourteen votes for U. S. Grant.

Massachusetts—Mr. President, the State of Massachusetts casts twenty-four votes for U. S. Grant.

Michigan—Mr. President, the State of Michigan, following the State of Massachusetts, gives sixteen votes for U. S. Grant.

Minnesota—Mr. President, the North Star State gives all she has, eight votes, for U. S. Grant.

Mississippi—Mr. President, the State of Mississippi, the

home of Jefferson Davis, repudiates that traitor, and offers you fourteen votes for General U. S. Grant.

Missouri—(Hon. C. Schurtz)—The State Convention of Missouri instructed the delegation to vote for the nomination of U. S. Grant on a radical platform, and with full confidence that General Grant will carry it out, Missouri gives Grant twenty-two votes.

Montana—The Missouri and Columbia Rivers are vocal with the name of Grant, and Montana gives him two votes. [Applause.]

Nebraska—Mr. Chairman, Nebraska, the last State admitted into the Union, and the first State to adopt impartial suffrage, gives six votes to U. S. Grant.

Nevada—Mr. President, the Silver State has but six votes to give, but it proposes soon to have six more to give. It gives all it has for Grant.

New Hampshire—New Hampshire gives ten votes for U. S. Grant.

New Jersey—The delegates from New Jersey, instructed by her convention, and, as they believe, expressing the voice of the Republican party within her borders, now deliver their fourteen votes for U. S. Grant, the most glorious of soldiers, the man noted for calmness, a man of justice and patriotism.

New York—The State of New York casts sixty-six votes for Ulysses S. Grant.

North Carolina—Mr. President, North Carolina commonly known as the land of the tar-heavers, gives eighteen votes for U. S. Grant, and will give twice eighteen, thirty-six thousand votes—all of which we think will stick. [Loud laughter and cheers.]

Ohio—Mr. President, Ohio has the honor of being the mother of our great Captain. Ohio is in line, and on that line Ohio proposes following this great Captain, that never knew defeat, to fight it out through the summer, and in the autumn, at the great end of the contest, and to be first in storming the intrenchments until victory shall be secured and all the stars that glitter in the firmament of our glorious constellation shall again be restored into their proper order, and all the sons of freedom throughout the whole earth shall shout for joy. [Good! Good!] Ohio gives forty-two votes for U. S. Grant.

Oregon—Mr. President, the State of Oregon—the most North-west State of this Union—the people of the State have directed their delegates here to cast six votes for U. S. Grant.

Pennsylvania—Mr. Chairman, Pennsylvania casts fifty-two votes for General U. S. Grant.

Rhode Island—Mr. President, bright-eyed "Little Rhody," your only sister, small in stature, and patriotic and noble, gives her eight votes for General U. S. Grant, and wishes she had more.

South Carolina—Mr. President, the State of South Carolina, the birth-place and the home of John C. Calhoun and the doctrine of State Rights, first to withdraw herself from the Union, directs me, through her representatives, sent here by a Republican majority of 43,470 [Applause], returning again to the councils of those who desire only to preserve the Union, arm in arm, and heart to heart with Massachusetts [Cheers and cries of "good!"] gives her twelve votes to General U. S. Grant.

Tennessee—Mr. President, Tennessee, being one of the Southern States that was thrust into the rebellion, and being the first to reconstruct and be readmitted to the Union, and to-day being in the enjoyment of a liberal republican government, casts twenty votes for Ulysses S. Grant, and hopes never again to vote for President or Vice-President for such a traitor as Andrew Johnson.

Texas—Texas, through her delegation here assembled, has instructed me to cast twelve votes for Ulysses S. Grant, from the Empire State of the South, having a territory of 275,000 square miles, and capable of sustaining the whole of the people.

Vermont—The Republicans of Vermont, through their delegation, give ten votes for Ulysses S. Grant.

Virginia—The State of New Virginia, raised from the grave that General Grant dug for her in the Appomattox, in in 1865, comes up here with her twenty votes and enlists under his banner, and they propose in next November to move on the enemy's works.

West Virginia—West Virginia, in the front of the rebellion, and which never gave a Democratic majority, gives freely and willingly her ten votes for Ulysses S. Grant for President. [Applause.] Mr. Chairman, West Virginia gives ten votes for U. S. Grant.

Wisconsin—Mr. Chairman: Wisconsin, the last on the roll of States, adds her voice to that of her sister States, and gives her sixteen votes for Ulysses S. Grant.

Mr. President: Wisconsin gives sixteen votes for U. S. Grant. The roll is completed with the following result:

THE VOTE FOR PRESIDENT.

States	No. of Delegates.	Votes for Grant.
Alabama	10	10
Arkansas	10	10
California	10	10
Colorado	6	6
Connecticut	12	12
Delaware	6	6
Florida	6	6
Georgia	18	18
Illinois	32	32

States.	No. of Delegates.	Votes for Grant.
Indiana	26	26
Iowa	16	16
Kansas	6	6
Kentucky	22	22
Louisiana	14	14
Maine	14	14
Maryland	14	14
Massachusetts	24	24
Michigan	16	16
Minnesota	8	8
Mississippi	14	14
Missouri	22	22
Nebraska	6	6
Nevada	6	6
New Hampshire	10	10
New Jersey	14	14
New York	66	66
North Carolina	18	18
Ohio	42	42
Oregon	6	6
Pennsylvania	52	52
Rhode Island	8	8
South Carolina	12	12
Tennessee	20	20
Texas	12	12
Vermont	10	10
Virginia	20	20
West Virginia	10	10
Wisconsin	16	16
Total	636	636

In addition to the above, Dakotah, Idaho, Montana, and the District of Columbia gave each two votes for General Grant.

The President. Gentlemen of the Convention, you have given six hundred and forty-four votes for General Ulysses

S. Grant, and he is unanimously nominated for the office of President of the United States.

HOW THE ANNOUNCEMENT WAS RECEIVED.

The announcement by the chair that General Grant had received the total vote of the Convention was received with the wildest applause. A curtain was withdrawn at the back of the stage, displaying a magnificent painting of the White House, with the Goddess of Liberty beckoning General Grant toward it. Words can not describe the enthusiasm that this produced. The Convention arose, the delegates swinging their arms and shouting while the galleries fluttered with handkerchiefs. Doves, colored red, white and blue, were launched from the galleries, and flying about the hall added a pleasing feature to the animated scene. A glee club came forward and sang a song composed expressly for the occasion, the burden of which was that they would "fight it out on this line if it takes all summer," while the Great Western Light Guard Band played several patriotic airs, to the intense delight of all in the Convention.

A delegate from Indiana. Mr. Chairman, I move that we try our throats on three times three with swinging hats and waving handkerchiefs.

They were given with a will, the band in the meantime playing "Rally round the flag," and delegates all joined in singing.

A DISPATCH TO GRANT.

A Delegate. I move that the President of this Convention be authorized and requested to transmit a telegraphic dispatch to General Grant.

A Delegate. I second the motion.

The delegates still remained standing, and it was difficult for the President to hear any thing.

The President. The Convention will come to order.

Three gentlemen then sang a song composed for the occasion. It was received with applause.

As soon as order could be restored, the Convention proceeded to nominate a candidate for Vice-President, of which we shall speak in another chapter. (See Life of Colfax.)

CHAPTER XX.

HOW GENERAL GRANT RECEIVED THE NEWS OF HIS NOMINATION—THE ENTHUSIASM IN WASHINGTON—PROCESSIONS—ADDRESS TO GENERAL GRANT BY GOVERNOR BOUTWELL—GRANT'S REPLY—RECEPTION OF THE SOLDIERS' AND SAILORS' COMMITTEE—PRESENTATION BY COLONEL ALLEMAN—GRANT'S REPLY—RECEPTION AT GRANT'S RESIDENCE IN THE EVENING—PRESENTATION OF THE REPUBLICAN NATIONAL CONVENTION'S RESOLUTIONS BY GOVERNOR HAWLEY—ABLE SPEECH BY HAWLEY—GENERAL GRANT'S REPLY—GRANT FORMALLY ACCEPTS THE REPUBLICAN NOMINATION—CONCLUSION.

GENERAL GRANT, who had been attending to his official duties all day, was at his head-quarters in Washington when the news was conveyed to him of his nomination. He puffed his cigar very vigorously for a few minutes, but said not a word. Soon callers began to drop in to congratulate him, and the modest General took the first opportunity to steal away and retire to his house.

In the evening a great throng of people, headed by a brass band, marched through the streets and proceeded to General Grant's residence.

After the band played "Hail to the Chief," calls were made for "Grant," when he appeared at the door and was greeted with prolonged cheers. Representative Boutwell, of Massachusetts, who was standing at his side, addressed him as follows:

General: This assemblage of your fellow-citizens, brought together without organization or previous arrangement, have desired me to express to you their gratification at your unanimous nomination for President of the United States by the Republican Convention recently assembled at Chicago. The unanimity with which you have been nominated, almost, if not altogether without a parallel in the history of our country, furnishes sufficient indication of the vast majority, if not entire unanimity, with which the nomination will be sustained by the loyal people of the country. The Republican party has not yet had an opportunity to test its capacity for the government of the Republic in time of peace. We have had a war of more than four years' duration, but the valiant and patriotic people of this country, under your leadership, quelled the mightiest rebellion the world has ever seen against the best government ever known to mankind. You will be supported in the contest upon which you have entered by the same heroic men who were with you at Shiloh, in the Wilderness, and before Richmond; and you are to meet with the opposition of a comparatively few of those who have returned, to the support of the Union, the Constitution, and the flag of the country, and, with but few exceptions, you are to be opposed by men animated by the same principles which animated the men engaged in the rebellion you were engaged in overthrowing.

After continuing in this strain for some time Governor Boutwell concluded, when General Grant stepped forward and said:

SPEECH BY GENERAL GRANT.

"Gentlemen: Being entirely unaccustomed to public speaking, and without any desire to cultivate that power, it is impossible for me to find appropriate language to thank you for this demonstration. All that I can say is this, that to whatever position I may be called by your will, I shall endeavor to discharge its duties with fidelity and honesty of purpose. Of my rectitude in the performance of public duties you will have to judge yourselves by my record before you."

It will be remembered that a committee of nine were appointed by the Soldiers' and Sailors' Convention to notify General Grant of his nomination by his old comrades in arms. On the 29th of May the committee discharged the duty assigned it. The affair came off at the house of General Grant, in Washington, and was witnessed by a crowd of people.

After a lively hand-shaking, Colonel Alleman, of Pennsylvania, delivered a few complimentary remarks.

General Grant spoke, in reply, as follows:

SPEECH OF GENERAL GRANT.

"Gentlemen of the Soldiers' and Sailors' Convention: I will say, while it was never a desire of mine to be a candidate for political office, it affords me great gratification to feel that I have the support of those who were with me in the war. If I did not feel I had the confidence of those, I would feel less desirous of accepting the position. The acceptance of the office is not a matter of choice, but of duty. Hoping, having accepted the nomination, I will receive your aid till next November, I must thank you, gentlemen, for the honor you have conferred upon me."

There were present all the Convention Committee, with whom were General Gregg, Generals Rawlins, Bódeau, Porter, Comstock, Dent, and Babcock, and Colonels Parker, Webster and Lee, of the General's staff.

After a few moments' conversation, General Grant extended a cordial invitation to the committee to be present at his residence in the evening, on occasion of the formal presentation of the nomination of the National Republican Convention.

In the evening the committee attended as invited, when a committee similar to their own, appointed by the citizen convention, officially notified General Grant of his nomination.

At the residence of General Grant about two hundred persons were present, including delegates to the Convention, several members of Congress, General Grant's staff, and the ladies of the families of General Grant and Speaker Colfax. These two gentlemen stood side by side, and the spectators formed in a semicircle in front of them, thus affording a full view of the proceedings. General Hawley, President of the Convention, delivered the following address:

"GENTLEMEN: The National Union Republican party assembled in national convention on the 20th of this month, appointed us, the officers of the Convention, to wait upon you. In obedience to its instructions we give you a copy of the record of its proceedings. You will perceive that it was governed by the most patriotic motives. Harmonious, enthusiastic, and determined; we mean, in your own words, 'to save in peace what we won in war.' We mean to make it a solemn, practical reality in the United States, that all men are created equal, endowed by their Creator with certain inalienable rights, among which are life, liberty, and the pursuit of happiness. We intend that there shall never be cause or opportunity for a civil war in this nation, originated either by those who would enslave their fellow-men, or those who must fight to regain their freedom. We believe there can be no permanent peace save in justice and equal rights, the equality of all men before the law. We hope to see our Government reaching to the remotest corner and to the humblest person, securing to him, by impartial and irresistible power, his personal safety, the right to the avails of his labor, and the right and the opportunity for physical, mental, and moral advancement. The best guarantee for the continuance of such a Government, is to give to all classes impartially a share in its management. We hear much of forgiveness and fraternity. We do most earnestly desire a speedy return of the policy and measures of peaceful time. None long more for a fully restored Union than those who sustained their Government during the late dreadful war. But the dead men have left a trust in our hands. We long for peace and good-will, but we have no friends who oppress their fellow-men. We do not idly and hopelessly ask for indemnity for the past. We do ask for security for the future. You will see that the Convention believes that integrity, simplicity, and economy in governmental affairs are the duties of good citizens and honorable men. It makes the strict fulfillment of national obligations a point of honor, never to be waived. While the civilized world recognizes a full and final payment as the only payment, the Union Republican party will never consent to tender any other. The equal rights of adopted citizens are clearly asserted, and all people who love our Government are hospitably invited to come and enjoy its benefits and contribute to its strength. The Convention spoke in nothing more warmly than in proffering a hearty welcome to all those who, lately in arms against the United States, are now frankly and honestly coöperating in restoring peace and establishing a truly free government. During the last three years countless indications of the people's choice for the next President have been converging upon yourself. Having made its statement of principles and purposes, the Convention deliberately and formally, State by State, Territory by Territory, recorded the will of its constituents, and unanimously nominated you for President of the United States, following the work by tumultuous and long-continued manifestations of joy, pride, and confidence. We know you will be faithful to the Constitution and the laws, and to the sympathies and principles that you are called to represent. We know that you will not seek to enforce upon the unwilling representatives of the people any policy of your own devising, for you have said that 'the will of the people is the law of the land.' The records of this war, and of your subsequent fidelity, afford the evidence that the nation can safely and wisely place you in the chair of Washington and Lincoln. In behalf of the Convention, we tender you its nomination for President, and solicit its acceptance. We can give you no higher proof of our gratitude for your past, or our confidence in your future. We propose to elect you."

After the applause with which the above speech was received had ceased, General Grant replied as follows:

"Mr. President, and gentlemen of the National Union Convention: I will endeavor, in a very short time, to write you, accepting the trust you have conferred upon me. [Applause.] Expressing my gratitude for the confidence you have placed in me, I will now say but little orally, and that is to thank you for the unanimity with which you have selected me as a candidate for the presidential office. I can say, in addition, that I looked on, during the proceedings at Chicago, with a great deal of interest, and am gratified with the harmony and the unity which seemed to have governed the deliberations of the Convention. If chosen to fill the high office for which you have selected me, I will give to its duties the same energy, the same spirit, and the same will that I have given to the performance of all the duties which have devolved on me heretofore. Whether I shall be able to perform these duties to your entire satisfaction, time will determine. You have truly said, in the course of your address, that I shall have no policy of my own to interpose against the will of the people."

As the General concluded his speech, there was long-continued applause.

The following is General Grant's letter to General Hawley, formally accepting the Republican nomination for President:

"WASHINGTON, D. C., May 29, 1868.

"*To General Joseph R. Hawley, President of the National Union Republican Convention:*

"In formally accepting the nomination of the National Union Republican Convention of the 21st of May, it seems proper that some statement of my views beyond the mere acceptance of the nomination should be expressed.

"The proceedings of the Convention were marked with wisdom, moderation, and patriotism, and, I believe, express the feelings of the great mass of those who sustained the country through its trials. I indorse their resolutions, and, if elected to the office of President of the United States, it will be my endeavor to administer all the laws in good faith, with economy, and with the view of giving peace, quiet, and protection every-where.

"In times like the present it is impossible, or at least eminently improper, to lay down a policy to be adhered to, right or wrong, through an administration of four years. New political issues, not foreseen, are constantly arising. The views of the public on old ones are constantly changing, and a purely administrative officer should be left free to execute the will of the people. I have always respected that will, and always shall.

"Peace and universal prosperity, its sequence, with

economy of administration, will lighten the burden of taxation, while it constantly reduces the national debt. Let us have peace. With great respect,

"Your obedient servant,

"U. S. GRANT."

Our task is done. Our life of Grant, such as it is, is written, and we send it forth, hoping it may contribute, in some small degree, to the election of the illustrious chieftain. We lay down our pen, feeling very confident, indeed, that the American people, with that good sense and judgment which has heretofore characterized their public action, will, in November next, confer upon him that civic crown of the republic—the Presidency—which is not only the highest office in this country, but in the world. Such action would be alike honorable to them and the man, a fit recognition by a grateful people of the eminent services he rendered in times of great public danger, and the cap-sheaf to a life which, for public worth and private purity, has not been surpassed since the days of Washington.

HON. SCHUYLER COLFAX

LIFE OF SCHUYLER COLFAX.

LIFE OF SCHUYLER COLFAX.

CHAPTER I.

BIRTH AND PARENTAGE OF COLFAX—DEATH OF HIS FATHER—POVERTY AND EARLY STRUGGLES OF THE FAMILY—HIS EDUCATION AND HABITS—HIS MOTHER MARRIES MR. MATTHEWS—SCHUYLER A CLERK—THEY REMOVE TO INDIANA—COLFAX DRIVES A WAGON ACROSS MICHIGAN—HIS STEP-FATHER SETTLES AT NEW CARLISLE—COLFAX A CLERK AGAIN—THE "STORE AND POST-OFFICE"—YOUNG COLFAX AS AN ORACLE—HIS FIRST ACQUAINTANCE WITH HON. JOHN D. DEFREES—A FRIEND IN NEED—GOES TO SOUTH BEND—READS LAW—IS DEPUTY COUNTY AUDITOR—THE MOOT LEGISLATURE—WRITES FOR THE NEWSPAPERS—IS APPOINTED SENATE REPORTER—ESTABLISHES THE VALLEY REGISTER, AND BECOMES AN EDITOR—HIS POVERTY AND STRUGGLES SUCCEEDS AT LAST—HIS POPULARITY WITH THE PEOPLE—HELPS TO FRAME THE CONSTITUTION OF INDIANA—OPPOSITION TO THE BLACK LAWS—IS NOMINATED FOR CONGRESS—HIS DEFEAT—IS A DELEGATE TO THE NATIONAL CONVENTIONS OF 1848 AND 1852, AND VOTES FOR TAYLOR AND SCOTT—HIS POLITICS—PURITY OF HIS CHARACTER—IS RENOMINATED AND TRIUMPHANTLY ELECTED TO CONGRESS—BEGINS HIS LEGISLATIVE CAREER.

FORTY-SIX years ago, in the summer of 1822, there lived in North Moore Street, in the city of New York, a young married couple, whose home has now become a matter of historical interest. The husband, a patient, hard-working young man, clerked in a bank, and the wife, a mere girl of fifteen, took care of the quiet home. These people were the parents of Schuyler Colfax, the next Vice-President of the United States. The same year, and before the subject of our sketch was born, Mr. Colfax died, and the mother, in affectionate remembrance of his father, named her child Schuyler. Left alone with her son, the grief-stricken young mother found it hard enough struggling with the world, but she bravely determined, by the help of God, to raise up the boy to be an honorable and useful man.

Schuyler Colfax first saw the light on the 23d day of March, 1823, and was a puny, delicate child. Had the ancient rule been enforced to slay all puny children, Colfax, Alexander, Napoleon, and Grant would not long have troubled the world, for they were all weakly children.

Schuyler grew up a slender, flaxen-haired, loving boy, seemingly too delicate to contend with the rough storms of life. Reared among grown people, he had no toys or children's plays, and was trying to earn a livelihood when he ought to have been in the nursery or at school. He was always a boy-man, and seemed from the first to understand and sympathize with his mother in her loneliness. To cheer and comfort her was his sole delight, and when, but a little child, he would appeal to her to know what he could do to help her along. The mother and son were all in all to each other, and though widowed and fatherless, each felt they were not entirely alone in the world. Forty years have passed away since the time of which we are writing, but the confidence of early affection is as bright and pure to-day as it ever was, and Schuyler Colfax and his mother, by their fireside, presents one of the pleasantest home pictures in America. Still the strong man, wise statesman, and distinguished citizen is the same simple-hearted, loving, and dutiful son; still the fond mother strokes, with tender hand, the head of her boy, though she is old now, and here and there threads of silver runs through her hair. See them on the Sabbath day, seated side by side in the house of God, listening to His divine word, praying earnestly for the peace and prosperity of the country, and the happiness of the people and each other. Such is the blameless life led by the second man in the nation, such the upright and honorable example set by him to the nation and the world.

Though hard pressed by poverty, Mrs. Colfax kept her boy steadily at school. In those days there were no public schools in New York, and the education of children was both troublesome and expensive to what it is now. Young Colfax was a wonderfully apt scholar, and learned rapidly, being always at the head of his class. His mental organization seemed as quick and retentive as he was physically delicate and sensitive.

The boy was a great reader, constantly borrowing books and newspapers, and poring over them for hours. Modest and reticent, he always had strong convictions and opinions of his own, and took great delight in maintaining them. Those who argued with him were surprised at the extent of his information and the skill and ease with which he debated questions.

When ten years of age he was well posted upon the political issues of the day, and was even then an earnest Whig. About this time Schuyler left school, and his mother soon afterward marrying Mr. Matthews, a commission merchant, of New York, the boy became a clerk in his stepfather's store. Young Colfax was prompt, energetic, and attentive to business, but could not give over his fondness for books, and whenever he could snatch an hour from his duties was always found with a volume in his hands. His polite deportment, and of affable disposition, made him a general favorite; and hundreds of persons yet living remember the pleasant boy-face that they met forty years ago. Mr. Matthews was not successful in business, and in

1836 determined to try his fortunes in the then fast-growing West.

Thousands were turning their faces toward the setting sun, and one morning, as the shadows of night were leaving the earth, the Matthews family, with all their earthly goods packed in a wagon, set out to seek a Western home. Crossing Michigan, young Schuyler, who was then thirteen years old, driving the wagon, the emigrants entered the then new State of Indiana, and halted at the little village of New Carlisle, fourteen miles west of South Bend, in St. Joseph County.

Here Mr. Matthews opened a small store, and Schuyler became his clerk. Again his genial smile, and kind and accommodating disposition won him hosts of friends, and young Colfax was a great favorite with the villagers and country people. He prevailed on his step-father to take the post-office into the store, engaging to open and change the mails. Thus he had free access to plenty of newspapers, and could keep himself thoroughly informed on all that was transpiring in the country.

Mr. Matthews' store soon became a place of resort, and on Saturday afternoon and at night the farmers and villagers would gather in to hear the news. Young Schuyler Colfax was their oracle, and even those who took the papers found it more pleasant to go and hear Schuyler tell over what was going on than to read the paper. He was always thoroughly informed, and could talk in a plain, intelligent way, so as to make himself perfectly understood by the simple-hearted, honest people about him. Foreign wars, markets, domestic news, accidents, what they were doing at Washington, speeches of the great men, were all at his command, and he related what was going on with wonderful accuracy and ease. That Schuyler Colfax was a "smart boy," was the verdict of many a villager, but not one of them dreamed for a moment that the pale, slender, flaxen-haired youth would, twenty years later, be the foremost man in Congress, Speaker of the House, a candidate for Vice-President, and a probable future President of the United States. Colfax had now been four years in the store of his step-father, and was seventeen years old, though small for his age.

It was mail day, and, as it came but once a week, the usual crowd had gathered at the "store and post-office" to get their mail, hear the news, and while away the evening. Among those gathered on that particular evening, was a stranger in the village, a tall, raw-boned young man, with intellectual face, who was a prominent lawyer at the neighboring county seat of St. Joseph. The lawyer was stopping over night in the village of Carlisle, and had come down to the post-office to borrow a paper and read the news. When the mail arrived, our legal friend observed that it was taken in charge by a light-haired, blue-eyed stripling, whom he had previously noticed behind the counter. There was something in the thoughtful but pleasant face, and in the quick and active movement of this youth, which at once attracted his attention and caused him to observe him closely. After the mail had been assorted and distributed, and the crowd of villagers measurably dispersed, he drew him into conversation. The longer he conversed with him the more he became charmed with his manners and the intelligence which he displayed. Small of stature, but evidently older than his appearance indicated, with eyes that fairly sparkled and danced when he became animated in conversation, with a face pleasing and handsome, both in repose and when agitated, he was a boy that could not fail to attract and interest the stranger. He seemed to take a deep interest in matters of public policy, and had already formed most decided political opinions. Those opinions, harmonizing with the views of the stranger, who was a leading Whig, and as such had several times represented the county in the legislature, led him to propose to the young man to accompany him home and enter his office as a student of law. While the proposition seemed to please him very much, his sense of duty to his mother and his step-father caused him to decline the generous offer. "For," said he, "while our business is neither large nor lucrative, I have principally attended to it myself; should I go away I fear it would decline and not even afford us a support. As we have nothing laid by, and no other income to look to for support, I could not think of leaving, at least for the present." Then his new-found friend explained to him that the legislature, which had just adjourned, had provided for the office of county auditor—that if he desired to read law he thought he might secure his step-father the appointment of auditor, which would give him a better income than he was now receiving; that in that event he could act as deputy auditor and pursue the study of law while not otherwise engaged. This proposition, on being submitted to the boy's step-father, was readily accepted, his appointment as auditor of the county secured, and Schuyler Colfax, soon to fill the second place in the gift of the American people, accompanied him to South Bend as his deputy, where he was to read law in the office of Hon. John D. Defrees, who was the generous stranger that had so kindly assisted him and his. This was the turning point in young Colfax's life. He was to read law during his leisure hours in Mr. Defrees' office, and he seems to have been very diligent in his studies, for it was not many months before he was an acknowledged expounder of State law. But he did not complete his legal education. We doubt if he had much of a relish for the dry details of statutes.

His reading of law, however, was not confined to that required for exercising an auditor's duties; he found time to make himself master of its great principles, rather, however, for the sake of the general culture it might afford him, than with the view of adopting it as a profession. During this period, too, he was practicing himself in that facility for putting his thoughts on paper, which was afterward of so much advantage to him. A gentleman, well known in the philanthropic circles of New York and Brooklyn, who had been a schoolmate of Mr. Colfax in the Crosby Street school, which was the last one he attended in New York City, kept up a correspondence with him during those years of his service as deputy auditor, and says: "Schuyler's letters in those days were very interesting; they were filled with details concerning his studies, knotty questions which he wanted me to aid him in clearing up, and brilliant thoughts often expressed with the same felicity which now marks his writings."

To such a youth, writing for the newspapers was almost a necessity. There had been a paper in South Bend, edited for some years by his friend John D. Defrees, and Colfax contributed often to its columns. Among the inevitable schemes of American village life, that of "a debating society" arose in 1843, at South Bend. In maturing outlines, somebody's prophetic soul caught the inspiration of a moot State Legislature. The ayes had it, whereupon Mr. Defrees, now congressional printer, was made "Mr. Speaker," and the future Speaker of "The Historic Congress" found himself "the honorable gentleman from Newton," now a county in his present congressionaldistrict. Thus our fledgling orators debated not hackneyed didactics, but "bills," and all proceedings were conducted according to strict parliamentary rules, which, doubtless, gave rural members much perplexing study; yet "Newton County" faltered not. The pages of Jefferson's and Cushing's Manuals were carefully and thoroughly conned, till "the gentleman from Newton" became as conversant with the rules and usages of "the House" as any presiding officer in our State Legislatures. This, and the habit of off-hand debate, were of great advantage to him in after years, and contributed much to make him, as he is acknowledged to be, by all parties, the best presiding officer the House of Representatives has had for many years.

Mr. Defrees, having now removed to Indianapolis and taken charge of the *State Journal*, procured from the Senate for his friend Colfax the position of Senate Reporter for the *Journal*. He was now fast laying the foundation for future usefulness. His two years' service at Indianapolis, as Senate reporter for the *State Journal*, gave Mr. Colfax a rarely clear solution of the perplexities of parliamentary usage, he little dreaming that the knowledge and skill thus obtained would later set boundaries to congressional debate and grandly historic legislation.

Like rays of Empire's star, white lines of covered wagons followed westward. Immigrants poured in. Franklin thrift longed for Franklin's printing-press, and yielding to the solicitation of a few enterprising men, Colfax, in 1845, with only two hundred and fifty subscribers, began the publication of the *St. Joseph Valley Register*. It was a small concern, being such a sheet as every Western settlement issues as a sort of flyer to a job printing business as soon as it has got its school-house, grocery, hotel, and blacksmith-shop, and begins to think about having a meeting-house. The "typo" out West frequently gets the start of the preacher, though the race is close. Those who saw Colfax then "at the case," describe him as a light, spindling, flaxen haired, boyish looking youth—clever rather in the Yankee than the English sense—with a delicacy of temperament which suggested a doubt whether he had the stamina to live to manhood, without the faintest suggestion that in his mature years he would be fifteen years in Congress, Speaker of the House, and the second choice of the people for President. The news in those days came to South Bend by stage from Detroit, or up the St. Joe River to the lake, and there was precious little of them at that. But Colfax made his paper readable, and often late in the night, he could be found at his desk or over "the case." Mr. Colfax was not, as many writers have supposed, a practical printer. He never had been apprenticed to the printing business, and knew nothing of the practical part of the "art preservative of all arts" until after he had commenced the publication of *The Register*. With his ready tact and quick perception, however, and great anxiety to economise, for his means were yet very limited, he soon mastered the art sufficiently to "help out of the drag," but he never attained to any great proficiency in the business, his editorial labors, the business of the office, and other duties soon claiming his entire attention. His paper was now prospering and acquiring influence; subscribers, advertising, and money coming in, and the poor editor saw *The Register* firmly established as a paying institution. Still Mr. Colfax gave his entire attention to his newspaper business. Every paragraph, however small, that went into his columns, was carefully examined, and bore the reflex of the elevated mind and thoughts of the editor. Colfax was a Whig, and his sympathies were with his party, and he ably defended its principles; but though often attacked, personally and with scurrilous abuse, by the Democratic papers of that section, he never allowed a discourteous or abusive word in his paper. He was too thoroughly a gentleman in word, and thought, and nature to stoop to scurrility, and his opponents soon found that they injured themselves in their efforts to injure him.

In South Bend every body liked him and believed in him. The magnetism of his genial face, his kindly nature, and his cordial hand grasp won all hearts. He was, the villagers said, a remarkable man, especially for a newspaper editor. He paid his debts; he drank no whisky; he was prudent and economical; he never uttered an oath; and though it was only by careful management that he avoided debt, he always seemed to have something to give to the poor.

He was, during this period, steadily gaining in reputation as a political writer and speaker, and had now fairly established his claim to intellectual superiority. His county always stood by him; and, in 1848, he was chosen a delegate to the Whig National Convention, which nominated General Taylor for the Presidency. He was elected and served as one of the secretaries of that convention; and, after its adjournment, returned home and entered actively into the canvass for the nominees.

Two years later, and at the age of twenty-seven, in 1850, he represented St. Joseph County in the convention which framed the present constitution of Indiana. In that convention, he opposed with all his ability the adoption of the clause preventing free colored men from settling in the State. His opposition to this measure caused his defeat for Congress the next year. In 1851, he was nominated for Congress, and had for a competitor Dr. Graham N. Fitch, an old, wily, and experienced Democratic politician, (subsequently the colleague of Jesse D. Bright, as Senator,) and in a district which for years had been Democratic by some thousands majority. Dr. Fitch used his opposition to the black laws mercilessly against him; but, despite the ability, tact, and shrewdness of the old political wire-worker, he only distanced his young competitor two hundred and thirty-eight votes, in a poll of over eighteen thousand.

In 1852, he was again elected a delegate, from Indiana, to the Whig National Convention. Of this body, as of its predecessor, Colfax was elected secretary, and took an active part in the nomination of General Scott for the

Presidency. He was an active worker in the campaign that followed, speaking often and writing much. In the spring of 1853, he was urged to accept another nomination for Congress, but declined, and Dr. Fitch was reëlected by a majority of more than a thousand votes.

It was the era of the Kansas-Nebraska swindle, and though the district which he represented was strongly opposed to this measure, and his constituents used all their influence to dissuade him from supporting it, yet Dr. Fitch was so mole-eyed and so wedded to slavery that he advocated and voted for it steadily.

This was too much for the good people of St. Joseph County. A majority of them had voted the Democratic ticket regularly, but they were determined to do so no longer. The young editor of the St. Joseph *Valley Register* was urged to accept the nomination for Congress, and did so. The canvass in that district, in 1854, was a memorable one. Colfax was very active; the "great deep" of Democracy in Indiana was broken up, and the old hunkers laid in a political grave from which, it is to be hoped, they may never be resurrected. Early in the campaign, young Colfax, who had now had considerable experience as a debater, and was familiar with State and National politics, challenged his competitor to travel the district with him, and discuss before the people the issues involved. Colfax proved himself more than a match in the hustings for his opponent, and the people every-where acknowledged his superiority as a debater. His mild and persuasive manners, his earnest and eloquent declamation, carried all hearts by storm, and he was elected by seventeen hundred and sixty-six majority. He was now thirty-one years of age when he commenced that brilliant career in Congress, of which we shall speak hereafter, and which has continued from that time up to the present without a single interruption.

CHAPTER II.

COLFAX AS AN ODD-FELLOW—HIS ENTRANCE INTO CONGRESS—SUPPORTS BANKS FOR THE SPEAKERSHIP—HIS FIRST SPEECH IN CONGRESS—IS A MEMBER OF IMPORTANT COMMITTEES—ENTERS THE PRESIDENTIAL CAMPAIGN OF 1856—IS RE-ELECTED TO CONGRESS—HIS IMMENSE POPULARITY—IS ELECTED SPEAKER OF THE XXXVIII CONGRESS—SUPPORTS THE WAR—MR. COLFAX'S VIEWS ON THE NATIONAL ENTERPRISES—HE SUPPORTS LINCOLN—MR. LINCOLN'S FRIENDSHIP FOR HIM—COLFAX ON THE STUMP—IS AGAIN RE-ELECTED TO CONGRESS—RE-ELECTED SPEAKER OF THE XXXIX CONGRESS—HIS POPULARITY IN THE HOUSE—THE BEST SPEAKER SINCE CLAY—REMARKABLE ABILITY OF MR. COLFAX AS A PRESIDING OFFICER.

MR. COLFAX has for many years been an active member of the order of Odd-Fellows. In 1849, he was a representative from Indiana to the Grand Lodge of the United States, and was on nearly all the important committees in that body. In 1850, he was one of a committee of three to report on the propriety of founding a degree for the wives and daughters of scarlet degree members and past officers. Messrs. La Rue and Kennedy, the other members of the committee, made a majority report against the new degree, but Mr. Colfax submitted so earnest a minority report that the majority report was overruled and a female degree ordered. Out of Mr. Colfax's report grew what is at the present day known as the Daughters of Rebecca.

In 1852, Mr. Colfax was again on all the important committees in the national body of Odd-Fellows, and in 1854 he was nominated for Grand Sire of the Order. On the first ballot he received the highest number of votes cast, but after a close contest was beaten by Mr. Elliston, of Massachusetts. A prominent Odd-Fellow said not long since he would rather be Grand Sire of the Order than President of the United States. We believe Mr. Colfax is still a prominent member of the organization.

. . . .

Exactly sixteen years from the time Colfax entered the office of his friend as a student at law, he entered, for the first time, the capitol of the nation as a representative of the people. Two years before, he had competed with the able and wily Dr. Fitch for the prize, which he then barely lost, and now, in the second race, triumphantly won, in a district largely Democratic.

He took his seat in Congress at the time of the protracted struggle in regard to the election of a Speaker, which terminated in the choice of Nathaniel P. Banks, and he gallantly plunged into the contest. His maiden speech took the whole House by surprise. It not only demonstrated that he was even then one of the ablest debaters in the House, but its eloquence, its logical power, and its graphic portrayal of the real condition of Kansas, and of the iniquity of the border ruffian movement made it one of the most effective speeches ever delivered in that body. It was a bold and fearless rebuke of the slave power, made in the teeth of its fire-eating representatives. It was methodical in arrangement and powerful in argument—every charge was clinched with such proofs as none dared to dispute. With the terrible experience we have since had—with the facts of all the villainies, rascality, and inhumanity of the leaders of the late rebellion still fresh in our memories, it is hardly possible to read and believe that all the charges he then made and sustained against the Democratic party were true. But such they were. No one dared to dispute them then, none will dare do so now. This speech, delivered by one of the youngest members of the House, became the principal Presidential campaign document of the contest of that year. Over one-half million copies of it were printed in Washington, Philadelphia, and New York, to say nothing of the wide circulation it received through the columns of the Republican press of the country. Such a compliment we believe was never before paid to any member of Congress—certainly not to the maiden speech of one of the youngest members of the House.

He was appointed Chairman of the Committee on Post-offices and Post-roads on the organization of the Thirty-seventh Congress, and did much to extend mail facilities throughout the West. He was one of the first advocates, and is still one of the warmest friends, of the Pacific Railroad. Indeed, he takes a warm interest in any movement looking to the development of the boundless resources of the great West.

Into the Presidential contest of 1856, the first of the Republican party, Mr. Colfax entered with all his zeal and enthusiasm. The banner of Fremont and Dayton was borne aloft in his paper, and his eloquent appeals in its behalf rang through all the States of the West. Victory was perhaps hardly to be expected for a new party at its first trial, but never was a fight more gallantly conducted.

The people of Northern Indiana knew and honored the talents and worth of their representative. By that personal magnetism which he possesses in larger measure than most men, he had drawn all hearts to him, and although the political causes which had aided him in 1854 no longer existed, the people still adhered to him, and in 1856 returned him to Congress by over one thousand majority. Perhaps the only cause of complaint Mr. Colfax has against his district is the continual majorities that have expelled him east of the mountains. Never for one moment has the confidence of the people in him flagged, and from 1855 to the present time they have cheerfully given him their votes. In 1860, he received thirty-four hundred more votes than his competitor, and in 1866, nearly twenty-two hundred more.

He was elected Speaker of the Thirty-eighth Congress in 1863, by a vote of 101 to 81, and has been reëlected Speaker of the Thirty-ninth and Fortieth. He was urged, but he declined, to accept a seat in the United States Senate, preferring his presiding chair in the House. For fourteen years he has been prominently identified with nearly every Republican measure in Congress, and during the war, was one of the best friends the soldiers had at the capitol. Every bill for men and money received his active support, and he gave liberally from his private means to the Christian Commission and hospital funds for the comfort and relief of the sick. To our knowledge, at one time Mr. Colfax donated $100, and at another time, all his mileage, amounting to over $500.

Mr. Colfax's position as presiding officer of the House has prevented him from obtaining that distinction as an orator he would otherwise have done, but it is only justice to say that during the short time he was on the floor, his great powers as a debater, his strong, clear, common sense, quick intuition, and devotion to the best interests of his country, made him so valuable a business member of the House of Representatives that he was early placed on important committees. If he had remained on the floor there can be little doubt but that he would have become one of the most distinguished business men of the body, and have been constantly kept at the head of the leading committees.

His views, in 1856, on many of the great national enterprises have since been adopted, and none more particularly than those regarding the Pacific Railroad, which he declared then was "a most important measure, not only for the prosperity of the nation, but as a means of binding together the distant sections of our great Republic."

Mr. Colfax plunged into the campaign of 1860 with all his energy. Mr. Lincoln had been from the first his favorite as a candidate, and he had foreshadowed his nomination, months before it occurred, in his paper. There were many points of resemblance in the characters of the two men, and Colfax's heart warmed toward him as toward a brother. Hardly any man in the United States did so much to secure the election of Mr. Lincoln as this Western editor, and this from pure love, and not from any hope or desire of reward. Mr. Colfax could have had, if he had sought it, a place in Mr. Lincoln's Cabinet, as he always had (a very warm one) in his heart; but he preferred to remain in Congress, and during the whole period of the war he was a bosom friend and a trusted adviser of the President. In his sound sense, his practical view of matters, and his freedom from hobbies, Mr. Lincoln could confide, with the assurance that his counsels would never lead him astray.

Hopeful, even in the darkest hours, and ever ready to cheer and encourage the drooping spirits of those whose duller vision could not pierce the cloud-rack and see the clear heavens beyond, his presence and influence were invaluable in the murky and treason-tainted atmosphere of the capital.

In 1862, when Mr. Colfax's fourth term in Congress was about to expire, the people were greatly depressed by the disasters that had befell the army. Many thought that the enthusiasm of the people was gone, and that at the coming elections the party in power would not be sustained. Hastening home to his district, Colfax took the rostrum and passed rapidly around among his people like a military evangel, pleading for freedom, for the country, and for the army, forgetful of self, and solicitous only to recruit our thinned lines of battle. Friends, believing that his reëlection was more valuable to the cause than a few Indiana volunteers could be to the army, almost sharply remonstrated against a course which, they thought, would secure his undeserved defeat. The characteristic reply, unstudied for effect, because made in private, was that he preferred that he, not our brave soldiers, should be in the minority, and that recruiting should go briskly and immediately forward.

We repeat, no man in Washington was more trusted or beloved by Mr. Lincoln than Colfax, and often when harassed by hasty friends or misrepresented by virulent enemies, the good President would appeal to the young statesman for advice. The friendship existing between them continued up to that sad night when the ball of the assassin robbed the country of its beloved ruler. Colfax was with Mr. Lincoln in his last moments, and was one of the heart-stricken little band that knelt around the bed of the dying martyr.

Mr. Colfax has been more honored by his fellow-members than any man who ever was in Congress except Henry Clay; and it is the testimony of members of all parties, that he is the best presiding officer the House has had since Henry Clay, and in some particulars he excels even Mr. Clay. He is always genial and courteous, never betrayed into impatience or vexation, and his marvelous quickness of thought, thorough knowledge of parliamentary usage, and talent for the rapid administration of details, and, above all, his extraordinary tact, enable him to control the House of Representatives, even in its most boisterous moods, with the skill and grace with which an accomplished pilot would manage the helm of one of our palace steamers on the Hudson. He is never at a fault in deciding a question of order, however delicate or difficult, and the whole array of precedents are at his command. Very seldom indeed are his decisions overruled, and in the rare cases in which they have been, the House have generally found that they, and not he, were in the wrong. It has been said that his talents were administrative and executive, rather than deliberative. While this is in itself high praise, we are inclined to doubt its entire truth. He does possess great executive ability, and inherits from his mother that faculty of rapid intuition, which has been very properly denominated "mother wit;" but he has also given indications of the possession of high reasoning and deliberative faculties, and both his editorials and speeches give evidence of fine logical as well as rhetorical power.

He possesses, in a remarkable degree, the power of reading character, and when called upon to select men for special duties he will not make mistakes. While a radical in his political views, he is still cautious, but will still faithfully execute the will of the people. His mind is well balanced, no undue predominance of any faculty being observable, but all uniting in such proportions as to make a sound, healthy-minded, judicious man; one who will not be a seer, far in advance of his age, nor a conservative, lagging in the rear of it, but an able leader, to whose position the whole host of patriots will rally, and whose views will meet with a hearty response from all lovers of their country.*

* NOTE.—I am indebted to Dr. L. P. Brockett, of Brooklyn, N. Y., the accomplished author of "Men of our Times," for much of the information contained in my sketch of Mr. Colfax.—AUTHOR.

CHAPTER III.

PERSONAL MANNERS OF MR. COLFAX—WHY THE WOMEN LIKE HIM—HIS WIFE—MR. COLFAX AT HOME—HIS RECEPTIONS—WHY THEY ARE POPULAR—COLFAX AND HIS MOTHER—A GOOD SON—GRANT AND COLFAX—EARLY STRUGGLES AND POVERTY OF COLFAX—SUPPER TO HIM BY THE PRESS OF WASHINGTON—HIS REMARKS—COLFAX AS A POLITICIAN—HIS TALENTS—GRANT SAFE FROM ASSASSINATION IF COLFAX IS VICE-PRESIDENT—COLFAX'S SPEECHES—HIS PIETY—COLFAX AT SOUTH BEND—WHAT HIS NEIGHBORS THINK OF HIM—A TEMPERANCE MAN—HIS LIBERALITY AND SUPPORT OF GOOD CAUSES—PERSONAL APPEARANCE—ANECDOTE—COLFAX IN HIS OFFICE—HIS RECORD.

Mr. Colfax is a polite man, but not proudly or haughtily so. He is genial and gentle from the necessities of his nature. The gentleman, in his case, as in all others, is not of necessity he who was gentle-born, but he who possesses a truly gentle nature. There are heart and kindness in his civility. Men leave his presence with the feeling that they have been with a good, kind, able, and honest man. Political opponents like him personally, as well as his political friends. The breath of slander has been silent toward his fair, spotless fame. Socially he is frank, lively, jolly. It may be that he feels his oats in some degree, but dignity has n't spoiled him. The everlasting I-hood and Us-ness of great men is forgotten in his presence. His manners are not quite so familiar as those of Lincoln, but nearly so. They are natural, graceful, with a bird-like or business-like quickness of thought and motion. But they are very far from the high and mighty style of Sumner, or the judicial coldness of Fessenden, Sherman, and Trumbull. American mothers believe in Schuyler Colfax. There are more babies named for him than for any public man since Clay. But not only American mothers believe in him, but he is a favorite with all good women; not only because he says very pleasant things to them, nor because he grew into manhood revering womanhood, through a good mother, wife, and sister; but because all true women know intuitively that he is a true man, holding his soul blameless in honor. To believe is a necessity of women, at least of a good woman. If she has unshaken faith in you, in the purity of your purpose, in the loftiness of your character, you may wound her with a thousand faults, yet to her uplifted eyes the nimbus of the god will hover about you still. "Do you think Schuyler Colfax a great man?" asked a gentleman of a lady, while listening to Mr. C.'s last speech in Cooper Institute. "I never think to inquire," was the reply; "because I know him to be what the country needs much more just now—a true man, through and through." "You can not think him as great as Chase?" "Intellectually! No. Morally he is greater. He is incapable of doing what Chase did for the sake of the presidency. He could not plan for the defeat of a friend, as Chase planned against Lincoln." We heard a lady say, not long since, "If the American women could vote, Schuyler Colfax would be the next President." If this be true, it is very much to his credit, for we all know that those public men who are believed in and supported by the best women, are the men who are supported and believed in by the best men. We know, also, that the most illustrious men of all ages and nations have drawn their highest inspiration and best success from the friendship and devotion of women.

But not only do the women believe in Colfax, but he believes in them. When a mere boy he learned to love one of his little playmates, and when only twenty-one married her. She was a good woman—pure, kind-hearted, lovely in person and disposition. With this devoted woman Mr. Colfax lived happily, surrounded by his mother, sisters, and friends, until 1863, when his wife sickened and died, leaving him childless. He never married again, and probably never will. There are no doubt many good and beautiful women in the United States, who would feel honored by the society of such a man, and would be willing to take upon themselves, at the holy fount, the name of Schuyler Colfax, but we doubt if he ever marries again. His heart lies buried in the grave with the choice of his youth, and for years past he has devoted himself entirely to the care of his mother and sisters. No more devoted brother or dutiful son ever lived than Schuyler Colfax, and those who have attended his brilliant receptions have not failed to notice his kind and affectionate treatment of his mother and sisters. People have wondered why Mr. Colfax's receptions were the most popular in Washington, but they need not go far to find out the cause, for they are the most home-like. There is heart, geniality, freedom, hospitality, welcome in them such as is not to be found elsewhere. They are the people's receptions, and as the Speaker enters all smiles, with his old mother on one arm and his sister Carrie on the other, every one present feels at home, and, instead of formalities, there is an evening of real enjoyment. There is a style about the Speaker's home which reminds one of the log-cabins of the West, with their wide chimnies and big roaring fires, where every traveler who passes that way is welcome. Nothing can exceed the chivalrous gallantry of the Speaker to his mother, his cherished companion from childhood. When she enters the gallery of the House, Mr. Colfax at once calls some member of the House to the Speaker's chair, and hastens to her, remaining, if possible, with her during the whole time she continues at the Hall of Representatives.

It is curious how destiny snatches her darlings from the arms of obscurity, and, mocking at birth and degree, sets them in the world's highest places. Scarcely a name has burst upon the world in transcendent luster that did not at the first emerge from the heavy cloud of defeat and humiliation.

Not many years ago the well-paid, little-to-do officers of the United States army used to cross the street to avoid meeting a young ex-captain, turned farmer, because he "bored" them by asking them to use their influence to assist him in obtaining a position. To-day no officer, whatever his rank, would be greatly bored by a conversation with this same ex-captain, nor very likely to cross the street to avoid meeting the General of all the armies, the certain-to-be President of the United States. Less than ten years ago the people of America had never heard of Ulysses Grant. He was poor, he was disappointed. He had neither social position nor political influence. Though he lived but a few doors away, he had never even spoken to Elihu Washburne, the brave congressman who afterward fought his battles through all defeat, and who washed his escutcheon white of blame long before Grant himself could lift it into the keen sunlight of renown.

Fifteen years ago a young man sat in a little office in a small town of the West, clipping and writing for the columns of an obscure newspaper. He could boast of brave blood and an honorable lineage, but the world did not know it. His name was historic by right of birth; yet, beyond the narrow arc of a few counties, no one had ever heard of him. Nature had not stinted his birthright. Adversity had trained him for life. He entered the service of his generation with a sunny courage, an endless patience, a clear head, and a true heart. One has said profoundly, "Temperament is greater than all." Temperament is fate. Not one of us is more nor less than our temperament makes us. Schuyler Colfax has the temperament of success. He began his career with an honorable ambition and dauntless faith in the future. Yet, through all the dreaming of youth, it is doubtful if the "narrow walls" of the newspaper office "stretched away in stately halls" of the capitol of the nation, or that he beheld himself the third in rank in the government of his country, and within less than twenty years presented by the most powerful of parties for the second office in the gift of his fellow-citizens.

Great, however, as has been Mr. Colfax's success in life, he never forgets, he remembers rather with peculiar tenacity, the humble circumstances of his early years, and honors, with peculiar love, those sons of toil, who, like himself, have, by diligent struggle and earnest endeavor, wrought their way up to a higher and more extended sphere of action.

A very pleasant illustration of this is contained in a speech which he delivered at a dinner given him by the representatives of the press, in December, 1866, at which the presiding officer, Samuel Wilkeson, Esq., had alluded to his passing his office at midnight eighteen years before, while waiting for the change of horses in the stage, and having seen him busily at work. Mr. Colfax replied as follows:

"I have had to listen to-night to a eulogy from your distinguished chairman, of which I can only wish I was worthy. What he has said has called back to my mind what is often before it, the years of my early manhood—and I see a friend seated at this table (Mr. Defrees) who knows much of it about as well as myself—when, struggling against poverty and adverse fortune, sometimes I sought in the profession to which you have devoted yourself, to earn an honest livelihood for myself and family, and a position, humble, but not dishonored, among the newspaper men of America. I can not remember the exact evening to which he alludes, when, eighteen years ago, a stranger then, as I am glad he is not now, he saw me through a window in my office, with the midnight lamp before me, and heard the commentary on my life from the lips of some too partial friend among those who from my boyhood had surrounded me with so much kindness and attention. But well do I remember, in the early history of the newspaper that numbered but two hundred and fifty subscribers when I established it, I was often compelled to labor far into the hours of the night. And little did I dream, at that time, I was ever to be a member of the American Congress; and far less that I was to be the recipient of the honor whose conferment you commemorate and indorse to-night. I can say of that paper that its columns, from its very first number, will bear testimony to-day that in all the political canvasses in which I was engaged, I never avoided a frank and out-spoken expression of opinion on any question before the American people; and that, as these opinions had always been honestly entertained, could not have hesitated to frankly and manfully avow them. Though the effect of these avowals was, from the political complexion of the district and the State, to keep me in a minority, the people among whom I live will bear testimony that I was no less faithful to them then than I have been when, in later years, that minority has, by the course of events, been changed into a majority."

In the course of this speech, he uttered the following noble thoughts in regard to the vocation of the editor, a vocation which he continued to honor by his own participation in it until his assumption of the Speaker's chair. Were these views more prevalent, journalism would be a far greater blessing to the nation and the world than it now is:

"Next to the sacred desk, and those who minister in it, there is no profession more responsible than yours. The editor can not wait, like the politician, to see the set of the tide, but is required, as new necessities arise, not only to avow at once his sentiments upon them, but to discuss them intelligently and instructively. It is also his duty to guide and protect public opinion in the proper channels, and to lay before the readers of his sheet such matter as shall tend to the elevation of their character. I have sometimes thought that newspapers in their sphere might be compared to that exquisite mechanism of the universe whereby the moisture is lifted from the earth, condensed into clouds, and poured back again in refreshing and fertilizing showers to bless the husbandman and produce the abundant harvests. So, with the representatives of the press, they draw from public opinion, condense public opinion, and finally reflect and re-distribute it back again in turn to its elevation and purification."

Schuyler Colfax is a politician in the highest sense of that much-abused term, for the best years of his active manhood have been devoted to the study of political science, and the administration of public affairs. Believing in the people, he has endeavored to faithfully carry out their will. He is, perhaps, to-day, the fittest man to fill the Vice-President's office, because he is, in the largest sense, a representative American. Of the people, and with the people, it is impossible for him to be purely sectional in his sympathies or in his ideas of legislation. He has greater personal familiarity with the resources and interests of the whole country than any other public man, having traveled in every State from Oregon to Maine, hailed every-where by the masses of the people as a beloved friend.

Some one has said that he has "no eccentricities, but great tact, and his talents are rather administrative and executive than deliberative." That is true so far as it enables him to make good appointments, and adopt sure policies. He would make a better President, or Speaker of the House, than Senator. He knows men well, estimates them correctly, treats them all fairly and candidly. No man will get through his business with you in fewer minutes, and yet none is more free from the horrid *brusqueness* of busy men.

If the experience of past years has proved the necessity of selecting, for the second executive of the government, a man who will be true to the platform and principles of his party and the people who elect him, then Colfax is the right man, for should any thing happen to Grant, it would not change the policy of the administration, unless to make it more radical. Rebels who know Schuyler Colfax will never kill Ulysses Grant, in order to have the former become President.

Of Mr. Colfax's speeches, it may be said that they are clear and convincing, with a vein of dignity and piety running through all their sentences. Thus he said to the Thirty-eighth Congress: "I invoke you to remember that sacred truth which all history verifies, that 'they who rule not in righteousness shall perish from the earth;'" and again: "The Creator is leading us in his own way rather than our own. He has put all men on an equality before Divine law, and demands that we shall put all men upon the same equality before human law;" or again, "Honesty to principle is our highest duty, and I would rather sacrifice my life than betray the people."

Thus he said of the employment of negro troops: "I do not call negro soldiers better than white ones. If I were to express my own opinion, it would be that those of my own color are better and braver. For I have always told you, in spite of charges to the contrary, that I believe the Anglo-

Saxon race was superior to any other that walks the footstool of God."

So he said of moral faithfulness in legislation: "Whether traveling in the valley of humiliation or disaster, or keeping my eye fixed on the heavens, I believe God reigns. I do n't believe his blessings will fall on the Confederacy. God's ways are sometimes dark, but sooner or later they reach the shining hills of day."

He first announced the Republican platform, after the breach with Mr. Johnson, thus: "Let us make haste slowly, and we can then hope that the foundations of our government, when thus reconstructed on the basis of indisputable loyalty, will be as eternal as the stars."

In like manner, on April 10, 1866, when he made mild but manly issue with Johnson, he said of the Civil Rights Bill, in the first moment of its enactment: "That law, misrepresented as it has been by its opponents in Congress, will never be repealed, and in the years that are coming, it will be the proudest recollection and the crowning honor of those men who stood up in the national councils, that they gave to that American Magna Charta their cordial support."

He treated in this way a taunt of the Democracy: "The new nickname flung at us is 'Radicals.' I had rather be called a radical than a rebel, at any time. I am a radical for right against wrong; for liberty against slavery; for justice against tyranny—a radical friend of my country and a radical enemy of every hater of my native land. I believe in a radical government of the people, by the people, the world over, and my sympathies go out toward the radicals who are trying to imitate our free institutions in Greece, Italy, France, Ireland, and Mexico. I wish to see a belt of republics encircle the globe."

Here is another curt passage: "I am for leveling up rather than leveling down. God do so to me, and more also, if I do aught more to crush any man down lower."

In short, this is Mr. Colfax, as described in the words of his pastor and poet at South Bend, his home:

"Thou art the clear,
Persuasive orator of right; the pure,
Unsullied patriot; the changeless, sure,
And genial friend, to many hearts how dear."

But after all, his oratory is more of the fervent and florid style than argumentative; he is always interesting and entertaining, and never speaks but he instructs his hearers, for he is a close student, and thoroughly studies his subjects. He is earnest and positive without being bitter; never in one of his speeches has he used the word copperhead. He speaks strongly of the acts and principles of the opposition, but never applies to them any abusive terms. This habit has been of great service to him, and it frequently has happened that men who one year were opposed to him, the next were found supporting him.

Some one has said that no one ever hated Mr. Colfax, and that he never had an enemy. That is not so; if it were true he were not worth writing about, but we happen to know a man who hates him most cordially, and, therefore, he stands acquitted of the woe pronounced on those of whom all men speak well. Still we confess Colfax is alarmingly popular for a man of brains and principle, and we wish the Democrats would curse him a little more frequently.

The home test is a severe one for most men. It is said "a prophet is not without honor save in his own country;" but Colfax is popular even at home, if we may judge from the manner in which he is received when he goes to South Bend. Thus, in 1866, when he returned from Washington, he was greeted in good, old-fashioned Hoosier style by earnest, loyal, political and personal friends. These, with heart-felt unanimity, seemed to share a common spirit of enthusiasm. When the morning train reached Laporte and South Bend, crowds were in waiting. At the depot of the latter place were old patriarchs who knew our "boy Schuyler," middle-aged men whom he had gracefully distanced in the race of life, and wondering children, to whom this was a holiday, attending carriages, wagons, nondescript vehicles of all sorts; flags, banners, and bands playing "Home, Sweet Home," all in waiting to honor the return of a distinguished yet simple-hearted citizen. Descending from the railway platform, Mr. Colfax was almost literally carried by the arms to an adjoining rostrum, where, in intense silence, the formal yet sincere and touching welcome was pronounced by Judge Wade, formerly colonel of the Seventy-third Indiana Infantry, who, during the war, was by Mr. Colfax delivered from actual squalid horrors and impending death in Libby Prison.

The orator, in substance, thanked Mr. Colfax in the name of his fellow-citizens for the honors he in his public life had won for them; in the name of national citizens, who feel that he is a prominent part of the trusty bulwark which shields them from public enemies; and, finally, in the name of soldiers who have learned by experience that he was patriotically, unselfishly, constantly, and unflaggingly devoted to their interests.

The speaker closed, and for a moment speech was silent on the lips of the silver-tongued statesman, who hitherto had gracefully addressed Presidents and Senates, but whose owner's heart seemed just then more ready to sit down and silently weep upon the threshold of its home, than to dictate the words whose meaning it were far easier to feel. But soon the ringing sentences began to flow and the returning guest to feel literally at home. Then the shouts, and the procession through the streets, whose doors and windows fairly shone with nodding heads and bright faces. For once in life, amid all this unostentatious, spontaneous excitement of that pure inland town, we discover a prophet having honor and enjoying "love in his own country."

Mr. Colfax's personal example at Washington is luminous. When twenty, he made vows of strict abstinence, which have never been broken. Liquors and wines are never used at his receptions, while Presidential dinners and diplomatic banquets are utterly powerless to abate one jot or tittle of his firmness. Many well remember his late speech at the congressional temperance meeting, and how he banished the sale of liquor from all parts of the Capitol within his jurisdiction.

At the National Republican Union Convention at Chicago, in May, 1868, at which he was nominated for the Vice-Presidency, the canvass for him was conducted by his special command without a drop of any intoxicating liquor. At the head-quarters of some of the other candidates, strong drink flowed freely, but Mr. Colfax would have preferred to lose the nomination, rather than to violate his temperance principles.

He is a member of the Dutch Reformed Church, and loves to talk in private of how God rules and how distinctly and how often in our history his holy arm has been revealed; and the ascription of praise comes from a worshiping heart, reliant on God through Christ.

He has always in all the relations of life, public and private, maintained an active and reputable Christian profession. The Sunday-school, the tract, the mission, and the Bible cause, have all found in him an earnest and cordial supporter; no matter whether it has been the Sanitary Commission, the Christian Commission, the Soldiers' Aid Society, or what benevolent institution that applied to him for help, he has always given freely a part of his earnings; and if an advocate was needed, his eloquent voice was immediately lifted up in the cities of the nation, now pleading for money, then for clothing, and still again for food comforts for the sick and wounded soldiers.

He is a smoker, and, indeed, indulges in this filthy habit almost as much as Grant. The following is told of the two candidates: The Speaker visited General Grant before the result of the vote at Chicago was known. The Speaker was smoking a fine cigar. "Where did you get that cigar, Colfax?" said Grant. "I get my cigars of a man at Danbury, Connecticut; he makes them himself," answered Colfax. "Well, that is one of the best cigars I have seen in some time," said Grant. "I will order some." Thereupon the General sat down and wrote to the Danbury man to send them one thousand Colfax cigars. When he had sealed the envelope, Colfax said: "General, let me frank that for you." Whereupon the Speaker wrote his signature on Grant's letter to the man at Danbury.

George Alfred Townsend, who visited Mr. Colfax not long ago, writes thus pleasantly about him:

"I found him in what he called 'his den,' a little closet-room, lighted by one basement window, under the Capitol. It was a curiosity-shop of manuscripts and documents, order reigning through superficial confusion. Here the Speaker hides himself away from pages and harpies, and works unassistedly at his speeches and his correspondence, the latter of itself a drudgery as great and exciting as any accountant's.

"But a light-house never grows old; after the hundred years its flame is as youthful as when it began. The pure, unaffected, radiant cheerfulness of Mr. Colfax keeps him as rosy and hopeful as a boy. Here he sits, smoking his cigar, surprised in the midst of a smile, for all his thoughts are good companions.

"I took a seat before him, and while he answered some questions I had brought, I tried to make out his face and character—a very difficult type were both of them, for a country of which the Speaker is so representative, and yet of a temperament so uncommon.

"We are a sober-minded people, with lines of thrift and anxiety in our faces, like the marks of whip and burden. We go to law and go to church with the same countenances. We want to make money fast, and on the way and after the end we have remorses, aches, wounded self-esteems, asceticisms. The air, the soil, the worry, and the hurry of American life provincialize the American into a hard, repellant, dreadfully overearnest man, with a skin, a stomach, and a soul, equally dyspeptic.

"Out of this population a face grows, now and then, like a clover head out of a stock-yard, all freshness and color, and quick to feel the earliest breezes. This is Mr. Colfax. His life is perennial hopefulness, having a good conscience for its compass, and for its ballast a temperament that is equal as an hour-glass."

There are some curious divisions of time connected with Mr. Colfax's career, which are worth mentioning. Six years after his first election to Congress he was elected Speaker of the House. He has been thrice elected to this position, and will have served in it exactly six years on his accession to the Vice-Presidency—stepping from the third to the second position within the gift of the people. Then we have, as the prominent periods in a more than ordinarily successful and brilliant life, first the age at which he entered the law office of his early and still devoted friend (sixteen.) Sixteen years later—at the age of thirty-two—we find him in the American Congress, and almost immediately recognized as one of the ablest champions of his party. Six years later he is elected as presiding officer of the lower House, reëlected twice, and at the end of his present term, which will constitute six years, he will be called to a still higher and more responsible position.

In the summer of 1866, in company with several friends, Mr. Colfax crossed the continent by the overland route, and received a hearty and cordial welcome in the Pacific States and Territories, and increased his already deep interest in the means of speedy and rapid communication with those portions of the Republic.

This trip prepared him for one of the most entertaining lectures ever delivered in this country. It has been listened to with rapt attention by the people of almost every city in the North. Pecuniarily, however, it has profited him but little, for with that liberality which has ever been a marked trait in his character, the entire proceeds of a lecture have as often been donated to some charitable object as they have found their way into his own pocket.

He has also published another lecture, on "The Education of the Heart," which has been widely circulated.

The following is a letter written by the patriot poet Whittier, to Mr. Colfax:

Colfax!—well chosen to preside
O'er Freedom's Congress, and to guide,
As one who holds the reins of fate,
The current of its great debate;
Prompted by one too wise, and good,
And fair, withal, to be withstood,
Here, from our northern river banks,
I send to thee my hearty thanks
For all the patience which has borne
The weary toot of Buncombe's horn,
The hissing of the Copperhead,
And Folly dropping words of lead!

Still wisely ready when the scale
Hangs poised to make the right prevail,
Still foremost, though Secession's head
Be crushed, with scornful heel to tread
The life out from its writhing tail!
As wise, firm, faithful to the end
God keep thee, prays thy sincere friend,

JOHN G. WHITTIER.

In personal appearance, Mr. Colfax is rather under the medium height, with form firmly and compactly molded. His hair is brown, now slightly sprinkled with gray; eyes blue, forehead high and arching, indicating great perceptive faculties and deep veneration. His face is open and frank, and as yet unmarked by age. He possesses great vitality, and can endure an extraordinary amount of labor with but little fatigue. This, coupled with his temperate habits, has caused him to wear his age so well, that but few persons would place him even at forty. He is yet in the prime and vigor of manhood, with all his cares and responsibilities as buoyant as most people at thirty.

His career in politics has been quite as successful as that of his illustrious colleague in arms. Here is the aggregate vote on either side at each election:

1851	Colfax	9,118	Fitch	9,356
1854	Colfax	9,989	Eddy	8,223
1856	Colfax	12,926	Stuart	11,890
1858	Colfax	14,541	Walker	12,610
1860	Colfax	16,860	Cathcart	13,458
1862	Colfax	14,775	Turpie	14,546
1864	Colfax	16,658	Turpie	14,978
1866	Colfax	20,221	Turpie	18,073

Thus we see that our candidate for Vice-President has proved as invincible in the arena of intellectual struggle for liberty and loyalty as our more illustrious candidate for President amid the stern alarms of war.

CHAPTER IV.

THE CHICAGO CONVENTION — NOMINATIONS FOR VICE-PRESIDENT — MR. PIERCE'S SPEECH—MR. CLAFLIN'S SPEECH—HON. HENRY LANE'S SPEECH —SPEECH OF MR. CUTCHESON—REMARKS OF FRED. HASSAUREK, CARL SCHURTZ, JUDGE JONES, ALEXANDER M'CLURE, AND OTHERS—HONS. BEN. WADE, COLFAX, WILSON, FENTON, HAMLIN, HARLIN, CURTIN, POMEROY SPEED, CRESWELL, AND KELLEY NOMINATED FOR VICE-PRESIDENT—FIRST BALLOT—SECOND BALLOT — THIRD BALLOT — FOURTH BALLOT — FIFTH BALLOT—COLFAX DECLARED THE UNANIMOUS NOMINEE OF THE CONVENTION—THE ENTHUSIASM—ADJOURNMENT.

It was part of the duty of the Convention which assembled at Chicago on the 20th of May, to nominate a candidate for Vice-President. After the nomination of General Grant had been made known, the President, General Hawley, directed the delegations to name their candidates for Vice-President. Mr. Pierce, of Virginia, in an eloquent speech, nominated Hon. Henry Wilson, of Massachusetts. Mr. Claflin, chairman of the Massachusetts delegation, in a speech highly complimentary to Mr. Wilson, seconded the motion. The Hon. Henry Lane, a venerable ex-senator from Indiana, then rose and said:

"Mr. Chairman: I am instructed by the delegation from the State of Indiana to present that tried, trusted, and true patriot, Schuyler Colfax. [Prolonged applause.] Of the purity of his life, in private and in public, of his distinguished public services, his long identification with congressional action, it is idle and unnecessary that I should go into any lengthy eulogy with reference to Mr. Colfax. He is an Indianian near to our hearts. We know him. The people are united for him, and I speak but one voice. He is well known there. He is the choice of the people, and although his residence is in Indiana, his fame, thank God, belongs to the whole continent. [Tremendous cheers.] To his past history I need but refer for a moment. He began public service an orphan boy, with no inheritance except those God-endowed gifts which marked him from the beginning a master and a leader of men. [Cheers.] He began his career as a Whig politician, under the standard of that pure and incorruptible patriot, that far-seeing statesman, that brightest representative of American character, that pure and peerless orator, Henry Clay, of Kentucky. [Cheers.] Faithful to his country, faithful to his friends, and faithful to his public allegiance, he has supported every candidate of the Whig party and every nomination of the Republican party. These are some of his claims to your confidence and consideration. He has supported every measure of congressional reconstruction. With other distinguished gentlemen presented for the same office we have no quarrel. They are proud sons of the republic. Their glory is a part of our common inheritance. We shall make no disparagement. When you shall make your nomination, we shall be there to roll up our sleeves in his behalf. [Cheers.] I assure the Convention that, with Mr. Colfax as our standard-bearer, we shall carry Indiana, sometimes slanderously called, by evil-minded men, a doubtful State. [Laughter.] We shall carry Indiana. We shall triumph in the election. We may do this with others. I trust, if another is nominated, we shall elect him, but we regard him as absolutely certain. It is an auspicious time to present a young man—a man representing the religious and moral sentiment of the country to a great extent. He is the chosen, tried, and true leader—no doubtful man. The painful experience of the past has admonished us that we must have no doubtful man to be our Vice-President. We present you no doubtful man. He has stood by reconstruction—thank God, he has also stood by impeachment. [Applause.] When the seven recreant senators, unlike the seven golden candlesticks, burning in no Christian temple—when their light shall have been extinguished, or when they shall be only dark lanterns, whose illumination is only seen in places fit for the light of dark lanterns. Schuyler Colfax, as Vice-President, or as Speaker, or as member of Congress, will be found true to his principles, true to the interest of the Republican party, and of the Union party—for they are synonymous—one and the same. Now, we have passed through the war, we have emerged from the storm and cloud of battle, and now stand, as the whole United States, represented, and properly represented; and the Scripture is now being fulfilled, for we find Ethiopia striking out her arms." [Applause.]

Mr. Parker, Chairman of the delegation from New Jersey:

"Mr. President: The Republican Convention of New Jersey gave to their delegates an instruction which they have fulfilled; a subsequent resolution upon the subject of the Vice-Presidency expressly declares that upon that subject no instructions were given, except that it was the duty of the delegates to aim at the nomination of the man most fit to occupy the place of Vice-President. In the spirit of that resolution these delegates are here to-day, and I am instructed, as chairman, to nominate as candidate to the office of Vice-President Schuyler Colfax, of Indiana.

[Applause.] We nominate him as a young man likely, in the Providence of God, to live; we nominate him as a candidate of the young men. [Applause.] We love him beyond all others because of the kindness of his heart, the power of his intellect. We nominate him because, coming from the great and glorious West, we believe he will add splendor to the galaxy of men which the West has furnished. We nominate him because we know that in our State we can live under his rule. Schuyler Colfax comes of Jersey blood—blood that has flowed throughout this land, and is always good and true. We nominate him for the virtues which have been mentioned by the gentleman from Indiana."

Mr. Cutcheson, of Michigan, said:

"MR. PRESIDENT: I rise in behalf of the electors and delegates of the Republican party of Michigan, to support the nomination of Schuyler Colfax. [Great applause.] At the State Convention, where the Republican party of the State was very fully represented, when the name of Schuyler Colfax was proposed there as a candidate for the office of Vice-President, we witnessed some such a scene as here to-day was seen when Ulysses S. Grant was declared the unanimous nominee of this Convention for President. In Michigan we have watched the course of Schuyler Colfax, who lives just on the border, and we believe there that no name can be proposed to the people of the United States for this high office that will excite greater enthusiasm; we believe none other can excite so great an enthusiasm. In the State of Michigan the name of Schuyler Colfax is powerful. [Cries, "True," applause, etc.] While we pledge the most hearty support to any nominee of this Convention, we feel that to Grant and Schuyler Colfax we can promise to this Convention, from the State of Michigan, for Grant and Colfax, to roll up thirty thousand majority. [Applause.] We have seen him, how true he is to principle, and how he has forced men to love him as the people all love the name of the man who gets so close to the people's heart." [Applause.]

The eloquent German orator, Fred. Hassaurek, in behalf of Ohio, then proceeded to nominate the "old war-horse," Ben. Wade. He was followed by General Carl Schurtz, who ably seconded the motion on behalf of the Missouri delegation. Judge Jones, of North Carolina, followed General Schurtz in an earnest speech, urging the nomination of Senator Wade. Judge Tremain nominated Governor Reuben E. Fenton for New York, amid great enthusiasm, and the motion was seconded by the Louisiana delegation through its chairman, Governor Warmouth. Mr. Wood, of Kentucky, nominated the Hon. James Speed, of Louisville. Mr. Sands, of Maryland, nominated Hon. A. J. Creswell. Mr. Forney, of Pennsylvania, nominated Hon. Andrew G. Curtin, and Mr. McClure seconded the motion in an able speech. General Williamson nominated Hon. James Harlan. Mr. Seymour, of Wisconsin, nominated Hon. Hannibal Hamlin, and Mr. Shepley, of Maine, seconded the nomination. Hon. Wm. D. Kelley, of Pennsylvania, was nominated by the Alabama delegation, and the delegation from Kansas nominated Senator Pomeroy, when the nominations were closed, and, by direction of the President, the Secretary proceeded to call the roll, with the following result:

THE BALLOT.

STATES.	Wilson.	Colfax.	Wade.	Fenton.	Hamlin.	Curtin.	Harlan.	Pomeroy.	Kelley.	Speed.	Creswell.
Alabama	4	4	2	2					6		
Arkansas	9		1								
California	1	2	5	2							
Colorado		6									
Connecticut	4	2	2	4							
Dakota		2									
Delaware	6										
District of Columbia			2								
Florida	2	2		2							
Georgia	6	2	3	6		1					
Idaho				2							
Illinois		3	15	3	11						
Indiana		26									
Iowa							16				
Kansas								6			
Kentucky										22	
Louisiana				14							
Maine					14						
Maryland			1								13
Massachusetts	24										
Michigan		16									
Minnesota			8								
Mississippi	5		5	3							
Missouri		2	20								
Montana			2								
Nebraska			6								
Nevada			2	4							
New Hampshire	10										
New Jersey		14									
New York				66							
North Carolina			18								
Ohio			42								
Oregon		6									
Pennsylvania		1	3			48					
Rhode Island	2	3	2		1						
South Carolina	12										
Tennessee		6	3	11							
Texas	11		1								
Vermont		10									
Virginia	18		2								
West Virginia	5	1	2								
Wisconsin		7		6	2	1					
Total	119	115	149	125	28	50	16	6	6	22	13

The President. Gentlemen of the Convention, I read the statement of the vote.

The total number of votes cast is	648
Necessary to a choice	325
Mr. Wade has	149
Mr. Fenton has	125
Mr. Wilson has	119
Mr. Colfax has	118
Mr. Curtin has	50
Mr. Hamlin has	28
Mr. Speed has	22
Mr. Harlan has	16
Mr. Creswell has	13
Mr. Kelley has	6

You have made no choice. Is it your pleasure to proceed to another call of the roll?

Mr. Wood of Kentucky. On behalf of the delegation from Kentucky, I withdraw the name of Mr. Speed.

The Secretary then proceeded to call the States, with the following result:

SECOND BALLOT.

STATES.	Wilson.	Colfax.	Wade.	Fenton.	Hamlin.	Curtin.
Alabama	11	1	2	2	....	....
Arkansas	10	....	....	....	....	....
California	1	2	5	2	....	....
Colorado	....	6	....	....	....	....
Connecticut	4	1	3	4	....	....
Dakotah	....	2	....	....	....	....
Delaware	....	5	....	....	....	1
District of Columbia	....	....	2	....	....	....
Florida	2	2	....	2	....	....
Georgia	2	2	7	7	....	....
Idaho	....	....	....	2	....	....
Illinois	....	3	14	3	11	....

SECOND BALLOT—Continued.

STATES.	Wilson.	Colfax.	Wade.	Fenton.	Hamlin.	Curtin.
Indiana		26				
Iowa		4		10	2	
Kansas		2	2	2		
Kentucky		9	13		2	
Louisiana				14		
Maine					14	
Maryland	1	2	10		1	
Massachusetts	24					
Michigan		16				
Minnesota			8			
Mississippi	4		5	4		
Missouri		2	20			
Montana			2			
Nebraska			6			
Nevada			2	4		
New Hampshire	10					
New Jersey		14				
New York				66		
North Carolina	9		9			
Ohio		4	38			
Oregon		6				
Pennsylvania		3	5			44
Rhode Island	5	3				
South Carolina	12					
Tennessee		6	3	11		
Texas			9	3		
Vermont		10				
Virginia	12	4	2	2		
West Virginia	6	3	1			
Wisconsin		7	1	6	2	
Total	113	146	169	144	30	44

THE ANNOUNCEMENT.

The President. Gentlemen, I read the statement of the vote:

Total number of votes cast........................ 647
Necessary to a choice........................ 324
Mr. Wade has........................ 169

Mr. Colfax has	146
Mr. Fenton has	142
Mr. Wilson has	113
Mr. Curtin has	45
Mr. Hamlin has	30

You have made no choice. Will the Secretary proceed with the call of the roll?

Voices. "The roll!"

The roll was called for the third time, when Alabama gave Wilson, 11; Wade, 2; Fenton, 2; Colfax, 1. Arkansas —Wilson, 10. California—Colfax, 1; Fenton, 1; Wade, 8. Colorado—Colfax, 6. Connecticut—Fenton, 7; Wade, 2; Colfax, 3. Dacotah—Colfax, 5; Fenton, 1. District Columbia—Wade, 2. Florida—Colfax, 2; Wilson, 2; Fenton, 2. Georgia—Colfax, 4; Wade, 6; Fenton, 8. Idaho—Fenton, 2. Illinois—Wade, 17; Hamlin, 6; Colfax, 4; Fenton, 3. Indiana—Colfax, 26. Iowa—Colfax, 8; Fenton, 8. Kansas—Colfax, 2; Wade, 2; Fenton, 2. Kentucky—Wade, 6; Colfax, 6; Fenton, 5. Maine—Hamlin, 14. Maryland—Wade, 10; Colfax, 2; Wilson, 1; Hamlin, 1. Massachusetts—Wilson, 24. Michigan—Colfax, 16. Minnesota—Wade, 7; Wilson, 1. Mississippi—Fenton, 5; Wilson, 2; Wade, 4; Colfax, 1. Missouri—Wade, 20; Colfax, 2. Montana—Wade, 2. Nebraska—Wade, 6. Nevada—Wade, 2; Fenton, 4. New Hampshire—Wilson, 10. New Jersey—Colfax, 14. New York—Fenton, 66. North Carolina—Wade, 9; Wilson, 9. Ohio—Wade, 37; Colfax, 5. Oregon—Colfax, 6. Pennsylvania—Curtin, 40; Wade, 7; Colfax, 5. Rhode Island—Colfax, 8. South Carolina—Wilson, 12. Tennessee—Fenton, 11; Colfax, 6; Wade, 3. Texas—Wade, 11; Fenton, 1. Vermont—Colfax, 10. Virginia—Colfax, 6; Wade, 2; Wilson, 10; Fenton, 2. West Virginia—Colfax, 2; Wilson, 7; Wade, 1. Wisconsin—Colfax, 8; Fenton, 5; Wade, 1; Hamlin, 2.

THIRD BALLOT.

The President. I read the statement of the vote:

Total number of votes cast	647
Necessary to a choice	324
Mr. Wade has	178
Mr. Colfax has	165
Mr. Fenton has	139
Mr. Wilson has	99
Mr. Curtin has	40
Mr. Hamlin has	25

Mr. McClure, of Pennsylvania, then read a letter withdrawing the name of Governor Curtin, when the Secretary proceeded to call the roll for a fourth ballot.

FOURTH BALLOT.

Alabama—Wilson, 11; Wade, 2; Fenton, 2; Colfax, 1. Arkansas—Wilson, 8; Wade, 2. California—Colfax, 1; Fenton, 2; Wade, 7. Colorado—Colfax, 6. Connecticut—Fenton, 8; Wade, 2; Colfax, 2. Delaware—Colfax, 5; Fenton, 1. Dakotah—Colfax, 2. District Columbia—Wade, 2. Florida—Wilson, 2; Fenton, 2; Colfax, 2. Georgia—Wade, 5; Colfax, 5; Fenton, 8. Idaho—Fenton, 2. Illinois—Wade, 7; Hamlin, 6; Colfax, 6; Fenton, 3. Indiana—Colfax, 26. Iowa—Colfax, 8; Fenton, 8. Kansas—Colfax, 2; Wade, 2; Fenton, 2. Kentucky—Wade, 12; Colfax, 10. Louisiana—Fenton, 9; Wade, 5. Maine—Hamlin, 14. Maryland—Wade, 10; Colfax, 3; Wilson, 1. Massachusetts—Wilson, 24. Michigan—Colfax, 16. Minnesota—Wade, 7; Wilson, 1. Mississippi—Fenton, 4; Wilson, 4; Wade, 5; Colfax, 1. Missouri—Wade, 20; Colfax, 22. Montana—Wade, 2. Nebraska—Wade, 6. Nevada—Wade, 2; Fenton, 4. New Hampshire—Wilson, 10. New Jersey—Colfax, 14. New York—Fenton, 66. North Carolina—Wade, 8; Wilson, 7; Fenton, 1. Ohio—Wade, 36; Colfax, 6. Oregon—Colfax, 6. Pennnsylvania

—Wade, 33; Colfax, 14; Hamlin, 3. Rhode Island—Colfax, 6; Wade, 2. South Carolina—Wilson, 7; Fenton, 5. Tennessee—Fenton, 11; Colfax, 6; Wade, 3. Texas—Wade, 11; Colfax, 1. Vermont—Colfax, 10. Virginia—Wade, 2; Wilson, 5; Fenton, 3. West Virginia—Wade, 1; Wilson, 5; Colfax, 4. Wisconsin—Colfax, 11; Fenton, 3; Hamlin, 3.

The President. I read the statement of the vote:

Total number of votes cast	646
Necessary to a choice	324
Mr. Wade has	204
Mr. Colfax has	186
Mr. Fenton has	144
Mr. Wilson has	87
Mr. Hamlin has	25

The Secretary then called the roll on the fifth ballot, when votes were cast as follows:

FIFTH BALLOT.

STATES.	Wade.	Colfax.	Fenton.	Hamlin.	Wilson.
Alabama	2	1	2		11
Arkansas	2				8
California	8	1	1		
Colorado		6			
Connecticut	2	4	6		
Dakotah		2			
Delaware	2	4			
District of Columbia	2				
Florida		1	5		
Georgia	5	3	10		
Idaho			2		
Illinois	19	8	3	2	
Indiana		26			
Iowa		8	8		
Kansas	2	2	2		
Kentucky	12	10			
Louisiana	5		9		
Maine				14	
Maryland	10	3			1
Massachusetts					24

FIFTH BALLOT—Continued.

STATES.	Wade.	Colfax.	Fenton.	Hamlin.	Wilson.
Michigan	....	16	....	....	....
Minnesota	7	....	....	....	1
Mississippi	5	1	4	....	3
Missouri	20	2	....	....	....
Montana	2	....	....	....	....
Nebraska	6	....	....	....	....
Nevada	1	....	5	....	....
New Hampshire	9	....	1	....	....
New Jersey	....	14	....	....	....
New York	....	....	66	....	....
North Carolina	9	7	....	....	2
Ohio	36	6	....	....	....
Oregon	....	6	....	....	....
Pennsylvania	20	30	1	1	....
Rhode Island	....	8	....	....	....
South Carolina	2	....	7	....	3
Tennessee	3	17	....	....	....
Texas	12	....	....	....	....
Vermont	....	10	....	....	....
Virginia	2	10	5	....	3
West Virginia	1	9	....	....	....
Wisconsin	....	11	2	3	....
Total	206	225	140	19	56

Before the result of this ballot was announced, Mr. Williamson, of Iowa, said: Iowa desires to change the votes cast for Fenton to Colfax, and casts its entire sixteen votes for Colfax.

Mr. McClure, of Pennsylvania. Pennsylvania votes unanimously for Colfax.

Mr. Warmouth. I am directed by the delegation from Louisiana to change its fourteen votes for Schuyler Colfax.

All the other States then changed their votes to Mr. Colfax, and his nomination was made unanimous, amid the greatest enthusiasm.

As soon as order could be restored, the President said: I have an important dispatch to read. It is one in which you will doubtless be much interested. It is addressed by the Hon. Schuyler Colfax to the Hon. J. B. Defrees, of Indiana, and he says, "I read, this morning, to General Grant, the midnight dispatches giving an abstract of the platform, and General Grant heartily approves its tone."

A committee, to consist of the officers of the Convention, was appointed to call on General Grant and Speaker Colfax and inform them of their nomination.

NATIONAL EXECUTIVE COMMITTEE.

The Secretary then called the States, and the following was announced as the National Executive Committee:

Alabama—James P. Stow.
Arkansas—B. F. Rice.
California—G. C. Gorham.
Connecticut—Henry H. Starkweather.
Delaware—Edward G. Bradford.
Florida—S. B. Conover,
Georgia—J. H. Caldwell.
Illinois—J. R. Jones.
Indiana—Cyrus N. Harns.
Iowa—Joshua Fletcher.
Kansas—John A. Barton.
Kentucky—Allen A. Burton.
Louisiana—M. H. Southworth.
Maine—L. Barker.
Maryland—C. C. Wulton.
Massachusetts—W. Claflin.
Michigan—Marsh Giddings.
Minnesota—J. T. Averill.
Mississippi—A. Z. Fisk.
Missouri—B. Loan.
Nebraska—E. P. Taylor
Nevada—C. E. DeLong.

New Hampshire—W. E. Chandler.
New Jersey—James Gopsill.
New York—Horace Greeley.
North Carolina—W. Sloan.
Ohio—B. R. Howell.
Oregon—H. W. Corbett.
Pennsylvania—W. H. Kemble.
Rhode Island—Lyman B. Frieze.
South Carolina—Joseph H. Jenks.
Tennessee—W. B. Stokes.
Texas—A. J. Hamilton.
Vermont—T. W. Parks.
Virginia—Franklin Stearns.
West Virginia—S. D. Karns.
Wisconsin—David Atwood.
Colorado—Daniel Witter.
Dakotah—N. Edwards.
Idaho—J. C. Henley.
Montana—E. M. Wilson.

ADJOURNMENT.

General Cochrane, of New York. I move that the convention do now adjourn, to meet again at the call of the National Committee.

The President. Such a motion has previously been made and carried. The question is, shall the Convention now adjourn? Carried unanimously, and the Convention adjourned.

CHAPTER V.

HOW MR. COLFAX RECEIVED HIS NOMINATION—GREETINGS FROM HIS BROTHER MEMBERS—THE CROWD AT THE CAPITOL—SERENADE TO MR. COLFAX—REPRESENTATIVE PIKE'S REMARKS—MR. COLFAX'S SPEECH—RECEPTION OF THE SOLDIER'S COMMITTEE—THE SPEECHES—RECEPTION OF THE REPUBLICAN COMMITTEE—SPEECH OF GOVERNOR HAWLEY—REPLY OF SPEAKER COLFAX—HIS FORMAL LETTER OF ACCEPTANCE—GENERAL REMARKS—THE END.

WHEN Mr. Colfax was nominated, he was at his room in the Capitol, where he was, throughout the day, the recipient of complimentary calls from distinguished members of the Government. Mr. Orton, the President of the Union Telegraph Company, forwarded dispatches to him every few minutes, and when the one announcing his nomination was received, the greatest enthusiasm prevailed, and his brother members of the House crowded around him, and warmly congratulated him on his merited promotion.

In the other wing of the Capitol a crowd of senators and members had gathered about the Vice-President's room, where dispatches were read every ten or fifteen minutes, announcing the progress of the ballots. When Mr. Wade heard that Colfax was nominated, the old "Ashtabula Chief" said: "Well, he deserves it, and will make a good run."

Next evening a large procession, headed by a band, marched to Mr. Colfax's residence, where he was addressed by Representative Pike, of Maine, who spoke in behalf of the people. At the conclusion of Mr. Pike's speech, Speaker Colfax said:

"MY FRIENDS: I thank you with all the fullness of a grateful heart for this flattering manifestation of your confidence and regard. I congratulate you on the auspicious opening of the eventful campaign on which we are entering. In the Chicago Convention, representing the entire continental area of the republic, every State, every Territory, every district, and every delegate, from ocean to ocean, declared that their first and only choice for President was Ulysses S. Grant. Brave, and yet unassuming; reticent, and yet, when necessary, firm as the eternal hills; with every thought, and hope, and aspiration for his country; with modesty only equaled by his merits—it is not extravagant for me to say that he is to-day, of all other men in the land, 'first in war, first in peace, and first in the hearts of his countrymen.' His name is the very synonym of victory, and he will lead the Union hosts to triumph at the polls as he led the Union armies to triumph in the field. But greater even than the conqueror of Vicksburg, and the destroyer of the rebellion, is the glorious inspiration of our noble principles, animated by the sublime truths of the Declaration of Independence. Our banner bears an inscription more magnetic than the names of its standard-bearers, which the whole world can see as it floats to the breeze, 'Liberty and Loyalty, Justice and Public Safety.' Defying all prejudices, we are for uplifting the lowly and protecting the oppressed. History records, to the immortal honor of our organization, that it saved the nation and emancipated a race. We struck the fetter from the limb of the slave, and lifted millions into the glorious sunlight of liberty. We placed the emancipated slave on his feet as a man, and put into his right hand the ballot, to protect his manhood and his rights. We staked our political existence on the reconstruction of the revolted States—on the sure and eternal corner-stone of loyalty—and we shall triumph. I know there is no holiday contest before us; but with energy and zeal, with principles that humanity will prove, and that I believe God will bless, we shall go through the contest conquering and to conquer, and on the 4th day of March next the people's champion will be borne by the people's votes to yonder White House, that I regret to say is now dishonored by its unworthy occupant. Then, with peace and confidence, we may expect our beloved country to enter upon a career of prosperity which shall eclipse the most brilliant annals of our past. I bid you God speed in this work, and now, good-night."

At the conclusion of the speech, many of the people entered the house and shook the Speaker by the hand.

On the 29th of May, 1868, at two o'clock, the committee from the Soldiers' and Sailors' National Convention, headed by their chairman, Colonel Alleman, of Pennsylvania, called on the Speaker at his rooms in the capitol, where a brief address was made by the chairman.

Mr. Colfax replied, alluding, in striking terms, to the perils by land and sea which were endured by the soldiers and sailors of the Union in defense of the Constitution and flag of their country. Great as were the obligations of the nation to those at home who stood by the Government in its hour of trial, greater still was the debt of gratitude it owed to those who, leaving home and all at the risk of life and limb, to save the republic from destruction, going forth from every portion of the republic, some in the freshness of life's June, and some in the ripe maturity of life's October. The land, South and North, is filled with the graves of the nation's patriot sons. Their memory will ever be inscribed in all patriotic hearts as long as time shall last or the republic endure. Thanking the committee who represented the survivors of the heroic defenders of the Union for this expression of their esteem and regard, he closed with the assurance that if the ballot-box should ratify the nominations at Chicago, his fidelity to principle and devotion to the Union would show that their confidence had not been misplaced.

A copy of the platform of principles was presented to the Speaker. The committee, after a few moments, retired, and the Speaker returned to his duties in the House of Representatives.

In the evening of the same day, Mr. Colfax being present at General Grant's house, Governor Hawley, with the committee from the citizen's National Convention, paid respect to Mr. Colfax. General Hawley said:

"MR. COLFAX: You have heard our declaration of principles at Chicago, and, therefore, I need not repeat them. You are aware that numerous candidates for the Vice-Presidency were presented. They were all loved and respected, and your selection was brought about by the good-will and friendship entertained for yourself. You are known to the American people by fourteen years of public service. We know you came from the people, and without false pretense, you are faithful to principle. The Convention tenders you the nomination for Vice-President, and asks your acceptance."

Mr. Colfax replied:

"MR. PRESIDENT HAWLEY AND GENTLEMEN: History has already proclaimed that the victories of the party you represent during the recent war always give increased hope and confidence to the nation, while its reverses and defeats ever increased the national peril. It is no light tribute, therefore, to the millions of Republicans in the forty-two States and Territories represented in the Chicago Convention, that our organization has been so inseparably interwoven with the best interests of the republic, that the triumphs and reverses of the one have been the triumphs and reverses of the other. Since the General of our armies, with his heroic followers, crushed the rebellion, the carrying out of its policy, that loyalty should govern what loyalty preserved, has been worthy of its honored record in the war. Cordially agreeing with the platform adopted by its National Convention, and the resolutions thereto attached, I accept the nomination with which I have been honored, and will hereafter communicate that acceptance to you in the more formal manner that usage requires."

There were long and continued demonstrations of applause.

The gentlemen present generally advanced and shook General Grant and Speaker Colfax by the hand, and congratulated them on the choice of the Convention. The party then withdrew to an adjoining room, where a collation had been provided.

On the 30th of May, 1868, Speaker Colfax addressed the following eloquent letter to General Hawley, accepting the nomination of the Republican party for the Vice-Presidency:

"WASHINGTON, D. C., May 30, 1868.

"*To Hon. J. R. Hawley, President of the National Union Republican Convention:*

"DEAR SIR: The platform adopted by the patriotic Convention over which you presided, and the resolutions which so happily supplement it, so entirely agree with my views as to a just national policy, that my thanks are due to the delegates as much for this clear and auspicious declaration of principles, as for the nomination with which I have been honored, and which I gratefully accept.

"When a great rebellion, which imperiled the national existence, was at last overthrown, the duty of all others devolving on those intrusted with the responsibilities of legislation evidently was to require that the revolted States should be re-admitted into participation in the Government against which they erred only on such a basis as to increase and fortify, not to weaken or endanger the strength and power of the nation. Certainly no one ought to have claimed that they should be re-admitted under such a rule that their organization as States could ever again be used at the opening of a war to defy the national authority or to destroy national unity. This principle has been the pole-star of those who have inflexibly insisted on the congressional policy your Convention so cordially indorsed. Baffled by executive opposition and by persistent refusals to accept any plan of reconstruction proposed by Congress, justice, and public safety, at last combined to teach us that only by an enlargement of suffrage in those States could the desired end be attained, and that it was even more safe to give the ballot to those who loved the Union than to those who had sought ineffectually to destroy it. The assured success of this legislation is being written on the adamant of history, and will be our triumphant vindication.

"More clearly, too, than ever before does the nation now recognize that the greatest glory of a republic is that it throws the shield of its protection over the humblest and weakest of its people, and vindicates the rights of the poor and the powerless as faithfully as those of the mighty and the powerful.

"I rejoice, too, in this connection, to find in your platform the frank and fearless avowal that naturalized citizens must be protected abroad at every hazard, as though they were native born. Our whole people are foreigners or descendants of foreigners. Our fathers established by arms their right to be called a nation. It remains for us to establish the right, and welcome to our shores all who desire, by oaths of allegiance, to become American citizens. Perpetual allegiance, as claimed abroad, is only another name for perpetual bondage, and would make all slaves to the soil where first they saw the light. Our national cemeteries prove how faithfully these oaths of fidelity to the adopted land have been sealed in the life blood of thousands upon thousands. Should we not, then, be faithless to the dead, if we did not protect their living brethren in full enjoyment of that nationality for which, side by side with the native born, our soldiers of foreign birth laid down their lives?

"It was fitting, too, that the representatives of a party which had proved so true to national duty in time of war, should speak so clearly in time of peace of the maintenance untarnished of the national honor and the national credit and good faith as regards its debt, the cost of our national existence.

"I do not need to extend this reply by further comment on a platform which has elicited such hearty approval throughout the land; the debt of gratitude it acknowledges to the brave men who saved the Union from destruction; the frank approval of amnesty, based on repentance and loyalty; the demand for the most rigid economy and honesty in the Government; the sympathy of the party of liberty with all throughout the world who long for the liberty we here enjoy, and the recognition of the sublime principles of the Declaration of Independence, are worthy of the organization on whose banners they are to be written in the coming contest. Its past record can not be blotted out or forgotten. If there had been no Republican party, slavery would to-day cast its baleful shadow over the republic. If there had been no Republican party, free press and free speech would be as unknown, from the Potomac to the Rio Grande, as ten years ago. If the Republican party could have been stricken from existence when the banner of the rebellion was unfurled, and when the response of 'no coercion' was heard at the North, we would have had no nation to-day. But for the Republican party daring the risk and the odium of tax and draft laws, our flag could not have been kept flying in the field until the long-hoped for victory came. Without a Republican party the Civil Rights Bill, the guarantee of equality under the law to the humble and defenseless, as well as to the strong, would not be to-day upon our national statute book.

"With such inspiration from the past, and following the example of the founders of the republic who called the victorious General of the Revolution to preside over the land his triumphs had saved from its enemies, I can not doubt that our labors will be crowned with success, and it will be a success that shall bring restored hope, confidence, prosperity, and progress South as well as North, West as well as East, and, above all, the blessings, under Providence, of national concord and peace.

"Very truly, yours,

"SCHUYLER COLFAX."

To sum up our estimate of Mr. Colfax's character, we have only to say farther, that the nation believes in him, trusts him, and is willing to confide its interests to him, confident that if either in the speedy or remote future he should be called to the Presidency, he will not disappoint the hopes of those who should elect him, or prove treacherous to the convictions he had previously avowed. He can not, and will not, under any temptation, be other than a true, honest, upright, God-fearing, manly man.

Thousands of young men will cast their first vote this fall, and we hope they will begin their political lives right, by voting for the Republican ticket. Hurrah for Grant and Colfax!

THE

GRANT AND COLFAX

Campaign Songster:

A Collection of Original, Stirring Campaign Songs,

Set to Popular and Familiar Airs.

BY GEN. JAS. S. BRISBIN.

Price, 10 Cents. - - Less by the quantity.

SAMPLE SONGS.

COME, SHOUT FOR U. S. GRANT.

A PARAPHRASE.

Air.—"Sunset Tree."

1 COME, shout for U. S. Grant,
The soldier, bold and true!
Hurrah! hurrah! hurrah!
For Schuyler Colfax, too.
With the Tanner of the West,
And the Indiana blue,
We 'll put the copperheads to rest,
With all their rebel crew.

CHORUS.

Come, shout for U. S. Grant,
Our country's pride and boast!
Hurrah! hurrah! hurrah!
We 're one determined host.

2 Ye men who till the land,
Your country's surest stay;
Come, boldly take your stand
For the hero of the day.
Come, for the nation's pride,
March up in bold array,
As brothers, side by side,
For the hero of the day.
Come, shout for U. S. Grant, etc.

3 Ye who in cities live,
Come forth in bold array,
And to your country give
Help on election day.
Come one, come all, and sing
Our last and sweetest lay,
And richest tribute bring
To the hero of the day.
Come, shout for U. S. Grant, etc

THE TANNER OF THE WEST.

A PARAPHRASE.

Tune.—"'Tis my delight of a shiny night.

1 Once more our glorious banner
Upon the breeze we throw;
Beneath its folds with song and shout
Let's charge upon the foe.
Our brave "Old Abe," alas! no more
Shall place his lance in rest;
But well we know the love he bore
The Tanner of the West.
The Tanner of the West, my boys,
The Tanner of the West.

3 Then, brothers, rise and rally round
The soldier ever true,
Until his name with trumpet sound
Shall wake the welkin's blue;
And millions with admiring eyes
Shall call him from his rest,
The hero of new victories,
The Tanner of the West, etc.

3 When rebels sought with flags unfurled
The empire of the Free,
Who, with his soldiers backward hurled
The Southrons to the sea?
Who greatest cheered our gallant tars,
And fired the soldier's breast,
Till victory hailed our stripes and stars?
'T was the Tanner of the West, etc.

4 Whene'er forgot the common weal,
And party waves run strong,
Till e'en the wisest halt and feel
That every thing goes wrong;
There 's one who light and quiet brings,
And lulls the storm to rest,
Till peace comes on her angel wings,
'T is the Tanner of the West, etc.

5 The honors which good Lincoln won,
Encircle not *his* head;
Like withered wreaths they rest upon
Another's brow instead.
The soldier, never faithless known,
The worthiest and the best,
Shall make them bloom again—*our own*—
The Tanner of the West, etc.

6 O! ever green the sods that lie
Above the sainted dead,
And o'er our path his memory
For aye his radiance shed.
Its hallowed light shall fall upon
Our flag, where'er it rests,
And write the name of ABE LINCOLN
With the Tanner of the West, etc.

"NO FAIL GRANT."

COMPOSED BY RICHARD MARSH, OF LEXINGTON, KY.

Air.—"Lucy Neal."

A SONG to our gallant chieftain,
A chieftain great and bold;
Whose deeds will rank in story,
With the proudest sung of old.
Hurrah for him who fails not
In the hottest battle's din
Whose command is but to "go in,"
To "go in" but to win.

2 Tho' at Belmont pressed back sternly,
He knew he had at hand
Men who ever would fight firmly
At his "no fail" command.
Hurrah for him who fails not, etc.

3 At Fort Donelson they rallied,
He knew their might full well,
But as numbers he ne'er tallied,
That haughty fortress fell.
Hurrah for him who fails not, etc.

4 While proud Pemberton at Vicksburg,
Stood thirty thousand strong,
With great battlements, a-deeming
His time he could prolong.
Hurrah for him who fails not, etc.

5 Soon Pem. heard a tramp a-coming,
And with it rang a name,
That with all his fuss and drumming,
Made him tremble for his fame.
Hurrah for him who fails not, etc.

6 The "on to Richmond" oft was tried
By leaders young and old,
But all by legions bold defied,
No victory could unfold.
Hurrah for him who fails not, etc.

7 McClellan's brilliant host gave way,
McDowell failed to win,
But when the "Tanner Boy" got sway,
He raked the victories in.
Hurrah for him who fails not, etc.

8 Hurrah, boys, for "no fail" Grant,
Who marched through weal or woe;
Who marched but to conquer,
To conquer every foe.
Hurrah for him who fails not
In the hottest battle's din;
Whose command is but to "go in,"
To "go in" but to win.